RSS and Atom in Action

 **W9-BFY-078**

RSS and Atom in Action

WEB 2.0 BUILDING BLOCKS

DAVE JOHNSON

MANNING

Greenwich
(74° w. long.)

For online information and ordering of this and other Manning books, go to
www.manning.com. The publisher offers discounts on this book when ordered in quantity.
For more information, please contact:

    Special Sales Department
    Manning Publications Co.
    209 Bruce Park Avenue   Fax: (203) 661-9018
    Greenwich, CT 06830   email: orders@manning.com

Manning Publications Co.   Copyeditor: Jody Gilbert
209 Bruce Park Avenue   Typesetter: Denis Dalinnik
Greenwich, CT 06830   Cover designer: Leslie Haimes

ISBN 1932394494

Printed in the United States of America
1 2 3 4 5 6 7 8 9 10 – VHG – 10 09 08 07 06

To Andi, Alex, Linus, and Leo

brief contents

contents

ix

foreword

Ever since Henry Ford told his customers they could have "any color so long as it's black," our consumer society has been driven by the vision and goals of just a few creators. But in the 1990s, the emergence of the worldwide Web led to the explosive popularization of the Internet, and it became clear that the one-way flow of ideas upon which the consumer society was based would soon be a memory. The ubiquity of the Internet is now thrusting us headlong into a new age, where the flow of ideas changes from one-way to many-way, and the key to society becomes participation instead of just consumption.

It was in that context that a few colleagues and I started the web site blogs.sun.com for Sun Microsystems. We could see that in a "participation age," a key to the company's success would be providing the means for Sun's staff to directly engage with the technology and customer communities in which they were participating. All over the world, in every corner of human interest, others have been coming to the same conclusion, and today blogs are proliferating as fast as web sites did in the early 1990s.

With these blogs, almost incidentally, comes another technology that may have an even greater effect on society: the syndication feed, a computer-readable list of blog contents. Used today by blog reader programs and by aggregators (such as the BlogLines[1] web site or the Planet Roller[2] aggregator,

---

[1] http://www.bloglines.com
[2] http://www.rollerweblogger.org

with which I build my summary blog "The Daily Mink"[3]), syndication feeds allow innovative repurposing of the content of blogs and open up new avenues for content sharing, such as podcasting. Although use of syndication feeds is in its infancy, I predict big things, as the ability to create and consume them gets built into the operating systems we use on computers and mobile devices.

It may seem simple, but the syndication feed, in whatever format it's found—RSS or Atom—is an important step in the evolution of the system at the heart of the Web, XML. The original authors of XML saw it as a universal document language, allowing a tree-structured representation of a document. Syndication feeds bring another powerful structure to XML—lists and collections.

Lists and collections (such as databases) are at the core of so much of computing already, and syndication feeds provide a means for programs to share data organically. They provide an avenue for easy SOA (service-oriented architectures) and unlock imaginative use of all the data that swirls around us—bank accounts, health records, billing information, travel histories, and so much more. Syndication feeds make the Web programmable. More than that, Atom standardizes the means by which feeds are accessed, providing an API to decouple the web site from the program that exploits its feeds.

A wave of people, the "Web 2.0" movement, is already using syndication feeds and Ajax to create web sites such as Flickr, del.icio.us, Bloglines, and Technorati, and they're just scratching the surface of what's possible.

This book is an important reference for people who want to be ready for the future. You may have picked it up for information about the technology side of blogging, but it offers much more than that. It's a launch pad for the future. Pioneers like Tim Bray, Sam Ruby, Dave Winer, and Mark Pilgrim had to make all this up as they went along.

For you, there's this book. The skills it teaches you may prove to be the key that unlocks a participation-age program that will change the world. Read on, program wisely, and create the future!

SIMON PHIPPS
Chief Open Source Officer
Sun Microsystems, Inc.

---

[3] http://www.webmink.net

preface

Whether you consider the first blogs to be the online journals started around the time Jorn Barger coined the term "weblog" in 1997, or the "what's new" pages at NCSA and Netscape shortly after the birth of the Web, or the political pamphlets of American Revolutionary War times, you have to acknowledge that the concept of blogging is not entirely new. Blogging is just another word for writing online.

What *is* new is the widespread adoption of *blog technology*—newsfeeds and publishing protocols—on the Web. In the late 1990s, blog software and web portal developers needed standard data formats to make it easy to syndicate content on the Web. Thus, RSS, Atom, and other XML newsfeed formats were born. They needed standard protocols for publishing to and programming the Web. Thus, XML-RPC, SOAP, and web services were born.

Now, thanks to the explosion of interest in blogging, podcasting, and wikis, those same developer-friendly blog technologies are everywhere. Newsfeeds are a standard feature of not just blogs, but also of web sites, search engines, and wikis everywhere. Computers, music players, and mobile devices are tied in, too, as newsfeed technologies become a standard part of browsers, office applications, and operating systems. Even if you don't see opportunities for innovation here, your users are going to ask for these technologies, and now's the time to prepare.

This book is about building applications with those blog technologies. For the sake of the cynical developers in the audience, we start with a few use stories that show some truly new ways of collaborating using blog technology. Then, we explain what you need to know about blog technology—and not just RSS and Atom. We also cover blog server architecture, blogging APIs, and web services protocols.

To help you get started, we've included what amounts to a blog technology developer's kit, including a complete blog server, newsfeed parsers, a blog client library and, in part 2, ten immediately useful blog applications, or *blog apps*, written in Java and C#. The blog server and the ten applications, known as the *Blogapps server* and *Blogapps examples*, are both maintained as an open source project at http://blogapps.dev.java.net, where you're welcome to help maintain and improve them.

I hope we've provided everything you need to start building great blog applications, and I look forward to seeing what you build. Enjoy!

acknowledgments

There's only one name on the cover, but a host of people helped out with the book and they all deserve my thanks.

I'll start with Rick Ross, who encouraged me to write and who introduced me to Manning Publications and publisher Marjan Bace. Manning was a joy to work with, thanks to Denis Dalinnik, Jody Gilbert, Mike Levin, Dottie Marsico, Sharon Mullins, Frank Blackwell, Mary Piergies, Karen Tegtmeyer, Helen Trimes and the rest of the crew.

Thanks also to reviewers Tim Bray, Simon Brown, Steven Citron-Pousty, Rick Evans, Jack Herrington, Frank Jania, Lance Lavandowska, Robert McGovern, John Mitchell, Jaap van der Molen, Yoav Shapira, Doug Warren, Henri Yandell, Peter George, Paul Kedrosky, Joe Rainsberger, Pim Van Heuven, Patrick Chanezon, Alejandro Abdelnur, and Walter Von Koch who all provided invaluable feedback in the early reviews of the book. And special thanks to Mike Levin who was the technical proofreader of the final manuscript.

Thanks to Simon Phipps, who wrote the foreword and who was brave enough to use the book's software to run his personal web site. And thanks to Masood Mortazavi, who provided the text about "Value at Risk" in the first screen shot that appears in chapter 1.

Once again, I have to thank my family, who are happier than anybody that the book is finally finished.

about this book

This book shows developers how to build applications using blog technologies. Part 1 explains the fundamentals of blog technology, including blog and wiki server architecture, RSS and Atom newsfeed formats, the MetaWeblog API, and the Atom protocol. Once we have the fundamentals out of the way, we focus on building applications. Each chapter in part 2 is devoted to one immediately useful blog application.

You will find a more detailed roadmap and introduction to the book in chapter 0, "What you need to know first."

Who should read this book

This book is intended for developers and IT innovators who need to understand blog, wiki, and newsfeed technologies. If you'd like to add newsfeed-reading capabilities to your applications or newsfeed-generation capabilities to your web sites, this is the book for you. If you'd like to automate the process of publishing to the Web, you'll find this book very useful. If you've been asked to deploy blog and wiki technologies and want to understand blog and wiki server architecture before selecting software, you'll find the answers you need here. And if you're just looking for new ideas and opportunities, you'll find a wealth of those here as well.

For most of the chapters, we assume that you understand web development with Java or C#. For more information about the prerequisites of the book and a complete roadmap of its contents, read chapter 0, which explains what you need to know first.

Downloads

All of the source code in this book is available online and is maintained as an open source project called Blogapps at Java.NET. The examples for each chapter are packaged separately. You can build the Java examples using Ant, but the C# and ASP.NET examples require Microsoft Visual Studio. You'll find complete instructions for building and running each example at the Blogapps project web site, http://blogapps.dev.java.net.

The Blogapps server is a complete blog and wiki server that supports all of the newsfeed formats and publishing protocols we cover in this book. Chapter 2 explains how to download, install, and start the Blogapps server, which you can download from the same web site as the examples.

You can also access the source code for this book from the publisher's web site at www.manning.com/dmjohnson.

Code conventions

We use the Courier font for Java, C#, and XML source code listings and for class names, constants, and other words used in code. We use **bold Courier** in some listings to highlight important sections. In longer listings, we use "cue balls," such as ❶, to indicate lines of code that we discuss in notes to the listings.

Author Online

Purchase of *RSS and Atom in Action* includes free access to a private web forum run by Manning Publications where you can make comments about the book, ask technical questions, and receive help from the author and from other users. To access the forum and subscribe to it, point your web browser to www.manning.com/dmjohnson. This page provides information on how to get on the forum once you are registered, what kind of help is available, and the rules of conduct on the forum.

Manning's commitment to our readers is to provide a venue where a meaningful dialog between individual readers and between readers and the author can take place. It is not a commitment to any specific amount of participation on the part of the author, whose contribution to the AO remains voluntary (and unpaid). We suggest you try asking him some challenging questions, lest his interest stray!

The Author Online forum and the archives of previous discussions will be accessible from the publisher's web site as long as the book is in print.

About the author

DAVE JOHNSON works at Sun Microsystems, where he develops, supports, and promotes blog technologies. Prior to joining Sun, Dave worked for a variety of software companies, including SAS Institute, HAHT Commerce, and Rogue Wave Software. In 2002, unable to satisfy his urge to create cool software at work, Dave worked nights and weekends to create the open source Roller blog server, which is now used by thousands of bloggers at Sun, IBM, and JRoller.com.

About the title

By combining introductions, overviews, and how-to examples, the *In Action* books are designed to help learning and remembering. According to research in cognitive science, the things people remember are things they discover during self-motivated exploration.

Although no one at Manning is a cognitive scientist, we are convinced that for learning to become permanent it must pass through stages of exploration, play, and, interestingly, retelling of what is being learned. People understand and remember new things, which is to say they master them, only after actively exploring them. Humans learn in action. An essential part of an *In Action* guide is that it is example-driven. It encourages the reader to try things out, to play with new code, and explore new ideas.

There is another, more mundane, reason for the title of this book: our readers are busy. They use books to do a job or to solve a problem. They need books that allow them to jump in and jump out easily and learn just what they want just when they want it. They need books that aid them "in action." The books in this series are designed for such readers.

About the cover illustration

The figure on the cover of *RSS and Atom in Action* is a "Dervish of Syria." Muslim dervishes lived in religious communities, much like Christian monks, withdrawing from the world and leading lives of poverty and contemplation; they were known as a source of wisdom, medicine, poetry, enlightenment, and witticisms. The illustration is taken from a collection of costumes of the Ottoman Empire published on January 1, 1802, by William Miller of Old Bond Street, London. The title page is missing from the collection and we have been unable to track it down to date. The book's table of contents identifies the figures in both English and French, and each illustration bears the names of two artists who worked on it, both of whom would no doubt be surprised to find their art gracing the front cover of a computer programming book…two hundred years later.

The collection was purchased by a Manning editor at an antiquarian flea market in the "Garage" on West 26th Street in Manhattan. The seller was an American based in Ankara, Turkey, and the transaction took place just as he was packing up his stand for the day. The Manning editor did not have on his person the substantial amount of cash that was required for the purchase and a credit card and check were both politely turned down. With the seller flying back to Ankara that evening the situation was growing hopeless. What was the solution? It turned out to be nothing more than an old-fashioned verbal agreement sealed with a handshake. The seller simply proposed that the money be transferred to him by wire and the editor walked out with the bank information on a piece of paper and the portfolio of images under his arm. Needless to say, we transferred the funds the next day, and we remain grateful and impressed by this unknown person's trust in one of us. It recalls something that might have happened a long time ago.

The pictures from the Ottoman collection, like the other illustrations that appear on our covers, bring to life the richness and variety of dress customs of two centuries ago. They recall the sense of isolation and distance of that period—and of every other historic period except our own hyperkinetic present.

Dress codes have changed since then and the diversity by region, so rich at the time, has faded away. It is now often hard to tell the inhabitant of one continent from another. Perhaps, trying to view it optimistically, we have traded a cultural and visual diversity for a more varied personal life. Or a more varied and interesting intellectual and technical life.

We at Manning celebrate the inventiveness, the initiative, and, yes, the fun of the computer business with book covers based on the rich diversity of regional life of two centuries ago, brought back to life by the pictures from this collection.

Part 1

Programming the writable web

In part I, we start by introducing the new ways of collaboration made possible by blog technologies. We show you how simple it is to install a blog server and to write your first blog application. Once we've given you a taste of the possibilities and shown you how easy it is to get started, we teach you everything you need to know about using blog technology in your applications. We cover blog and wiki servers, newsfeed formats, parsing and producing newsfeeds, and blog publishing protocols. By the end of part I, you'll be ready to start writing your own blog applications.

What you need to know first

Here's what you need to know about Java (or C#), web development, and XML to get the most out of RSS and Atom in Action.

RSS and Atom in Action is a developer's and IT innovator's guide to developing applications with blog technologies, newsfeed syndication, and publishing protocols. In this chapter, we'll explain what that means and what you need to know to get the most out of the book.

First, because this is primarily a developer's book, we'll look at what you need to know about development. You need to understand either Java or C#, web development, and XML. For those who don't, we'll provide some pointers to good books and web sites that cover these topics. Next, to help you get oriented, we'll present a quick guide to blog technology terminology and introduce you to the software building blocks that are developed and used in the example applications. We'll wrap up by reviewing the structure and chapters of the book, so you can pick your own path through the material.

Let's get started by explaining the prerequisites. First are Java and C#. If you're already comfortable with the prerequisites, you can safely skip to Section 0.4, and start with blog technology terminology.

0.1 What you need to know about Java or C#

The majority of the examples in this book are about evenly split between Java and C#, so you'll need to know one or the other. Fortunately, Java and C# are similar. If you know one you should find it easy to follow all of the examples. There are also a couple of short examples in Python, which should be easy for Java or C# programmers to follow.

If you'd like to learn Java, start with Sun's free Java Tutorial. You can find it online at http://java.sun.com/tutorial. Manning also has available an introductory Java book titled *JDK 1.4 Tutorial* by Gregory M. Travis, which will give you the Java background necessary for understanding *RSS and Atom in Action*. Most of the Java examples include Ant-based build scripts, so knowledge of Ant is also useful. You can learn more about Ant in the Manning title *Java Development with Ant*, by Erik Hatcher and Steven Loughran.

If you'd like to take the C# route, you might start instead with Manning's *Microsoft .NET for Programmers* by Fergal Grimes. Note that you'll need a copy of Microsoft Visual Studio C# and Microsoft Visual Web Developer to build the examples, but you don't need to buy anything; you can use the free "express" versions of these products, as we did to develop and test the C# examples.

Now that we've covered programming languages, let's discuss what you need to know about the Web.

0.2 *What you need to know about web development*

As a web developer, you should have a basic knowledge of web standards HTTP, HTML, XML, CSS, and JavaScript. For this book, HTTP and XML are the most important of those standards. You don't need to be an HTTP guru, but you need to know that HTTP is a protocol for creating, retrieving, updating, and deleting resources on the Web. You also need to know about request parameters, HTTP headers, URIs, and content-types. You can learn about most of these by reading a good book on C# or Java web development, and we'll cite a couple of those below. But don't be afraid of the HTTP specification itself. It's short, to the point, and available online at http://www.ietf.org/rfc/rfc2616.txt.

0.2.1 *Web services*

We do *not* assume that you know much about web services. We'll teach you what you need to know about XML-RPC and REST-based web services in chapter 8 and chapter 9, respectively.

Now that we've covered the fundamentals, let's discuss the specific APIs that C# and Java programmers will to need know.

0.2.2 *Java web development*

The Java web development examples in the book use only Java's built-in support for web development. We assume you know the Servlet API in the Java package `javax.servlet` and are comfortable writing a Java Server Pages (JSP) page or a Servlet. We stick to the basics and avoid using any third-party web frameworks (such as Struts, Spring, or Tapestry).

If you'd like to learn more about Java web development, refer to these Manning titles:

- *Web Development with JavaServer Pages* by Duane K. Fields, Mark A. Kolb, and Shawn Bayern
- *Java Servlets by Example* by Alan R. Williamson

0.2.3 *C# web development*

The C# web development examples use only ASP.NET. To run them, you'll need Microsoft Visual Web Developer, which includes a built-in web server for testing, and optionally Internet Information Server (IIS). To learn more about ASP.NET, we recommend the Addison-Wesley title *Essential ASP.Net with Examples in C#,* by Fritz Onion.

0.2.4 *Running scheduled tasks*

Some of the examples in this book are designed to run on a schedule, every hour or every day. To use these examples, you'll need to know how to set up a scheduled task on your computer. On UNIX-based systems such as Linux, Mac OS, and Solaris you can do this with the cron command. On Windows, you can do the same thing with the Scheduled Task facility in the Windows Control Panel.

Now that we've covered web development, let discuss the XML prerequisite.

0.3 *What you need to know about XML*

As a C# or Java web developer, you can't escape XML. XML tools are built into both Java and .NET platforms. XML is used for system configuration files and is a part of almost every application. So we assume that you have a basic knowledge of XML. Again, you don't have to be a guru, but you should at least know about Document Type Definitions (DTDs) and XML Schema Definitions (XSDs) and how to use XML namespaces to add new XML elements to an XML format.

We also assume that you are familiar with the common techniques for parsing XML. Java and C# both support Document Object Model (DOM)-based parsers, which read an entire XML file into an in-memory tree representation, but they offer alternative approaches. If you'd like to learn more about XML, refer to the Addison-Wesley title *Essential XML: Beyond MarkUp*, by Don Box, Aaron Skonnard, and John Lam.

Since Java and C# parsing techniques are different, let's touch briefly on the Java and C# XML parsing tools we use in this book.

0.3.1 *Java XML tools*

In the Java examples, we use Java's built-in support for DOM- and SAX-based parsers. We also use JDOM, which is a popular open source DOM alternative designed to make the DOM more Java-like. If you understand DOM, you should have no problem following the JDOM examples.

0.3.2 *C# XML tools*

In the C# examples, we use only the built-in .NET XML classes, which are found in the .NET namespace System.Xml. We use both the DOM-based XmlDocument parser and the pull-based XmlTextReader parser.

That wraps up our discussion of prerequisites. Now let's get oriented by quickly reviewing the blog application terminology we'll be using in the book.

0.4 Blog technology terminology

Like most technologies, blog technology has its own collection of jargon and ordinary words that have been assigned special meaning. Jargon can be confusing, so let's kick-start the learning curve by defining some of the most commonly used blog technology terms.

- *Blog*—Short for *weblog*, a web-based personal journal or news site that makes it easy, even for nontechnical users, to publish on the web.

- *Wiki*—A free-form web site that anybody can edit and add pages to using a simple syntax.

- *Newsfeed Syndication*—Providing a newsfeed, or feed for short, a constantly updated XML representation of blog posts, wiki changes, or any other type of data that can be distributed as a collection of discrete items.

- *RSS*—a family of competing and not completely compatible XML newsfeed formats. The proponents of each format define the acronym RSS in different ways. Often used generically to describe newsfeeds in any format including Atom.

- *Atom publishing format*—The new Internet Engineering Task Force (IETF) standard newsfeed format that is likely to replace RSS in the coming years.

- *XML-RPC*—A simple web services protocol, and precursor to SOAP, that is the basis for most of today's commonly used blogging APIs, the most significant being the Blogger and MetaWeblog APIs.

- *MetaWeblog API*—An XML-RPC based protocol for publishing to a blog.

- *Atom publishing protocol*—The new IETF standard web services protocol for publishing to a blog, wiki, or other web content management system; it's likely to replace the XML-RPC based protocols over the next year.

- *Podcasting*—A technique for distributing files as attachments to newsfeed items; typically used to deliver audio files to digital media players, such as the Apple iPod.

- *Aggregator*—Software that combines multiple newsfeeds for display, for further syndication, or both.

- *Newsfeed reader*—A type of aggregator that is designed to make it easy for an individual to follow hundreds or even thousands of newsfeeds.

- *Outline Processor Markup Language (OPML)*—A simple XML format for representing outlines. Newsfeed readers use OPML as an import/export format for lists of subscription URLs.

- *Permalink*—each blog entry can be referred to and accessed by a permanent link. This enables bloggers to point to specific blog entries when they write about what they read on other blogs.

- *Ping*—In blog jargon, a notification message sent using XML-RPC protocol to a central server to indicate that a blog has been updated.

With the new terms fresh in your mind, let's move on to discuss the components we'll develop and use in the rest of the book.

0.5 *The components we'll use*

It's possible (and helpful) to think of blog applications, or *blog apps* for short, as Lego-like creations assembled from standard building blocks or, to use the term loosely, components. Both Java and C# provide extensive class libraries of components for doing everything from low-level IO to sending mail, to parsing XML. Numerous open-source projects offer even more building blocks for blog application development. And we'll develop some useful building blocks right here in the pages of this book.

0.5.1 *Blog application building blocks*

Thinking of blog applications as Lego-like creations gives us a shorthand notation for visualizing blog application architecture. Here we'll use that notation to introduce the blog applications we present in part II. Once you see the blocks and how we combine them, you'll get your own ideas for new combinations and interesting new applications. First, let's look at some of the book's most commonly used building blocks, shown in figure 0.1. Then, we'll look at some examples of how the blocks can be combined to form interesting blog applications.

As you can see, there are two types of blocks in figure 0.1: inputs and outputs. We show them in pairs; each input appears with its corresponding output. Let's discuss each block.

Figure 0.1 Starter set of building blocks for blog application development

- *Feed fetcher*—Fetches a feed from a web site or other location and parses that feed into data structures needed by a blog application. We discuss how to build a feed parser in chapter 5, how to use the Windows RSS Platform's built-in parser and fetcher in chapter 6, and how to use the Java-based ROME newsfeed parser and fetcher in chapter 7.

- *Feed provider*—Generates a feed and makes it available on the Web. We discuss how to build a feed server in chapter 8.

- *Publishing endpoint*—A server-side component that accepts and responds to incoming web services requests for a publishing protocol (such as Meta-Weblog API or the Atom protocol).

- *Publishing client*—Publishes to a blog, wiki, or content management system via web services protocol (such as MetaWeblog API or Atom protocol). We show how to build an XML-RPC based publishing client in chapter 9 and an Atom protocol-based client in chapter 10.

- *Mail receiver*—Can monitor an email inbox via POP or IMAP protocol, looking for new messages and downloading and processing those that meet some predefined criterion. We first use a mail receiver in chapter 14.

- *Mail sender*—Can send mail via SMTP protocol. We first use a mail sender in chapter 15.

- *File download*—Downloads files from a file server. We use file download first in chapter 19.

- *File server*—A server-side component that makes files available for download via HTTP, FTP, or another protocol. We create a simple web-based file server in chapter 18.

- *Ping endpoint*—A server-side component that accepts notification pings.

- *Ping sender*—Sends notification pings via an XML-RPC based protocol.

With that simple set of blocks, we can build all sorts of blog applications. Let's use those blocks to visualize a real-world example: the Flickr.com photo-sharing service. Figure 0.2 shows how you'd represent Flickr.com using our blocks.

To make the distinction between inputs and outputs clear, we show inputs on the left and outputs on the right. On the input side, Flickr.com provides a publishing endpoint so that programs can automatically upload photos. This is what enables you to post photographs to Flickr.com directly from your camera phone.

On the output side, Flickr.com allows you to subscribe to newsfeeds of newly uploaded photos via its feed server component. It can automatically post new

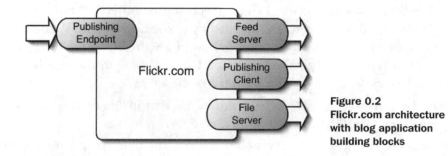

**Figure 0.2
Flickr.com architecture
with blog application
building blocks**

photos to your blog by using its publishing client component. And it allows you to view and download photos using its file server component.

Now that we've covered the prerequisites and reviewed our building materials, it's time to help you find your way around the book.

0.6 Organization of the book

RSS and Atom in Action is organized into two parts. The first part introduces you to blog technologies of newsfeed formats and publishing protocols—the building blocks. The second part shows you how to put those blocks together to assemble some interesting and useful blog applications.

To make it easy for you to pick and choose the chapters you want to read and to use the book as a reference, let's review the organization of the book chapter by chapter, listing the prerequisites for each.

Part I: Programming the writable web

- Chapter 1, "New ways of collaborating"—This chapter illustrates the potential of blog technologies using a series of user stories. The characters and stories are fictional, but they're composites of real-world experiences. Prerequisites: no programming experience required.

- Chapter 2, "Development kick-start"—In this chapter, we'll show you how to get started by setting up a blog server and writing a simple blog app in Java or C# that publishes to the server using XML-RPC. Prerequisites: basic knowledge of Java or C#.

- Chapter 3, "Under the hood"—This chapter will teach you everything a blog app developer needs to know about blog and wiki server architecture. It also offers some guidelines for selecting blog and wiki servers. Prerequisites: no programming experience required.

- Chapter 4, "Newsfeed formats"—In this chapter, we'll discuss the contentious history of RSS newsfeed formats, detail the most widely used newsfeed formats, and introduce the new IETF standard Atom newsfeed format. Prerequisites: knowledge of XML.

- Chapter 5, "How to parse newsfeeds"—This chapter will show you how to parse RSS and Atom newsfeeds into data structures you can use in your blog applications. We'll show you how to use the XML parsers built into Java and C#, and specialized newsfeed parsing libraries. Prerequisites: knowledge of XML and Java or C#.

- Chapter 6, "The Windows RSS Platform"—With the introduction of Internet Explorer 7 and Vista, Microsoft is adding comprehensive RSS and Atom support to Windows. In this chapter, you'll learn how to manage subscriptions, fetch, and parse newsfeeds with Microsoft's new Feeds API. Prerequisites: knowledge of XML and C#.

- Chapter 7, "The ROME newsfeed utilities"—The open source ROME project provides the premier RSS and Atom toolset for Java. We'll show you how to use ROME to parse, generate, and fetch newsfeeds. We'll also show you how to use ROME's flexible plug-in architecture to extend ROME to support new newsfeed extensions and variants. Prerequisites: knowledge of XML and Java.

- Chapter 8, "How to serve newsfeeds"—In this chapter, you'll learn how to share data in newsfeed formats, and you'll learn what you need to know about generating newsfeed XML and serving it efficiently on your web site or in your web application. Prerequisites: knowledge of web development, XML, and Java or C#.

- Chapter 9, "Publishing with XML-RPC based APIs"—We'll build a simple blog client library in this chapter using the XML-RPC based web service protocols to publish to and interact with a remote blog server. Prerequisites: knowledge of C# (example code is also available in Java).

- Chapter 10, "Publishing with Atom"—In this chapter, we'll implement the same blog client library we developed in chapter 9, but this time with the new IETF Atom protocol. Prerequisites: knowledge of web development and Java.

Part II: Blog apps

- Chapter 11, "Creating a group blog via aggregation"—A group aggregator combines a set of blogs to form one blog with its own newsfeed. In this chapter, we'll introduce the Planet Tool aggregator. Prerequisites: knowledge of Java helpful, but not required.

- Chapter 12, "Searching and monitoring the Web"—Search engines now index newsfeeds and offer search results in newsfeed formats. In this chapter, you'll learn about the most popular of the newsfeed search engines. We also present a blog app that uses a Technorati API (TAPI) to save a blog's incoming or outgoing links to Outline Processor Markup Language (OPML) format, which is a popular format for exchange lists of blogs and newsfeeds. Prerequisites: no programming experience required, except for the Technorati-to-OPML example.

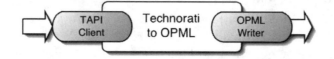

- Chapter 13, "Keep your blog in sync"—If you have multiple blogs, consider using a cross poster, like the C# one we'll present in this chapter, to gather posts from your secondary blog's newsfeeds and repost them to your primary one. Prerequisites: knowledge of C# (example code is also available in Java).

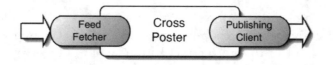

- Chapter 14, "Blog by sending email"—You can blog by sending email using the C# program we'll present in this chapter. Prerequisites: knowledge of C# (example code is also available in Java).

- Chapter 15, "Sending a daily blog digest"—You can notify your readers of new blog posts via email with the C# program presented in this chapter. Prerequisites: knowledge of C# (example code is also available in Java).

- Chapter 16, "Blog your software build process"—You can build a software project blog by publishing build messages, unit test results, and other build events to a blog using the custom Ant tasks presented in this chapter. Prerequisites: knowledge of Java and the Ant build system.

- Chapter 17, "Blog from a chat room"—In this chapter, we'll present a chatbot, a program that enables you to blog from an IRC chat room. Prerequisites: knowledge of Java.

- Chapter 18, "Distribute files podcast style"—Use podcasting as a technique for distributing any type of file with the Java-based web application discussed in this chapter. The example is FileCaster, a web application that allows users to upload files and provides a newsfeed of most recent files uploaded. Prerequisites: knowledge of web development and Java.

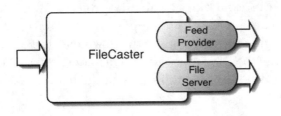

- Chapter 19, "Automatically download podcasts"—Use the Java program outlined in this chapter to automatically download podcasts and route them to different directories on your computer. The example is File-Catcher, a command-line program that subscribes to a newsfeed and downloads any podcasts it finds. Prerequisites: knowledge of Java.

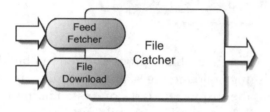

- Chapter 20, "Validate newsfeeds automatically"—The best way to validate newsfeeds is the Python-based Feed Validator. In this chapter, we'll show you how to write a Python script to automatically validate your newsfeeds and notify you via email of any failed validation.

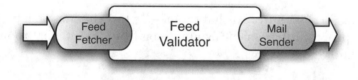

- Chapter 21, "The best of the rest"—In the final chapter of the book, we'll present more than two dozen additional blog technology applications we just couldn't fit in the book. Prerequisites: no programming experience required.

0.7 The Blogapps examples

The example programs in this book are maintained as an open source project called Blogapps, which is hosted at Sun Microsystem's Java.NET open source community site. To get the examples, go to the project's Web site at http://blogapps.dev.java.net and download the Blogapps examples. You can find instructions for building and running the examples in the download and on the Web site. That's also where you'll find the Blogapps server, which we'll cover in chapter 2, a complete blog and wiki server designed to work with the book's examples.

0.8 Summary

At this point, you should be prepared for *RSS and Atom in Action*. You know what you're expected to know, you're familiar with the components we'll be using, and you can find your way around the book.

New ways of collaborating

Thanks to blogs, wikis, and news-feeds, reading and writing the Web has become simple and convenient.

Even the most casual observer can see that blogs, wikis, and newsfeeds have taken over the Internet and sparked a revolution in citizens' media, corporate communications, and collaboration on the Web. The reason for this revolution is simplicity. Blogs, wikis, and newsfeeds make it simple for anybody to read and write the Web. Not only that, but they also make it easy for your software to do the same thing. Newsfeed formats RSS and Atom enable your software to monitor the Web and to extract meaningful data from web sites. Publishing protocols such as MetaWeblog API and Atom Protocol make it easy for your software to publish to the Web.

In this chapter, we'll introduce you to the new world of opportunities created by blog technologies. You don't have to be a programmer to recognize these opportunities. All you need is a basic knowledge of web technologies and a good imagination. Let's start by taking a look at how blogs, wikis, and blog technologies took root at FinModler, a fictional medium-size technology firm in Research Triangle Park, N.C.

1.1 *Research blogging*

Carl is a marketing strategist who works for FinModler. He specializes in competitive analysis for his company's suite of financial modeling applications and is responsible for tracking three vertical market segments. Carl's job is to keep the rest of the company informed about competitors in the equities trading, insurance, and banking industries. He does this by maintaining a blog for each of his three topic areas. The blog is hosted on an internal blog server that is accessible only to company employees. Whenever a notable development occurs in one of his three markets, he writes a short blog entry to offer some analysis of the development and to provide reference links so that his readers can learn more.

Readers often ask questions by leaving comments on Carl's blogs, and Carl takes pleasure in answering each question in great detail. His blog is part of the FinModler corporate intranet, and it is indexed by the company's internal search engine. Whenever folks are looking for information about the equities trading, insurance, or banking markets, a quick search will usually take them to one of Carl's informative blog entries.

When he first started blogging, Carl found it difficult to post to three separate blogs. He considered using just one blog, with three categories of posts, but he decided that his topic areas were different enough to warrant three separate blogs. Eventually, Carl found a blog editor called MarsEdit (figure 1.1) that makes blogging a lot easier and more like sending email, with spell checking, drafts, and

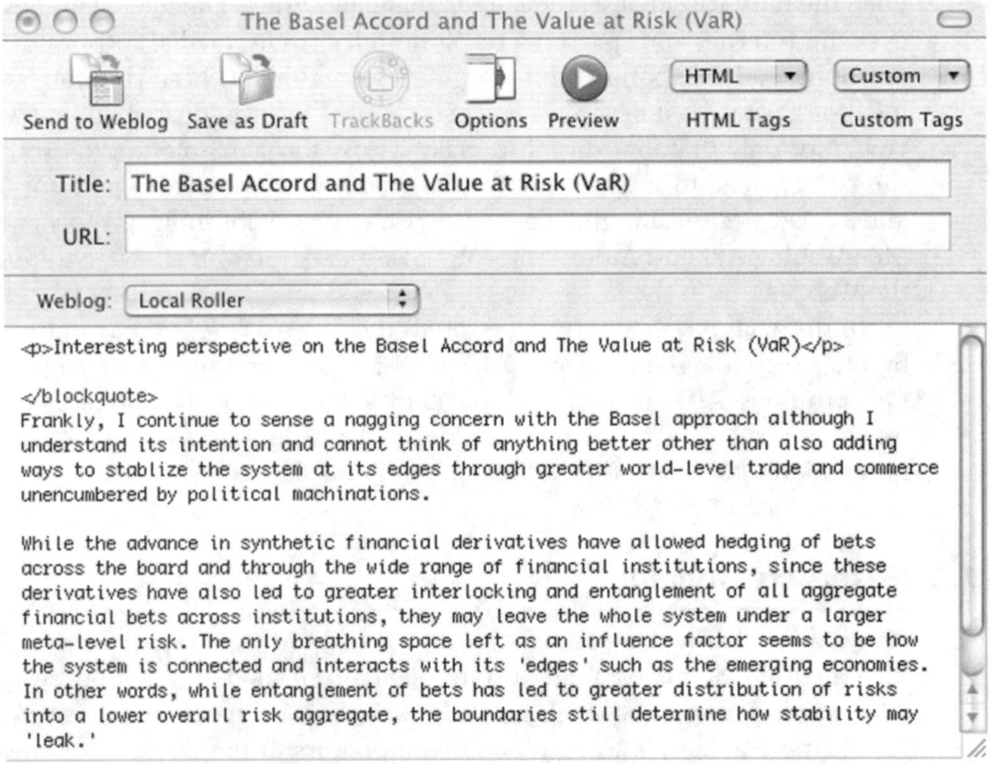

Figure 1.1 The MarsEdit blog client

support for posting to multiple blog servers. Carl has also used Ecto, an alternative to MarsEdit that runs on both Windows and Mac OS.

Carl tracks his three vertical markets by doing a lot of reading and skimming. He subscribes to numerous journals and research services. He also watches online forums and blogs where customers and potential customers discuss FinModler products. Obviously, Carl can't read every single new research paper, news item, and discussion forum in each of his topic areas. But blog technology makes his job a lot easier.

Each of the web sites Carl follows provides a *newsfeed*, an XML representation of the recent news items posted to the site. Carl uses a *newsfeed reader* called NetNewsWire (figure 1.2) to subscribe to and read newsfeeds from hundreds of web-based news sources. Thanks to his newsfeed reader, Carl doesn't have to visit the sites he is tracking. When a site is updated, the news

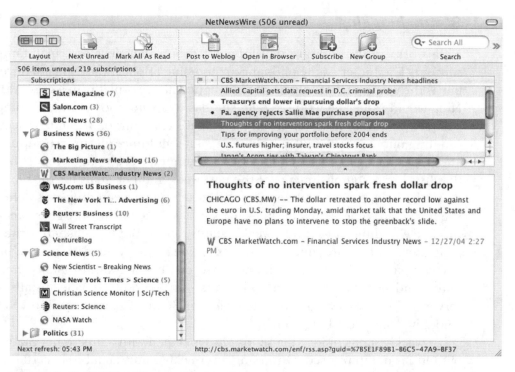

Figure 1.2   The NetNewsWire newsfeed reader

is delivered right to his desktop. NetNewsWire is not the only choice; some of Carl's associates prefer BlogLines, a web-based newsfeed reader that provides the same functionality.

Banks that are interested in risk management methodologies, such as Value at Risk and Basel II, are potential customers for FinModler's software, so Carl wants to be informed of any news stories or blog entries that mention these terms. By using Feedster, a search engine that subscribes to and indexes newsfeeds of all varieties, Carl can search for exactly what he wants. And because Feedster subscribes to newsfeeds rather than crawling the entire Web, the results are more accurate and timely. On top of that, Feedster can return search results in the form of newsfeeds. So Carl uses his newsfeed reader to subscribe to Feedster searches for the phrases *Value at Risk* and *Basel II*. Whenever one of these phrases is mentioned in a newsfeed, Carl's newsfeed reader delivers the news to him via Feedster.

1.2 *Status blogging*

Nina works in the software development group that develops, maintains, and supports FinModler's suite of financial modeling applications. She is a developer, but as the group's UNIX expert she is assigned all cross-platform issues. Although Nina would rather be writing code, she has to spend a lot of time dealing with complex application server installs, database configurations, and projects that can drag out over several days and necessitate multiple calls to tech support.

Nina's manager, Otto, requires her to submit a weekly status report by email that lists her accomplishments of the past week and her goals for the next week. Unfortunately, Nina is multitasking and switching between projects so often that she has a hard time remembering what she has done during any given week, and this makes it difficult to write a weekly status report. But Nina likes to write and is a blogger in her spare time, so she gets an idea. She decides to set up a blog on her company's private network and to record her accomplishments, her work notes, and her thoughts on a daily basis—as blog entries. She installs a blog server and creates a blog with categories for Status, Goals, Notes, and Random Thoughts. She starts blogging.

At weekly status time, Nina sends Otto an email with a link to her Status blog, but Otto is not impressed. Otto wants his weekly status emails. He certainly does not want to have to visit each of his team members' blogs and try to piece together their accomplishments and goals. To Nina, this represents a challenge, but not for long. Nina knows how easy it is to parse the newsfeed that her blog server produces.

In a couple of hours, Nina writes a simple blog app that fetches the newsfeed from her blog, parses the newsfeed, and then composes and sends an email that lists all of her Status blog entries and all of her Goals blog entries (figure 1.3). Her blog application formats the email to look just like the ones she used to write by hand. She creates a `cron` task on her favorite Linux box to run the blog application every Friday. She is particularly tickled by the fact that for a while, Otto remains unaware. He doesn't realize that she has automated her status report until she calls in sick one Friday and her status report still arrives in his inbox at 2:00 P.M. sharp.

If you'd like to send a daily or weekly summary of posts to a blog, chapter 15 will show you how to do it.

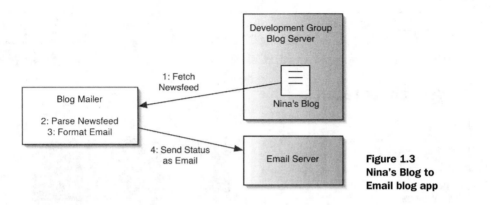

**Figure 1.3
Nina's Blog to
Email blog app**

1.3 *Build blogging*

Nina's coworker Rangu also works for Otto in the development department at FinModler. Rangu started as the build guy, but his role in the group has expanded to include source code control, issue tracking, and managing the group's wiki. Part of Rangu's job is to keep other groups within FinModler informed of each new software build.

Otto, impressed with Nina's and Carl's use of blogs, asks Rangu to start a blog to announce new builds. Rangu thinks a build blog is a good idea, but he does not want to add a manual step to his completely automated nightly build process. Rangu starts thinking about ways to automatically blog his builds.

After work, Rangu, who happens to be an avid photographer, is shopping for an online photo service so that he can share his photographs with his friends. He looks at a number of web sites, including Shutterfly, Snapfish, and Flickr (figure 1.4). Flickr impresses him because it provides a newsfeed for each user, so his friends can subscribe to his new photos. When he reads that Flickr allows users to post photographs to their blogs, Rangu is intrigued.

The next day, Rangu asks Nina how Flickr can post photos to so many different blog servers. Nina says, "That's easy, Rangu. Just about every blog server in existence supports the MetaWeblog API." Rangu quickly locates the documentation for the MetaWeblog API, fires up his favorite IDE, and gets to work. In only an afternoon, he writes a simple blog application, a plug-in for the group's Ant-based build system. The app allows the build system to post messages to the blog via a web services-based publishing protocol. When a release build is created, the build script automatically updates the blog—problem solved.

Figure 1.4   The Flickr photo-sharing web site

If you'd like to create an Ant task that can post to a blog, chapter 16 will show you how to do it.

1.4 *Blogging the business*

At his weekly staff meeting, the CIO mentions that on a recent flight, he read an interesting article about the benefits of blogs and wikis in the workplace. He tells Otto and Kate, who manages the marketing communications group, that the CEO has always been concerned that the groups and divisions in the company are not communicating and collaborating effectively.

Otto takes the opportunity to tell the CIO about Nina's status report blog and Rangu's build system blog. And Kate mentions Carl's vertical market blogs and describes how he uses a newsfeed reader and newsfeed searches to monitor developments on the Web. The CIO is intrigued. Before you can say "leveraging intergroup synergies," Otto and Kate are heading up the new blog and wiki implementation task force. When they return to their office, they schedule a meeting with the existing bloggers in the development and marketing groups.

At next week's meeting, Otto starts by wondering aloud about the effectiveness of blogging in the workplace. He says, "Getting my staff to write status reports is like pulling teeth. How can I expect them to become bloggers?" Carl chimes in. "Yeah, and most developers are horrible writers." Fortunately, Nina and Rangu have spent some time preparing for the meeting and are ready for these questions. "We're not going to ask anybody to do what they are not already doing. We're just going to make it easier for everybody to share information," Rangu says. He turns on the projector and shows everybody a slide of what he calls *use cases*, specific tasks that people will perform with blog and wiki software. The slide lists these use cases:

- Reporting progress and status
- Recording research activities
- Sharing build and test results
- Documenting test plans and configurations
- Sharing corporate news
- Monitoring the market
- Building the FinModler customer community

Rangu explains that these use cases all represent activities they're already doing. For example, they already ask employees to write weekly status reports and to record research activities. By asking them to use blogs instead of email, they'll gain visibility, as anybody in the company will be able to read, search, and even subscribe to these writings. This will help the company communicate and collaborate more closely.

"The CIO has always wanted us to announce corporate news, build results, and test results on the internal Web; blogs and wikis make this much easier to do," Rangu says. "We won't have to edit, upload, and maintain individual web pages anymore. Plus, we'll be able to use web services to automate the sharing of build and test reports."

Otto asks, "What about that last bullet, 'Building the FinModler customer community'—we are definitely not doing that now." Carl says, "I know. Don't you think that's a problem? Every day I watch as our customers and potential customers grouse about our products and services on web forums and blogs, and I wish we had some way to join in the conversation. Microsoft and Sun Microsystems are doing that by allowing their employees to blog publicly, and it has done wonders for their public images. Maybe we should do the same."

After a lively discussion of the legal implications of public blogs, Nina takes a turn at the projector. "We've discussed how blog and wiki technologies make it easy to write the Web; now let's talk about how they make it easy to read the Web." She quickly explains the newsfeed concept and how newsfeeds enable people like Carl to follow numerous sources of news and information. "Newsfeeds are not just for blogs anymore," she tells them. "Any data source that changes over time could potentially produce a newsfeed." She advances to the next slide and shows the group a list of newsfeed use cases:

- Content syndication
- Web search results
- Issue tracking
- Monitoring wiki changes
- Monitoring source code changes
- File distribution: audio, video, software patches

Nina explains that *content syndication*—or, more simply, making web content available to other web sites and applications—is the classic newsfeed use case. That's the use case that makes thousands upon thousands of news sources available to Carl for his market research. Carl also takes advantage of web search results in newsfeed form.

Nina explains that many of the software applications they use in-house are starting to provide newsfeeds. For example, the development team uses the JIRA issue tracker, which provides newsfeeds of newly added bugs, newly resolved bugs, and user-defined queries against the issue database. Wikis also provide newsfeeds to inform users of each change made.

To explain the file distribution use case, Nina tells the group about *podcast* newsfeeds, special newsfeeds that can contain binary file attachments, such as audio files. Nina says, "I use this software called iPodder to subscribe to podcast newsfeeds. Whenever a new audio file appears on one of my subscriptions, iPodder downloads it and transfers it to my iPod, so I always have interesting things to listen to during my early morning run."

The group starts talking about podcasts, iPods, and other MP3 players until Otto realizes that they've run out of time. Otto calls an end to the meeting and tells Nina and Rangu, "Let's meet again next week to talk about what software we'll need to deploy. This stuff sounds great, but we'll need to get a handle on the costs before we can go much further."

1.5 *Nina's and Rangu's grand plan*

The next week when they reconvene, Nina goes first. She starts by telling the group, "We won't have to deploy any expensive or complex software at all to get started with blogs and wikis. Blog and wiki server software will work with our existing web servers, and most of it is either open source or relatively inexpensive." Nina notices that managers Otto and Kate are smiling and obviously pleased with her presentation so far.

"But we will want to set aside some development resources, because once we get started we are going to discover all sorts of interesting ways to integrate blogs

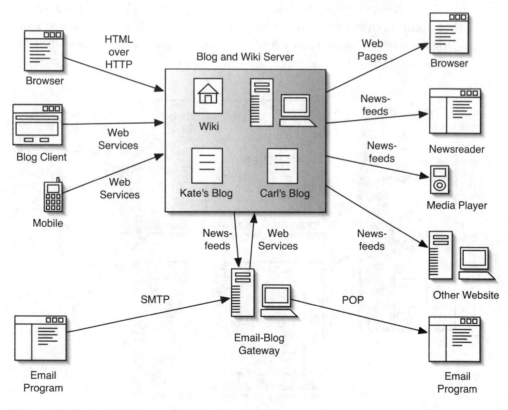

Figure 1.5   Blog and wiki server inputs and outputs

and wikis with our existing software and business processes." Nina turns to her laptop, starts her presentation software, and shows the attendees her first slide. It's a diagram with blog and wiki inputs on the left and blog and wiki outputs on the right (figure 1.5). "This slide shows some of the software and devices that already work with blogs and wikis today."

Nina explains the input side first. "Most people will use a web browser to post and edit blog entries and wiki pages. But web services protocols make it possible to blog via specialized blog clients, like Carl's MarsEdit blog editor, mobile-phone blogging, or *moblogging* software, or even via email. We can use those protocols too. In fact, just the other week, Rangu used them to enable our build script to post build announcements to a blog." Next, Nina explains the output side. "Most people start off using a web browser to read blogs but eventually switch to a news-feed reader once they understand the benefits. And as we learned last week, an iPod lets users listen to an audio blog, thanks to the magic of podcasting."

Once Nina wraps up her discussion of blog and wiki server inputs and outputs, Rangu takes over to explain their plan. "What we'd like to do is seed a network of blogs and wikis." Rangu uses Nina's laptop to advance to the next slide of the presentation (figure 1.6).

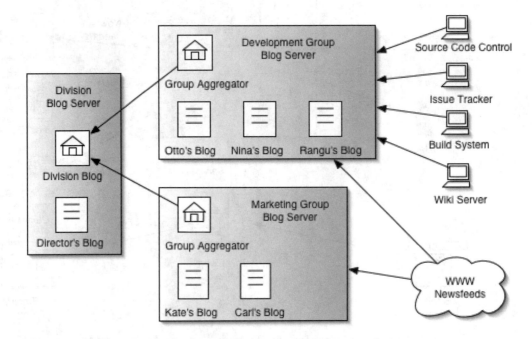

Figure 1.6 Network of blogs, wikis, and aggregators

Rangu explains the plan: "We'll provide the development group, the marketing group, and the division director's office with a blog server. Each group member will have his own blog, and each group will have an *aggregator* that combines the group members' individual newsfeeds to form a new group blog with its own aggregated newsfeed. Anything that produces a newsfeed can be added to the aggregator, including source code control systems, issue trackers, build systems, and wiki servers. Employees will be expected to report status on their blogs rather than via email and encouraged to journal their daily activities and observations."

Otto and Kate are pleased with Nina's and Rangu's plan because it offers clear benefits and can be implemented easily with inexpensive components and a small amount of programming. The resulting network of blogs and blog aggregators will enable groups to communicate and collaborate more effectively, allow managers to monitor status at any level of the organization, and build a searchable web of corporate knowledge that is useful to all.

1.6 *Summary*

You can do the same things that Carl, Nina, Rangu, and friends are doing. In this book, we'll show you how. In part I we will cover blog application development in detail. After teaching you what every developer needs to know about blog and wiki server internals, we'll show you how to read, parse, and serve RSS and Atom newsfeeds. We'll also show you how to use XML-RPC and Atom Protocol web services interfaces to automate blog and wiki tasks. In part II, we'll provide you with a collection of interesting blog applications, including a web-based aggregator and a podcast server. Let's get started. In the next chapter, we'll hit the ground running by developing our first blog application.

Development kick-start

2

With the help of the MetaWebLog API, we'll get our feet wet and build a simple blog application.

In this chapter, we'll walk you through the installation of a blog server and the development of your first blog app, a simple console program that can post to a blog.

2.1 *Blog server setup*

The examples in this book should work with just about any blog server, but to make things easy for you, we provide an easy to install blog server, *Blogapps server*, based on the Roller blog server, which you can use to run the examples. Blogapps server is exceedingly easy to install, includes an integrated wiki, and supports all of the blog and wiki features we need for the blog apps in the book. You don't have to use Blogapps server—other blog servers will work. But it is the easiest way to get started. You can install Blogapps server by following the steps below:

Step 1 Install the J2SDK. Before installing Blogapps server, you will need to install the Java 2 Software Development Kit (J2SDK) version 1.4 or later on your computer. You can download the J2SDK from the Sun Microsystems Web site (http://java.sun.com). Follow the instructions on the Sun site to download and install the J2SDK. Then, you'll need to set the environment variable JAVA_HOME equal to the directory path where you installed the J2SDK.

> **NOTE** Windows users: set the JAVA_HOME variable by right-clicking on the My Computer icon on your desktop, clicking the Properties menu item, and then clicking the Environment Variables button on the Advanced tab of the System Properties dialog. You may set JAVA_HOME as either a User or a System variable.
>
> UNIX users: set the JAVA_HOME variable in your shell's run command file.

Step 2 Download and unpackage Blogapps server. Download the latest version from the Blogapps project home page on Java.NET(http://Blogapps.dev. java.net). Unpackage the downloaded file into a directory on your computer and make sure that the directory's name and path do not include any spaces.

NOTE Windows users: download Blogapps server and use WinZip or Cywin tar to uncompress and untar it into a directory on your computer.

UNIX users: download Blogapps server and use GNU tar to uncompress and untar the demo into a directory on your computer. For example:

```
% cp blogapps-server-1.0.tar.gz /usr/local
% cd /usr/local
% tar xzvf blogapps-server-1.0.tar.gz
```

Step 3 Start Blogapps server. Before you attempt to start Blogapps server, make sure that the variables CATALINA_HOME and CATALINA_BASE are *not* defined in your environment. To start the Blogapps server server, just run the appropriate startup script. You can find the startup script in the bin directory of the Blogapps server installation. The Windows version of the script is called startup.bat, and the UNIX version is called startup.sh. The script takes no arguments, so all you have to do is run it.

NOTE Windows users: open the Blogapps server directory using Windows Explorer and double-click on startup.bat to start Blogapps server.

UNIX users: change directory to the bin directory of the Blogapps server installation and run the script startup.sh. For example:

```
% cd /usr/local/blogapps-server/bin
% ./startup.sh
```

Step 4 Verify that Blogapps server is running. Start your favorite web browser, type the address *http://localhost:8080/roller* into the address bar, and hit Enter. You should see the web page shown in figure 2.1.

Step 5 Shut down Blogapps server. When you have finished using the Blogapps server, you should shut it down properly. To do this, run the shutdown script the same way you ran the startup script. The Windows version of the shutdown script is called shutdown.bat and the UNIX version is called shutdown.sh.

Now that we have a running blog server, we're ready to start developing our first blog application.

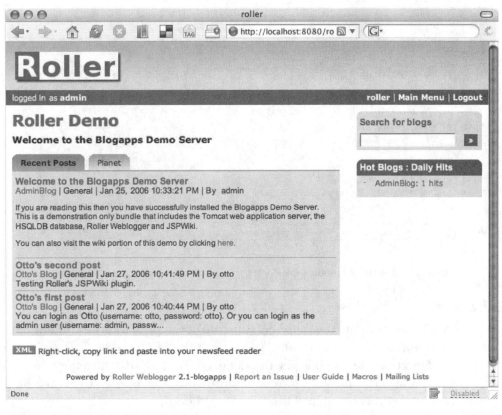

Figure 2.1   Welcome to Blogapps server

2.2 *The Blog Poster example*

We'll create Blog Poster by using a web services protocol known as the Meta-Weblog API, which is supported by most popular blog servers. We will use the MetaWeblog API `newPost` method to post to a blog.

The MetaWeblog API is based on XML-RPC, a simple web services specification that is the predecessor to SOAP. Like SOAP, XML-RPC allows you to make remote procedure calls by sending and receiving XML files over HTTP. We will discuss XML-RPC and other Web services specifications in more detail in chapter 9. For now, all you need to know is that XML-RPC is a remote procedure call mechanism and that XML-RPC client libraries exist for both Java and C#, which makes using XML-RPC a simple task.

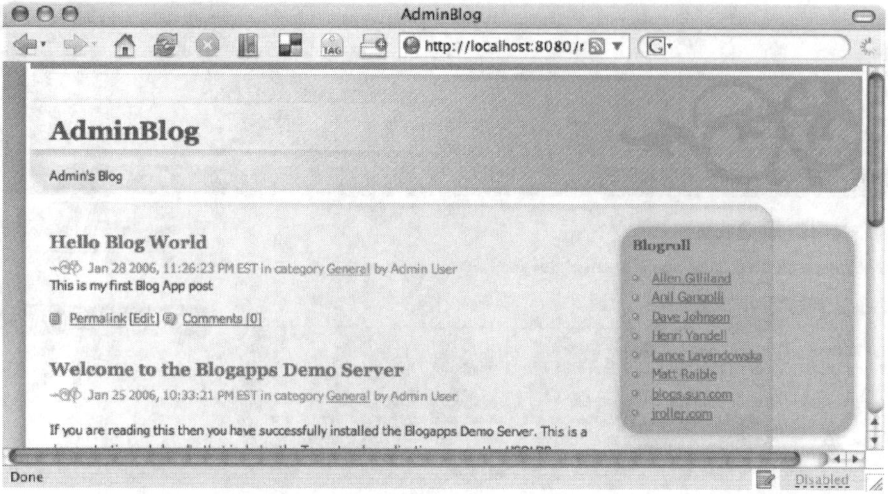

Figure 2.2   Results of running Blog Poster

2.2.1 *Invoking Blog Poster*

Blog Poster takes two parameters, the title of the post and the content of the post. The address of the target blog server and the login credentials are read from a configuration file. We'll cover the details of running the Java and C# versions of Blog Poster later, but let's look at a simple usage example. To invoke Blog Poster from a Windows command line, you would do this:

```
c> BlogPoster "Hello Blog World" "This is my first Blog App post"
```

The result would be that a message with the title "Hello Blog World" and the content "This is my first Blog App post" would be posted to the blog server specified in the application's configuration file. On the example blog server, the post would look like figure 2.2.

Now that we have seen the results of Blog Poster, let's take a look at the code.

2.3 *Blog Poster for Java*

The Java version of Blog Poster is a single Java class called `BlogPoster`. Most of the code in the example involves parsing input arguments and reading the configuration file. We use the Apache XML-RPC client library to invoke the Meta-Weblog API `newPost` method, and that takes only about a dozen lines of code. The complete source code for Blog Poster for Java is shown in listing 2.1.

Listing 2.1 BlogPoster.java

```java
package com.manning.blogapps.chapter02;
import java.util.Date;
import java.util.Hashtable;
import java.util.Properties;
import java.util.Vector;
import org.apache.xmlrpc.XmlRpcClient;

public class BlogPoster {

    public static void main(String[] args) throws Exception {    ◄─❶

        System.out.println("Simple MetaWeblog Client in Java");
        String title = null;
        String description = null;
        if (args.length == 1) {    ◄─❷
            description = args[0];
        }
        else if (args.length == 2) {
            title = args[0];
            description = args[1];
        }
        else {
            System.out.println("USAGE: BlogPoster [desc]");
            System.out.println("USAGE: BlogPoster [title] [desc]");
            return;
        }

        Properties config = new Properties();
        config.load(BlogPoster.class.getResourceAsStream(    ◄─❸
            "config.properties"));
        String target = config.getProperty("target");    ◄─❹
        String blogid = config.getProperty("blogid");    ◄─❺
        String username = config.getProperty("username");    ◄─❻
        String password = config.getProperty("password");

        Hashtable post = new Hashtable();    ◄─❼
        post.put("dateCreated", new Date());
        if (title != null) post.put("title", title);
        post.put("description", description);

        Vector params = new Vector();    ◄─❽
        params.addElement(blogid);
        params.addElement(username);
        params.addElement(password);
        params.addElement(post);
        params.addElement(Boolean.TRUE);

        XmlRpcClient xmlrpc = new XmlRpcClient(target);    ◄─❾
            String result = (String)xmlrpc.execute (
            "metaWeblog.newPost", params);
```

```
        System.out.println("newPost result: " + result);   ◄—❿
    }
}
```

We start by creating a simple command-line program, a class called `BlogPoster` with a static `main()` ❶ method as the entry point and by parsing the command-line arguments ❷.

Next, we read the blog server connection parameters from the properties file ❸. To post to a blog server, we need the URL of the target blog server's XML-RPC interface ❹, a valid blog account ID ❺, and a valid username-password pair for that blog account ❻. We do not want the user to have to type this information on every invocation, so we look for it in a simple properties file called config.properties. In the next section of code, we load the properties file and retrieve the blog server connection parameters.

Apache XML-RPC expects us to package the blog post structure as a `java.util.Hashtable` object, so next we add the three post fields `dateCreated`, `title`, and `description` to a hashtable called `post` ❼.

We now have all of the information we need to post to the blog server, and we are ready to make our post by calling the MetaWeblog API `newPost` method.

To call `newPost` using the Apache XML-RPC library, we must first package the parameter list as a `java.util.Vector`, so here we create a vector ❽ and add to it the necessary parameters. The signature of the `newPost` method is shown below. As you can see, the order and type of the parameters we put into the vector match this signature.

```
String newPost(
    String blogid,
    String username,
    String password,
    Struct post,
    Boolean publish)
```

Finally, we make the actual call to `newPost` by creating an `XmlRpcClient` ❾ and calling its `execute()` method ❿ with the name of the RPC method and the arguments we have packaged for the call. If the call succeeds, the method will return the ID of the blog entry that was posted to the server. If the call fails, an exception will be thrown and the user will see a stack trace printed to the console.

So there you have it. A small amount of Java code and an XML-RPC client library are all it takes to write a simple blog application. Now it's time to run the example.

2.3.1 *Running Blog Poster for Java*

The examples directory contains the source code for this example in Blog-Poster.java, an Ant script to build it, and a command script to run it. Below are the steps required to build and run BlogPoster:

Step 1 Start the Blogapps server server or your preferred blog server.

Step 2 Ensure that the properties file is set up properly for calling the blog server. As an example, this config.properties file shows the correct parameters for posting to a Blogapps server blog server running on the same machine:

```
blogid=adminblog
username=admin
password=admin
target=http://localhost:8080/roller/xmlrpc
```

Step 3 Build the example. Open a command-line window, change directory to the proper directory, and run Ant. For example, if you are running Windows and you have unpackaged the examples into c:\blogapps, you would do the following:

```
c> cd c:\blogapps\java
c> ant
c> ch ch02
c> ant
```

Step 4 Run the example. From that same command-line window, run the start script. For Windows, use the batch script BlogPoster.bat. For UNIX, use the shell script BlogPoster.sh. For example, on Windows you might do the following:

```
c> BlogPoster "Hello Blog World" "This is my first Blog App post"
```

Now that we know how to develop and run Blog Poster for Java, let's turn our attention to the C# version.

2.4 *Blog Poster for C#*

The C# version of Blog Poster is also a single class called BlogPoster. As in the Java version, most of the code involves parsing input arguments and reading the configuration file.

We'll use the Cook Computing XML-RPC.NET client library, which uses a dynamic proxy approach to make calling XML-RPC methods as easy as calling normal C# methods. Because of this approach, the code that invokes the newPost method looks quite different from the equivalent code in the Java version.

We will implement the whole example in one C# file called BlogPoster.cs, which is shown in listing 2.2.

Listing 2.2   BlogPoster.cs

```csharp
using System;
using System.Configuration;
using System.Collections.Specialized;
using CookComputing.XmlRpc;

namespace BlogApps_Chapter02 {

    public struct Post {
        public DateTime dateCreated;
        public string description;
        public string title;
    }
    public interface IMetaWeblog {
        [XmlRpcMethod("metaWeblog.newPost")]          <--①
            string metaweblog_newPost(
            string blogid,
            string username,
            string password,
            Post post,
            bool publish);
    }

    class BlogPoster {          <--②

        static void Main(string[] args) {          <--③

            System.Console.WriteLine("Simple MetaWeblog Client in C#");
            string title = null;
            string description = null;
            if (args.Length == 1) {          <--④
                description = args[0];
            }
            else if (args.Length == 2) {
                title = args[0];
                description = args[1];
            }
            else {
                System.Console.WriteLine(
                    "USAGE: BlogPoster [description]");
                System.Console.WriteLine(
                    "USAGE: BlogPoster [title] [description]");
                return;
            }

            NameValueCollection settings =
                ConfigurationSettings.AppSettings;          <--⑤
```

```
        string target = settings.Get("target");    ←─6
        string blogid = settings.Get("blogid");     ←─7
        string username = settings.Get("username");   ←─8
        string password = settings.Get("password");

        Post post = new Post();    ←─9
        post.dateCreated = System.DateTime.Now;
        post.title = title;
        post.description = description;

        IMetaWeblog metaWeblogProxy =
            (IMetaWeblog)XmlRpcProxyGen.Create(    ←─10
            typeof(IMetaWeblog));
        XmlRpcClientProtocol metaWeblogProtocol =
            (XmlRpcClientProtocol)metaWeblogProxy;
        metaWeblogProtocol.Url = target;
        string result = metaWeblogProxy.metaweblog_newPost(    ←─11
            blogid, username, password, post, true);

        System.Console.WriteLine("newPost result=" + result);
    }
  }
}
```

Before we can make our XML-RPC call, we must declare an interface to represent the method we will call. So first, we declare the IMetaWeblog interface ❶ and the MetaWeblog.newPost method. The MetaWeblog specification defines many methods, but for this simple example, all we need to declare is the newPost method.

In the next section of code, we declare the class BlogPoster ❷ with a static main() method ❸ as the entry point, and we handle the command-line arguments ❹.

Next, we gather the connection parameters from the .NET Configuration-Settings object ❺. To post to a blog server, we also need the URL of the target blog server's XML-RPC interface ❻, a valid blog account ID ❼, and a valid username-password pair ❽ for that blog account. We do not want the user to have to type this information on every invocation, so we look for it in a simple properties file called app.config.

Next, we package the blog post as a C# struct with fields dateCreated, title, and description ❾.

In the final section of code, we make the actual call to metaWeblog.newPost by calling XmlRpcProxyGen.Create() ❿ to create a dynamic proxy for the IMeta-Weblog interface, setting the target URL for that proxy, and calling the proxy's metaweblog_newPost() method ⓫. If the call succeeds, the method will return the ID of the blog entry that was posted to the server. If the call fails, an exception will be thrown and the user will see a stack trace printed to the console. In approximately the same amount of code as the Java version, we have created a C# blog app that can post an arbitrary message to a blog server using the MetaWeblog API.

2.4.1 Running Blog Poster for C#

The examples directory contains the source code for BlogPoster.cs and a Visual Studio project for building it. Below are the steps required to build and run Blog Poster.

Step 1 Start the Blogapps server server or your preferred blog server.

Step 2 Start Visual Studio and open the solution called BlogApps_Chapter02. The Solution contains a project called BlogPoster, which contains Blog-Poster.cs. If you have unpackaged the examples into c:\blogapps, you will find this Solution in the directory c:\blogapps\csharp\ch02.

Step 3 Ensure that the configuration file is set up correctly for calling your blog server. Below is an app.config file with the correct parameters for posting to the Blogapps server blog server:

```
<?xml version="1.0" encoding="utf-8" ?>
<configuration>
<appSettings>
   <add key="blogid" value="adminblog" />
   <add key="username" value="admin" />
   <add key="password" value="admin" />
   <add key="target" value=http://localhost:8080/roller/xmlrpc />
</appSettings>
</configuration>
```

Step 4 Build the example. In Visual Studio, click the Build Project button to compile the source code and build the executable.

Step 5 Run the example. Open a command-line window, change directory to the Solution directory, and run the executable, found in the directory bin\Debug. For example, if you have unpackaged the examples into c:\blogapps, you would do the following:

```
c> cd c:\blogapps\csharp\ch02\BlogPoster
c> bin\Debug\BlogPoster "Hello World" "This is my first Blog App post"
```

We've developed our first blog application in both Java and C#, and now it is time to summarize what we have covered.

2.5 *Summary*

Here's a recap of what we have learned so far:

- Blogapps server is an easy-to-install blog and wiki server that supports all of the blog and wiki features we need for the blog apps in the book.
- XML-RPC is a web services protocol for making remote procedure calls. It works by sending and receiving XML files via HTTP.
- XML-RPC is versatile because client libraries exist for both Java and C#.
- Apache XML-RPC is an easy-to-use XML-RPC client library for Java.
- XML-RPC.NET is an easy-to-use XML-RPC client library for C# and other .NET languages.
- The MetaWeblog API is a widely supported XML-RPC based web services protocol that allows retrieving, posting, and updating blog entries.

In the next chapter, we'll learn what every blog and wiki application developer needs to know about blog and wiki internals.

Under the hood

*An understanding of blog and wiki
server technologies will give you the
background you need to make the
best of newsfeeds and publishing
protocols.*

In this chapter, you'll learn what every RSS and Atom developer needs to know about blog and wiki servers. We'll discuss server data models to provide some background on newsfeed formats and blog publishing APIs, covered in later chapters. We'll also discuss blog and wiki server architecture so that you'll understand what these servers offer your blog apps.

We'll start by describing the anatomy of a typical blog server, then the same for a typical wiki server. Once we've covered the two separately, we'll discuss why blogs and wikis work so well together and the typical ways in which they are integrated. By the end of the chapter, you'll know enough about blog and wiki server technology to choose a blog or wiki server, so we'll provide you with software selection guidelines and a table that summarizes some of the best blog and wiki server options.

3.1 Anatomy of a blog server

There are many varieties of blog server, created for every operating system and written in every programming language. There are large servers designed to support many users and small servers designed to support just one blogger. Fortunately for us, blog servers are more alike than they are different, and the old saying "seen one, seen them all" holds some truth.

Let's learn about blog servers by examining a typical one, starting with its features. Most blog servers support the following set of features:

- Web-based user interface for editing blog entries and administering the server
- Ability to organize blog entries by category
- Customizable page templates, so each blog can have unique visual design
- Support for feedback in the form of comments, trackbacks, and referrers
- Email notification of new blog entries and comments
- Newsfeeds for blog entries and blog entry comments
- Standard web services interface to support desktop blog editors and other blog apps
- Management and display of bookmarks for blogroll
- Support for file upload of image, audio, and video files

Now, let's discuss the data model needed to support those features.

3.1.1 Blog server data model

A data model defines the types of objects that are stored in a system and how those objects are related. Figure 3.1 shows the types of objects you'll find in a typical blog server data model. Let's discuss each.

- *Users*—A blog server has users, and a user may or may not have a blog. Some users might have more than one blog on a server. We'll discuss user privileges below.

- *Blogs*—A blog server has blogs; each user may have one or more blogs; and each blog may have more than one user.

- *Blog entries*—The most important part of any blog is the collection of blog entries written by the author or authors of the blog. Each blog entry has a title, content, a timestamp, and one or more categories. We will discuss blog entries in more detail in the section "Anatomy of a blog entry."

- *Categories*—A blog has a set of categories that may be assigned to each blog entry. Some blog servers allow a blog entry to have only one category, and some allow multiple categories per blog entry. Some blog servers support hierarchical categories, which is why the Categories box in figure 3.1 has a parent association. Some blog servers also support *tags*, free-form categories chosen by the blog author and not selected from a pre-defined list.

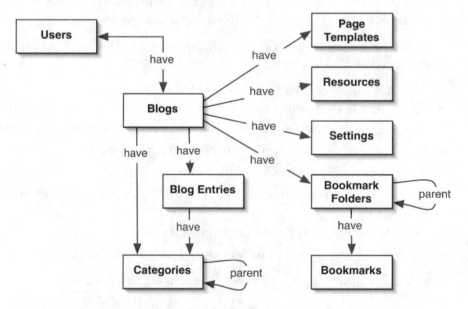

Figure 3.1 Objects in a typical blog server data model

- *Page templates*—Typically, the visual appearance of a blog is determined by a set of HTML page templates that contain special macros indicating where blog components are to be placed.
- *Resources*—A blog may also have a set of resources, such as images, audio files and documents. Typically, the user uploads these files and then references them from page templates and blog entries.
- *Bookmarks*—A blog may also have a collection of bookmarks so that bloggers can keep track of their favorite blogs, web sites, and online resources. This makes it easy for a blogger to display a blogroll, a list of links to her favorite blogs.
- *Settings*—Each blog has a set of preferences, such as the number of blog entries to show on each page, the default category for new blog entries, and whether comments are enabled.

3.1.2 Anatomy of a blog entry

A blog entry is the fundamental unit of content in a blogging system. When a blogger creates a blog entry, he enters some text, known as the *content* of the blog entry. He may also enter some additional data to be associated with the blog entry, such as a title, summary, publication date, and category. When he clicks the button to post the blog entry, the blog server stores it as a blog entry object with properties and associated objects.

Properties of a blog entry

Figure 3.2 shows a typical blog entry object with its properties and associated objects. Let's first discuss the properties of a blog entry object:

- *Id*—Globally unique and permanent identifier for blog entry.
- *Permalink*—Permanent URL for the blog entry.
- *Title*—A short text string that describes the blog entry.
- *Content*—The content of the blog entry is the body, the text of the blog entry itself. This might be stored as HTML, XHTML, or wiki syntax, or as some other type of markup, but when the blog server displays the blog entry, it will be transformed into HTML.
- *Summary*—A short excerpt from the blog entry, suitable for use as a teaser.
- *Link*—If the blog entry references one specific URL above all others mentioned, the author might specify that URL as the link for the entry.

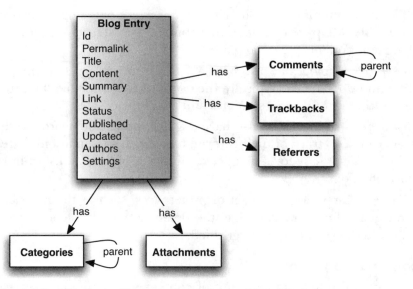

Figure 3.2   A blog entry, its properties, and associated objects

- *Status*—The state of a blog entry in the publishing process, for example: *draft* if the entry has not been made public, *approved* if it has been approved for publication, or *published* if it has been made available to the general public.

- *Published*—The time that the blog entry was or is to be made public.

- *Updated*—The time that the blog entry was last updated.

- *Authors*—The users who authored and contributed to this blog entry.

- *Settings*—A blog entry may have settings that specify the language of the entry, whether comments are allowed on the entry, and which plug-ins should be used to display the entry.

Objects associated with a blog entry

These are the objects that may be associated with a blog entry:

- *Categories*—A blog entry may be assigned one or more categories (or tags). Some blog servers allow a blog entry to exist in multiple categories, and some support only one. Some support hierarchical categories, and others support only a flat list of categories. Some allow you to assign arbitrary metadata to blog entries, and others do not. Take a little time up-front to plan how you will be categorizing blog entries in your system.

- *Attachments*—A blog server might allow each blog entry to have a number of uploaded file attachments.

- *Comments*—Visitors can respond to your blog entry by adding comments. A comment is typically made up of a title, text, timestamp, and an email address. Comments may be threaded, with each comment having a parent comment, as shown in figure 3.2.

- *Trackbacks*—Other bloggers might prefer to respond to your blog entry by writing about it on their own blogs and then sending a trackback. The Trackback protocol, devised by Movable Type developers Benjamin and Mena Trott, is a simple web services protocol that enables one blog server to notify another that a blog entry on the former refers to a blog entry on the latter. The notification itself is known as a trackback, and it includes a title, excerpt, URL, and blog name.

- *Referrers*—If another web site responds to your blog entry by linking to your blog entry, your blog server may be able to capture the referring URL from the incoming web request or by processing the web server logs. By looking at your referrers, you can tell which sites are writing about and linking to your blog entries.

3.1.3 *Users, privileges, and group blogs*

A typical blog server controls user access to blog data by assigning each user a different set of privileges. Here are the common types of user privileges:

- *Reader*—A reader is allowed to read one or more blogs. Most blogs are configured so that anybody, including anonymous visitors, can read, but some blogs allow only registered users with reader privilege to do so. For example, if you are setting up a family blog, you might wish to restrict access to family members only.

- *Commenter*—A commenter is allowed to add comments to blog entries on one or more blogs. Most blogs are configured so that anybody can leave comments, but some blogs allow only registered users with commenter privilege to do so. Now that unscrupulous advertisers are spamming blog comments, you will see more and more blogs that allow only registered users to post comments.

- *Editor*—An editor is allowed to create, edit, and publish blog entries on one or more blogs. Some blog servers support a concept called *workflow*, whereby any blog author can create new blog entries, but only editors can approve blog entries for publication on the Web. This is an important feature for corporate news blogs, some of which require management approval of all new blog posts.

- *Author*—In a blog server that supports workflow, an author is a user who is allowed to create blog entries on one or more blogs but not to publish them. An author may or may not be able to create and modify categories, page templates, bookmarks, and resources.

- *Administrator*—An administrator is allowed to edit blog settings categories, page templates, bookmarks, and resources.

Different blog servers have different levels of support for users and privileges, with the most limited allowing only one user per blog, and most capable of allowing each user to have multiple blogs and *group blogs,* blogs with more than one user. If your blog server does not support group blogs, you can approximate one by using an aggregator, as described in chapter 12.

Now that we understand how data is stored in a blog server, let's move on to architecture.

3.1.4 *Blog server architecture*

To develop a simple blog or wiki server, all you need is a place to store data and a transformer to turn that data into HTML for web browsers and into XML for newsfeed readers. This basic architecture, shown in figure 3.3, is so simple that it's possible to develop a useful blog or wiki sever with only a single page of code. Some developers have done just that. For example, Rael Dornfest's popular Bloxsom blog software was originally implemented in only 61 lines of Perl code.

But those core components are not enough for a full-featured multiuser blog server. Users want a friendly user interface for blogging, uploading files, and managing the server. Developers want a plug-in architecture so they can customize the system and a web services interface so they can write programs that

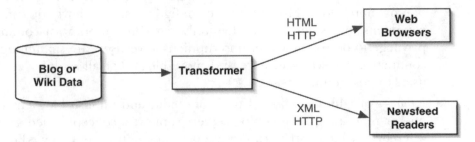

Figure 3.3 Core components of blog server architecture

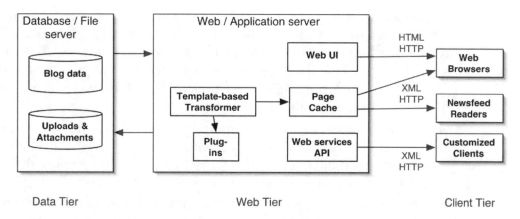

Figure 3.4   Architecture of a typical blog server

blog. IT managers want a system that can scale to handle an increasing number of users and visitors. To meet those additional requirements, most blog servers use a multitiered design, as shown in figure 3.4.

Let's discuss each of the tiers of blog server architecture shown in figure 3.4.

Data tier

The data tier is responsible for storing the entities and relationships we covered in the previous section. These entities could be stored as records in a relational database, such as Oracle or MySQL, as files in a filesystem, or a combination of both. For example, some blog servers store blog entries in a relational database, but they store any uploaded files in a filesystem.

When shopping for a blog or wiki server, you will probably have to choose between using a relational database or a filesystem for storage. If you are setting up a server for a small group and you just want to avoid the overhead of installing a relational database system, you should consider a filesystem-based blog server. If you are setting up a large multiuser installation and you may eventually need to use clustering, or if you simply prefer storing your data in a database, you should consider a relational database-based blog server.

Web tier

The web tier is responsible for transforming blog data into HTML and XML representations, providing a user interface for both blog authors and blog readers, and for supporting a web services interface for blog clients. The web tier is made up of a number of components:

- *Template-based transformer*—This component is responsible for transforming blog entries and other blog data into HTML representation for web browsers and into XML representation for newsfeed readers. To render the HTML for a blog, the transformer will fetch the blog's entries from the data store, fetch the blog's page templates from the data store, and use the templates to format the HTML output.

- *Plug-ins*—Some blog servers support a plug-in mechanism to enable developers and users to customize the transformation process. Currently, there is no standard interface for this type of plug-in, and therefore there is no way to write a plug-in that will work across all blog servers.

- *Web user interface*—A typical blog server provides a web-based user interface for blog authors, editors, and administrators. Bloggers may have a choice of different blog editors, ranging from a simple text editor to a WYSIWYG HTML editor. Some blog servers allow users to change the templates that define the layout and style of their blogs through the web user interface.

- *Page cache*—To make most efficient use of computer system and network resources, most blog servers use caching wherever possible. Whenever the transformer creates a new HTML page or XML file, it places that file into a server-side cache. Whenever an HTML page or XML file is served, the blog server sets HTTP cache control headers to enable proxy servers to cache the page and sets the HTTP Last-Modified header to enable browsers to do the same.

- *Web services* API—A typical blog server also provides a web services interface that allows remote client programs to create, post, and edit blog entries and other blog data. Most servers support XML-RPC based interfaces, such as the MetaWeblog API, described in chapter 9, and many are adding the new Atom Publishing Protocol, described in chapter 10.

Client tier

The client tier is made up of web browsers, newsfeed readers, and blog clients that interact with the blog server through the web tier.

Newsfeed readers use HTTP to fetch newsfeeds in XML formats, and if they are well behaved, they maintain a client-side cache of pages and use HTTP conditional GET to avoid fetching pages more often than necessary. You'll learn how to use conditional GET when fetching newsfeeds in chapter 5 and how to support conditional GET for newsfeeds you generate in chapter 8.

Custom blog clients are programs like MarsEdit, the blog editor that Carl used in chapter 1, which interact with a blog server via web services interfaces. You'll learn how to write blog clients based on XML-RPC and Atom Protocol in chapters 9 and 10.

3.2 *Anatomy of a wiki server*

As with blog servers, there are many varieties of wiki servers, and most are more similar than they are different. So let's apply the *seen one, seen them all* rule again and learn about wikis by examining a typical wiki server, starting with features. A wiki server generally supports the following set of features:

- Web-based user interface for editing wiki pages and administering the server
- Ability to partition wiki pages and user privileges via namespaces
- Newsfeeds for recent wiki changes
- Support for feedback in the form of comments, trackbacks, and referrers
- Email notification of wiki page changes and comments
- Standard web services interface
- Support for file upload of wiki page attachments

3.2.1 *Wiki server data model*

At the most basic level, a wiki is simply a collection of pages with links to other pages. Anybody can edit any page and anybody can create new pages. That simple model has worked well for wikis on the Web, where each wiki serves one project and all visitors are encouraged to participate as equals. In an organizational setting, however, things get a little more complicated, and wikis have adapted.

Many wikis now support partitioning, user access controls, and blog-like features such as comments, trackbacks, and referrer tracking. Let's start our discussion of the wiki data model, shown in figure 3.5, with users and namespaces.

Users and namespaces

A *namespace* is a portion of a wiki, a partition that is reserved for one topic area or one set of users. A user can be assigned to one or more namespaces, and a namespace can have one or more users. Some wikis do not support the concept of namespaces. Such wikis can be thought of as having only one namespace.

Namespaces are an important feature for wikis that are used by multiple groups or projects. For example, take our friend Nina from chapter 1. Nina's team works on multiple software products, each has its own installation guide, and each is going to want to use the wiki page name "Installation Guide," but that is not possible unless the wiki is divided into namespaces.

Wiki pages

A wiki page is the fundamental unit of wiki content. A wiki page is simply a hypertext document that links to other hypertext documents in the wiki or to external pages on the Web. As you can see in figure 3.5, a wiki server can allow wiki pages to have attachments, user comments, trackbacks, and referrers, just as blog entries do.

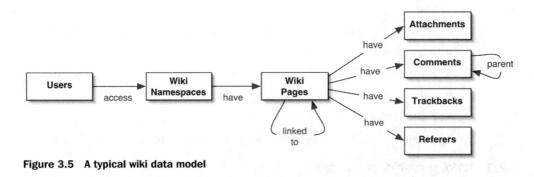

Figure 3.5   A typical wiki data model

Most wiki servers support *versioning* of wiki pages, which is equivalent to storing every old version of each page. This allows you to examine the history of every page in the wiki and see who changed what and when each change was made. Most wikis also support a visual *diff* facility that allows you to compare two page revisions with colors to indicate which areas of text were added, modified, or removed.

Wiki pages are usually edited and stored using a special markup language, known as *wiki syntax*, which is designed to be easier to write than HTML and to look as much like plain text as possible. Let's look at an example. Below is some text written in the wiki syntax of the JSPWiki wiki server.

```
Some examples of wiki markup:
* Some wikis use underbars to make words __bold__.
* Some use double apostrophes to ''italicize''.
* Link to new or existing pages via WikiWords
* [External links|http://example.com] are also supported.
```

JSPWiki transforms that into the following HTML:

```
<p>Some examples of wiki markup:</p>
<ul>
   <li>Some wikis use underbars to make words <b>bold</b>.</li>
   <li>Some use double apostrophes to <i>italicize</i>.</li>
   <li>Link to new or existing pages via <u>WikiWords</u>
       <a href="Edit.jsp?page=WikiWords">?</a></li>
   <li><a class="external" href="http://manning.com">External links</a>
       are also supported.</li>
</ul>
```

Wiki syntax makes it a little easier to publish formatted text, but it has one big drawback: There is no standard. Every brand of wiki uses slightly different markup, and there does not seem to be any movement toward standardization. This makes it difficult for users to move from one wiki to another, and it makes it almost impossible for developers to create applications that target more than one type of wiki. Now that we understand what is stored in a typical wiki server, let's move on to architecture.

3.2.2 *Wiki server architecture*

Wiki server architecture is similar to blog server architecture. Wiki servers are based around the same core components: a data store and a transformer that transforms that data into HTML and XML representations. Full-featured wiki servers typically use a multitiered design, like that shown in figure 3.6.

The wiki server architecture shown in figure 3.6 is almost identical to the blog server architecture we saw in figure 3.3, so let's just focus on the components that are different.

- *Data tier*—The wiki data tier is responsible for storing and versioning wiki pages. It also stores page attachments and possibly feedback, like comments, trackbacks, and referrers. Some wiki servers use a Version Control System to manage pages and a filesystem to store page attachments and feedback. Some wikis use a relational database to store everything.

- *Wiki syntax transformer*—Every wiki server has some form of wiki syntax transformer that converts wiki pages stored in wiki syntax to HTML or XHTML format.

- *Recent changes transformer*—Wiki servers also provide newsfeeds to keep users notified of changes to pages, namespaces, or the wiki as a whole. So a recent changes transformer is needed to transform change information into newsfeed format.

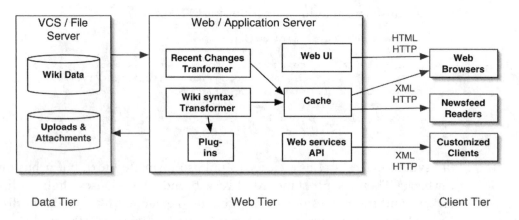

Figure 3.6 Architecture of a typical wiki server

- *Web services* API—Wikis don't support the same web services interfaces that blogs do. Wikis may eventually adopt the Atom Publishing Protocol. For now, the closest thing to a standard web service API for wikis is the XML-RPC based WikiRPCInterface.

3.3 *Choosing a blog or wiki server*

Choosing a blog or wiki server is like choosing any other software. First, you figure out how you're going to use it. You document your use cases and the requirements for each. Next, you determine which of the available software packages most closely meets your requirements. You install the most suitable candidates in-house, evaluate each, and make a choice.

3.3.1 *Narrowing your choices*

We can't decide for you how you are going to use blogs and wikis, but we can give you some guidelines to help you narrow the options. Here are a couple of questions to ask yourself as you start to shop for a blog or wiki server.

Do you need a blog, a wiki, or both?

Blogs and wikis are technologically similar and share the goals of making the Web into a better environment for writing and collaboration, but they are fundamentally different. If you're selecting software, you're going to have to choose one or the other, or both. Here are some guidelines to help you decide:

- *Reasons to choose a blog server*—Blogs are good for individuals and conversations. A blog is essentially a personal space, a home for one person or a group that writes about related topics. A blog works well for information that is issued by one party and organized along the axis of time, such as news stories, announcements, and status reports. Most blog servers now support limited wiki integration, allowing you to write blog entries using wiki syntax and easily link into an external wiki.

- *Reasons to choose a wiki server*—Wikis are good for groups and collaborations. A wiki provides a shared space where a group can come together to collaborate on documents and share information. Most wiki servers now support limited blogging capabilities, allowing you to establish a blog within a wiki page or a wiki namespace, create blog entries using wiki syntax, accept comments, and provide a newsfeed of your blog.

- *Reasons to choose both a blog and a wiki server*—If you need full-featured blog and wiki capabilities and you are not satisfied by the limited blogging capabilities offered by most wikis, the best option is to set up both blog and wiki servers and to integrate them wherever possible.

Do you have a preferred platform and programming language?

If you have a preferred platform in terms of operating system, web server, database system, or programming environment, you might want to limit your search to include only those blogs and wikis that work well on that platform.

If you think you might want to customize your blog or wiki server by developing plug-ins or by tweaking the server's source code, consider blog or wiki servers written in your preferred programming language.

How many users must you support?

If you are setting up a blog or wiki server for large number of users and lots of traffic, features such as caching, support for clustering, and database storage become essential. On the other hand, if your system will be serving only a small number of users, a simple filesystem-based blogging system might be more convenient.

3.3.2 Comparing blog and wiki servers

With those questions in mind, let's compare some of the most widely used and well-known blog and wiki server options. Table 3.1 lists some of the most popular blog and wiki choices and the platform, language, storage, and license for each.

Table 3.1   Well-known blog and wiki servers for a variety of platforms

	Type	Platform	Language	Storage	License
.Text	Blog	Windows	C#	RDBMS	Open source (BSD)
Blojsom	Blog	Any/Java	Java	Files	Open source (BSD)
Bloxsom	Blog	Any/Apache	Perl	Files	Open source (MIT)
Confluence	Wiki	Any/Java	Java	RDBMS	Commercial
Das Blog	Blog	Windows	C#	Files	Open source (BSD)
Drupal	Blog	Any/Apache	Perl	RDBMS	Open source (GPL)
Greymatter	Blog	Any/Apache	PHP	Files	Open source
JSPWiki	Wiki	Any/Java	Java	VCS or files	Open source (LGPL)
Moin Moin	Wiki	Any/Apache	Python	VCS or files	Open source (GPL)
Movable Type	Blog	Any/Apache	Perl	RDBMS or files	Commercial
Pebble	Blog	Any/Java	Java	Files	Open source (BSD)
PyBloxsom	Blog	Any/Apache	Python	Files	Open source (MIT)
Roller	Blog	Any/Java	Java	RDBMS	Open source (Apache)
SnipSnap	Wiki	Bundled app server	Java	Bundled database	Open source (GPL)
SocialText	Wiki	Any/Apache	Perl	VCS or files	Commercial
Tiki Wiki	Wiki	Any/Apache	PHP	VCS or files	Open source (LGPL)
Traction	Blog	Any/Java	Java	RDBMS	Commercial
Twiki	Wiki	Any/Apache	Perl	VCS or files	Open source (GPL)
Wordpress	Blog	Any/Apache	PHP	RDBMS or files	Open source (GPL)

Different types of storage are abbreviated as follows:

- RDBMS—Relational database-based
- Files—Filesystem-based
- VCS—Version control system-based

That brings us to the end of our exploration of blog and wiki server technologies. Let's summarize what we have learned.

3.4 Summary

- There's a wide variety of blog servers, but they all share similar feature sets, data models, and architectures. The same applies to wiki servers.

- Not all blog servers support group blogs, publishing workflows, hierarchical categories, or user-customizable templates; so if you need those features, shop carefully.

- Most wiki servers support limited blogging capabilities but don't offer all the features and flexibility that blog servers offer.

- For single-blog sites, consider using an easy-to-install file-system based blog server such as Pebble or Blojsom.

- For large multi-user blog sites, consider using a database-backed blog server with good support for caching, clustering and user-management features such as Roller.

- If you have a preferred operating system platform or programming language, choose a blog or wiki system that works well there.

Newsfeed formats

A little history lesson on newsfeed formats will help you understand the choices you have and the direction that newsfeed technology is headed.

One of the first challenges developers face when building applications with RSS and Atom is making sense of the many slightly different XML newsfeed formats. The most popular newsfeed format is RSS, but RSS is not really a single format. RSS is a family of informally developed and competing formats that has forked into two opposing camps, which can't even agree on what the letters RSS stand for. In this chapter, we'll help you through this confusion by explaining the history of RSS, the RSS fork, and the details of the most widely used RSS formats.

We'll also explain that, at least in the world of newsfeed formats, there is hope for the future. The Internet Engineering Task Force (IETF) has developed a new newsfeed format, known as the Atom Publishing Format, or Atom for short, which will eventually replace the RSS family of formats. We'll cover the details of the Atom format in this chapter and look at its sister specification, the Atom Publishing Protocol, in chapter 10. But for now, let's get started with our RSS history lesson.

4.1 The birth of RSS

RSS began life at Netscape as part of the My Netscape project. It was given the name RDF *Site Summary* (RSS) because it was an application of the Resource Description Framework (RDF), a sophisticated language for describing resources on the Web. Netscape used RSS to describe news stories and to allow users to build their own information portal, called My Netscape, by selecting the news sources they wanted to have displayed in their personal portal. RSS caught on quickly, as web sites scrambled to provide newsfeeds compatible with Netscape's innovative new portal.

By the time Netscape developer Dan Libby produced the first specification, RSS 0.9, in January 1999, the RSS user community was already starting to divide into two camps. One camp wanted Netscape to make better use of RDF in RSS, and the other wanted to simplify RSS by removing RDF altogether. Influential blogger Dave Winer of Userland Software was among those arguing for simplicity and the removal of RDF. In the end, Winer's camp won.

4.1.1 RSS 0.91

When Netscape released the RSS 0.91 specification, all references to RDF were removed. Since RDF was no longer part of the specification, the acronym RSS no longer made sense. Dave Winer declared, "There is no consensus on what RSS stands for, so it's not an acronym, it's a name." It was around this time that he started his stewardship of RSS. In July 2000, he released his own version of the RSS 0.91 specification. He reformatted the document to make it shorter and easier to read. He also removed the specification's document type definition (DTD), making it more difficult for XML parsers to validate RSS newsfeeds.

RSS 0.91 is still in use today and is the oldest ancestor of RSS 2.0, which is currently the most widely used newsfeed format. Let's take a closer look at RSS 0.91, starting with an example newsfeed.

Listing 4.1   Example of an RSS 0.91 format newsfeed

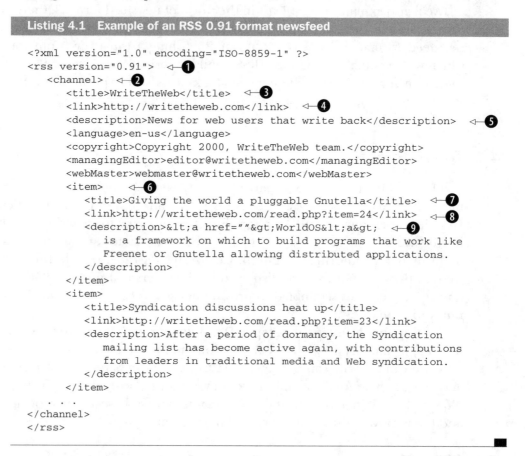

```
<?xml version="1.0" encoding="ISO-8859-1" ?>
<rss version="0.91">      ←1
   <channel>   ←2
      <title>WriteTheWeb</title>   ←3
      <link>http://writetheweb.com</link>   ←4
      <description>News for web users that write back</description>   ←5
      <language>en-us</language>
      <copyright>Copyright 2000, WriteTheWeb team.</copyright>
      <managingEditor>editor@writetheweb.com</managingEditor>
      <webMaster>webmaster@writetheweb.com</webMaster>
      <item>      ←6
         <title>Giving the world a pluggable Gnutella</title>   ←7
         <link>http://writetheweb.com/read.php?item=24</link>   ←8
         <description>&lt;a href=""”&gt;WorldOS&lt;a&gt;   ←9
            is a framework on which to build programs that work like
               Freenet or Gnutella allowing distributed applications.
         </description>
      </item>
      <item>
         <title>Syndication discussions heat up</title>
         <link>http://writetheweb.com/read.php?item=23</link>
         <description>After a period of dormancy, the Syndication
            mailing list has become active again, with contributions
            from leaders in traditional media and Web syndication.
         </description>
      </item>
   . . .
   </channel>
   </rss>
```

Listing 4.1 is a newsfeed in RSS 0.91 format. The root element of an RSS newsfeed is `<rss>` **1**. Within the root element there is one `<channel>` element, and within that, a channel header **2**, which consists of metadata elements, including `<title>` **3**, `<link>` **4**, and `<description>` **5**.

Within a channel are the most recent news items from the channel's web site. As you can see, an <item> ❻ contains a <title> ❼, a <link> ❽, and a <description> ❾. The description is meant to hold the HTML content of the newsfeed item. In some newsfeeds, the item descriptions include the full content of the news story or blog item they represent. In others, the descriptions include just an excerpt, and the reader must visit the web site to read the full story.

Escaped content

Note that the HTML content in the <description> elements in listing 4.1 is *escaped*. That's why it's so hard to read the link <a href="http://www.worldos. com">World OS</a> that is embedded in the text. We do this to follow the rules of XML. Special characters that have meaning in XML must be replaced with escape codes. So we replace any left brackets (<) with <, any right brackets (>) with > and any ampersands (&) with &. We'll discuss some other ways to represent content in newsfeeds, but escaped content is the common practice for representing HTML within an RSS newsfeed.

4.1.2 The elements of RSS 0.91

The definitive source of information about RSS 0.91 is the specification itself, but for your convenience we have provided a summary diagram in figure 4.1. Each box in the diagram represents an XML element, and the arrows indicate containment. For example, the <rss> element contains the <channel> element, which contains <description>, <link>, <language>, and so on.

We saw the <rss>, <channel>, and <item> elements in listing 4.1, but some new elements here deserve mention:

- <image>—This element allows a web site to specify an icon or logo image to be displayed when the newsfeed is displayed in a newsfeed reader or on another web site.

- <lastBuildDate>—This element specifies the last time any item in the newsfeed changed.

- <pubDate>—This element specifies the time that the newsfeed was last published, using RFC 822 date format. Note that the channel itself has a publication date, but the individual items in the newsfeed do not. That's a serious limitation for applications that rely on item dates to sort items (such as the group aggregator example presented in chapter 11).

- `<textInput>`—Another rarely used element, `<textInput>` offers a way for a publisher to allow a reader to query the publisher's web site.
- `<skipDays>` and `<skipHours>`—These elements allow publishers to specify the times during which a newsfeed is unlikely to be updated. Most newsfeed readers ignore these values.

Let's get back to our history lesson, picking up the story with RSS 1.0.

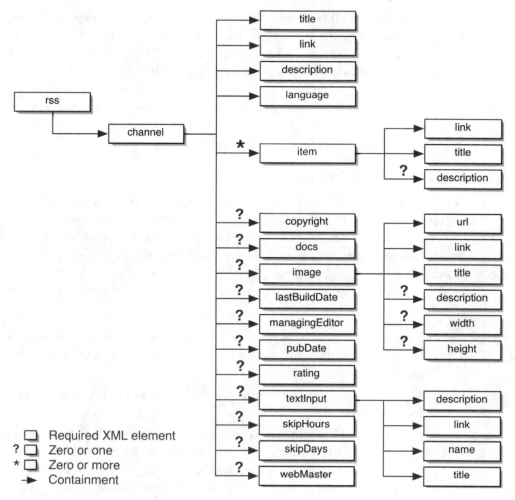

Figure 4.1 The XML elements that make up RSS 0.91

4.2 The RDF fork: RSS 1.0

RSS 0.91 was clearly useful, but just about everybody agreed that it needed some improvement and additional metadata. Unfortunately, the RSS user and developer community was divided about how RSS should be improved. A group of RDF advocates wanted to bring the full power of RDF back into RSS. Dave Winer, on the other hand, wanted to keep RSS as simple as possible. The two sides did not get along well and eventually, in December 2000, the RDF advocates released what they called RSS 1.0—a new version of RSS with RDF back in the mix and with support for extension modules.

RSS 1.0 was well received. It was adopted by the popular Movable Type blogging system and as a result is still in widespread use. Let's take a close look at it, starting with the sample RSS 1.0 newsfeed shown in listing 4.2. This feed is taken from the specification itself. Some optional elements have been removed for the sake of brevity.

Listing 4.2   Example of an RSS 1.0 format newsfeed

```
<?xml version="1.0"?>
<rdf:RDF     ⟵❶
    xmlns:rdf="http://www.w3.org/1999/02/22-rdf-syntax-ns#"
    xmlns="http://purl.org/rss/1.0/">
<channel rdf:about="http://www.xml.com/xml/news.rss">     ⟵❷
    <title>XML.com</title>     ⟵❸
    <link>http://xml.com/pub</link>     ⟵❹
    <description>
        XML.com features a rich mix of information and services     ⟵❺
        for the XML community.
    </description>
    <items>
    <rdf:Seq>     ⟵❻
    <rdf:li resource="http://xml.com/pub/2000/08/09/xslt/xslt.html"/>
    <rdf:li resource="http://xml.com/pub/2000/08/09/rdfdb/index.html"/>
    </rdf:Seq>
    </items>
</channel>
<item rdf:about="http://xml.com/pub/2000/08/09/xslt/xslt.html">     ⟵❼
    <title>Processing Inclusions with XSLT</title>
    <link>http://xml.com/pub/2000/08/09/xslt/xslt.html</link>     ⟵❽
    <description>
        Processing document inclusions with general XML tools can be
        problematic. This article proposes a way of preserving inclusion
        information through SAX-based processing.
    </description>
</item>
<item rdf:about="http://xml.com/pub/2000/08/09/rdfdb/index.html">
```

```
<title>Putting RDF to Work</title>
<link>http://xml.com/pub/2000/08/09/rdfdb/index.html</link>
<description>
    Tool and API support for the Resource Description Framework
    is slowly coming of age. Edd Dumbill takes a look at RDFDB,
    one of the most exciting new RDF toolkits.
</description>
</item>
</rdf:RDF>
```

The first thing to note is that the newsfeed is an RDF document ❶. Next, notice that the containment hierarchy is different from that of earlier forms of RSS. The <item> elements are not contained within the <channel> element ❷. The channel is essentially the header for the file. It contains the <title> ❸, <link> ❹, and <description> ❺ of the newsfeed, as well as an RDF-style table of contents ❻ that lists the items in the newsfeed.

Each <item> contains the same <title>, <link>, and <description> elements as in previous versions of RSS, except that the item permalink is specified twice— once in the rdf:about attribute ❼ and once in the <link> element ❽. Note that an item-level <date> element is still not part of the format, but it is common practice for RSS 1.0 newsfeeds to include the Dublin Core extension module and a <dc:date> element in each item. We'll show you how to do that in section 4.2.2.

4.2.1 *The elements of RSS 1.0*

As we did with RSS 0.91, let's take a look at a summary diagram of RSS 1.0. Figure 4.2 shows the XML elements that make up RSS 1.0, the containment hierarchy, and the optional and required elements. We use the same notation we used in figure 4.1, along with a new notation: required XML attributes are marked with an "at" sign (@).

By comparing the RSS 0.91 and RSS 1.0 diagrams, you can see that the formats are significantly different. Here are the key differences:

- A typical RSS 1.0 newsfeed is longer and more complex, but it does not include as much metadata as the equivalent RSS 0.91 newsfeed.

- RSS 1.0 is more complex, but only because it is more flexible and extensible.

- The root element is <RDF:rdf> rather than <rss>.

- News items exist as children of the document's root element and not as children of the <channel> element, as they do in RSS 0.91.

- News items must be declared inside the <channel> as RDF resources.

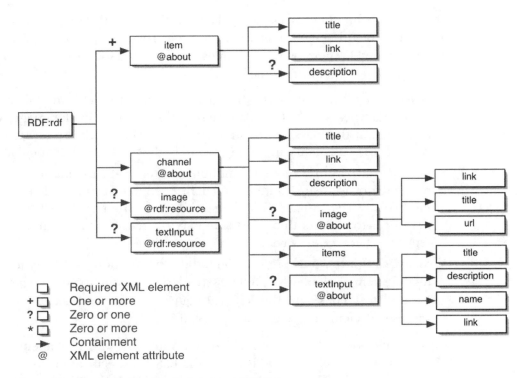

Figure 4.2   The XML elements that make up RSS 1.0

- `<image>` and `<textInput>` elements must be declared inside the `<RDF:rdf>` element as RDF resources if they are to be included inside the `<channel>` element.

- Many metadata elements, such as `<pubDate>`, `<lastBuild-Time>`, `<skipDays>`, `<skipHours>`, `<managingEditor>`, and `<webMaster>` are missing from the format. These can be added as needed by using RSS 1.0 modules, which are described in the next section.

As you might imagine, these differences were significant enough to break all existing RSS parsers, but RSS 1.0 was released years ago and RSS parsers have been updated to handle both formats. Later in this chapter, we will show you how to write a parser that can handle RSS 0.91 and RSS 1.0 newsfeeds.

4.2.2   Extending RSS 1.0 with modules

Unlike RSS 0.91, RSS 1.0 is extensible in the same ways that XML is extensible. The RDF Site Summary 1.0 Modules specification (http://web.resource.org/rss/

1.0/modules/) defines how this is done. The specification allows producers of RSS 1.0 newsfeeds to add new XML elements to their newsfeeds as long as those elements are defined in their own XML namespaces. The RSS 1.0 Modules specification defines three standard modules:

- *Dublin Core* (http://purl.org/rss/1.0/modules/content/)—This module defines basic data types, such as title, date, description, creator, and language, which are useful at the newsfeed or item level. The Dublin Core `<dc:date>` and `<dc:creator>` elements are often used in both RSS 1.0 and 2.0 newsfeeds.

- *Content* (http://purl.org/rss/1.0/modules/content/)—This module defines elements for web site content and defines content formats. The Content module's `<content:encoded>` element is often used in RSS 1.0 and 2.0 newsfeeds to allow both a short summary (in `<description>`) and full content (in `<content:encoded>`).

- *Syndication* (http://purl.org/rss/1.0/modules/syndication/)—The syndication module defines elements to tell newsreaders how often to poll the newsfeed for updates. These are the RSS 1.0 equivalents for the `<skipHours>` and `<skipDays>` elements we present in RSS 0.91.

Using a module is easy. For example, if you want to add a `<date>` element to your RSS 1.0 newsfeed, something that is not in the RSS 1.0 specification, you can use the `<date>` element defined by the Dublin Core Metadata Initiative to do just that. Simply declare the XML namespace in the standard way and add your new element. The newsfeed fragment below shows how you would do this. The Dublin Core namespace declaration attribute is shown in bold inside the `<rdf:RDF>` element, and the usage of the Dublin Core `<dc:date>` element is also shown in bold. Note that Dublin Core dates use the ISO 8601 date format.

```
<?xml version="1.0"?>
<rdf:RDF
    xmlns:rdf="http://www.w3.org/1999/02/22-rdf-syntax-ns#"
    xmlns="http://purl.org/rss/1.0/"
    xmlns:dc=" http://purl.org/dc/elements/1.1/">
<channel rdf:about="http://www.xml.com/xml/news.rss">
    <title>XML.com</title>
    <link>http://xml.com/pub</link>
    <dc:date>2004-08-19T11:54:37-08:00</dc:date>
    . . .
```

In addition to the three standard modules, there are a number of user-contributed modules. Here are some of the more interesting ones:

- *mod_annotation*—This module defines an `<annotate:reference>` element that can be used to annotate newsfeed items.

- *mod_audio*—This module defines a series of `<audio>` elements that can be used to add metadata such as song name, artist, and album to audio tracks referenced by items in a newsfeed.

- *mod_link*—This module defines a `<link>` element, modeled on the HTML element of the same name, that can be used to provide links to resources referenced in a newsfeed.

- *mod_taxonomy*—This module defines a series of `<taxo>` elements that can be used to add tags or category information to items in a newsfeed. For example, the popular del.icio.us bookmark-sharing site uses this module in its newsfeeds to represent bookmark tags.

You can learn more about these modules' specifications and many others at http://web.resource.org/rss/1.0/modules.

4.3 *The simple fork: RSS 2.0*

Let's return to the RSS history lesson. Not everybody was happy about the new RSS 1.0 format, especially Dave Winer, who had argued against RDF and lobbied to keep RSS as simple as possible. Winer rejected RSS 1.0 and released a new version of RSS, a minor revision of RSS 0.91, which he called *Really Simple Syndication* (RSS) 0.92. Thus, RSS was forked. The RDF advocates urged users to go with the RDF-based RSS 1.0 specification, and Winer urged users to stick with simple, safe, and compatible RSS 0.92.

Winer continued to develop the simple fork of RSS. He published new specifications for RSS 0.93 and RSS 0.94. With each release, he tweaked the format and added more metadata. In RSS 0.93, he added new subelements to the `<item>` element: `<pubDate>` and `<expirationDate>`. In RSS 0.94, he dropped `<expirationDate>` from the specification. Eventually, Winer published what he called the final version of RSS, dubbed RSS 2.0.

4.3.1 *The elements of RSS 2.0*

The RSS 2.0 specification provides a detailed description of each element allowed in an RSS 2.0 newsfeed. You can find the specification here: http://blogs.law.harvard.edu/tech/rss. Figure 4.3 summarizes the XML elements that make up RSS 2.0, using the same notation as our previous figures, with one twist. Elements shown in gray were added subsequent to RSS 0.91.

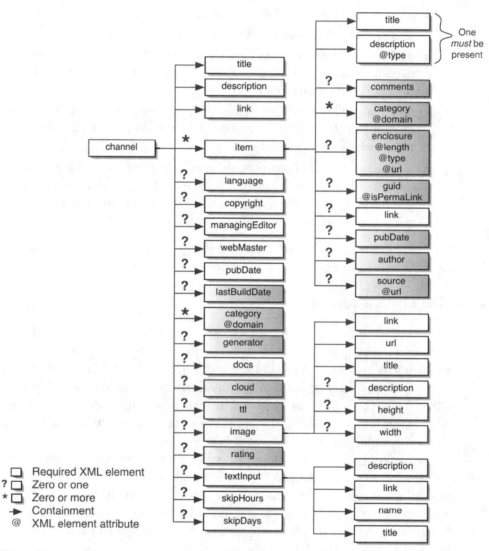

Figure 4.3   The XML elements that make up RSS 2.0

Some of the new elements added since RSS 0.91 deserve explanation:

- You can now specify categories at the channel level or at the item level by using the `<category>` element. Multiple categories are allowed. If you are using a well-known *taxonomy* or categorization system, you can note that by specifying the URI of the taxonomy in the optional `domain` attribute.

- The item-level `<comments>` element may be used to specify the URL of the comments page for a specific weblog entry.

- The item-level `<guid>` element can be used to specify a globally unique ID (GUID) for each item. Unless you specify the attribute `ispermalink=` `"false"`, the GUID will be considered the permanent link to the web representation of the newsfeed item. Unfortunately, this introduces the opportunity for confusion because the `<link>` element is sometimes used as the permanent link to the item.

- The item-level `<author>` element lets you specify an author's email address. If you want to specify the author's name, you can use the Dublin Core module's `<dc:creator>` element.

- The item-level `<enclosure>` element can be used to attach a file to an item. To include a file, you must specify the file's URL, content-type, and length.

4.3.2 *Enclosures and podcasting*

The `<enclosure>` element was added to RSS 0.92 in 2002 and it remains in RSS 2.0, but it was not widely used until 2004, when the podcasting craze began. Podcasting is the practice of distributing audio files via RSS. Specialized podcast client software looks for enclosures, downloads each enclosed file, and copies it to your Apple iPod. The word *podcasting* is something of a misnomer because any sort of file can be distributed as an `<enclosure>`, not just audio files destined for an iPod or other digital audio player.

For more information about podcasting, see chapter 18, which presents a podcast server, and chapter 19, where we build a download podcast client you can use to automate the download of RSS enclosures.

4.3.3 *Extending RSS 2.0*

By the time RSS 2.0 was released in August 2002, everybody recognized the value of RSS 1.0-style extension modules. Winer decided to allow the same type of extensions to RSS. He did so by adding this sentence to the RSS 2.0 specification: "An RSS feed may contain elements not described on this page, only if those elements are defined in a namespace."

Funky RSS

At the same time that Winer added extensions to RSS, he also he made all of the subelements of `<item>` optional. You must specify either a title or a description, but nothing else is required. Because of this, some users started to substitute elements from other XML specifications, such as Dublin Core, for the optional standard elements. For example, they started using the Dublin Core `<dc:date>` instead of the native RSS `<pubDate>`. And some started to use the Content Module `<content:encoded>` element to include item content instead of using the native RSS `<description>` element. Winer discourages this practice because it makes parsing RSS more complex. He calls newsfeeds that employ it *funky*, but such newsfeeds are perfectly valid according to the RSS 2.0 specification. Unfortunately, funky RSS is a fact of life, and if you are writing an RSS parser, you'll have to take it into account. We'll show you how to do this in chapter 5.

4.4 *The nine incompatible versions of RSS*

After learning the history of the RSS specifications, the fork, and the funkiness, you may not be too surprised to learn that parsing RSS is tricky. The RSS specifications on both sides of the fork are informal and simple—perhaps too simple. Simplicity and informality can be virtues, but for specifications, they cause problems. No version of RSS has gone through a rigorous standardization process, and it shows.

An influential blogger named Mark Pilgrim has been following the development of RSS closely, and he has made some important contributions. Working with Sam Ruby, another influential blogger, Pilgrim developed a newsfeed validation service at http://www.feedvalidator.org/ that handles all of the commonly used RSS and Atom newsfeed formats. He also wrote one of the best newsfeed parsers available, the Universal Feed Parser, which we'll cover in chapter 5. Pilgrim pointed out that there were nine incompatible versions of RSS. Table 4.1 summarizes these incompatible versions and the author, date, and status of each.

Table 4.1   The nine incompatible versions of RSS

	Released by	**Date**	**Status**	**Notes**
RSS 0.90	Libby / Netscape	January 1999	**Obsolete** and rarely found in the wild	RDF-based format.
RSS 0.91 (Netscape)	Libby / Netscape	July 1999	**Obsolete** but widely used	XML-based with DTD; dropped all RDF elements; added support for modules.
RSS 0.91 (UserLand)	Winer / Userland	June 2000	**Obsolete** but widely used	Dropped DTD.

continued on next page

Table 4.1 The nine incompatible versions of RSS *(continued)*

	Released by	Date	Status	Notes
RSS 1.0	RSS-DEV	December 2000	**Viable** and widely used	RDF-based format again.
RSS 0.92	Winer / UserLand	December 2000	**Obsolete** but widely used	Content type of `<description>` element changed from plain text to HTML.
RSS 0.93	Winer / UserLand	April 2001	**Obsolete** and rarely found in the wild	Added `<pubDate>` and `<expirationDate>` items. Also allows multiple `<enclosure>` elements per `<item>`.
RSS 0.94	Winer / UserLand	Summer 2002	**Obsolete** and rarely found in the wild	Dropped `<expirationDate>` element. Specification is no longer available online.
RSS 2.0	Winer / UserLand	August 2002	**Viable** and widely used. Final version of RSS.	Allows addition of new elements as long as they are defined by XML namespaces.
RSS 2.0.1	Winer / Harvard	July 2003	Minor change to RSS 2.0.	Added `<rating>` element.

For more information on each of these versions of RSS, see the specifications found on the Web at the following addresses:

- RSS 0.90—http://www.purplepages.ie/RSS/netscape/rss0.90.html
- RSS 0.91 (Netscape)— http://my.netscape.com/publish/formats/rss-spec-0.91.html
- RSS 0.91 (UserLand)—http://backend.userland.com/rss091
- RSS 0.92—http://backend.userland.com/rss092
- RSS 0.93—http://backend.userland.com/rss093
- RSS 0.94—No longer available online
- RSS 1.0—http://web.resource.org/rss/1.0/spec
- RSS 2.0—No longer available online
- RSS 2.0.1—http://blogs.law.harvard.edu/tech/rss

From a developer's perspective, the RSS situation looks like a nightmare, but it's really not that bad. The good news is that if you stick to the basic elements—`<item>`, `<title>`, `<description>`, `<pubDate>`, and `<link>`—or you use a good parsing library, you'll be able to parse RSS with relative ease. We'll show you how to do it in the next chapter. The even better news is that help is on the way, and its name is Atom.

4.5 *The new standard: Atom*

In 2003, a group of bloggers who were disillusioned with the state of newsfeed and publishing API standards came together to create a new standard, which would later be known as Atom. They wanted to start fresh and do things right this time. Because the group was led by well-known bloggers and XML experts Joe Gregorio, Mark Pilgrim, and Sam Ruby, it attracted the attention and involvement of all the major blog server developers.

The Atom group hoped that by including all the right people, building on existing HTTP and XML specifications, and creating carefully worded complete specifications, they could build a better newsfeed format and publishing protocol. In 2004, they joined with the Internet Engineering Task Force (IETF) and created the Atom Publishing Format and Atom Publishing Protocol. In 2005, IETF released Atom as an Internet standard known formally as RFC-4287 Atom Syndication Format.

Whether you think Atom is an improvement over RSS or just another format, as a blog application developer you'll need to learn Atom. All the major blog servers either support Atom now or have plans to do so, and Blogger.com, one of the largest blogging services, offers only Atom newsfeeds—no RSS.

4.5.1 *Atom by example*

Let's take a look at an example. Listing 4.3 shows a typical Atom newsfeed with one news item. Items are known as *entries* in Atom lingo.

Listing 4.3 A minimal Atom newsfeed

```
<?xml version='1.0' encoding='UTF-8'?>
<feed xmlns= 'http://www.w3.org/2005/Atom' xml:lang='en-us'>     <-1
    <title>Finmodler</title>     <-2
    <link href='http://www.finmodler.com/blog' />     <-3
    <link rel='self' href='http://www.finmodler.com/blog/index.atom' />     4
    <icon>http://www.finmodler.com/favicon.ico</icon>
    <updated>2005-04-06T20:25:05-08:00</updated>     <-5
    <author><name>Nina Carter</name></author>     <-6
    <subtitle>FinModler Update Blog</subtitle>
    <id>http://www.finmodler.com/updateblog</id>
    <generator>FinModler Newsfeed Servlet</generator>
    <entry>     <-7
```

```
<title>Product patch 454-B available</title>     ←❽
<link href=     ←❾
'http://www.finmodler.com/blog/2005/04/06/Patch454B' />
<id>http://www.finmodler.com/blog/2005/04/06/Patch454B</id>   ←❿
<published>2005-04-06T13:00:00-08:00</published>     ←⓫
<updated>2005-04-06T20:25:05-08:00</updated>     ←⓬
<category
    scheme='http://www.finmodler.com/categories'
    term='Software/Patches' label='Software/Patches' />
<content type='xhtml'>     ←⓭
    <div xmlns='http://www.w3.org/1999/xhtml'>
        Patch is available in the
        <a href="http://finmodler.com/downloads">Download center</a>
    </div>
</content>
    </entry>
</feed>
```

The newsfeed shown in listing 4.3 is unlike those we've seen before. Gone are the <rss>, <channel>, and <item> elements found in RSS. In Atom, they've been replaced by <feed> ❶ and <entry> ❼.

An Atom feed must specify a <title> ❷, a <link> ❸ to the source web site, the most recent instant when the feed was updated ❺, and the <author> ❻ (unless the author is specified for each entry). The feed includes a <link> element with rel="self", which contains the URL of the newsfeed ❹.

Each Atom entry must specify a <title> ❽, at least one <link> ❾, and an <id> ❿. The entry in listing 4.3 contains both a <published> ⓫ and an <updated> ⓬ date, but only the updated date is required. Note that these and all other dates in Atom conform to RFC 3339, which allows the ISO 8601 date format.

An entry may contain one <content> element. In listing 4.3, the <content> element ⓭ is marked as type="xhtml" because it contains XHTML (as opposed to escaped HTML, as we've seen in the previous newsfeed examples).

4.5.2 *Atom common constructs*

Atom defines a number of common constructs, attributes, and elements that are reused throughout the format. The most significant are date, text, and person. Dates are simple. A date construct is defined as an element that contains a date in date-time format as defined by RFC 3339. The text and person constructs require explanation.

Text construct

A text construct is an element that contains text. The way the text is stored is indicated by a type attribute. If the type attribute is "text", the element contains plain text and no markup of any kind. If it's "html", the element contains text and escaped HTML markup. If type is "xhtml", the element contains unescaped XHTML markup in the form of XHTML XML elements and text. Figure 4.4 summarizes this.

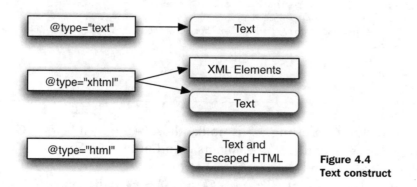

Figure 4.4
Text construct

Person construct

Some constructs involve more than one XML element. For example, Atom defines a person construct that is used to represent authors and contributors, such as the `<author>` element ❻ in listing 4.3. As you can see in figure 4.5, a person construct must contain a name and may contain an email address and a URL. Just as you can extend Atom by adding new elements under `<feed>` and `<entry>`, you can do the same for a person construct.

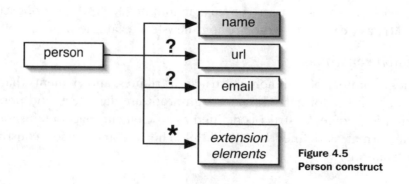

Figure 4.5
Person construct

4.5.3 *The elements of Atom*

Figure 4.6 is our standard newsfeed summary diagram for Atom. We've used the notation <<text>>, <<person>>, and <<date>> to indicate which elements are common constructs. Required elements are shaded.

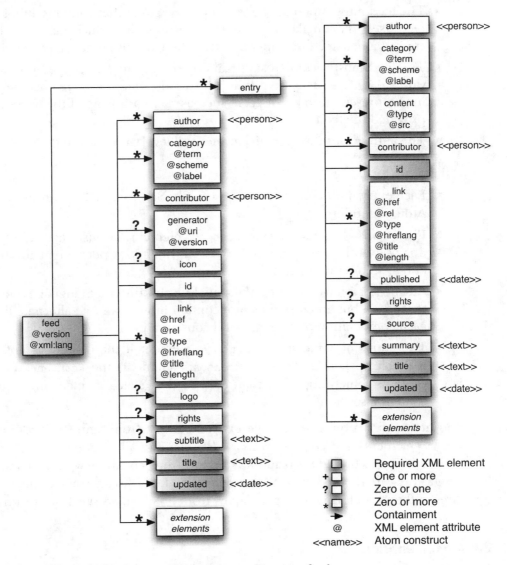

Figure 4.6   The XML elements that make up an Atom newsfeed

Some important requirements are not apparent from this Atom format diagram, so let's review them. First, the feed-level requirements:

- The feed must contain an `<id>` element. See section 4.5.4 for more about Atom identifiers.

- The feed must contain a `<link>` with `rel="self"` that contains a link to the feed itself. This makes it possible for a program, which may have only a copy of a newsfeed document, to find the URL of the newsfeed.

- The feed must include a single alternate link, meaning a `<link>` element with `rel="alternate"`—typically a feed's alternate link references an alternate representation of the feed, such as the main page of the web site that provided the feed.

- The author must be specified at the feed level or in each individual entry.

And now, the entry-level requirements:

- Each entry must contain an `<id>` element. See section 4.5.4 for more about Atom identifiers.

- If the entry does not have a `<content>` element, it must have an alternate link. An entry's alternate link is its permalink, a permanent link to the entry's web representation.

- An entry can have multiple alternate links for different languages and content types, but an entry must not contain more than one alternate link for each combination of language and content type.

- The entry must include a `<summary>` element if the content is not easily readable, i.e., if there is no `<content>` element, the `<content>` element contains something other than text, or the `<content>` element references content elsewhere.

And notice that Atom is extensible. As you can see from figure 4.6, `<feed>` and `<entry>` elements may contain *extension elements*. This allows Atom to be extended in the same ways that RSS 1.0 and RSS 2.0 are. You can add new XML elements as long as they are defined in an XML namespace. Let's discuss some of the key features of the Atom format that set it apart from RSS formats. We'll start with ids.

4.5.4 *Atom identifiers*

Unlike earlier formats, Atom format requires that you provide a unique and permanent identifier for each feed and each entry. Each `<feed>` and `<entry>` element must contain an `<id>` element that contains an Atom identifier. An Atom identifier must be:

- Unique. An Atom `<id>` must be universally unique.

- Permanent. An Atom `<id>` must not change when the feed or entry is republished, exported to another system, or relocated to another host.

- Formatted as an IRI. An Atom `<id>` must be a valid Internet Resource Identifier (IRI) in accordance with RFC 3987, which is a special form of URI that is allowed to contain Unicode characters.

That last bullet about RFC 3987 sounds a little intimidating, but generating ids for your feeds and entries is really not that difficult. In fact, you can use URLs because every URL is a valid IRI. That's probably the easiest route. Use a feed's alternate link as the feed's id and use each entry's alternate link as its id. That's what we did in the Atom feed shown in listing 4.3.

4.5.5 *The Atom content model*

To include content in an Atom entry, you use the `<content>` element. The `<content>` element is similar to a text construct, but it's more complex because it is designed to support six types of content. These types of content can be included inline within the body of the entry or out-of-line at a web location specified by a URI. Here are the six types of content supported by Atom:

- *Plain text*—Text without any markup or any escaped markup

- *XHTML*—Text that may contain XHTML markup. Since XHTML markup is valid XML, it need not be escaped. If you use XHTML in a feed, you must first declare the XHTML namespace, as we did in listing 4.3.

- *Text with escaped HTML*—Text that may contain HTML markup, but with all markup escaped so that it is not interpreted as XML.

- *XML*—Content may contain XML from a declared XML namespace. In this case, set the type attribute to the content-type of the XML data (and note that content-types for XML data must end with "+xml" or "/xml").

- *Inline content of any type*—A `<content>` element can contain data of any content-type if that data is encoded using Base64 encoding. Set the type attribute to the content-type of the data.

- *Out-of-line content of any type*—A `<content>` element can reference remote content by providing a link to that content in the src attribute of the `<content>` element and setting the type to the content-type of the remote content.

To specify the type of content in a `<content>` element, you use the type attribute. Like the type attribute in a text construct, the type can be text, xhtml or html. Let's take a look at some simple examples. Here is an example of a `<content>` element with `type="text"` (no HTML is allowed in text content):

```
<content type="text">
   Read all about it here http://example.com/blog.
</content>
```

And here is one with `type="xhtml"`; we've made the URL into a link:

```
<content type="xhtml">
   Read all about it <a href="http://example.com/blog">here</a>.
</content>
```

Here's one with `type ="html"` and the same link; note that all markup is escaped:

```
<content type="html">
   Read all about it
   &lt;a href="http://example.com/blog"&gt;here&lt;a&gt;.
</content>
```

As you can see, Atom has a well thought-out, flexible, and well-specified content model. Now let's discuss how Atom's `<link>` element can be used to support podcasting.

4.5.6 *Podcasting with Atom*

Podcasting originated as a feature of RSS, but as the world moves to Atom as the new standard, the podcasters will too—and for good reason. Atom can support podcasting through the `<link>` element. As is the case with RSS 2.0-based podcasts, you can have only one podcast per entry. But with Atom, you can have a different representation for each language and for each content-type. For example, if you want to make a podcast available in both English and German and in both MP3 and WMV formats, you can do it like this:

```
<link href="http://example.com/podcasts/show001-usenglish.mpg"
   rel="enclosure" hreflang="en-US" length="21472922" type="audio/mpg" />
<link href="http://example.com/podcasts/show001-usenglish.wmv"
   rel="enclosure" hreflang="en-US" length="23889921" type="audio/wmv" />
<link href="http://example.com/podcasts/show001-german.mp3"
   rel="enclosure" hreflang="de-DE" length="20032879" type="audio/mpg" />
<link href="http://example.com/podcasts/show001-german.wmv"
   rel="enclosure" hreflang="de-DE" length="19907766" type="audio/wmv" />
```

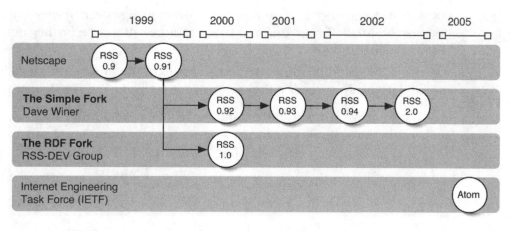

Figure 4.7   Newsfeed format family tree

4.6 *Summary*

Perhaps the best way to summarize this chapter is with the newsfeed format family tree, shown in figure 4.7. You can clearly see the simple vs. RDF fork and Atom's clean break with the past.

Here are some of the key points we covered in this chapter:

- Atom Publishing Format and the various forms of RSS are XML newsfeed formats; originally invented to allow Netscape portal to syndicate news items from other Web sites.

- Dave Libby and Dave Winer wrote the first RSS specifications in 1999; but since then RSS has forked into two incompatible versions: the RSS 1.0 RDF fork and Dave Winer's RSS 2.0 simple fork.

- Atom and RSS formats can be extended; you can add your own new XML elements to the formats as long as you do it in a declared XML namespace.

- Podcasting is a way to distribute any sort of file (not just MP3s for your iPod) via newsfeed, using either an `<enclosure>` element in RSS 2.0 or `<link>` elements in Atom format.

- Podcasting client software, sometimes called podcatchers, and newsfeed readers use newsfeed metadata to decide which podcast files are to be downloaded.

- RSS 1.0 and RSS 2.0 are the most common newsfeed formats, but both are essentially frozen and the specifications will not be further developed or clarified.

- Atom Publishing Format (RFC-4287) is the IETF standard newsfeed format, and it's likely to replace the many incompatible forms of RSS now in use.

Now that we have a good understanding of newsfeed format history and the details of the most important formats, let's turn our attention to programming and learn how to parse newsfeeds using C# and Java.

How to parse newsfeeds

Learn how to use standard XML parsing techniques and specialized newsfeed libraries to parse all forms of RSS and Atom format newsfeeds.

Now that you know the history of newsfeeds and understand the differences between the RSS and Atom formats, you're ready to learn how to parse newsfeeds—how to read in and use newsfeed data in your programs. We'll also discuss how to fetch newsfeeds—how to efficiently (and politely) retrieve them from the Web.

We'll start the chapter by discussing how to use XML techniques to parse newsfeeds, with examples in both C# and Java. Along the way, we'll help you learn how to solve the problems you encounter as you apply these techniques to the numerous slightly different newsfeed formats you'll find in the wild.

After we show you how to parse newsfeeds "by hand" with only an XML parser, we'll introduce you to newsfeed parser libraries, which are designed to make fetching and parsing newsfeeds simple and easy. In the following two chapters, we'll focus on the two most useful libraries: the Windows RSS Platform and the ROME newsfeed utilities.

To wrap up the chapter, we'll show you how to write your own simple parser and fetcher that can handle RSS 1.0, RSS 2.0, and Atom.

But before we get started, let's check in with our fictional friends from chapter 1, Nina, Rangu, and Otto.

5.1 *The possibilities*

As you may remember, Nina, Rangu, and Otto develop financial modeling software. Their main product, Finmodler, requires frequent updates, and the team is constantly releasing new patches and datasets. Keeping users up to date is an ongoing problem.

Nina is responsible for providing new datasets and patches. Several times a month, she'll get a call from the company's chief analyst, who tells her it's time for a new dataset to be distributed. It usually takes a morning for her to combine the required data from a number of sources, package it as a dataset, and make it available to users by uploading it to an online file repository. When she's finished, Nina sends an email to the Finmodler community mailing list to announce the new dataset. Users are then supposed to download, install, and start using the new data.

The problem is that from Nina's point of view, most users are either too busy or inexperienced to download and install the datasets themselves. She spends way too much of her time helping users with these new datasets, and she wants to find a way to automate the process. One day, as she gets ready for her morning run, Nina comes up with a solution to this problem.

Nina has an Apple iPod, which she carries on every run. She listens to her music collection and to *podcasts*—audio files that are automatically downloaded to her iPod. She uses *podcatcher* software, special newsfeed reader software, which monitors newsfeeds for attachments. Whenever an attachment is found, the podcatcher software downloads it and transfers it to her iPod so that it's available the next time she goes for a run.

Nina realizes that she can use podcasting as a technique to download and install the Finmodler dataset and patch files. To make this work, she'll need to build podcatcher capabilities into the Finmodler software. She'll also need a podcast server to host the files and to provide a newsfeed that is updated every time a new file is available for download.

When Nina tells her manager, Otto, about the idea, he's thrilled about this new way to communicate with customers. He wants to build not only a podcatcher into Finmodler, but also a newsfeed reader. With a newsfeed reader, users will be able to read the latest Finmodler news, tips, and tutorials from within the application itself. Otto asks Nina to lead the development of the new Finmodler newsfeed reader and podcatcher feature, and Nina gladly accepts.

In this chapter, we'll present everything Nina needs to know to create a simple newsfeed reader and podcatcher. We won't develop a podcatcher here, but you can find one in chapter 19.

5.2 *Parsing with an XML parser*

You'd think parsing newsfeeds would be easy. After all, they're just XML. But if you've read chapter 4, you probably suspect that's not the case. You're right. There are nine newsfeed formats, and (except for Atom) the specifications are imprecise and open to different interpretations. Parsing newsfeeds is tricky, so we'll start with some simple parsers and guide you past the *gotchas*—the unexpected problems you'll encounter as you parse newsfeeds in the wild.

In this section, we'll show you how to use DOM-based XML parsers to parse RSS 1.0, RSS 2.0, and Atom with C# and Java. Let's start with RSS 1.0.

5.2.1 *Parsing RSS 1.0*

To develop a simple newsfeed reader like the one Nina is building, you must be able to parse a newsfeed into individual news items. For each item, you'll want to display the item title, an excerpt or the item's full content, and a link to the item on the Web. You'll need a date for each item, so they can be displayed in chronological or reverse-chronological order. Let's look at a simple example that shows how to get just those elements.

Listing 5.1 shows how to loop through the news items in a newsfeed and print out the elements for title, description, link, and date using C# and the DOM-based XML parser that is built into .NET.

Listing 5.1   Parsing an RSS 1.0 feed with C# and a DOM-based XML parser

```
XmlDocument feedDoc = new XmlDocument();
feedDoc.Load(inputStream);    ←❶
XmlElement root = feedDoc.DocumentElement;

XmlNodeList items = root.GetElementsByTagName("item");    ←❷
for (int i=0; i<items.Count; i++) {
   XmlElement item = (XmlElement)items.Item(i);

   XmlNode title = item.GetElementsByTagName("title").Item(0);    ←❸
   Console.Out.WriteLine("Title: " + title.FirstChild.Value);

   XmlNode link = item.GetElementsByTagName("link").Item(0);    ←❹
   Console.Out.WriteLine("Link: " + link.FirstChild.Value);

   XmlNodeList descNodes = item.GetElementsByTagName("description");    ←❺
   if (descNodes.Count > 0) {
      Console.Out.WriteLine("Description: "
         + descNotes.Item(0).FirstChild.Value);
   }
   XmlNodeList dateNodes = item.GetElementsByTagName("date",    ←❻
      "http://purl.org/dc/elements/1.1/");
   if (dateNodes.Count > 0) {    ←❼
      Console.Out.WriteLine("Date: " + DateTime.Parse(
         dateNodes.Item(0).FirstChild.Value));
   }
}
```

Let's break it down. The first thing we do in our simple parser is create a DOM document object by reading from an input stream ❶, which could represent a newsfeed file stored on our hard drive or a newsfeed read over the Web. Next, we get the document's root element, get the list of the <item> elements that are its children ❷, and loop through those items one by one.

For each item, we print out the text of the <title> ❸, <link> ❹, and <description> ❺ elements. We don't check for empty node lists for the <title> and <link>elements, because they're required elements in RSS 1.0. Besides, we're trying to keep things simple. If you're not happy with a newsfeed parser that throws exceptions when it encounters an invalid feed, you are welcome to add more error checking. We do check for an empty node list for the description element because it is optional.

Recall from chapter 4 that RSS 1.0 does not provide an item-level date element. Fortunately for us, most RSS 1.0 newsfeeds include item-level dates by using the Dublin Core `<dc:date>` element from the XML namespace http://purl.org/dc/elements/1.1. So next we look for `<dc:date>` **❻**. The date element is not required, so we check for its existence **❼** before we print it out. Note that we use the built-in .NET `DateTime` class to parse the date, which works just fine because .NET can handle ISO8601 format dates.

RSS 1.0 gotchas

Because it's based on RDF, RSS 1.0 looks more complex, but it's actually pretty easy to handle. Only a couple of issues can cause confusion. One issue is extensibility. RSS 1.0 is designed to be a small extensible format that allows users to add in metadata by using extension modules, which we covered in chapter 4, section 4.2.2. The use of Dublin Core `<dc:date>` element is a good example of this. The same goes for author, which is commonly specified by `<dc:creator>`, and category, which is commonly specified by `<dc:subject>`.

Another potentially confusing issue is the optional `<description>` element. Because the RSS 1.0 item `<description>` element has a suggested maximum length of 500 characters, some RSS 1.0 newsfeeds use the Content Module's `<content:encoded>` element instead. So if you really want to display the text of each item, you might want to check for both description and content. To print data from the `<content:encoded>` element, if it is included, you'd add the following inside the `for-loop` in listing 5.1.

```
XmlNodeList encNodes = item.GetElementsByTagName(
    "encoded", "http://purl.org/rss/1.0/modules/content/");
if (encNodes.Count > 0) {
   Console.Out.WriteLine("Content: "
      + encNotes.Item(0).FirstChild.Value);
}
```

Now that we've covered the basics of parsing the RDF fork of RSS, let's move on to the simple fork.

5.2.2 Parsing RSS 2.0

In chapter 4, we saw that RSS 2.0 is not a sequel of RSS 1.0. It's a totally different format. But for our needs, the differences are minimal. Newsfeed items are contained inside the `<channel>` element instead of the root element. Items still have

<title> and <link>, but both are optional now. And there is an item-level <pub-Date> element. With a couple of if statements, you could write a parser that handles both formats, and we will do that later in this chapter. For now, let's look at another simple example that parses RSS 2.0 and prints just the <title>, <description>, <link>, and date elements needed for a simple aggregator—like the one that Nina is building.

Listing 5.2 shows how to parse and print an RSS 2.0 newsfeed using Java and JDOM. We're using the JDOM XML parsing API because it provides a more pleasant and easy-to-use API than the standard org.w3c.dom API that is built into Java. And, as you'll see later, there are a couple of JDOM tricks that are useful for handling embedded XHTML.

Listing 5.2   Parsing an RSS 2.0 newsfeed with Java and JDOM

```
SAXBuilder builder = new SAXBuilder();      ←①
Document feedDoc = builder.build(inputStream);    ←②
Element root = feedDoc.getRootElement();    ←③
Element channel = root.getChild("channel");    ←④

Iterator items = channel.getChildren("item").iterator();    ←⑤

SimpleDateFormat rfc822_format =
   new SimpleDateFormat( "EEE, dd MMM yyyy hh:mm:ss z" );    ←⑥

while (items.hasNext()) {
   Element item = (Element) items.next();    ←⑦

   System.out.println("Title: " + item.getChildText("title"));    ←⑧
   System.out.println("Link: " + item.getChildText("link"));

   String dateString = item.getChildText("pubDate");    ←⑨
   if (dateString != null) {
      Date date = rfc822_format.parse(dateString);
      System.out.println("Date: " + date.toString());
   }
   System.out.println("Description: "    ←⑩
      + item.getChildText("description"));
   System.out.println("\n");
}
```

In listing 5.2, we start by creating a JDOM SAXBuilder parser ① and using it to parse an input stream in to a JDOM Document object ②. We get the root element ③ and from that we get the <channel> element ④. From the channel, we get the <item> elements ⑤, which we will loop through. Before we get into the loop, we create a `SimpleDateFormat` object ❻ that we'll use inside the loop to parse dates, which are in RFC 822 format.

Next, we use a `while-loop` to go through the items one by one. For each item ❼, we print the title and link ❽, but these are optional elements in RSS 2.0, so we may be printing out nulls. If an item has a `<pubDate>` element ❾, we parse it into a `java.util.Date` object and print it out. If it has a description, we print that as well ❿. That's all it takes to parse simple RSS 2.0.

RSS 2.0 Gotchas

The main gotchas in parsing RSS are the optional elements. An item must contain either a `<title>` or a `<description>`, but everything else is optional. Plus, newsfeed producers are free to use alternative elements to represent item content and date. Some consider the use of alternative elements to be *funky*, as we learned in chapter 4, but they are a fact of life, and we need to deal with them in our parsers.

The parser we presented in listing 5.2 can't handle funky RSS, so let's fix that. Let's add in support for two of the most commonly used alternative elements: the Dublin Core date element `<dc:date>` and the Content Module `<content:encoded>` element. Listing 5.3 shows the `while-loop` from listing 5.2, but rewritten to handle funky RSS 2.0.

Listing 5.3   The while-loop from listing 5.2, rewritten to handle funky RSS 2.0

```
Namespace dcNS = Namespace.getNamespace(      ◁─❶
    "dc","http://purl.org/dc/elements/1.1/");
Namespace contentNS = Namespace.getNamespace(      ◁─❷
    "content","http://purl.org/rss/1.0/modules/content/");

while (items.hasNext()) {
   Element item = (Element) items.next();

   System.out.println("Title: " + item.getChildText("title"));
   System.out.println("Link: " + item.getChildText("link"));

   String dateString = item.getChildText("pubDate");
   if (dateString != null) {
      Date date = rfc822_format.parse(dateString);
      System.out.println("Date: " + date.toString());
   }
   else if ((dateString = item.getChildText("date", dcNS)) != null) {  ◁─❸
      Date date = ISO8601DateParser.parse(dateString);
      System.out.println("Date: " + date.toString());
   }
   String description = item.getChildText("description");
```

```
    if (description == null) {
        description = item.getChildText("encoded", contentNS);    ←—❹
    }
    System.out.println("Description: " + description);
    System.out.println("\n");
}
```

Let's cover the new code we added. First, we set up Namespace objects for the Dublin Core ❶ and Content Module ❷ namespaces. Then, inside the loop, if we don't find a `<pubDate>`, we look for a `<dc:date>` and use it instead ❸. The same goes for the description. If we fail to find a `<description>`, we look for `<content:encoded>` and use it instead ❹.

Now that we've covered the two major flavors of RSS, let's move on to the format of the future, Atom.

5.2.3 *Parsing Atom*

We're going to look at the same example of parsing and printing a newsfeed, but this time for Atom. Atom, of course, is a totally different format, with different element names and rules about when and how each element is to be included. Despite that, our simple parser is pretty similar in structure to the previous parsers we've developed. Take a look at listing 5.4, which shows how to parse and print an Atom newsfeed using C# and the `System.Xml` parser that is built into .NET.

> **Listing 5.4   Parsing Atom with C# and System.Xml**

```
XmlDocument feedDoc = new XmlDocument();    ←—❶
feedDoc.Load(inputStream);
XmlElement root = feedDoc.DocumentElement;    ←—❷

Uri baseUri = FindBaseUri(root);    ←—❸

XmlNodeList entries = root.GetElementsByTagName("entry");    ←—❹
for (int i=0; i<entries.Count; i++) {
    XmlElement entry = (XmlElement)entries.Item(i);

    XmlNode title = entry.GetElementsByTagName("title").Item(0);
    Console.Out.WriteLine("Title: " + title.FirstChild.Value);    ←—❺

    XmlNodeList links = entry.GetElementsByTagName("link");    ←—❻
    foreach (XmlNode link in links) {
        string href = link.Attributes["href"].Value;
        Console.Out.WriteLine(
            "A link: " + ResolveUri(baseUri, link, href));    ←—❼
    }
```

```
XmlNode dateNode = entry.GetElementsByTagName("updated").Item(0);
Console.Out.WriteLine("Date: "
   + DateTime.Parse(dateNode.FirstChild.Value));        ←❽

XmlNodeList descList =
   entry.GetElementsByTagName("content");        ←❾
if (descList.Count < 1) {
   descList = entry.GetElementsByTagName("summary");        ←❿
}
if (descList.Count > 0) {
   XmlElement desc = (XmlElement)descList.Item(0);
   String type = desc.GetAttribute("type");        ←⓫
   if ("text".Equals(type) || "html".Equals(type)) {        ←⓬
      Console.Out.WriteLine(
         "Description: " + desc.FirstChild.Value);        ←⓭
   }
   else {
      Console.Out.WriteLine(
         "Description: " + desc.InnerXml);        ←⓮
   }
}
}
```

Let's discuss listing 5.4 line by line. We start with an XmlDocument object and an input stream that contains the newsfeed we want to parse. The first step is to load the document with the newsfeed ❶. At this point, the newsfeed XML is parsed into a DOM, and we're ready to use the .NET DOM API to pull out the information we need.

Next, we get the root element ❷ from the DOM and use that to get the baseURI of the newsfeed by calling findBaseURI() ❸, a method we'll explain in the next section. We need that baseURI so that we can resolve any relative URIs we come across during parsing.

Now we're ready to loop through the entries in the newsfeed. From the root, we get the newsfeed's collection of <entry> elements ❹. For each entry, we print out the title ❺ and any links we find ❻. Note that we call ResolveURI(), another method to be explained later, to ensure that relative URIs are handled properly ❼. We parse the <updated> date using the built-in DateTime class and print it ❽.

For the description we use the <content> element ❾, and if that is not found, we use <summary> ❿. The way we get the text depends on the value of the element's type attribute ⓫. If the type is "text" or "html" ⓬, we simply print out the text and rely on XmlElement to un-escape any escaped text ⓭. If it's "xhtml," we use the InnerXml field to get the XHTML in plain text form and we print that out ⓮.

That seemed pretty easy, but we still need to explain how to handle relative URIs.

Resolving relative URIs in Atom newsfeeds

We didn't have to worry about relative URIs before because they're not allowed in RSS. With Atom, newsfeed creators can use the xml:base attribute, defined in the W3C XML Base recommendation, to define base URIs against which relative URIs must be resolved.

Not all Atom newsfeeds use relative URIs, but since they're allowed by the Atom format, we need to be able to handle them. First, let's look at the simple one-entry example in listing 5.5 so we can understand how relative URIs work.

Listing 5.5   Example Atom newsfeed with relative URIs

```
<?xml version='1.0' encoding='UTF-8'?>
<feed xmlns='http://www.w3.org/2005/Atom'
    xml:base='http://www.example.com/blog/atom.xml'>    ◀─❶
<title>Example feed</title>
<link href='./' />    ◀─❷
<updated>2005-09-25T00:16:04-08:00</updated>
<author><name>Otto</name></author>
<subtitle>Example feed</subtitle>
<id>http://example.com/blog/</id>
<entry xml:base='archives/2005/10/18'>    ◀─❸
   <title>Test post one</title>
   <link href='test_post_one' />    ◀─❹
   <id>http://example.com/blog/archives/2005/10/18/test_post_one</id>
   <published>2005-09-25T13:00:00-08:00</published>
   <updated>2005-09-25T00:16:02-08:00</updated>
   <content type='text'>Test post one content<content>
</entry>
</feed>
```

In the <feed> element, the newsfeed specifies its base URI using the xml:base attribute ❶. Since that's the root element, all relative URIs in the newsfeed must be resolved relative to http://www.example.com/blog/atom.xml, but with the filename atom.xml stripped off the end. According to the XML Base rules, the first relative URI we encounter, './' in the feed's <link> element ❷, resolves to http://www.example.com/blog.

The xml:base attribute can be used in any XML element within the document, and when it appears, all relative URIs within the element must take the base into account. Depending on how the base attribute is used, you may have to

take multiple bases into account. For example, in the newsfeed above, the
<entry> element also has a base attribute 'archives/2005/10/18' ❸, and that base
is itself relative. So when we find the relative URI 'test_post_one' inside the
entry's <link> element ❹, we have to take both the entry base and the feed base
into account. The resulting entry link is feed base + entry base + relative URI,
which equals http://www.example.com/blog/archives/2005/10/18/test_post_one.

Now let's examine the implementation of the ResolveUri() method that we
used in our simple Atom parser. Listing 5.6 shows the code.

Listing 5.6   C# method for resolving URIs in an Atom newsfeed

```csharp
private string ResolveUri(Uri baseUri, XmlNode parent, string uri) {
    uri = (uri.Equals(".") || uri.Equals("./")) ? "" : uri;
    if (IsRelativeUri(uri) && parent != null && parent == XmlElement) {    ❶
        String xmlBase = ((XmlElement)parent).GetAttribute("xml:base");
        xmlBase = (xmlBase == null) ? "" : xmlBase;
        if (!IsRelativeUri(xmlBase) && !xmlBase.EndsWith("/")) {    ◁❷
            xmlBase = xmlBase.Substring(0, xmlBase.LastIndexOf("/")+1);
        }
        return ResolveUri(baseUri, parent.ParentNode, xmlBase + uri);    ◁❸
    }
    else if (IsRelativeUri(uri) && parent == null) {    ◁❹
        return baseUri + uri;
    }
    else if (baseUri != null && uri.StartsWith("/")) {    ◁❺
        string hostUri = baseUri.Scheme + "://" + baseUri.Host;    ◁❻
        if (!baseUri.IsDefaultPort) {
            hostUri = hostUri + ":" + baseUri.Port;
        }
        return hostUri + uri;
    }
    return uri;    ◁❼
}
private bool IsRelativeUri(String uri) {    ◁❽
    if (  uri.StartsWith("http://")
       || uri.StartsWith("https://")
       || uri.StartsWith("/")) {
        return false;
    }
    return true;
}
```

The ResolveUri() method uses recursion to walk from the current element back
toward the root of the XML tree, stopping only when it has enough information to
create an absolute URI or when it reaches the root of the tree. The method takes

three parameters: the base URI of the newsfeed, the parent element of the URI we are resolving, and the URI to be resolved.

First, we check for a relative URI by calling a helper method called `IsRelative-Uri()` ❶. If we don't have a relative URI, we check for an `xml:Base` attribute in the parent element ❷. If we find one, we prepend it to the URI and make a recursive call back to the `ResolveUri()` method, but this time using the parent of the parent element ❸.

Next, if we still have a relative URI, but we're at the top of the tree, we simply prepend the `baseUri` on the URI and return that ❹.

If we have a `baseUri` and the URI we're resolving begins with a slash, we form an absolute URI by appending the URI to the URI of the host ❺. We have to do a little work to determine the scheme, hostname, and port number based on the `baseUri` ❻. If we fall off the bottom of the `if-else` block, we simply return the URI that was passed on ❼. And finally: the `IsRelativeURI()` method is simple ❽. It returns true for all URLs that don't start with http:// or https://.

Now let's cover the last missing piece of the puzzle.

Determining the base URI of an Atom newsfeed

The `ResolveUri()` method above needs to know the base URI of the newsfeed itself. In the simple Atom parser in listing 5.7, we use the `FindBaseUri()` method to determine that. Let's take a look at the code.

Listing 5.7   C# method for finding the base URI of an Atom newsfeed

```
private Uri FindBaseUri(XmlElement root) {
    Uri baseUri = null;
    XmlNodeList links = root.GetElementsByTagName("link");     ←❶
    foreach (XmlNode link in links) {
        if (!root.Equals(link.ParentNode)) break;
        string href = link.Attributes["href"].Value;
        if (  link.Attributes["rel"] == null
           || link.Attributes["rel"].Value.Equals("alternate")) {
            href = ResolveUri(null, link, href);     ←❷
            baseUri = new Uri(href);
            break;
        }
    }
    return baseUri;
}
```

The algorithm is simple. We loop through the `<link>` elements at the top level of the feed ❶ and we use the first alternate link we find as the base URI. Because the link might be relative, we call `ResolveUriI()` ❷ to resolve it properly.

Now that you know how to use an XML parser to parse RSS and Atom newsfeeds, let's turn our attention to specialized newsfeed parsing libraries.

5.3   *Parsing with a newsfeed library*

A *newsfeed library* is a programming library that's designed to make fetching, parsing, and producing newsfeeds easy. The big advantage of newsfeed libraries is that they abstract away the differences between the numerous newsfeed formats so that you don't have to deal with them. Newsfeed libraries also provide convenient methods to make it easy to detect, fetch, and cache newsfeeds.

In this section, we'll discuss four newsfeed libraries–one for Python, two for Java and one for .NET. We'll discuss the pros and cons of each so that if you use a newsfeed library, you'll know which one you should prefer. We'll start with the most stable and widely used library of the lot, the Universal Feed Parser.

5.3.1   *The Universal Feed Parser for Python*

The Universal Feed Parser by Mark Pilgrim is written in Python. We're mentioning it in this book, which focuses on C# and Java, because it's probably the most powerful and popular newsfeed parser around. The Universal Feed Parser can parse all forms of RSS and Atom. It can handle 50 different extension modules. It's supported by more than 2,000 unit tests. The parser's main claim to fame is that it can parse just about anything. It's a *liberal parser*, which means it's very forgiving of errors in newsfeeds.

Let's take a look at the example we've been using in this chapter, but this time in Python with the Universal Feed Parser. The Python script below is all it takes to parse any version of RSS or Atom and print out the title, description, link, and date for each item.

```
import feedparser
import sys
feed = feedparser.parse(sys.argv[1])
for item in feed["items"]:
   print "Title: "       + item["title"]
   print "Description: " + item["summary"
   print "Link: "        + item["link"]
   print "Date: "        + item["modified"]
```

That's much easier than anything we've seen so far. Let's break it down. First, we import the feedparser and sys packages. Next, we call the feed parser and pass in sys.argv[1], which is the first argument passed to the script on the command line. That argument may be either the path to a newsfeed file in the local filesystem or the URL of a newsfeed on the Web. The parser returns the parsed newsfeed as a dictionary, whose keys correspond to newsfeed element names. The Universal Feed Parser stores items as an array of dictionaries, which can be retrieved by using the key "items." So next, we loop through the items in the items array. For each item, we print the title, description, link, and summary.

You can download the Universal Feed Parser, full documentation, and source code from the project's web site at http://feedparser.org. The Universal Feed Parser is the best choice for Python developers. Now let's move on to ROME, the best choice for Java developers.

5.3.2 *The ROME newsfeed utilities*

The ROME newsfeed parser was created by developers at Sun Microsystems. Their goal was to create an open source Java newsfeed parser and generator that can handle all forms of RSS and Atom with minimal dependencies and a high degree of extensibility. Let's take a brief look at ROME's advantages and disadvantages so that we can compare it to our other options. In chapter 7, we'll cover ROME in depth.

Unlike the Universal Feed Parser, which models each newsfeed as a dictionary, ROME uses object models to represent newsfeeds at different levels of abstraction. ROME can parse an RSS newsfeed into an RSS-like object model for those who wish to operate in terms of RSS constructs. ROME can parse an Atom newsfeed into an Atom-like object model for those who wish to work in terms of Atom. But most developers will work instead with ROME's simple *SyndFeed* model, an abstract model designed to represent all forms of Atom and RSS.

ROME is designed around a simple core, which includes parsers, converters, and generators for all of the commonly used RSS and Atom newsfeed formats. ROME's subprojects, which are distributed separately, provide newsfeed extension support, a newsfeed parser, a facility for storing ROME objects in a database, and the ROME Fetcher for efficient fetching of newsfeeds.

Below is our parse and print example, written in Java using ROME. It shows how to parse an RSS or Atom newsfeed to a SyndFeed model and print each item's title, description, link, and date.

```
SyndFeedInput input = new SyndFeedInput();
SyndFeed feed = input.build(new InputStreamReader(inputStream));
Iterator items = feed.getEntries().iterator();
while (items.hasNext()) {
    SyndEntry item = (SyndEntry)items.next();
    System.out.println("Title: "       + item.getTitle());
    System.out.println("Description: " + item.getDescription());
    System.out.println("Link: "        + item.getLink());
    System.out.println("Date: "        + item.getPublishedDate());
}
```

If you'd like to learn more about ROME, skip ahead to chapter 9. Before we move on to the Jakarta Feed Parser for Java, let's discuss the pros and cons of ROME.

Advantages of ROME

- *Easy to use*—ROME parses to any of three easy-to-use object models: RSS, Atom, or the abstract SyndFeed model.

- *Supports generation and conversion*—ROME is not just a parser. It can also generate and convert between any of the 10 forms of RSS and Atom newsfeeds.

- *Highly flexible*—Not only can you add support to ROME for new newsfeed extensions, but you can also override ROME's built-in parsers, generators, and converters.

- *Cross-platform*—Since ROME is written in Java, it will run on just about any operating system platform.

Disadvantages of ROME

- *DOM-based*—ROME uses a DOM-based XML parser and therefore is not well suited to parsing or generating extremely large newsfeeds.

- *Not liberal*—ROME includes some error correction features but is still not a true liberal parser.

- *Under development*—The ROME community is active and supportive, but at the time of this writing it has yet to reach the milestone of a 1.0 release.

ROME isn't the only newsfeed library option for Java developers. Next let's examine Kevin Burton's Jakarta Feed Parser.

5.3.3 *Jakarta Feed Parser for Java*

Kevin Burton originally developed Jakarta Feed Parser for his NewsMonster newsfeed reader, but it's now part of the Apache Jakarta project. You can find the Jakarta Feed Parser documentation and source code repository at http://jakarta.

apache.org/commons/feedparser/. And, it's been battle-tested in a couple of high-volume web applications, including the Rojo.com aggregator and the Tailrank. com search engine (you can find the Tailrank.com fork of the Feed Parser at http:// tailrank.com/code.php).

Like ROME, Jakarta Feed Parser can parse all varieties of RSS and Atom newsfeeds. Unlike ROME, it's a SAX-based parser. So instead of handing you a complete object model representing a newsfeed, Jakarta Feed Parser calls your code at key points in the parsing process. To use Jakarta Feed Parser, you must provide an implementation of the interface FeedParserListener. The easiest way to do this is to extend the included DefaultFeedParserListener class and override just the methods you need.

The code below shows our parse-and-print example implemented in Java with Jakarta Feed Parser. Before we call the parser, we extend DefaultFeedParserListener and override its onItem() and onCreated() methods so we can print title, description, link, and date for each item. When we call parser.parse(), our listener will be called.

```
FeedParserListener listener = new DefaultFeedParserListener() {

    public void onItem(FeedParserState state,
            String title, String link,
            String description, String permalink)
            throws FeedParserException {
        System.out.print("\n");
        System.out.println("Title: " + title);
        System.out.println("Description: " + description);
        System.out.println("Link: " + link);
    }
    public void onCreated(FeedParserState state, Date date)
            throws FeedParserException {
        System.out.println( "Date: " + date );
    }
};
FeedParser parser = FeedParserFactory.newFeedParser();
parser.parse(listener, inputStream);
```

Notice that the onItem() method has only four string arguments: title, link, description, and permalink. If you need to get any other subelements, you can get the underlying JDOM Element object from FeedParserState object using the JDOM API.

Now that we've seen a simple example, let's discuss why and why not to use Jakarta Feed Parser.

Advantages

- *High performance*—According to developer Kevin Burton, the Jakarta Feed Parser, which uses a SAX-based approach to parsing newsfeeds, is up to 15 times faster than ROME.

- *SAX-based*—Because it uses a SAX parser, Jakarta Feed Parser can handle extremely large newsfeeds without using an extremely large amount of memory.

- *Production tested*—You can count on the Jakarta Feed Parser because it does the parsing for the Tailrank.com and Rojo.com services, each of which process millions of newsfeeds per day.

- *Cross-platform*—Jakarta Feed Parser, like ROME, is written in Java, so it will run on just about any operating system platform.

Disadvantages

- *Difficult to use*—Using a SAX-based parser like Jakarta Feed Parser is generally more difficult and requires more code than using a DOM-based parser like ROME.

- *Lack of documentation*—Documentation for the Jakarta Feed Parser is scarce. An API reference is available, but you won't find a wiki full of documentation and tutorials like ROME offers.

- *Not liberal*—Jakarta Feed Parser includes some error correction features but is still not a true liberal parser.

- *Under development*—Although used in a number of production newsfeed aggregation services, the Jakarta Feed Parser has not reached a 1.0 release. Also, it's not clear who will control future development of the project: Apache Jakarta or Tailrank.com.

That takes care of the Java newsfeed libraries. Now let's see what Microsoft has to offer.

5.3.4 *The Windows RSS Platform*

Starting with Internet Explorer 7 and Windows Vista, Microsoft is building RSS and Atom newsfeed support directly into the Windows operating system. Microsoft's new Windows RSS Platform includes a newsfeed parser, subscription management, and a complete download manager for efficient downloads of both newsfeeds and enclosures. Your programs can use all of these features via the Feeds API, which is packaged as a COM component callable from C/C++ and all of the .NET languages.

Below is our simple parse and print example, written in C# using the Windows RSS Platform's Feeds API. It shows how to parse an RSS or Atom newsfeed specified by url and print each item's title, description, link, and date.

```
FeedsManager fm = new FeedsManagerClass();
IFeed feed = (IFeed)fm.GetFeedByUrl(url);
foreach (IFeedItem item in (IFeedsEnum)feed.Items) {
  Console.Out.WriteLine("item.Title:       " + item.Title);
  Console.Out.WriteLine("item.Description: " + item.Description);
  Console.Out.WriteLine("item.Link:        " + item.Link);
  Console.Out.WriteLine("item.PubDate:     " + item.PubDate);
}
```

Let's take a brief look at Windows RSS Platform pros and cons so we can compare it with our other newsfeed library choices. In chapter 8, we'll cover the Windows RSS Platform in depth.

Advantages of Windows RSS Platform

- *Easy to use*—The Windows RSS Platform can parse any form of RSS and Atom newsfeeds to a simple abstract object model.

- *Integrated fetcher and cache*—The platform fetches and caches newsfeeds using the bandwidth-saving techniques we'll discuss later in this chapter.

- *Subscription management*—Via the Feeds API, your programs can add and remove newsfeed subscriptions for the current user, set download preferences, and mark individual newsfeed items as read or unread.

Disadvantages of the Windows RSS Platform

- *Not liberal*—The Windows RSS Platform won't parse invalid XML.

- *Not general purpose*—The platform is designed to support the needs of Internet Explorer 7 and other client-side desktop applications. It's not designed for general-purpose use and is not intended for use in server-side applications.

- *Windows only*—In case it's not obvious, the Windows RSS Platform will work on only one platform: Windows.

That brings us to the end of our review of newsfeed libraries. We'll cover both the Windows RSS Platform and ROME in depth in the next two chapters, but now it's time to learn how to develop your own newsfeed parser.

5.4 *Developing a newsfeed parser*

If you're not happy with the newsfeed library options, you'll be glad to hear that it's not that hard to build your own simple newsfeed parser. We've already created simple parsers for RSS 1.0, RSS 2.0, and Atom. Now let's look at a larger example. We'll use the XML parsing techniques we covered earlier in the chapter to develop a newsfeed parser in Java that can handle all three types of newsfeeds. We'll call it *AnyFeedParser*.

To keep things simple, AnyFeedParser will parse newsfeeds into hashtable and array form, just like the Universal Feed Parser does. We won't try to handle every RSS and Atom element, just the basics we need for the examples in this book—and that includes RSS `<enclosure>` elements so we can handle podcasts.

Figure 5.1 illustrates the hashtable and array representation we'll use to represent newsfeeds. In the top-left is the feed hashtable, which contains feed-level metadata title, description, and link. Under the hashtable key "Items," we have an array of items. Each item is represented by a hashtable in the array. The item hashtable, in the lower-left corner, contains item-level metadata plus a hashtable to hold enclosure information. We use RSS and Atom element names as the key names, and in some cases, we key with both the Atom and RSS name so you can use either Atom or RSS terminology in your code. For example, you can use either "items" or "entries" to get the items array.

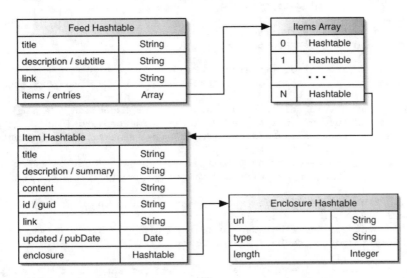

Figure 5.1 Hashtable and array representation of a newsfeed

In Java, we'll use a `Map` interface to represent the hashtable and a `List` to represent the array. In C#, we'll use an `IDictionary` for the hashtable and an `IList` for the array. We know how our parser will return newsfeed data, and we've defined the interface to be used by calling code, so we're ready to write the code for AnyFeedParser.java.

5.4.1 *AnyFeedParser for Java*

We'll implement AnyFeedParser.java using JDOM as our XML-parsing API, but someday you might want to implement it using a newsfeed library or some other technique. We'll code to an interface so that you can switch out your implementation later. AnyFeedParser.java will implement this Java interface:

```
public interface IFeedParser {
    public Map parseFeed(Reader reader) throws Exception;
    public Map parseFeed(String fileName) throws Exception;
}
```

Let's take a look at the code, shown in listing 5.8 in its entirety.

Listing 5.8   Complete source code of the Java and JDOM-based AnyFeedParser

```
package com.manning.blogapps.chapter05;
import java.io.*;
import java.net.*;
import java.util.*;
import java.text.SimpleDateFormat;
import org.jdom.*;
import org.jdom.input.SAXBuilder;
import org.jdom.output.XMLOutputter;

public class AnyFeedParser implements IFeedParser {
    Namespace ns = Namespace.getNamespace("http://www.w3.org/2005/Atom");

    public static void main(String[] args) throws Exception {        ◁─❶
        Map parsedFeed = new AnyFeedParser().parseFeed(args[0]);
        FeedPrinter.displayFeed(parsedFeed, new PrintWriter(System.out));
    }
    public Map parseFeed(String feedFileName) throws Exception {      ◁─❷
        return (parseFeed(new FileReader(feedFileName)));
    }
    public Map parseFeed(Reader reader) throws Exception {            ◁─❸
        SAXBuilder builder = new SAXBuilder();
        Document feedDoc = builder.build(reader);
        Element root = feedDoc.getRootElement();

        if (root.getName().equals("feed")) return parseAtom(root);    ◁─❹
            return parseRSS(root);        ◁─❺
    }
```

```java
public Map parseAtom(Element root) throws Exception {      ◄━❻
    URL baseURI = findBaseURI(root);      ◄━❼

    Map feedMap = new HashMap();
    put(feedMap,"title", parseAtomContent("title", root, ns));      ◄━❽
    put(feedMap,"link", parseAtomLink(baseURI, root, ns));      ◄━❾
    put(feedMap, new String[] {"subtitle","description"},      ◄━❿
        parseAtomContent("subtitle", root, ns));

    List itemList = new ArrayList();
    put(feedMap, new String[] {"entries","items"}, itemList);      ◄━⓫

    Iterator items = root.getChildren("entry",ns).iterator();      ◄━⓬
    while (items.hasNext()) {
        Element item = (Element) items.next();
        Map itemMap = new HashMap();
        itemList.add(itemMap);
        put(itemMap, new String[] {"id","guid"},      ◄━⓭
            item.getChildText("id", ns));
        put(itemMap, "title",  parseAtomContent("title", item, ns));
        put(itemMap, new String[] {"summary", "description"},      ◄━⓮
            parseAtomContent("summary", item, ns));
        put(itemMap, "link",    parseAtomLink(baseURI, item, ns));◄━⓯
        put(itemMap, "content", parseAtomContent("content", item, ns));
        String dt = item.getChildText("updated", ns);
        if (dt != null) {
            put(itemMap, new String[] {"updated","pubDate"},      ◄━⓰
                ISO8601DateParser.parse(dt));
        }
    }
    return feedMap;      ◄━⓱
}
Map parseRSS(Element root) throws Exception {      ◄━⓲
    Namespace contentNS = Namespace.getNamespace(      ◄━⓳
        "content","http://purl.org/rss/1.0/modules/content/");
    Namespace dcNS = Namespace.getNamespace(      ◄━⓴
        "dc","http://purl.org/dc/elements/1.1/");
    Namespace ns = null;
    if (root.getName().equals("rss")) {      ◄━㉑
        ns = Namespace.NO_NAMESPACE;
    } else {
        ns = Namespace.getNamespace("http://purl.org/rss/1.0/");
    }
    Element channel = root.getChild("channel",ns);      ◄━㉒
    Map feedMap = new HashMap();
    put(feedMap, "title", channel.getChildText("title",ns));
    put(feedMap, "link", channel.getChildText("link",ns));
    put(feedMap, new String[] {"description","subtitle"},
        channel.getChildText("description",ns));
```

```
        Iterator items = null;
        if (root.getName().equals("rss")) {      ◄─㉓
            items = channel.getChildren("item",ns).iterator();    ◄─㉔
        } else {
            items = root.getChildren("item",ns).iterator();    ◄─㉕
        }
        List itemList = new ArrayList();
        put(feedMap, new String[] {"entries", "items"}, itemList);
        SimpleDateFormat rfc822_format =
            new SimpleDateFormat( "EEE, dd MMM yyyy hh:mm:ss z" );    ◄─㉖
        while (items.hasNext()) {    ◄─㉗
            Element item = (Element) items.next();
            Map itemMap = new HashMap();
            itemList.add(itemMap);

            Element link = item.getChild("link", ns);    ◄─㉘
            Element guid = item.getChild("guid", ns);
            put(itemMap, new String[] {"id", "guid"}, guid);
            if (link != null) {
                put(itemMap, "link", link.getText());
            } else if (guid != null    ◄─㉙
            && "true".equals(guid.getAttributeValue("isPermaLink"))) {
                put(itemMap, new String[] {"link","guid"}, guid.getText());
            }
            put(itemMap,"title", item.getChildText("title", ns));
            put(itemMap,"content",
                item.getChildText("encoded", contentNS));    ┃
            put(itemMap,new String[] {"description","summary"},   ㉚
                item.getChildText("description", ns));

            if (item.getChild("pubDate", ns) != null) {    ◄─㉛
                put(itemMap, new String[] {"pubDate","updated"},
                    rfc822_format.parse(item.getChildText("pubDate", ns)));
            }
            else if (item.getChild("date", dcNS) != null) {    ◄─㉜
                put(itemMap, new String[] {"pubDate","updated"},
                    ISO8601DateParser.parse(item.getChildText("date", dcNS)));
            }
            Element enc = item.getChild("enclosure", ns);    ◄─㉝
            if (enc != null) {
                Map encMap = new HashMap();
                encMap.put("url",    enc.getAttributeValue("url"));
                encMap.put("length", enc.getAttributeValue("length"));
                encMap.put("type",   enc.getAttributeValue("type"));
                itemMap.put("enclosure", encMap);
            }
        }
        return feedMap;    ◄─㉞
    }
```

```
    void put(Map map, String key, Object value) {      <-⑤
        if (value != null) map.put(key, value);
    }
    void put(Map map, String[] keys, Object value) {      <-⑥
        if (value != null) for (int i=0; i<keys.length; i++) {
            map.put(keys[i], value);
        }
    }
    String parseAtomLink(URL baseURI, Element elem, Namespace ns) {      <-⑦
        String link = null;
        Iterator links = elem.getChildren("link", ns).iterator();
        while (links.hasNext()) {
            Element linkElem = (Element) links.next();
            String rel = linkElem.getAttributeValue("rel");
            if (rel == null || rel.equals("alternate")) {
                link = resolveURI(baseURI, linkElem,
                        linkElem.getAttributeValue("href"));
                break;
            }
        }
        return link;
    }
    String parseAtomContent(String name, Element elem, Namespace ns) {   ⑧
        String value = null;
        Element contentElem = elem.getChild(name, ns);
        if (contentElem != null) {
            String type = contentElem.getAttributeValue("type");
            if ("text".equals(type) || "html".equals(type)) {
                value = contentElem.getText();
            } else if ("xhtml".equals(type)) {
                XMLOutputter outputter = new XMLOutputter();
                value = outputter.outputString(contentElem.getChildren());
            } else {
                value = elem.getChildText("title", ns);
            }
        }
        return value;
    }

    private String resolveURI(URL baseURI, Element parent, String url) {}
    private boolean isRelativeURI(String uri) {}
    private URL findBaseURI(Element root) {}                         ⑨
}
```

Listing 5.8 is quite long, so we'll break our discussion of it into sections for the
parseFeed() methods, the parseAtom() method, the parseRSS() method, and
the helper methods. First, let's discuss the class itself. The AnyFeedParser class
implements the IFeedParser interface and provides a main()method ❶ so that

you can call it from the command line. When you call `AnyFeedParser` from the command line, you must pass in one argument, the path to a newsfeed file to be parsed. The `main()` method ❶ calls `parseFeed()` to parse that file and then calls a FeedPrinter utility class (which you can find in the online examples) to print the parsed feed out to the console.

AnyFeedParser parseFeed() methods

The first `parseFeed()` method ❷ takes a string argument, which specifies the newsfeed file to be parsed, and uses it to create a `FileReader`, which it passes on to the other version of `parseFeed()`, which can handle any sort of `Reader`.

The second `parseFeed()` method ❸ accepts a `Reader` argument and passes it to a JDOM `SAXBuilder` to parse the newsfeed XML into the form of a JDOM `Document`. We use the name of the root element to decide whether to parse the newsfeed as Atom or RSS. If the name is "feed," we call `parseAtom()` to parse the newsfeed as Atom ❹. Otherwise, we call `parseRSS()` to parse it as RSS ❺. Let's examine `parseAtom()`.

AnyFeedParser parseAtom() method

The `parseAtom()` method ❻ accepts one argument, the root of an XML document that contains an Atom newsfeed, and returns a map representing the contents of that newsfeed. First, we call `findBaseURI()` ❼, just as we did in the Atom feed parser in listing 5.4, to determine the base URI of the newsfeed. Next, we create the feed map and start populating it with feed-level metadata. Note that we use our own convenience method called `put()` to put items into the map. The `put()` method will put items into the map only if they are non-null. The title is an Atom text construct and needs special handling so we use the `parseAtomContent()` method (which we'll discuss later) to extract it ❽. There may be multiple links in the feed, so we call `parseAtomLink()` (which we'll also discuss later) to get the right one ❾.

Subtitle needs special handling ❿. We call `parseAtomContent()` to get the content value, and a second version of `put()` to put the value into the feed map with both keys "subtitle" and "description."

Once we're finished with the feed-level metadata, we create the items array and put it into the feed map with the keys "entries" and "items" ⓫. Next, we loop through those items one by one ⓬. We get the Atom ID and put it in the item map, keyed by both "id" and "guid" ⓭. We use `parseAtomContent()` to parse the item summary and put it into the item map, keyed by "summary" and "description" if it exists ⓮. We call `parseAtomLink()` to parse and resolve the entry's link **⓯**. And finally, we put the date, if there is one, into the item map as both "updated" and "pubDate" **⓰**.

That's all there is to parsing an Atom newsfeed, so we return the resulting feed map **⓱** and we're done. Now on to RSS.

AnyFeedParser parseRSS() method

The parseRSS() method **⓲** accepts one argument, the root of an XML document that contains an RSS newsfeed, and returns a map representing the contents of that newsfeed. This method can parse both simple fork RSS (e.g., 0.91, 0.92, 0.93, 2.0) and RDF fork RSS (RSS 1.0). Before we start, we set up JDOM Namespace objects contentNS for the Content Module namespace **⓳** and dcNS for the Dublin Core namespace **⓴**.

Next, we use the name of the root element to determine the type of newsfeed we're reading so that we can set the default namespace **㉑**. If the root is <rss>, we're dealing with simple fork RSS and we have no namespace. Otherwise, we assume that we're reading RSS 1.0, and we set the RSS 1.0 namespace. Whether we're reading the simple or the RDF flavor of RSS, we need to get feed-level meta-data from the <channel> element **㉒**. We get the title, link, and description and add them to the feed map.

Once we've read the feed-level metadata, it's time to handle the individual items. Again, we use the name of the root element to determine the type of news-feed **㉓**. If the root is <rss>, we have simple RSS and we get the collection of <item> elements from the <channel> element **㉔**. Otherwise, we get the collection directly from the root **㉕**.

After we set up a date parser **㉖** for use inside the item loop, we start looping **㉗**. For each item, we get the <link> and <guid> elements **㉘**. If there is no link and the guid is a permalink, we use it as the link **㉙**. We get the content and the description **㉚**. We look for <pubDate> **㉛** or a <dc:date> **㉜**. Finally, we save the enclosure as a hash map of its attributes, if there is one **㉝**.

Once we're finished looping through the items, we're done, and we return the resulting feed map **㉞**. And now, some words about the helper methods.

AnyFeedParser helper methods

We used a number of convenience methods to make parsing easier:

㉟ void put(Map map, String key, Object value) puts a value into a map, but only if that value is not null.

㊱ void put(Map map, String[] keys, Object value) puts a value into a map with each of the keys specified in a string array, but only if the value is not null.

㊲ `String parseAtomLink(Element elem, Namespace ns)` returns the href attribute of the first link found under `elem` with attribute `rel="alternate"` or null if none is found. We're taking a shortcut here by assuming that there will be only one alternate link. It is possible for a feed or entry to have multiple alternative links, one for each language.

㊳ `String parseAtomContent(String name, Element elem, Namespace ns)` returns Atom content found in element `elem` in string form, with special handling for XHTML, but not for the full Atom content model since the src attribute and Base64 content are not handled.

㊴ The `resolveURI()`, `isRelativeURI()`, and `findBaseURI()` methods are essentially the same as the three methods we used for relative URI resolution in the simple Atom parser, so we don't include the code in the listing and we don't need to explain them again.

And that's all there is to our simple newsfeed parser. We'll use this parser, or the C# version of this parser, in most of the examples in part II, and you're welcome to use it freely in your applications as well. You can find a copy of the source code for AnyFeedParser.java in the online examples that accompany this book. The java examples from this chapter are in the directory java/ch05. There is also a C# implementation, which you can find in the directory csharp/ch05.

Now that we've covered parsing, let's move on to the topic of fetching newsfeeds.

5.5 *Fetching newsfeeds efficiently*

In the examples we've seen so far, we haven't worried at all about fetching newsfeeds. We've assumed that newsfeeds are available via input stream and that's all we need. But if you're writing an application that parses newsfeeds, you're going to have to download, or *fetch*, those newsfeeds from the Web. For best performance and to conserve network bandwidth, you'll want to limit the number of times you download newsfeeds and download only when a newsfeed has been updated. So how do you know when a newsfeed has been updated?

5.5.1 *HTTP conditional GET*

You can use HTTP conditional GET to detect when a newsfeed—or any other web resource—has been updated. Here's how it works. When you get a resource from a web server, the server sets the HTTP `Last-Modified` header to indicate the time the resource was last modified. You save that value. Then, when you want to check for a new version of that resource, you set the HTTP `If-Modified-Since` header with the last-modified value you saved. If the resource hasn't been modified, the server will return an HTTP status code 304, known as HTTP_NOT_MODIFIED, instead of wasting bandwidth to return a resource that has not been updated.

If you want to use HTTP conditional GET in your application, you'll have to maintain a cache of newsfeeds that you have already downloaded. When you need to access a newsfeed, you'll retrieve it from your cache and check to see if it is up to date. If it is, you use it. Otherwise, you fetch a fresh copy from the Web. Wouldn't it be nice if your newsfeed parser did that for you?

To demonstrate, let's extend the AnyFeedParser we developed in section 5.4 to support fetching newsfeeds from the Web, HTTP conditional GET, and caching. Listing 5.9 shows our new caching implementation of AnyFeedParser.

Listing 5.9   Extending AnyFeedParser.java to support HTTP conditional GET

```
public class AnyFeedParserCaching extends AnyFeedParser.java {      ◄─①
    String cacheDir = "/tmp/feed_cache";      ◄─②
    public static void main(String[] args) throws Exception {      ◄─③
        new AnyFeedParserCaching().parseFeed(args[0]);
    }
    public Map parseFeed(String fileName) throws Exception {      ◄─④
        if (!fileName.startsWith("http://")) {
            return (super.parseFeed(new FileReader(feedFileName)));      ◄─⑤
        }
        URL url = new URL(fileName);
        HttpURLConnection conn =
            (HttpURLConnection)url.openConnection();      ◄─⑥
        CachedFeed cachedFeed = getCache(url);
        if (cachedFeed != null) {
            conn.setIfModifiedSince(cachedFeed.lastModified);      ◄─⑦
        }
        if (conn.getResponseCode() == HttpURLConnection.HTTP_NOT_MODIFIED) {
            return parseFeed(new StringReader(cachedFeed.feed));      ◄─⑧
        }
        String feedString = inputStreamToString(conn.getInputStream());   ⑨
        putCache(url, feedString, conn.getLastModified());      ◄─⑩
        return parseFeed(new StringReader(feedString));      ◄─⑪
    }
    public static class CachedFeed implements Serializable {      ◄─⑫
        URL url;
        String feed;
        long lastModified;
        public CachedFeed(URL url, String feed, long lastModified) {
            this.url = url;
            this.feed = feed;
            this.lastModified = lastModified;
        }
    }
```

```
    private void putCache(URL url, String feed, long lastModified) {  ◁─⓭
        // . . .
    }
    private CachedFeed getCache(URL url) {    ◁─⓮
        // . . .
    }
    public static String inputStreamToString(InputStream is)//    ◁─⓯
        throws IOException {
        // . . .
    }
}
```

Let's examine `AnyFeedParserCaching` in detail. First, we declare the class to extend AnyFeedParser ❶. We specify that the cache directory is /tmp/feed_cache ❷. You'll probably want to make this configurable. We provide a main method that creates `AnyFeedParserCaching` and calls its `parseFeed()` method ❸. Next, we override AnyFeedParser's `parseFeed()` method with our own ❹. We're interested in handling only files whose names start with "http://". We assume that anything else is a local file, and we hand it off to the `super` class ❺.

Assuming that we have a newsfeed URL, we open up a connection to it ❻. We also check the cache to see if we have a cached copy of the newsfeed. If we find a copy in the cache, we take its `lastModified` time and use it to set the `If-Modified-Since` HTTP header in the connection we just opened ❼. If the newsfeed hasn't been modified, we'll receive a status code of HTTP_NOT_MODIFIED. We'll know that our cached copy of the newsfeed is up to date, and we'll parse and return it instead of fetching a new one from the Web ❽. If the newsfeed has been updated, we fetch it from the Web and read it into a string ❾. We store the newsfeed url, string, and last-modified time in our cache ❿ and, finally, we parse and return the feed we fetched from the Web ⓫.

The remainder of the code in our examples involves the newsfeed cache. We use a class `CachedFeed` to cache each newsfeed ⓬. We use a method `putCache()` ⓭ to store newsfeeds in the cache and a method `getCache()` ⓮ to get them from the cache. And finally, the `inputStreamToString()` method, which makes it easy for us to read a stream into a string ⓯. We've omitted the body of these methods, but you can find them in the online examples that come with the book.

5.5.2 *Other techniques*

At a minimum, when fetching newsfeeds, you should use HTTP conditional GET, but it's not the only option for minimizing bandwidth usage. Below are some other techniques you can use, listed in order of usefulness.

- *HTTP Entity Tags (ETags)*—Many web servers use the HTTP ETag header to indicate that a resource has been updated. An ETag is a string that uniquely identifies one version of a resource; it could be a time stamp (e.g., the last-modified time), a hash of the resource content, or some other version iden-tified. You use an ETag header much as you'd use a Last-Modified header, except that you pass it back to the server using the If-None-Match header instead of If-Modified-Since. For more information on ETags, see the HTTP 1.1 specification RFC-2616 (http://www.w3.org/Protocols/rfc2616).

- *Compression*—Many web servers will automatically compress newsfeeds and other resources using GZIP compression. If you want to retrieve a compressed version of a newsfeed, set the HTTP Accept-Encoding header to "gzip" when you send your request to the web server. Both Java and .NET include support for reading and writing GZIP data, so adding sup-port for compression to the AnyFeedParser should not be too difficult. We'll leave that as an exercise for the reader.

- *RSS Time To Live (TTL)*—The simple fork of RSS includes a time-to-live ele-ment <ttl>, which indicates the number of minutes that a newsfeed should be cached. For example, if a newsfeed provider includes <ttl>60</ttl> in a newsfeed, it's asking you not to fetch that newsfeed more often than once every 60 minutes. Very few newsfeeds include a <ttl>element, and even fewer newsfeed readers support <ttl>.

- *Syndication Module*—Some newsfeeds use the Syndication Module's <sy: updatePeriod> and <sy:updateFrequency> to indicate how often a newsfeed should be polled. Like <ttl>, this technique is not widely used.

- *Delta Encoding*—The IETF Delta Encoding (RFC 3229) defines a mecha-nism for requesting only the parts of a resource that have changed. For newsfeeds, you can use this to request only the new items that have been added since the last time you fetched a newsfeed. Unfortunately, at this time, only a tiny number of blog servers support Delta Encoding.

It would take a fair amount of code to support all of those techniques, but you don't have to write that code yourself. The newsfeed fetcher that's built into the Windows RSS Platform, which we cover in the next chapter, supports all of those techniques. And Java developers can use the ROME Fetcher, covered in chapter 7, which supports ETags, compression, and Delta Encoding. Before we move on to the Windows RSS Platform and ROME, let's sum up what we've learned about parsing newsfeeds.

5.6 Summary

- RSS and Atom newsfeeds can be parsed using the XML parsing tools that are built into Java and .NET.

- To effectively parse funky RSS, you'll need to look for elements from the Dublin Core and Content Module namespaces.

- Mark Pilgrim's Universal Feed Parser is probably the most powerful and popular newsfeed parser available.

- Universal Feed Parser is a liberal parser; it can handle newsfeeds that are not well-formed XML and that would be rejected by an ordinary XML parser.

- The open source ROME newsfeed library is the best choice among newsfeed libraries for Java developers, but it is still under development.

- The open source Jakarta Feed Parser for Java uses a SAX-based approach for better performance than ROME, but it is also still under development.

- If you're developing a desktop application specifically for Windows XP or Windows Vista, then consider using the Windows RSS Platform Feeds API to fetch and parse newsfeeds.

- When fetching newsfeeds, you should use HTTP Conditional GET to avoid downloading newsfeeds too often and putting a strain on network bandwidth and computer resources.

The Windows
RSS Platform

6

Use the new Windows RSS Platform to parse newsfeeds, manage newsfeed subscriptions, and synchronize data between applications.

In the previous two chapters, you learned the history of RSS and Atom newsfeed formats, the details of each, and how to fetch and parse newsfeeds by hand using the tools built into Java and C#. You also learned about newsfeed parser libraries, but we didn't explore them in depth. Before you move on to learn about serving newsfeeds, which you'll do in chapter 8, you need to learn what a full-featured newsfeed parser library can do for you. In some cases, such a library can save you a lot of work.

In this chapter, we'll cover the newsfeed parser library and other newsfeed-handling tools that are built into the Windows RSS Platform. The Windows RSS Platform is a development platform that enables your programs to access and manage newsfeed subscriptions, automate newsfeed and enclosure downloads, and access parsed newsfeeds via a simplified object model. It supports all of the common newsfeed formats: RSS 0.9X, RSS 1.0, RSS 2.0, and Atom 1.0.

If you're building client-side software that specifically targets IE7 or Windows, read this chapter carefully. You'll probably want to build on the Windows RSS Platform. On the other hand, if you're building cross-platform or server-side software, you can skip ahead to chapter 7, which covers the premier Java newsfeed parser library, ROME.

Let's start by learning what the Windows RSS Platform is and why Microsoft chose to add it to Windows.

6.1 Windows RSS Platform overview

In the five years since Microsoft Internet Explorer 6.0 (IE6) shipped in 2001, the ways in which people use the Web have changed significantly. Mainstream users adopted blogs, wikis, and other forms of social software at home and in the workplace. Newsfeeds and podcasts became a part of nearly every Web site. As the old version 4.X browsers faded into the background and Firefox rose to challenge Microsoft's browser dominance, developers started to trust in JavaScript again—and an old technique with the new name AJAX—to add desktop application-like interactivity to Web sites. These changes, known collectively by the buzzword *Web 2.0*, started a new round of investment in Web technology.

As Microsoft worked to update Internet Explorer for this new era of the Web, the company realized that RSS and Atom newsfeeds are not just for blogs, news, and podcasts. These new formats, which enable applications to share all kinds of data, should be part of the underlying infrastructure in Windows and available to all applications. So instead of simply adding RSS and Atom support to Internet Explorer 7.0 (IE7), Microsoft created the Windows RSS Platform, a set of newsfeed-handling APIs available to all Windows applications.

A word of warning

At the time of this writing, the Windows RSS Platform has not been released except in beta form. So the APIs and capabilities of the platform are likely to change. The information and examples in this chapter are based on the version of the Windows RSS Platform that came with the March 2006 IE7 beta release (build 5335.5). Once IE7 is released, we'll update the online examples to work with the final APIs. Second, this chapter is not meant as a reference, so we're not going to cover each method in the Windows RSS Platform's Feeds API. For full documentation on the methods in these and other Feeds API interfaces, see the Microsoft Developer Network (MSDN) section on the Microsoft Feeds API.

Now that we have that out of the way, let's look at what's possible with the Windows RSS Platform and examine the components of the platform at a high level.

6.1.1 Browse, search, and subscribe with IE7

Microsoft describes the new "Web" usage model using the words *browse, search, and subscribe*. Browsing and searching have been the primary ways people use the Web for quite some time. Newsfeeds have added the ability to easily subscribe to things of interest. But in this new world of newsfeeds, IE6 and the older browsers don't do much for you. When you visit a newsfeed-enabled Web site in IE6, there is no good indication that the site has a newsfeed except for an obscure link labeled XML or at best, a little orange XML icon on the margin of the page. And if you click on that link or icon, you see a page of raw XML data—not very friendly at all.

IE7 addresses this problem in a couple of ways. First, when you use IE7 to visit a Web page that offers newsfeeds, you'll see a button with an orange newsfeed icon (next to the home button). Figure 6.1 shows the top portion of IE7 viewing my blog, which has both RSS and Atom feeds.

If you click that button, you'll see a list of the newsfeeds offered by the Web page. If you click on one of the newsfeed choices, you won't see the raw XML. With IE7, when you click on a newsfeed link you see the newsfeed displayed with easy-to-read formatting, a summary of the content, a filter control for filtering by

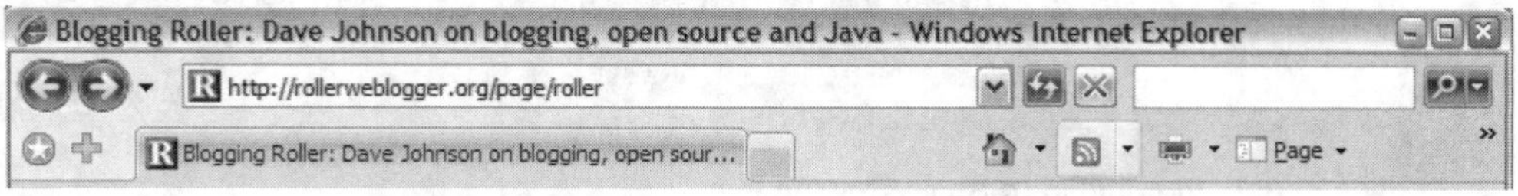

Figure 6.1 Newsfeed auto-discovery in IE7

category, and a sorting control so you can sort the feed's content by date, title, and author. Figure 6.2 shows my blog's newsfeed as it appears in IE7. Since I'm not subscribed to my blog in IE7, a message at the top of the page explains how I can subscribe to this feed.

Once you subscribe to a feed in IE7, it's added to your subscription list and appears in the IE7 Favorites Center so you can easily see when the feed is updated. That subscription list, known as the Common Feed List, is available not only to IE7 but to any Windows application via the Feeds API. We'll cover the Common Feed List and the Feeds API in the next section, but first, a word about auto-discovery.

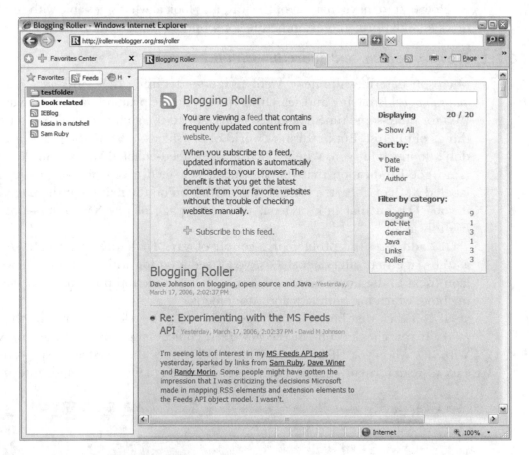

Figure 6.2   Viewing an RSS newsfeed in IE7

Newsfeed auto-discovery

How do IE7 and Firefox determine that a Web page has newsfeeds? The answer is *auto-discovery*, a technique that uses the HTML `<link>` element to indicate links to resources related to a web page. For example, if you look at the HTML of my blog, shown in listing 6.1, you can see that it includes auto-discovery links to my newsfeeds. (These appear in bold.) Note that the links indicate type "alternate" because the newsfeeds are to be considered as alternate representations of the web page. The links also include a title, the content-type of the newsfeed, and the URL where the newsfeed can be found.

Listing 6.1 HTML from the author's blog that shows newsfeed auto-discovery links

```
<!DOCTYPE html PUBLIC "-//W3C//DTD HTML 4.01 Transitional//EN" "http://
   www.w3.org/TR/html4/loose.dtd">
<html>
<head>
   <meta http-equiv="Content-Type" content="text/html; charset=utf-8" >
   <script type="text/javascript"
      src="http://rollerweblogger.org/theme/scripts/roller.js"></script>
   <link rel="stylesheet" type="text/css" media="all"
      href="http://rollerweblogger.org/page/roller/css.css" />
   <link rel="alternate" type="application/rss+xml"
      title="RSS" href="http://rollerweblogger.org/rss/roller" />
   <link rel="alternate" type="application/atom+xml"
      title="Atom" href="http://rollerweblogger.org/atom/roller" />
```

Most blog sites include auto-discover links like these, and if you're serving newsfeeds on your Web site or in your Web application, you'll want to do the same thing. For more information on newsfeed auto-discovery, see chapter 8, section 8.2.2. Next, we'll introduce you to the Feeds API and the other components of the Windows RSS Platform.

6.1.2 Components of the Windows RSS Platform

Microsoft sees newsfeeds as a way to wire together all sorts of applications, both on the desktop and on the Web. Your calendar program will use newsfeeds to synchronize your schedule with your business associates'. Business-to-business e-commerce applications will use newsfeeds to synchronize price information. Your screensaver will use newsfeeds to show you the latest news or to present a slideshow of the latest photos from your friends and family. And of course, your media player will use newsfeeds to download podcasts and video-casts. The components of the Windows RSS Platform are designed to support those use cases.

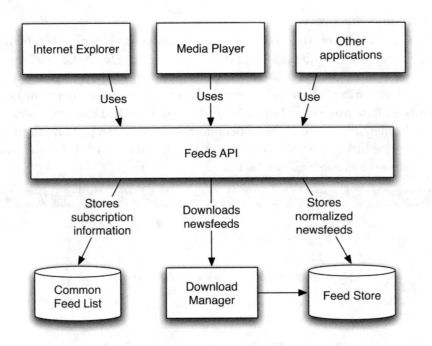

Figure 6.3   How the Windows RSS Platform components work together

Before we discuss each of the individual components of the Windows RSS Platform, let's look at how they work together.

As you can see in figure 6.3, Windows applications use the Feeds API to access the underlying components of the Windows RSS Platform, the Common Feed List, Download Manager, and Feed Store. The Feeds API stores subscription information in the Common Feed List, it calls on the Download Manager to download newsfeeds and enclosures, and it stores normalized newsfeed data and enclosures in the Feed Store. The Feeds API is the key player, so we'll start with it and then discuss each of the other components in turn.

The Feeds API

The Feeds API serves as much more than just a newsfeed parser. It manages subscriptions, caches downloaded newsfeeds, stores downloaded enclosures, and gives you access to downloaded newsfeeds via a simple object model. Through the API, you can control the download interval of each newsfeed. You can also monitor events by registering to be notified when the subscription list changes or when a download has completed. The Feeds API does a lot, but Microsoft has

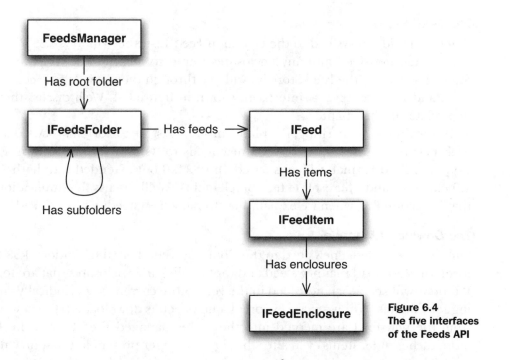

**Figure 6.4
The five interfaces
of the Feeds API**

done a good job of keeping the API simple. There are only five interfaces in the API, which are shown in figure 6.4.

At the top of figure 6.4 is the IFeedsManager interface. It's the entry point to the Feeds API, and once you have an instance of it, you can access the Common Feeds List and gain access to the newsfeed data that is cached in the Feed Store. Next are the IFeedsFolder and IFeed interfaces, which provide access to the Common Feed List.

The Common Feed List

The Common Feed List is the list of newsfeeds managed by the Windows RSS Platform. The word *Common* is used because the list is available to all of your applications, not just IE7. As illustrated in figure 6.4, the list is maintained as a folder hierarchy. From the IFeedsManager interface, you can get the root folder in the hierarchy. Folders are represented by the IFeedFolder interface, and each folder can contain other folders and feeds, which are represented by the IFeed interface. You'll learn how to manage feeds and folders in section 6.2, but now let's continue our discussion of the components.

The Feed Store

When you add a newsfeed to the Common Feed List, the Windows RSS Platform fetches that newsfeed and any enclosures found to a cache known as the Feed Store. The data in the Feed Store is available through the Feeds API `IFeed`, `IFeed-Item`, and `IFeedEnclosure` interfaces, shown in figure 6.4. We'll discuss them in depth later in this chapter.

At the time of this writing, the platform *does not* store the original XML data for each newsfeed. Instead, it converts newsfeeds to its own format, known as the Common Feed Format, which is based on RSS 2.0 but extended with both Atom 1.0 elements and Microsoft extension elements. We'll discuss the implications of that in section 6.3, when we explain how to parse newsfeeds with the Feeds API.

The Download Manager

Once you've added a newsfeed to the Common Feed List, the Windows RSS Platform will download that newsfeed and (optionally) any enclosures that are found. Windows will keep each newsfeed in the Feed Store current by periodically checking for updates. When a new version of a newsfeed is downloaded, the new items from the newsfeed are merged into the cache-managed Feed Store. The Feed Store caches older items even after they are no longer present in the source newsfeed. That's true for all feeds except those that are declared to be lists. When a list is updated, the new items completely replace the old items in the Feed Store. You can use an extension element (see section 6.4.2) to declare a newsfeed to be a list, and that brings us to the next component of the Windows RSS Platform.

Newsfeed list and sharing extensions

Microsoft has also created a set of newsfeed extensions for RSS and Atom. Although not pictured in the overview diagram presented in figure 6.3, these extensions are an important component of the Windows RSS Platform. There are three sets of extensions. The Common Feed (CF) extensions keep track of the read/unread status of each item and the download status of each enclosure. The Simple List Extensions (SLE) allow sorting and grouping information within newsfeeds. And the Simple Sharing Extensions (SSE) allow newsfeeds to be used for bidirectional synchronization of data between applications. We'll explain these extensions in section 6.4.

Now that you've seen the new newsfeed features in IE7 and are familiar with the components of the Windows RSS Platform and how they work together, let's put the Feeds API to work, starting with subscription management.

6.2 Managing subscriptions with the Common Feed List

In this section, you'll learn how to call the Feeds API from C# and use it to manage newsfeed subscriptions in the Common Feed List. We'll use a simple example to demonstrate how to walk the folder hierarchy. Then, we'll show you how to add new subscriptions. Finally, we'll show you how to use the event monitoring features of the Feeds API. Before we do that, let's take a closer look at the Feeds API interfaces used for managing subscriptions: the `IFeedsManager`, `IFeedsFolder`, and `IFeed` interface. Figure 6.5 shows these three interfaces and the properties and methods of each. Properties are listed first, followed by methods. Properties that correspond directly to RSS 2.0 elements are indicated by (rss).

Managing subscriptions

The three interfaces shown in figure 6.5 provide the methods you need to manage subscriptions in the Common Feed List.

The `IFeedsManager` interface provides access to the root folder of the hierarchy and a set of shortcut methods so you can find and delete feeds without navigating to the folder that contains them. For example, the `GetFeed()` method returns a Feed specified by folder-path, and `GetFeedByUrl()` returns a feed specified by URL. The `IFeedFolder` interface represents one folder and provides methods for managing subscriptions and subfolders within that folder. And the `IFeed` interface represents an individual newsfeed subscription.

Keeping track of what's been read

One interesting aspect of the Feeds API is that it keeps track of which newsfeed items you have marked as read. Note the `TotalItemCount` and `TotalUnreadCount` in the `IFeedFolder` interface in figure 6.5. The Feeds API keeps track of those numbers at the folder, feed, and individual item level. So applications that use the Feeds API won't annoy and inconvenience you by showing you items you've already seen before, even if you saw the item in a different application.

Now that introductions are out of the way, let's get started with our first code example.

6.2.1 Getting started with the Common Feed List

In our first Feeds API programming example, we'll explore the folder hierarchy of the Common Feed List. Since this is our first example, let's discuss how to get started with the Feeds API.

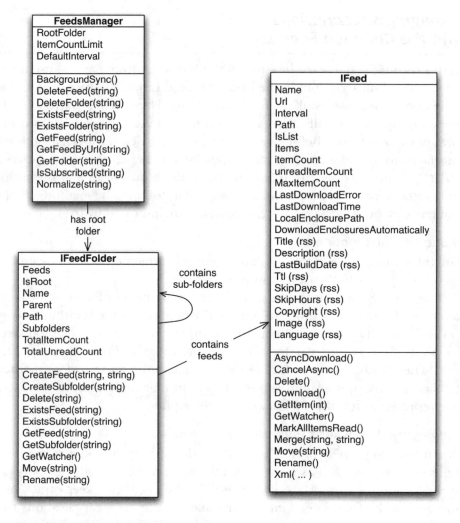

Figure 6.5 The IFeedsManager, IFeedsFolder, and IFeed interfaces

Adding the Feeds API to your C# project

The Feeds API is packaged as a set of Component Object Model (COM) objects, so it's possible to call it from any of the Microsoft-supported languages, including Visual Basic.NET, C++, and of course C#. But before you can use the Feeds API, you need the Windows RSS Platform. If you're running Windows Vista, you're all set, but if you're running Windows XP, the best way to get the Windows RSS Platform is to download and install IE7.

Once you've got the Windows RSS Platform, using it in your Visual Studio projects is easy. To use the Feeds API in your C# project, first add a reference to the Feeds API. In Visual Studio, use the **Project->Add Reference** menu to do this. When the Add Reference window appears, select the COM tab, scroll down to the Microsoft Feeds line, which includes msfeeds.dll. Then, select it and click OK to add it to your project. When you have the Feeds API in your project, you can use it in your C# code.

Walking the feed folder hierarchy

Let's take a look at the Feeds API in action with a simple C# console program example that recursively walks the folder hierarchy tree and prints out the name of every folder and newsfeed it finds, using indentation to indicate the structure of the tree. The complete source code for the program, called PrintFolderTree.cs, is shown in listing 6.2.

Listing 6.2 PrintFolderTree.cs recursively traverses and prints the Common Feed List

```
using System;
using Microsoft.Feeds.Interop;      ←❶
namespace BlogApps_Chapter06 {
   class PrintFolderTree {
      static void Main(string[] args) {
         IFeedsManager fm = new FeedsManagerClass();      ←❷
         IFeedFolder rootFolder = (IFeedFolder)fm.RootFolder;      ←❸
         PrintFolder(rootFolder, "");      ←❹
      }
      static void PrintFolder(IFeedFolder fd, string indent) {
         Console.Out.WriteLine(indent + "folder: " + fd.name);      ←❺
         foreach (IFeed feed in (IFeedsEnum)fd.Feeds) {      ←❻
            Console.Out.WriteLine(indent + "feed: " + feed.name);
         }
         foreach (IFeedFolder sub in (IFeedsEnum)fd.Subfolders) {      ←❼
            PrintFolder(sub, indent + "   ");
         }
      }
   }
}
```

Let's discuss how PrintFolderTree.cs works. First, we bring in the Feeds API by declaring that we are using the `Microsoft.Feeds.Interop` namespace ❶. Next, inside the `Main()` method of the class, we create an instance of the Feeds manager ❷. From the manager, we get the root folder ❸, and we call the `PrintFolder()`

method ❹. We pass the root folder and for the indent parameter, we pass the empty string because the root folder will be printed with no indentation.

Inside the `PrintFolder()` method, we first print the name of the folder ❺. Next, we loop through the feeds in the folder ❻ and print the name of each. After that, we loop through the subfolders ❼ and for each we make a recursive call to the `PrintFolder()` method, passing in the subfolder object. We add a three-space-long string to the indentation so that subfolders are indented by three spaces for each level of depth in the hierarchy.

PrintFolderTree.cs and the other examples in this book are included in the online examples as a Visual Studio C# Solution called BlogApps_Chapter06.sln in the directory csharp/ch06. See the readme file that accompanies the examples for instructions on building and running the code.

Now that we know how to find our way around the Common Feed List, let's discuss how to create subscriptions.

6.2.2 Creating subscriptions

To create a new newsfeed subscription in the Common Feed List, you need three things: the URL of the newsfeed, a nice friendly name for the subscription (which can be anything you want), and a folder. You also need to make sure that you are not already subscribed, because you can't subscribe to the same newsfeed twice with the Windows RSS Platform. For example, let's say you want to subscribe to my blog "Blogging Roller" and you want to create the subscription in a folder called "blogs." Here's how you'd do that with the Feeds API:

```
string feedUrl = "http://rollerweblogger.org/rss/roller";
string subName = "Blogging Roller";
string folderName = "blogs";

FeedsManager fm = new FeedsManagerClass();
if (!fm.IsSubscribed(feedUrl)) {
   IFeedFolder rootFolder = (IFeedFolder)fm.RootFolder;
   IFeedFolder newFolder = rootFolder.CreateSubfolder(folderName);
   IFeed feed = newFolder.CreateFeed(subName, feedUrl);
} else {
   // already subscribed
}
```

Newsfeed update interval

When you create a new subscription, Windows will download the newsfeed, normalize it, and cache it in the Feed Store. Windows will keep the newsfeed current by periodically checking for updates, using the HTTP conditional GET technique described in chapter 5, section 5.5.1.

Windows will use the `FeedManager`'s `DefaultInterval` property, which defaults to 1440 minutes (24 hours) to determine how often to poll a newsfeed for updates. If you want to control the update interval of each individual subscription, you can set the `IFeed.interval` property for each new subscription you create. However, if an RSS newsfeed includes a Time To Live `<ttl>` element, Windows will make sure it doesn't poll more often than the TTL value.

Download enclosures or not

If you would like Windows to automatically download enclosures it finds in a feed, you must set the `IFeed.DownloadEnclosuresAutomatically` property to true. It defaults to false. You can allow Windows to download enclosures and newsfeeds automatically or you can manage them yourself. You can use the Feeds API event system to monitor your downloads, and that brings us to the next topic.

6.2.3 Monitoring events

If you're writing a desktop application that uses the Feeds API, you may need to monitor events in the Windows RSS Platform. For example, if you're writing a newsfeed reader that displays the user's newsfeed subscriptions in a tree control, you'll want to update that tree whenever the user subscribes to a new newsfeed. Or, if you're writing a podcasting client, you might want to alert your users when a new podcast has been downloaded. You can do both of those things and more with the Feeds API's support for feed and folder events. Table 6.1 lists the folder- and feed-level events you can monitor using the Feeds API.

Table 6.1 Events that can be monitored via the Feeds API

Folder-level events	Feed-level events
Folder added	Feed deleted
Folder deleted	Feed renamed
Folder renamed	Feed URL changed
Folder moved	Feed moved
Folder's item count changed	Feed downloading
Feed added	Feed download completed
Feed deleted	Feed item count changed
Feed renamed	
Feed's URL changed	
Feed moved	
Feed downloading	
Feed download completed	
Feed item count changed	

To better understand the Feeds API event system and subscription management, let's take a look at a simple example that shows how to add a subscription, delete a subscription, and monitor subscription events in the root folder of the Common Feed List.

Listing 6.3 shows SubscribeEvents.cs, a C# console program that accepts two arguments: a command, which can be "sub" or "unsub," and a URL to be subscribed to or unsubscribed from.

Listing 6.3   SubscribeEvents.cs: a subscribe and unsubscribe utility with events

```csharp
using System;
using System.Threading;
using Microsoft.Feeds.Interop;      ◄─❶

namespace BlogApps_Chapter06 {

    class SubscribeEvents {
        static void Main(string[] args) {      ◄─❷
            new SubscribeEvents(args);
        }
        public SubscribeEvents(string[] args) {
            if (args.Length < 2) {      ◄─❸
                Console.Out.WriteLine(
                    "USAGE: SubscriberEvents <command> <url>");
                return;
            }
            string command = args[0];
            string url = args[1];
            FeedsManager fm = new FeedsManagerClass();
            IFeedFolder rootFolder = (IFeedFolder)fm.RootFolder;      ◄─❹
            IFeedFolderEvents_Event events =      ◄─❺
                (IFeedFolderEvents_Event)rootFolder.GetWatcher(
                    FEEDS_EVENTS_SCOPE.FES_SELF_AND_CHILDREN_ONLY,      ◄─❻
                    FEEDS_EVENTS_MASK.FEM_FOLDEREVENTS);
            events.FeedAdded +=
                new IFeedFolderEvents_FeedAddedEventHandler(Added);      ◄─❼
            events.FeedDeleted +=
                new IFeedFolderEvents_FeedDeletedEventHandler(Deleted);      ◄─❽

            if (command.Equals("sub")) {      ◄─❾
                if (!fm.IsSubscribed(url)) {
                    rootFolder.CreateFeed(url, url);
                }
            } else if (command.Equals("unsub")) {      ◄─❿
                if (fm.IsSubscribed(url)) {
                    fm.DeleteFeed(url);
                }
            }
```

```
        Thread.Sleep(500);    <-- 11
    }
    private void Added(string path) {
        Console.Out.WriteLine("Subscribed to " + path);    <-- 12
    }
    private void Deleted(string path) {
        Console.Out.WriteLine("Unsubscribed from " + path);    <-- 13
    }
  }
}
```

Let's take a closer look at SubscribeEvents.cs. First, we declare that we're going to use the Feeds API namespace `Microsoft.Feeds.Interop` ❶. Next, we declare the `SubscribeEvents` class and a `Main()` method ❷ so the class can be called from the console. In the main method, we create an instance of the class and pass the command-line arguments into the class constructor.

Since this is just a simple console program, we do all the work in the constructor, first checking that we have two arguments ❸. If we don't have two, we print a usage message and exit.

We're ready to register for events, so we create an instance of the `FeedsManager`, we get the Common Feed List's root folder ❹, and we get a reference to its `IFeedFolderEvents_Event` object ❺, passing in the right flag ❻ to restrict events to only the folder and its immediate children. To monitor new subscriptions, we add our `Added()` method as a handler for feed-added events ❼. And to monitor unsubscriptions, we add our `Deleted()` method as a handler for feed-deleted events ❽.

Now we're ready to get down to business. If the command passed in is "sub" ❾ and we're not already subscribed to the requested URL, we call `rootFolder.Create-Feed()` to create a new subscription. When that happens, the feed-added event will fire, resulting in a call to the `Added()` method ⑫ to print out the "Subscribed to…" message. If the command passed in is "unsub" ❿ and we are subscribed to the indicated URL, we call `fm.DeleteFeed()` to unsubscribe, which will cause the feed-deleted event to fire and call our `Deleted()` method ⑬. The last statement in the program is a call to `Thread.Sleep()` ⑪ so that we don't exit before printing out our event message.

Now that we've mastered subscriptions and the Common Feed List, let's move on to parsing newsfeeds with the Feeds API.

6.3 *Parsing newsfeeds with the Feeds API*

The Windows RSS Platform can parse all of the common newsfeed formats: RSS 0.9X, RSS 1.0, RSS 2.0, and Atom 1.0. How does it work? When you add a newsfeed subscription to the Common Feed List, you can access the newsfeed via a simple and abstract object model made up of just three interfaces. In this section, we'll show you how to parse newsfeeds using the Feeds API and get at the information you need, even if that information is not exposed through the Feeds API interfaces.

Before we start, let's look at the three interfaces in the Feeds API's simple newsfeed object model. Figure 6.6 shows the interfaces and their containment

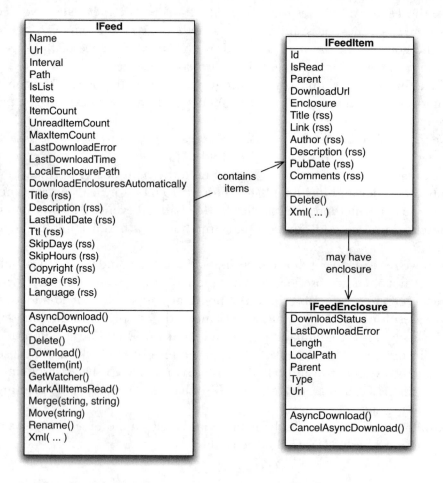

Figure 6.6   The IFeed, IFeedItem, and IFeedEnclosure interfaces

relationships. The interfaces are `IFeed`, `IFeedItem`, and `IFeedEnclosure`. Properties are listed first, followed by methods. Properties that correspond directly to RSS 2.0 elements are indicated by (rss).

If you remember what we learned about parsing newsfeeds in chapter 5, you might be wondering how such a simple object model can be used to represent RSS, funky RSS, and Atom newsfeeds. That's a good question.

Is the Feeds API object model too simple?

At the time of this writing, the Feeds API object model is too simple to correctly model all the types of newsfeeds currently in use on the Web. Take, for example, the problem of summary and content. Recall from chapter 5 that some RSS newsfeeds use the RSS `<description>` element to hold a short summary of each item and the `<content:encoded>` element to hold the full content. And some Atom newsfeeds use `<summary>` and `<content>` to do the same thing. The problem is this: the Feeds API doesn't support having both summary and content. All you get is `IFeed.Description`.

Another example is the Atom `<author>` element. In Atom, `<author>` can contain a `<name>` element for the author's name, an `<email>` element for the author's e-mail address, and a `<uri>` element for the author's URL. But the Feeds API provides only an Author property, which contains the e-mail address of the author.

There are other examples of this problem in the Feeds API, so for some more advanced applications you might have to resort to parsing the feed XML as you learned to do in chapter 5. Fortunately, the Feeds API makes this easy by allowing you to access the XML for the individual items in the newsfeed. We'll show you how to access and parse item XML in the next section. Hopefully, by the time IE7 is finally released, a more complete object model will be in place and the need for XML parsing will be reduced, if not eliminated entirely.

Despite these problems, the Feeds API really does make parsing easy. Let's take a look at how it works and how to get around the problems.

6.3.1 A simple newsfeed parsing example

Let's start with a simple example, like the ones we used to explain newsfeed parsing in the beginning of chapter 5. PrintFeed.cs, in listing 6.4, is a C# console program that accepts one argument, the URL of a newsfeed to be parsed, and prints out the title, publication date, and description for each item found.

Listing 6.4 PrintFeed.cs: parses and prints a newsfeed

```
using System;
using Microsoft.Feeds.Interop;    ←❶

namespace BlogApps_Chapter06 {

    class PrintFeed {    ←❷
        static void Main(string[] args) {
            if (args.Length < 1) {
                Console.Out.WriteLine("USAGE: PrintFeed <url>");    ←❸
                return;
            }
            string url = args[0];
            FeedsManager fm = new FeedsManagerClass();
            IFeed feed = null;
            if (fm.IsSubscribed(url)) {    ←❹
                feed = (IFeed)fm.GetFeedByUrl(url);    ←❺
            } else {
                IFeedFolder rootFolder = (IFeedFolder)fm.RootFolder;    ←❻
                feed = (IFeed)rootFolder.CreateFeed(url, url);    ←❼
            }
            foreach (IFeedItem item in (IFeedsEnum)feed.Items) {    ←❽
                Console.Out.WriteLine("item.Title:       " + item.Title);
                Console.Out.WriteLine("item.PubDate:     " + item.PubDate);
                Console.Out.WriteLine("item.Description: " + item.Description);
            }
        }
    }
}
```

Let's walk through the code. The only namespaces we need in PrintFeed.cs are System and Microsoft.Feeds.Interop ❶. Inside the class ❷, we declare a Main() method and that's where we'll do our work. First, we check that we have one argument and if not, we print a usage message and exit ❸. Next, we get the IFeed object for the newsfeed. If we're already subscribed ❹, we get it from the Feeds-Manager ❺. If we're not subscribed, we get the root folder ❻ and create a new subscription ❼. Once we've got the IFeed object, we loop through each of the items ❽ and print out each item's title, publication date, and description. That's all it takes to parse a simple feed with the Feeds API. Now, let's get funky.

6.3.2 Parsing extension elements and funky RSS

Parsing most common forms of RSS and Atom with the Feeds API is pretty easy, but if you need to parse a newsfeed with extension elements, you may have to parse the XML yourself. In this section, we'll help you understand when you need to resort to parsing XML and we'll explain how to do it.

The Feeds API represents newsfeeds in two ways. You've already seen the first way, the simple object model that consists of the `IFeed`, `IFeedItem`, and `IFeed-Enclosure` interfaces. If you can't get the information you need from the properties exposed in those interfaces, you'll need to resort to parsing XML. For example, if you're trying to extract the latitude and longitude values from the `<geo:lat>` and `<geo:long>` extension elements in a GeoRSS newsfeed, you'll need to parse XML. And that brings us to the second way the Feeds API represents newsfeeds: XML.

The Feeds API gives you access to the underlying XML for each newsfeed so you can parse it yourself. But you'll need to parse with care, because the Feeds API does not store the original newsfeed XML. Instead, it stores all newsfeed data in its own normalized format.

Microsoft Common Feed Format

The Windows RSS Platform stores all newsfeeds, regardless of their original form, in a normalized XML format known as the Microsoft Common Feed Format, which is based on RSS 2.0 but with Atom 1.0 and Microsoft-defined extension elements. You can see an example newsfeed in Common Feed Format in listing 6.6 later in this chapter.

Why did Microsoft choose to normalize to a single format? One reason is ease of development. It's much easier for developers to deal with data if it is presented in a uniform way. Another reason is funky RSS. Many RSS newsfeeds use extension elements such as the Dublin Core `<dc:date>` and `<dc:creator>` elements and the Content Module `<content:encoded>` element in place of the standard RSS elements. By converting these to normalized representation, these values can be made available in a uniform way through the interfaces in the Feeds API.

To better understand how the normalization process works, let's look at a few specific examples. First, let's examine how author elements are normalized and made available through the Feeds API object model. Table 6.2 shows how the different author elements are normalized to one representation in the Windows RSS Platform. Since the RSS 2.0 author element can't carry both author name and e-mail address, the Atom 1.0 `<author>` element is used instead.

Note that even though the Windows RSS normalized form can carry both author name and email address, the Feeds API cannot. If both name and email are specified, the `IFeedItem.Author` property will return the email address. In that case, if you want to get the author's name, you'll have to parse it out yourself.

Table 6.2 Normalization example: author elements in the Windows RSS Platform

Newsfeed form	Normalized form	Available in the Feeds API

`<dc:creator>`
`   Dave`
`</dc:creator>`
	`<author>`
	`   Dave`
	`</author>`
	`<atom:author>`
	`   <atom:name>`
	`      Dave`
	`   </atom:name>`
	`</atom:author>`
		`item.Author = "Dave"`

`<author>`
`   dave@example.com`
`</author>`
	`<author>`
	`   dave@example.com`
	`</author>`
	`<atom:author>`
	`   <atom:email>`
	`      dave@example.com`
	`   </atom:name>`
	`</atom:author>`
		`item.Author =`
		`   "dave@example.com"`

`<dc:creator>`
`   Dave`
`</dc:creator>`
`<author>`
`   dave@example.com`
`</author>`
	`<atom:author>`
	`   <atom:name>`
	`      Dave`
	`   </atom:name>`
	`</atom:author>`
	`<atom:author>`
	`   <atom:email>`
	`      dave@example.com`
	`   </atom:email>`
	`</atom:author>`
		`item.Author =`
		`   "dave@example.com"`

Let's examine how content elements are normalized in table 6.3. If an item has its content in a standard RSS `<description>` element or Content Module `<content:encoded>` element, the normalized form is `<description>`. But a lot of newsfeeds use the `<description>` element for a short summary and `<content:encoded>` for the full content of each item. Again, the standard RSS elements can't handle both summary and content, so the normalized form uses the `<atom:summary>` element for the summary and the RSS `<description>` element for the full content.

Table 6.3 Normalization example: Content elements in the Windows RSS Platform

Newsfeed form	Normalized form	Available in the Feeds API

`<description>`
`   Content of item`
`</description>`
	`<description>`
	`   Content of item`
	`</description>`
		`item.Description =`
		`   "Content of item"`

continued on next page

Table 6.3 **Normalization example: Content elements in the Windows RSS Platform** *(continued)*

Newsfeed form	Normalized form	Available in the Feeds API

`<content:encoded>`
`   Content of item`
`</content:encoded>`
	`<description>`
	`   Content of item`
	`</description>`
		`item.Description =`
		`   "Content of item"`

`<description>`
`   Short summary of item`
`</description>`
`<content:encoded>`
`   Full content of item`
`</content:encoded>`
	`<atom:summary>`
	`   Short summary of item`
	`</atom:summary>`
	`<description>`
	`   Full content of item`
	`</description>`
		`item.Description =`
		`   "Full content of item"`

In the third row of table 6.3, you can see that the `IFeedItem`'s `Description` property contains the full content of the item. If you want to get the summary, you'll have to parse it yourself, so that's what we'll do next.

Parsing item summary using the Feeds API

We already have a simple example program called PrintFeed.cs in listing 6.4 that parses a newsfeed and prints the title, publication date, and description of each item found. Let's take that code, copy it to a new file called PrintFeedFunky.cs, and retrofit it to parse out the summary too. The only part of the code that needs to change is the code inside the `foreach` loop. Listing 6.5 shows that loop and the new code within.

Listing 6.5   Partial listing of PrintFeedFunky.cs that shows how to parse summaries

```
foreach (IFeedItem item in (IFeedsEnum)feed.Items) {
    Console.Out.WriteLine("item.Title:      " + item.Title);
    Console.Out.WriteLine("item.PubDate:      " + item.PubDate);
    Console.Out.WriteLine("item.Description: " + item.Description);    ← ❶

    string xml = item.Xml(FEEDS_XML_INCLUDE_FLAGS.FXIF_NONE);    ← ❷
    XmlDocument doc = new XmlDocument();
    doc.LoadXml(xml);    ← ❸

    XmlNamespaceManager nsm =
        new XmlNamespaceManager(doc.NameTable);
    nsm.AddNamespace("atom", "http://www.w3.org/2005/Atom");    ← ❹

    XmlNode summary =
        doc.SelectSingleNode("/item/atom:summary", nsm);    ← ❺
    if (summary != null) {
        Console.Out.WriteLine(
```

```
              "Summary: " + summary.FirstChild.Value);    ⬋—❻
       }
   }
```

Within the `foreach` loop, we print out the title, publication date, and description
❶, just as we did before, so there are no changes there.

To pull out the summary, we need the XML representation of the item. We get
it in string form by calling the `item.Xml()` method ❷ and passing in the flag value
`FXIF_NONE`, which tells the Feeds API that we don't need the Common Feed extensions, just the basic XML data. We wrap the XML string in a `StringReader` and pass
it into an `XmlDocument` to parse it into an XML DOM ❸. We know from table 6.3
that the Feeds API represents the item summary using the Atom `<atom:summary>`
element, so we add the Atom namespace to the XML namespace manager ❹.

The final step is to use an XPath expression to pull out the item summary ❺. If
the summary exists, we print it to the console ❻ and continue with the next loop
iteration.

And with that, we're done with our foray into parsing newsfeeds with the Feeds
API. Now, we'll look at the newsfeed extensions Microsoft has created for the Windows RSS Platform.

6.4 Windows RSS Platform newsfeed extensions

To support the Windows RSS Platform, Microsoft has added a set of extensions for
RSS and Atom newsfeeds. Some of these extensions are designed for use in the
internals of the Windows RSS Platform, but some of them might be useful in your
applications too. In this section, we'll help you understand these extensions and
decide whether you should use them in your applications.

To refresh your memory, let's review the extension concept. Newsfeed extensions were first introduced in RSS 1.0 and are now part of both RSS 2.0 and Atom.
As we explained in chapter 4, section 4.2.2, you can extend a newsfeed format by
adding your own new XML elements anywhere in the newsfeed as long as your
new elements exist inside their own XML namespace. That explains what extensions are, but it doesn't explain why Microsoft needs to use them.

Why are extensions necessary?

Microsoft uses newsfeed extensions to accomplish two goals in the Windows RSS
Platform. The first goal is to provide a normalized newsfeed format, known as the
Common Feed Format, which we discussed in section 6.3.2. The Common Feed

Format, which is based on RSS 2.0, uses Atom 1.0 elements so that it can model all of the common forms of RSS and Atom. It also uses Microsoft's own Common Feed (CF) extensions to track the read/unread state of newsfeed items and the download status of enclosures.

Microsoft's second goal is to enable applications to share data in ways not possible with ordinary newsfeeds. To achieve this goal, Microsoft created two extensions: the Simple List Extensions (SLE) for sharing lists of items and the Simple Sharing Extensions (SSE) for bidirectional synchronization of items.

We'll cover all three of the Microsoft extensions, CF, SLE, and SSE, in this section. You'll learn how they're used and how you might use them in your own applications. Let's start with the CF extensions.

6.4.1 *Common Feed (CF) extensions*

The CF extensions are a set of new XML elements and attributes that the Windows RSS Platform uses in the Common Feed Format, which is the internal RSS 2.0 format the platform uses to store newsfeeds. These extensions exist to allow the Windows RSS Platform to keep track of the read/unread status of newsfeed items and the download status of enclosures and to clarify the meaning of some of the RSS 2.0 elements.

The beta warning applies here. The CF extensions and documentation exist only in beta form, so this information may change by the time the Windows RSS Platform is released in IE7.

The CF extensions include new item-level elements and new attributes. The elements exist within an XML namespace (with the URI http://www.microsoft.com/schemas/rss/core/2005) and use the namespace prefix "cf". First, let's discuss the new item-level elements.

New item-level elements

The CF extensions provide two new item-level elements:

- The `<cf:id>` element holds an integer value, which is an item's unique ID within the Windows RSS Platform. This element is mapped to the `IFeedItem.Id` property in the Feeds API.

- The `<cf:read>` element holds a boolean value, which indicates whether the item has been marked read by the user. This element is mapped to the `IFeedItem.IsRead` property in the Feeds API.

New type attribute

The CF extensions provide a new type attribute intended for use in RSS `<title>`, `<copyright>` and `<description>` elements to indicate the type of content carried by the element. This is necessary because the RSS 2.0 specification does not spell out where escaped HTML content is allowed. There are two possible values for this attribute:

- The value `cf:type="text"` indicates that the element contains only plain-text.

- The value `cf:type="html"` indicates that the element contains a mix of plain text and escaped HTML markup.

New enclosure attrbibutes

To track the download status of item enclosures, Microsoft has added this pair of new attributes to be used inside `<enclosure>` elements:

- The `cf:downloadstatus` attribute indicates the download status of the associated enclosure. Possible values are Not Downloaded, In Progress, Downloaded, and Error.

- The `cf:path` attribute specifies the full path to the downloaded enclosure file, even if the file has not yet been downloaded.

- Now that we've covered the CF extension elements and attributes, let's see them in action.

An example Common Feed Format newsfeed

Listing 6.6 shows a simple example newsfeed in Common Feed Format with the CF extension elements shown in bold. It was produced by a C# program called Normalizer.cs, which you can find in the online examples that accompany the book (in the directory csharp\ch06\Normalizer). Normalizer.cs can take any RSS or Atom newsfeed and convert to Common Feed Format. See the readme in the csharp\ch06 directory for instructions on building and running Normalizer.cs.

> **Listing 6.6 Example Common Feed Format newsfeed with CF extensions**

```
<?xml version="1.0" encoding="utf-8"?>
<rss version="2.0"
   xmlns:atom="http://www.w3.org/2005/Atom"
   xmlns:cf="http://www.microsoft.com/schemas/rss/core/2005">    ⟵❶
<channel>
<title cf:type="text">Example CF feed</title>    ⟵❷
<description cf:type="text">Example CF feed </description>    ⟵❸
```

```
<lastBuildDate>Mon, 20 Mar 2006 20:43:55 GMT</lastBuildDate>
<link>http://example.com/blog/link1</link>
<item>
    <cf:id>0</cf:id>        ←❹
    <cf:read>false</cf:read>      ←❺
    <title cf:type="text">Item title</title>
    <link>http://example.com/blog/link1</link>
    <pubDate>Mon, 20 Mar 2006 21:43:55 GMT</pubDate>
    <guid isPermaLink="false">http://example.com/blog/link1</guid>
    <atom:author>
        <atom:name>Dave</atom:name>
    </atom:author>
    <atom:summary type="html">      ←❻
        Short summary of item
    </atom:summary>
    <description cf:type="html">      ←❼
        Full content of item
    </description>
    <enclosure url="http://example.com/podcast/file1.mp3"
        length="395012" type="audio/mpeg"
        cf:downloadstatus="Not Downloaded"      ←❽
        cf:path="C:\ …full path omitted… \file1.mp3" />      ←❾
    </item>
</channel>
</rss>
```

Let's discuss how the CF extensions are used in this example newsfeed. Before an extension can be used, you must declare it by adding a namespace declaration to the newsfeed. In this case, Windows declares the namespace in the root element using the prefix "cf" ❶.

The first extension is the cf:type attribute. It's used to indicate that the feed-level <title> ❷ and <description> ❸ elements are plain text only.

The next time an extension is used is inside the one item in the feed. Windows uses the <cf:id> element to hold the item's unique ID ❹. On the following line, a <cf:read> element with the value "false" ❺ indicates that this item has not yet been marked as read.

Note that the item's <atom:summary> element ❻ *does not* use the cf:type attribute because Atom has its own type attribute, which will suffice, but the <description> element does use it ❼.

The last place the extensions are used is in the item's <enclosure> element. The cf:downloadstatus attribute ❽ is used to indicate that the enclosure has not been downloaded and the cf:path attribute ❾ specifies the path to the enclosure once it is downloaded.

That's all you need to know about the Common Feed extensions, so let's move on to the next set of extensions.

6.4.2 *Simple List Extensions (SLE)*

Unlike the Common Feed extensions, which were invented for use in the internals of the Windows RSS Platform, the Simple List Extensions (SLE) were created for use in application-produced newsfeeds. You can use them in your newsfeeds to enable intelligent sorting and grouping of newsfeed items. Consider using them if you want to define a default sort order for your newsfeeds or you want to enable sorting and grouping on newsfeed extension elements you have added.

The SLE are easy to use and fully documented in the Simple List Extensions Specification, which is available online at http://msdn.microsoft.com/XML/rss/sle/. Let's look at the new elements available in SLE and then examine a simple example newsfeed to demonstrate how they are used.

The elements in SLE

The new elements in SLE are intended for use at the top level of an RSS or Atom newsfeed. They exist in the same namespace as the Common Feed extensions and can therefore use the same "cf" prefix. Here are the elements available in SLE:

- The `<cf:treatAs>` element contains the string value "list" and by including it in a newsfeed, you are declaring the newsfeed to be a list. A list is different from a normal newsfeed because it is a complete list of items, like a top-ten list, and not a subset of a larger collection that will be updated over time, like a blog.

- The `<cf:listinfo>` element is a container element that can hold either or both of the next two elements.

- The `<cf:sort>` element can exist only inside a `<cf:listinfo>` element. Use it to define a default sort order for your newsfeed or to declare how your newsfeed extension elements should be sorted.

- The `<cf:group>` element can also exist only inside a `<cf:listinfo>` element. Use it to define groupings based on your extension elements.

To help understand how to use the SLE elements, let's look at an example. Listing 6.7, taken from Microsoft's SLE specification, shows a simple example newsfeed that uses extension elements to define a list of books. SLE elements are shown in bold.

Listing 6.7 Example newsfeed that represents a list of books

```
<rss version="2.0"
      xmlns:cf="http://www.microsoft.com/schemas/rss/core/2005"   ←①
      xmlns:book="http://www.example.com/book">   ←②
  <channel>
    <cf:treatAs>list</cf:treatAs>   ←③
    <title>Books in My Collection</title>
    <link>http://www.example.com/collectionofbooks.htm</link>
    <cf:listinfo>   ←④
      <cf:sort label="Relevance" default="true" />   ←⑤
      <cf:sort ns="http://www.example.com/book"   ←⑥
          element="firstedition" label="First Edition" data-type="date" />
      <cf:group ns="http://www.example.com/book"   ←⑦
          element="genre" label="Genre" />
    </cf:listinfo>
    <item>
      <title>Great Journeys of the Past</title>
      <author>Bob</author>
      <description>A wonderful history of great journeys</description>
      <book:firstedition>Sat, 07 Sep 2002 00:00:01 GMT</book:firstedition>
      <book:genre>Travel</book:genre>
    </item>
    <item>
      <title>Horror Stories, vol 16</title>
      <author>Steve</author>
      <description>Our favorite horror author provides us with
          another great collection</description>
      <book:firstedition>Thu, 25 Aug 2005 00:00:01 GMT</book:firstedition>
      <book:genre>Horror</book:genre>
    </item>
  </channel>
</rss>
```

Before we can use the SLE elements in a newsfeed, we must declare the SLE namespace ①. This example uses a special newsfeed extension for book information, so we have to declare that too ②.

The first SLE element is the <cf:treatAs> element ③, which we use to declare that this newsfeed is a list. The rest of the SLE elements are contained in the <cf:listinfo> element ④.

The first one, <cf:sort> ⑤, declares that the initial and default sort order of the list is called "Relevance." The next <cf:sort> element ⑥ declares that the list can be grouped by the values in the <book:firstedition> elements, the label for that element is "First Edition", and the element's value is a date. After that, we have the final SLE element, a <cf:group> element ⑦ that declares that the items in the list can be grouped by the values in the <book:genre> elements.

That's all there is to the SLE. Let's move on to the last set of extensions we'll cover in the chapter.

6.4.3 Simple Sharing Extensions (SSE)

Like the SLE, the Simple Sharing Extensions (SSE) were created to allow applications to share data in ways not possible with ordinary newsfeeds. Specifically, SSE was created to enable bidirectional synchronization of data between applications. SSE can be used in RSS and Atom newsfeeds to enable synchronization of items and in OPML outlines to enable synchronization of outline data.

SSE is documented in the specification titled Simple Sharing Extensions for RSS and OPML, which you can find at http://msdn.microsoft.com/xml/rss/sse/. At the time of this writing, the SSE specification is not final and there are not yet any applications that support it. But it's clearly an important specification for Microsoft, so let's examine how it works. First, let's talk about the concept of bidirectional synchronization.

Bidirectional synchronization

What does bidirectional synchronization mean in this context? Consider the simple example of calendar sharing, which Microsoft uses to explain the utility of SSE. Let's say you want to make your calendar available on the Web. You want to allow others to subscribe to your calendar newsfeed so that they can be notified whenever you add a new event to your schedule. Each item in the newsfeed represents one calendar event. That's possible today with ordinary newsfeeds, but there are some problems.

One problem is data loss. For example, your wife subscribes to your calendar newsfeed via her newsfeed-smart calendar program. One weekend she goes on a mountain-biking trip with her girlfriends but without her laptop. By the time she gets back online, several important calendar events have scrolled off the bottom of your calendar feed and she misses them. She doesn't get the automatic notification about your upcoming beach weekend trip with the boys until you happen to mention it during dinner the week before the trip, and wow, is she upset.

Another problem is deletions. When you delete an event from your calendar, how do your subscribers' calendar programs know to delete the event?

But the larger issue is bidirectionality. Your wife is not going to be satisfied with read-only access to your calendar, as unpleasant as this sounds; she's going to want to add and maybe even remove events from your schedule. (She might be the one who cancels your beach weekend.)

SSE is designed to solve these problems. With SSE, your wife can subscribe to your calendar newsfeed and be assured that she will not miss any events added to or deleted from your schedule. And if you'd like to allow her to add and remove items from your calendar, you can subscribe to the newsfeed from her copy of your calendar.

How does SSE work?

SSE defines a new set of XML elements for use in newsfeeds and OPML files. These new elements are designed to address the problems we outlined above in the following ways:

- Enable applications to determine the date range of changes in a newsfeed, so they know if they might have missed some updates. This is implemented via the `<sx:sharing>` element, which can be placed in the `<channel>` of an RSS file to specify the since and until dates of the changes in the file.

- Enable applications to access the full list of items, so that they can recover in those cases when they did miss some updates. This is implemented by the `<sx:related>` element, which can be nested within `<sx:sharing>` to point to the full list of items.

- Allow newsfeed items to carry delete flags so that subscribers know that items have been deleted. SSE implements this via the `delete` attribute of the `<sx:sync>` element, which must be included in every RSS `<item>` element in an SSE-enabled feed.

- Allow newsfeed items to carry conflict flags so that subscribers know when they have conflicting changes. SSE implements this via the `conflict` attribute of the `<sx:sync>` element and the `<sx:conflict>` element, which can be nested within `<sx:sync>`.

- Allow newsfeed items to carry a complete change history. SSE implements this with the `<sx:history>` and `<sx:update>` elements, which can be nested inside `<sx:sync>`.

To help you understand how these new elements are used, let's consider a couple of examples from the SSE specification. First, let's look at how the `<sx:sharing>` element can be used inside an RSS `<channel>` element:

```
<channel>
  <sx:sharing
      since="Tue, 1 Nov 2004 09:43:33 GMT"
      until="Fri, 1 Mar 2005 09:43:33 GMT"
      version="0.91" >
```

```
        <sx:related link="http://x.com/all.xml" type="complete" />
        <sx:related link="http://y.net/B.xml" type="aggregated"
           title="Family Contacts (Dad's Copy)" />
        <sx:related link="http://y.net/C.xml" type="aggregated"
           title="Family Contacts (Suzy's Copy)" />
     </sx:sharing>
     ...
  </channel>
```

As you can see, the `<sx:sharing>` element carries the since and until attributes so that applications can know the date range of changes contained in the newsfeed. Nested within are `<sx:related>` elements. The first one indicates the complete collection of items, a shared family address book. The second one is Dad's copy of the address book, and the third one is Suzy's copy.

Next, let's take a look at an example of the `<sx:sync>` element and see how it is used inside an RSS `<item>` to carry the change history of an item:

```
<item>
    <description>This is a test item</description>
    <sx:sync id="0a7903db47fb0ae8" version="6">
        <sx:history when="Thu, 26 May 2005 09:43:33 GMT" by="REO1750">
            <sx:update when="Wed, 25 May 2005 09:43:33 GMT"
                    by="REO1750" />
            <sx:update when="Tue, 24 May 2005 09:43:33 GMT"
                    by="REO1750" />
            <sx:update when="Mon, 23 May 2005 09:43:33 GMT"
                    by="REO1750" />
        </sx:history>
    </sx:sync>
</item>
```

The `<sx:sync>` element must be included in every `<item>` of an SSE-enabled newsfeed and it must carry a globally unique ID in the id attribute and a version number. Each `<sx:sync>` element must contain an `<sx:history>` element that carries the complete change history of the item. Each change is recorded by a `<sx:update>` element, which specifies the time of the change and who made it.

That brings us to the end of our quick tour of SSE. In summary, SSE is a simple solution to a complex problem. It looks to be an important specification for Microsoft, but be forewarned: it hasn't gone through the extensive community review that RSS has or the rigorous standardization process that Atom has. And that brings us to the end of the chapter and time to sum up what we have learned.

6.5 *Summary*

- IE7 will provide extensive support for all varieties of RSS and Atom, making it easy to find and subscribe to newsfeeds and to download podcasts.

- The new RSS and Atom features in IE7 will be provided by the Windows RSS Platform, which is designed to allow other applications to access and manage the same newsfeed subscription data that is used by IE7.

- The Windows RSS Platform will be part of the new Windows Vista operating system and will be built into IE7, which means that it will also be available on Windows XP.

- The Windows RSS Platform is designed to support the use of newsfeeds for blogs and podcasts as well as other applications, such as calendar-sharing, photo-sharing, and business applications.

- The components of the Windows RSS Platform are the Feeds API, Common Feed List, Download Manager, and a set of newsfeed extensions.

- The Feeds API is packaged as a set of COM objects and is therefore available to programmers using any other Microsoft-supported programming languages, including C, C++, and C#.

- The Feeds API makes newsfeeds subscriptions, newsfeeds, newsfeed items, and enclosures available via a simple object model.

- The Windows RSS Platform stores newsfeed data in a normalized form known as Common Feed Format, which is based on RSS 2.0 and Atom 1.0.

- The simple object model provided by the Feeds API does not support newsfeed extensions, so if you need to parse them, you must parse the XML yourself.

- To allow applications to share data in ways not possible with ordinary newsfeeds, the Windows RSS Platform includes two newsfeed extensions, the Simple List Extensions (SLE) and the Simple Sharing Extensions (SSE) for RSS and OPML.

The ROME
newsfeed utilities

7

Learn how to use the ROME newsfeed utilities to fetch, parse, and generate all varieties of RSS and Atom newsfeeds with ease.

In the last chapter, you learned how to use the newsfeed parser and other newsfeed-handling tools that are built into the new Windows RSS Platform. In this chapter, you'll learn how to use ROME, the premier newsfeed parser library for the Java platform. ROME provides many of the same features as the Windows RSS Platform, but ROME can generate as well as parse newsfeeds, it's highly customizable, and it's based on Java, so it's not limited to Windows.

We'll start with an in-depth introduction that covers ROME's history and design goals and how it works. After that, we'll look at how to use ROME. You'll learn how to parse and generate RSS and Atom newsfeeds with ROME, how to support newsfeed extensions, and how to cache newsfeeds with the ROME fetcher. We'll wrap up the chapter with a detailed explanation of ROME's plug-in architecture and show you how to extend and even override ROME.

If you're a C# programmer who wants to stick to C#, you can safely skip this Java-only chapter. If not, let's get started with introductions.

7.1 *Introducing ROME*

ROME is a free and open source Java class library that provides a newsfeed parser, generator, and other tools for working with RSS and Atom newsfeeds. You can find ROME, along with documentation and full source code, on Java.NET at http://rome.dev.java.net.

Sun employees Alejandro Abdelnur, Patrick Chanezon, and Elaine Chen developed ROME because they found it difficult to parse and generate all the different newsfeed formats. They needed ROME for their work on Sun's portal product, and they wanted to share ROME with others. That's why they released ROME under the open source Apache Software License and that's why they carefully designed ROME for reuse.

ROME design goals
The primary design goal of ROME is to make parsing and generating newsfeeds easy, but it's also designed to be complete, lightweight, and highly flexible. Let's discuss how it achieves each of those goals.

- *Easy-to-use*—Using ROME to parse and generate newsfeeds is easy. ROME can represent any newsfeed as a simple abstract Java object model.
- *Complete*—ROME can differentiate, parse, and generate every commonly used variant of RSS and Atom, including extensions.

- *Lightweight*—ROME has minimal dependencies; its core depends only on the built-in Java SDK class libraries and the JDOM XML processing API. To use ROME, you don't have to bring a lot of new jars into your application.

- *Highly flexible*—You can plug your own newsfeed parsers and generators into ROME to override ROME behavior for any newsfeed type. You can also plug in your own extension modules.

A word of warning

ROME comes pretty close to achieving the above goals, but it's not perfect and, in fact, it's not quite finished. At the time of this writing, the current version of ROME is 0.8, and it's likely that the ROME API will change before ROME version 1.0 is released. Once ROME version 1.0 is available, we'll update the example code in the book to use the final ROME API.

Now that you understand the whys and wherefores of ROME and have been suitably warned about ROME's prerelease status, it's time to learn how ROME works.

7.1.1 How ROME works

In this section, we'll introduce the concepts that will help you understand how ROME works. You'll learn about ROME's three object models, and you'll learn how the ROME parsers, generators, and converters work with those object models.

The three ROME object models

Why does ROME need the three object models shown in figure 7.1? ROME makes it easy to work with newsfeeds using a simple Java object model, known as the *SyndFeed* model, which is designed to represent any type of RSS or Atom newsfeed. Using the SyndFeed model is easy because you can treat RSS and Atom newsfeeds in a generic way, without knowing or caring what the underlying newsfeed format is.

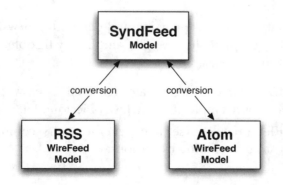

Figure 7.1
The three ROME newsfeed object models

For some applications, however, the SyndFeed model is too abstract. And it doesn't model every construct found in RSS or Atom. What if you need access to the RSS <cloud> element, which is not included in the SyndFeed model? What if you're interested only in Atom and you want to work in terms of an Atom object model, as we do in chapter 10 when we implement the Atom Publishing Protocol? Those things are not possible with the SyndFeed model.

If the SyndFeed model is too abstract for your needs, ROME also allows you to work with newsfeeds using either an RSS or an Atom object model. The RSS and Atom object models are known as *WireFeed* models, because RSS and Atom are the formats that actually pass over the wire (i.e., the Internet). We'll explain how to use the WireFeed models later in the chapter. For now, let's focus on the SyndFeed model.

The SyndFeed model

If you need to parse feeds of all formats, you'll probably want to work with the SyndFeed model. Take a look at the SyndFeed object model, which is shown in figure 7.2. As you might expect, there is feed object SyndFeed, which can contain entry objects of type SyndEntry. With content, link, person, and category objects, the SyndFeed model is rich enough to represent Atom or RSS.

Recall from chapter 4 what we learned about extending newsfeed formats with modules. A module is a set of new XML elements that exist in their own namespace, which are intended for use in an RSS or Atom newsfeed. Modules are useful, and they're widely used and supported in the SyndFeed model. As you can see in figure 7.2, SyndFeed and SyndEntry objects each have a collection of zero or more Module objects. You'll find diagrams of the RSS and Atom WireFeed models in section 7.2, where you'll learn how to parse newsfeeds to all three of the ROME object models. You'll learn how to create your own module implementations in section 7.4. That's enough about object models for now; let's move on to the next topic.

Parsers, generators, and converters

The other parts of the ROME core are parsers, generators, and converters. A ROME *parser* is a class that parses a newsfeed in JDOM XML document form and produces a WireFeed object model. A *generator* is a class that takes a WireFeed model and converts it to a newsfeed in JDOM XML document form. And a *converter* can convert a WireFeed model to a SyndFeed model and vice versa.

To understand how parsers, generators, and converters work together with the ROME object models, take a look at figure 7.3, which shows them in action.

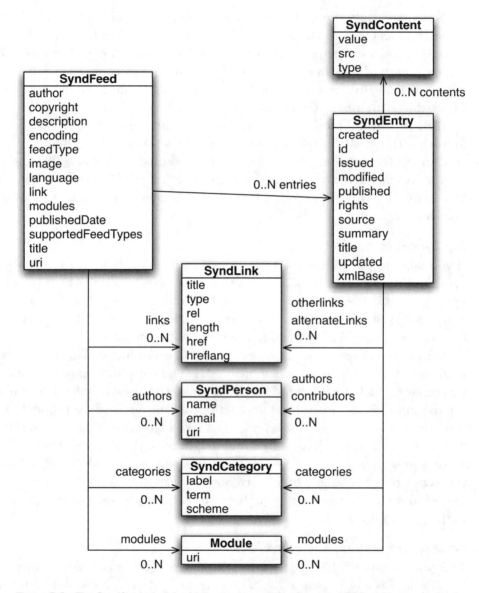

Figure 7.2   The Syndfeed model, which can represent any type of RSS or Atom newsfeed

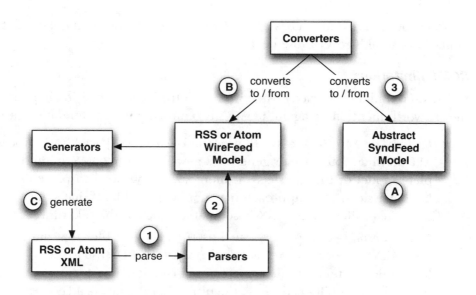

Figure 7.3   ROME parsers, generators, converters, and object models in action

The parsing process

Let's see how the parsing process works by following the numbered circles in figure 7.3. The parsing process starts with an RSS or Atom newsfeed. When you ask ROME to parse a newsfeed to SyndFeed form using the SyndFeedInput class (not shown), ROME examines the newsfeed and picks the right parser to parse the feed ①. The parser walks the XML elements in the newsfeed and creates a WireFeed model for the newsfeed ②. Finally, ROME picks the right converter and uses it to convert the WireFeed representation to SyndFeed form ③. If you don't want to parse all the way to SyndFeed form, you can use the WireFeedInput class instead of SyndFeedInput. Coming up in section 7.2, you'll learn to parse all types of newsfeeds to both SyndFeed and WireFeed form.

The generation process

Next, let's discuss the generation process by following the lettered circles in figure 7.3. To generate a newsfeed based from a SyndFeed representation, you call the WireFeedOutput class (not pictured) and pass it a SyndFeed object Ⓐ and the type of newsfeed to be generated. ROME will pick the right converter and use it to convert the SyndFeed to a WireFeed model Ⓑ. Finally, ROME picks the right generator to generate the specific newsfeed format you requested Ⓒ.

You should have enough basic knowledge of ROME now to understand its two limitations, so let's cover those next

7.1.2 ROME limitations

We covered limitations briefly when we first introduced ROME in chapter 5, but they're worth mentioning again. ROME's two most significant limitations are:

- *It's based on XML DOM*—ROME uses the DOM-based JDOM XML processing API. So when you parse or generate a newsfeed with ROME, it builds a complete model of the newsfeed in memory. If you need to parse extremely large newsfeeds, this approach may not be workable. If that's the case, you should consider using a SAX-based parser, such as the Jakarta Feed Parser.

- *It's not liberal*—XML parsers, such as JDOM, reject files that are not well-formed XML. Since ROME is based on JDOM, ROME has the same problem. It does attempt to do some error correction, but if you really need to be forgiving, you'll need to use the ultra-liberal Universal Feed Parser.

It's possible that both of those limitations will be addressed in future releases of ROME, but for now you'll have to keep them in mind. Next up, the last topic in our introduction to ROME: the ROME subprojects.

7.1.3 The ROME subprojects

In addition to the core ROME parser, generator, and converter API, the ROME developers are working on a set of subprojects. These projects are released separately from ROME and most are versioned separately from ROME. Some are more complete than others, and some are far from being finished. The ROME subprojects fall into two main categories: extension modules and others. Let's start with the extension modules.

Extension modules

ROME hosts eight extension module subprojects, all of which are in various states of completion.

- *Content Module*—Supports `<content:encoded>` and the rest of the Content Module elements.

- *Creative Commons Module*—Supports the Creative Commons License metadata elements.

- *Google-Base Module*—Supports new elements based on the Google Base schema.

- *Apple iTunes Module*—Supports new podcast metadata tags for use with Apple iTunes.

- *Slash Module*—Supports department and comment count metadata provided by Slash-based Web sites.

- *MediaRSS*—Supports Yahoo's MediaRSS extensions, which provide additional metadata for podcasting applications.

- *GeoRSS*—Supports the GeoRSS extensions, which add XML elements for adding longitude and latitude information in newsfeeds.

- *OpenSeach*—Supports the A9 OpenSearch extensions, which add new elements for returning search results in newsfeed form. (See chapter 12, section 12.4 for more about OpenSearch.)

Later in this chapter, you'll learn how to use the Content Module to parse and generate newsfeeds with the `<content:encoded>` element. Now let's move on to the other subprojects.

Other subprojects

ROME's other subprojects focus on components needed to build an aggregator, a newsfeed fetcher, and SyndFeed persistence libraries:

- *Fetcher*—The ROME Fetcher fetches and caches newsfeeds using HTTP conditional GET and ETags and can even support IETF Delta Encoding (RFC-3229). You'll learn how to use the Fetcher in section 7.3, and you'll see it in action in the PlanetTool aggregator presented in chapter 11.

- *Aqueduct*—The goal of this ongoing project is to provide persistence for the ROME SyndFeed model objects by defining a Data Access Object (DAO) layer and then providing DAO implementations using Prevayler and Hibernate.

- *Hibernate*—This project aims to provide SyndFeed persistence using Hibernate, but it seems to have been superceded by the Aqueduct project.

Of those three projects, only the Fetcher is ready for production use. You'll learn how to use it later in this chapter and you can also see it in action in the PlanetTool aggregator we present in chapter 11. That brings us to the end of our introduction to the ROME project. Let's dive into some examples and learn how to parse newsfeeds with ROME API.

7.2 *Parsing newsfeeds with ROME*

In this section, you'll learn how to use ROME to parse all varieties of RSS and Atom into a nice, easy-to-handle SyndFeed object model. You'll also learn how to parse RSS newsfeeds to the RSS WireFeed model, how to parse Atom newsfeeds to the Atom WireFeed model, and how to plug in your own parser classes to override ROME's default parsing behavior.

A simple parsing example

To show you how to parse newsfeeds with ROME, we'll use the same type of example we used in previous chapters—a command-line program that parses and prints a newsfeed. For each newsfeed item, we'll print the id, title, link, dates, and content. You'll learn the steps involved in parsing newsfeeds with ROME, and you'll see how ROME maps newsfeed elements to its three object models. We've got a lot of example code to present, so let's get started with parsing to the SyndFeed model.

7.2.1 *Parsing to the SyndFeed model*

The easiest way to use ROME is to work with the SyndFeed model, which we saw in figure 7.2, so that you can handle all newsfeeds the same way. In this example, you'll learn how to parse any type of newsfeed to the SyndFeed model, iterate through entries in the newsfeed, and print the important information for each.

Listing 7.1 shows the relevant portions of the command-line Java program ParseFeed.java. You can find the complete code for ParseFeed.java and the other examples in this chapter in the directory java/ch07, along with a readme file that explains how to build and run each one.

> **Listing 7.1   ParseFeed.java: Parses RSS or Atom via SyndFeed model; prints items**

```
package com.manning.blogapps.chapter07;      ◁─①
import com.sun.syndication.feed.synd.*;      ◁─②
import com.sun.syndication.io.SyndFeedInput;
import java.io.*;
import java.util.*;

// ... class definition omitted

SyndFeedInput input = new SyndFeedInput();      ◁─③
SyndFeed feed = input.build(new InputStreamReader(is));      ◁─④

Iterator entries = feed.getEntries().iterator();
while (entries.hasNext()) {   ◁─⑤
    SyndEntry entry = (SyndEntry)entries.next();
```

```
System.out.println("Uri: " + entry.getUri());           ◄─❻
System.out.println(" Link:        " + entry.getLink());   ◄─❼
System.out.println(" Title:       " + entry.getTitle());
System.out.println(" Published: " + entry.getPublishedDate());
System.out.println(" Updated:     " + entry.getUpdatedDate());

if (entry.getDescription() != null) {
    System.out.println(" Description: "    ◄─❽
        + entry.getDescription().getValue());
}
if (entry.getContents().size() > 0) {    ◄─❾
    SyndContent content = (SyndContent)entry.getContents().get(0);
    System.out.print(" Content type=" + content.getType());
    System.out.println(" value=" + content.getValue());
}
for (int i=0; i < entry.getLinks().size(); i++) {    ◄─❿
    SyndLink link = (SyndLink)entry.getLinks().get(i);
    System.out.println(
        "  Link type=" + link.getType() +
        " length="    + link.getLength() +
        " hreflang=" + link.getHreflang() +
        " href="     + link.getHref());
}
System.out.println("\n");
}
```

ParseFeed.java starts out with a package declaration ❶ and the imports necessary for parsing a newsfeed from a file to a SyndFeed model. We need the `java.io` classes to read a file, the `SyndFeedInput` class to parse the file, and the SyndFeed model classes themselves, which are in the package `com.sun.syndication.feed.synd` ❷. For the sake of brevity, we've omitted the declaration of the `ParseFeed` class, the declaration of the `main()` method, the code that reads the newsfeed file-name from the command-line arguments, and the code that opens an input stream to read the file. The next code you see is inside the main method.

The action begins when we create a `SyndFeedInput` object ❸, which we use to parse the newsfeed from a `java.io.InputStream` object named is ❹. Once we've got the resulting `SyndFeed` object, we're ready to start looping through the entries within and printing the properties of each ❺.

For each entry, we print the id, link, title, dates, description, content, and links collection. The title and dates work as you might expect and require, but the other properties need some explanation:

The uri property—ROME uses the uri property to represent the entry's unique identifier, if one is available. For RSS newsfeeds, ROME maps the `<guid>` to the uri property. For Atom, the `<id>` is used.

 The link property—ROME uses the link property to carry the entry's permalink. For RSS newsfeeds that have a `<guid>` element with the attribute `isPerma-Link="true"` ROME uses the `<guid>` value here. For Atom newsfeeds, ROME uses the first alternate `<link>` element found in the entry.

 The description property—ROME maps the RSS `<description>` element and the Atom `<summary>` element to the description property, which is an object of type `SyndContent`.

 The contents collection—If not empty, the first element of this collection is a `Synd-Content` object, which holds the content for the entry. For RSS newsfeeds, the object will be the same one that is returned by the description property. For Atom, the object represents the `<content>` element.

 The links collection—ROME uses the links collection to represent the collection of enclosures or links associated with the entry, each represented as an object of type `SyndLink`. ROME maps any RSS `<enclosure>` or Atom `<link>` elements found into this collection.

That's all there is to parsing a simple RSS or Atom newsfeed to the SyndFeed model, but what about funky RSS?

7.2.2 Parsing funky RSS

You may remember from chapter 4 that some RSS newsfeeds are funky—that is, they use XML elements from extension modules instead of the ones defined by the specifications. Funky RSS makes the parsing process more complex, but it's widely used, so let's discuss how to handle its most common forms with ROME.

Parsing Dublin Core elements

Some newsfeed producers prefer to use the Dublin Core `<dc:date>` element because they'd rather use the ISO 8601 than the RFC-822 date format that is mandated by RSS. Some prefer to use the Dublin Core `<dc:creator>` element because they want to identify authors by name rather than email address, which is required by the RSS `<author>` element.

Because Dublin Core is so widely used, ROME includes a Dublin Core module and applies it to all formats of newsfeeds. If you want to parse for the Dublin Core elements, all you need to do is add some code. To demonstrate, let's enhance the ParseFeed.java example from listing 7.1 so that it can print `<dc:date>` and

<dc:creator> values for each entry. First, we bring in the DCModule class by adding an import statement:

```
import com.sun.syndication.feed.module.DCModule;
```

Next, inside the entries' while loop ❺, we add the following code to get the DCModule by using the module's namespace URI as a key and print the module's date and creator values:

```
DCModule dc = (DCModule)entry.getModule(DCModule.URI);
if (dc != null) {
    System.out.println("dc:date:    " + dc.getDate());
    System.out.println("dc:creator: " + dc.getCreator());
}
```

How to handle <content:encoded>

One of the most popular applications of funky RSS is to provide both summary and content for each item in a newsfeed. Currently, both of the blogging services Wordpress.com and Typepad.com put summary in <description> and content in the Content Module <content:encoded> element.

At the time of this writing, ROME does not include the Content Module. So before you can use it, you have to download the Content Module jar separately and include it in your classpath. We've done that for you, and you'll find the jar (content-0.4.jar) in the java/ch07/lib directory of the online example and included in the scripts that run the examples.

To see how this works, let's enhance the ParseFeed.java example from listing 7.1 so that it can print the <content:encoded> values for each entry. First, we add an import statement to bring in the ContentModule class:

```
import com.sun.syndication.feed.module.content.ContentModule;
```

Next, inside the entries' while loop ❺, we add the following code to get the Content-Module by using the module's namespace URI as a key and print the module's <content:encoded> value:

```
ContentModule contentModule = (ContentModule)
    entry.getModule(ContentModule.URI);
if (contentModule != null) {
    if (contentModule.getEncodeds().size() > 0) {
        System.out.println("  content:encoded: "
            + contentModule.getEncodeds().get(0));
    }
}
```

If you want to see the new version of ParseFeed.java, which has been retrofitted to support funky RSS using the above two code examples, take a look at ParseFeed-Funky.java in the online examples.

That's not the end of the story for extension modules. In section 7.4, you'll learn how to generate newsfeeds that use the Dublin Core and Content Modules and in section 7.5, you'll learn how to create and use your own extension modules in ROME. Now that we've mastered parsing to the SyndFeed model, let's move on to the RSS WireFeed model.

7.2.3 Parsing to the RSS model

It's convenient to be able to parse all forms of newsfeeds to the SyndFeed model, but for some applications, you should work directly with ROME's RSS WireFeed

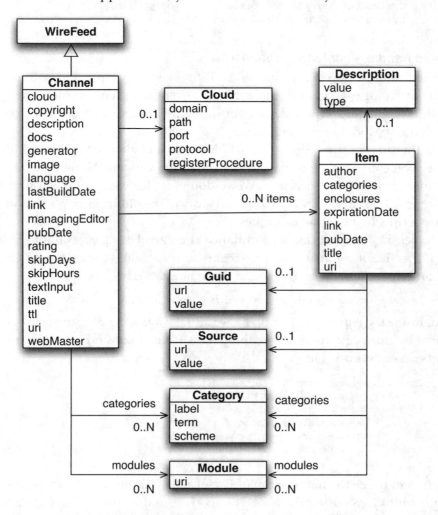

Figure 7.4   The RSS WireFeed model can represent all forms of RSS 0.9, 1.0, and 2.0

model. The SyndFeed model doesn't model every element in RSS. For example, if you need to access values from RSS-only elements, such as <skipHours>, <skip-Days>, and <ttl> elements, which some newsfeeds use to indicate how often you should check for newsfeed updates, the SyndFeed model won't help you. It doesn't model those elements. If you need to access RSS-only elements or you are working exclusively with RSS formats, you should work with ROME's RSS Wire-Feed model, which is shown in figure 7.4. In this section, we'll show you how.

The RSS WireFeed model is designed to represent all forms of RSS newsfeed, from the old 0.9 version to RDF fork RSS 1.0 and simple fork RSS 2.0. As you can see in figure 7.4, it most closely resembles the simple fork of RSS, with a Channel object that contains a collection of Item objects. It supports all of the RSS-specific elements, such as the <skipHours> and <guid>, and even the rarely used <cloud> element. Note that extension models are supported at both the Channel and Item levels, so you can use the same funky RSS parsing techniques we used with the SyndFeed model in listing 7.2.

Now that you're familiar with the RSS WireFeed model, let's put it to use. Take a look at listing 7.2, which shows how to use it to parse an RSS newsfeed.

Listing 7.2   Parses an RSS newsfeed to the RSS WireFeed model; prints items

```
package com.manning.blogapps.chapter07;    <--❶
import com.sun.syndication.feed.WireFeed;   <--❷
import com.sun.syndication.feed.rss.*;
import com.sun.syndication.io.WireFeedInput;
import java.io.*;
import java.util.Iterator;

// ... Class definition omitted

WireFeedInput input = new WireFeedInput();    <--❸
WireFeed wireFeed = input.build(new InputStreamReader(is));    <--❹
if (!(wireFeed instance of Channel)) {    <--❺
    System.out.println("Not an RSS feed");
    return;
}
Channel channel = (Channel)wireFeed;    <--❻
Iterator items = channel.getItems().iterator();
while (items.hasNext()) {    <--❼
    Item item = (Item)items.next();

    System.out.println("Guid:        " + item.getGuid());    <--❽
    System.out.println("  Title:     " + item.getTitle());
    System.out.println("  Published: " + item.getPubDate());
    System.out.println("  Link:      " + item.getLink());
```

```
        if (item.getDescription() != null) {    ◄━❾
            System.out.println("  Desc: "
                + item.getDescription().getValue());
        }
        for (int i=0; i < item.getEnclosures().size(); i++) {    ◄━❿
            Enclosure enc = (Enclosure)item.getEnclosures().get(i);
            System.out.println(
                "  Enclosure type=" + enc.getType() +
                " length="          + enc.getLength() +
                " url="             + enc.getUrl());
        }
        System.out.println("\n");
    }
```

Let's review this simple example. After the package declaration ❶, we import the WireFeed interface ❷ and the RSS WireFeed model classes. We also bring in the WireFeedInput and the java.io classes we'll need to read and parse newsfeed files. Again, for the sake of brevity, we've omitted the class declaration, main() method declaration, and the code that opens the input stream.

The action begins when we create a WireFeedInput object ❸, which we use to parse the newsfeed from a java.io.InputStream object named is ❹. Next, we check to ensure that we're reading an RSS newsfeed ❺. If the feed is not an instance of the RSS Channel class, we print an error message and return to end the program.

If we do have RSS, we cast the WireFeed object to an RSS model Channel object ❻ and start iterating through the items within ❼. For each item, we print the guid ❽, title, published date, and link. The description requires special handling ❾ because it is modeled as an object.

Finally, we print out the item's enclosures ❿, if there are any. Each enclosure is modeled as an Enclosure object. In case you're wondering why there might be more than one enclosure, the RSS specifications are not clear about how many enclosures are allowed in an RSS item, so ROME plays it safe and models enclosures as a collection.

That's it for the RSS model. Let's move on to the Atom WireFeed model.

7.2.4 *Parsing to the Atom model*

If you work only with Atom format newsfeeds and you'll never need to parse or generate RSS, you really don't need the SyndFeed model. Instead, you should work directly with the Atom WireFeed model, which is shown in figure 7.5.

The Atom WireFeed model is designed to represent newsfeeds in Atom 1.0 and the deprecated Atom 0.3 formats. That's why it supports the <created>

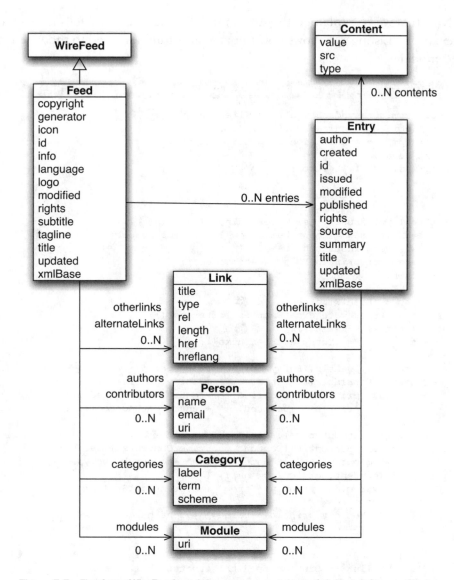

Figure 7.5   The Atom WireFeed model can represent Atom 1.0 (and 0.3) newsfeeds

and <issued> date elements, and that's why it allows an Entry object to have more than one Content object. Those things are not allowed in Atom 1.0, but ROME models them because there are still a large number of Atom 0.3 newsfeeds in circulation.

Now that we've explained the Atom model's idiosyncrasies, let's take a look at an example. Listing 7.3 shows how to parse an Atom newsfeed to the Atom Wire-Feed model.

Listing 7.3 ParseFeedAtom.java: Parses Atom via WireFeed model; prints items

```java
import com.sun.syndication.feed.WireFeed;            ←①
import com.sun.syndication.feed.atom.*;
import com.sun.syndication.io.WireFeedInput;
import java.io.*;
import java.util.Iterator;

// ... class definition omitted

WireFeedInput input = new WireFeedInput();           ←②
WireFeed wireFeed = input.build(new InputStreamReader(is));   ←③
if (!(wireFeed instanceof Feed)) {    ←④
    System.out.println("Not an Atom feed");
    return;
}
Feed feed = (Feed)wireFeed;            ←⑤
Iterator entries = feed.getEntries().iterator();
while (entries.hasNext()) {    ←⑥
    Entry entry = (Entry)entries.next();

    System.out.println("Entry id: " + entry.getId());    ←⑦
    System.out.println(" Title:    " + entry.getTitle());
    System.out.println(" Modified: " + entry.getModified());
    System.out.println(" Updated:  " + entry.getUpdated());

    if (entry.getContents().size() > 0) {    ←⑧
        Content content = (Content)entry.getContents().get(0);
        System.out.print(" Content type=" + content.getType());
        if (content.getSrc() != null) {
            System.out.println(" src=" + content.getSrc());
        } else {
            System.out.println(" value=" + content.getValue());
        }
    }
    for (int i=0; i < entry.getAlternateLinks().size(); i++) {    ←⑨
        Link link = (Link)entry.getAlternateLinks().get(i);
        System.out.println(
            " Link type=" + link.getType() +
            " rel="       + link.getRel() +
            " length="    + link.getLength() +
            " hreflang="  + link.getHreflang() +
            " href="      + link.getHref());
    }
    for (int i=0; i < entry.getOtherLinks().size(); i++) {    ←⑩
        Link link = (Link)entry.getOtherLinks().get(i);
```

```
System.out.println(
    "  Link type=" + link.getType() +
    " rel="        + link.getRel() +
    " length="     + link.getLength() +
    " hreflang="   + link.getHreflang() +
    " href="       + link.getHref());
}
System.out.println("\n");
}
```

Listing 7.3 starts with the usual preamble of import statements. To parse Atom, we'll need the `WireFeedInput` class ❶. We'll need the Atom WireFeed model classes and `java.io` classes too. Once that's out of the way, we can get started.

Again, we've omitted the class and `main()` method declarations and the action begins when we create a `WireFeedInput` object ❷, which we use to parse the newsfeed from a `java.io.InputStream` object named is ❸. Once we've parsed the newsfeed to a `WireFeed` object, we can check to ensure that we're dealing with an Atom format newsfeed. If the feed is not an instance of the Atom `Feed` class ❹, we print an error message and return to end the program.

Once we know we're processing an Atom newsfeed, we can safely cast the `Wire-Feed` object to an Atom `Feed` object ❺ and start looping through the entries within ❻. For each, we print out the simple properties: id ❼, title, and the modified and updated dates. Next, we print out the entry's content, alternate links, and other links. Let's discuss each of these.

❽ *The contents collection*—We print out the first object in the contents collection, which is of type `Content`. We print the content type. Then, we print either the src, which is the URL for out-of-line content, or the value, which is a string containing the HTML, XHTML, or text that exists inside the Atom `<content>` element. See chapter 4, section 4.5.5 for more information on the Atom content model.

❾ *The alternate links collection*—Here, we print the collection of `Link` objects. For most newsfeeds, you can assume that the first object in this collection is the entry's permalink. An Atom entry can have one or more alternate links, one for each language, where language is indicated by the hreflang property.

❿ *The other links collection*—Any `<link>` without `rel="alternate"` is included in this collection. This collection might include podcasts (with `rel="enclosure"`) and other files associated with the entry.

That brings us to the end of our discussion of parsing newsfeeds. Next, you'll learn how to fetch newsfeeds efficiently.

7.3 Fetching newsfeeds with ROME

In the examples you've seen so far in this chapter, we've been keeping things simple by reading newsfeeds from files on disk using a `java.io.InputStream`. Clearly, that's not good enough. For most newsfeed applications, you'll want to fetch newsfeeds directly from the Web, and you'll want to conserve bandwidth by doing so efficiently.

The ROME Fetcher is a Java class library that builds on ROME to provide an efficient newsfeed fetcher. It supports many of the bandwidth-saving techniques we covered in chapter 5, section 5.5, including HTTP conditional GET, Entity Tags (ETags), GZIP compression, and Delta Encoding. The fetcher also provides a simple event system so that your application can be notified when newsfeeds are polled, fetched, or found to be unchanged. We'll show you how to use the ROME Fetcher, but first let's discuss how it works.

7.3.1 How the ROME Fetcher works

Figure 7.6 shows the key interfaces and classes in the ROME Fetcher. The most important of these is the `FeedFetcher` itself, which defines the `retrieveFeed()` method you'll use to retrieve newsfeeds in SyndFeed form.

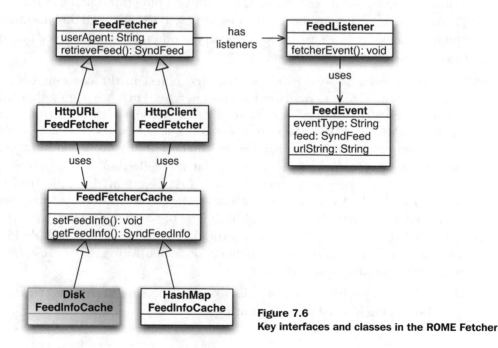

Figure 7.6
Key interfaces and classes in the ROME Fetcher

There are two implementations of the `FeedFetcher` interface. The `HttpURLFeed-Fetcher` implementation uses the Java SDK's built-in `java.net` classes to fetch newsfeeds. The `HttpClientFeedFetcher` implementation uses the Apache HTTP-Client classes to do the same thing. Which one should you use? For some applications involving proxies, authentication, or HTTPS, you might need to use the HTTPClient implementation, but first try `HttpURLFeedFetcher` because it's the easiest to use and requires only the two ROME and ROME Fetcher jars.

The `FeedListener` interface and the `FeedEvent` class provide event handling for the ROME Fetcher. As you'll see in the example code below, you can use these to be notified about when newsfeeds are polled, fetched, or found to be unchanged.

Both of the ROME Fetcher implementations use the `FeedFetcherCache` interface to manage the cache of newsfeeds. Currently, the ROME Fetcher includes only one implementation of this interface; `HashMapFeedInfoCache`, which caches newsfeeds in memory. Caching in memory is not ideal because the cache must be rebuilt every time you run your application. So we've provided you with a disk-based cache implementation called `DiskFeedInfoCache`, which you can find in the online examples that accompany this chapter. Now, let's put the ROME Fetcher and the `DiskFeedInfoCache` to use in a simple example.

7.3.2 *Using the ROME Fetcher*

To understand how to use the ROME Fetcher, let's look at a simple example. Listing 7.4 is a partial listing of FeedFetcherTest.java, a command-line program that fetches, caches, and parses newsfeeds using the ROME Fetcher using either a disk cache via `DiskFeedInfoCache` or a memory cache via `HashMapFeedInfoCache`.

Listing 7.4 FeedFetcherTest.java

```
public class FeedFetcherTest implements FetcherListener {      ◄─❶
    public static void main(String[] args) throws Exception {
        if (args.length < 2) {      ◄─❷
            System.out.println(
                "USAGE: FeedFetcherTest [disk|memory] <feed-url>");
            return;
        }
        new FeedFetcherTest(args[0], args[1]);      ◄─❸
    }
    public FeedFetcherTest(String type, String url) throws Exception {
        FeedFetcherCache feedInfoCache = null;
        if ("disk".equals(type)) {      ◄─❹
            File cache = new File("./cache");
            if (!cache.exists()) cache.mkdirs();
            feedInfoCache = new DiskFeedInfoCache(cache.getAbsolutePath());
```

```
        } else {
            feedInfoCache = new HashMapFeedInfoCache();     ◄──❺
        }
        FeedFetcher feedFetcher =     ◄──❻
            new HttpURLFeedFetcher(feedInfoCache);
        feedFetcher.addFetcherEventListener(this);     ◄──❼
        SyndFeed feed =
            feedFetcher.retrieveFeed(new URL(url));     ◄──❽
    }
    public void fetcherEvent(FetcherEvent ev) {     ◄──❾
        System.out.println("FetcherEvent received");
        System.out.println("  eventType: " + ev.getEventType());
        System.out.println("  urlString: " + ev.getUrlString());
    }
}
```

Let's discuss the finer points of listing 7.4. First, note that the class FeedFetcher-Test implements the FetcherListener interface ❶ so we can listen to all events fired by the Fetcher.

FeedFetcherTest requires two arguments. The first is the cache type, which must be either "disk" to cache to disk or "memory" to cache to memory. The second argument is the URL of the newsfeed to be fetched. In the main() method, we check to ensure that we have two arguments ❷ and if we don't, we print a usage message and exit. Otherwise, we create an instance of the FeedFetcherTest class ❸, passing in args[0] for the cache type and args[1] for the newsfeed URL. FeedFetcherTest does all of its work in its constructor.

If the cache type is "disk" ❹, we create a directory to serve as the cache and we create an instance of class DiskFeedInfoCache to manage the cache. This class is not part of ROME; we had to create it ourselves. (You can find the source code for DiskFeedInfoCache.java in the online examples.) Otherwise, we assume that the cache type is "memory" and we create an instance of the class HashMapFeedInfo-Cache ❺, which *is* part of the ROME Fetcher, to manage the in-memory cache.

Once we've got the cache set up, we create an instance of the HttpURLFeed-Fetcher ❻, add the FeedFetcherTest object as an event listener ❼, and use it to parse from the specified newsfeed URL ❽. When the ROME Fetcher retrieves the newsfeed, it will check to see whether the newsfeed has been updated since the last time it was fetched and fire a FEED_POLLED event. The fetcherEvent() method ❾ will print that out to the console. If the newsfeed has been updated, the Fetcher will fetch it, parse it, and fire a FEED_RETRIEVED event. Otherwise, it will fire a FEED_UNCHANGED event and simply return the SyndFeed found in the cache.

Running the examples

You can find complete instructions for building and running FeedFetcherTest in the directory java/ch07 of the online examples that accompany the book. Under the same directory, you'll also find the code for DiskFeedInfoCache.java and a version of the ParseFeed.java example, called ParseFeedFetcher.java, which has been retrofitted to use the ROME Fetcher. That should be more than enough to get you started with the ROME Fetcher.

We've reached the end of our discussion of parsing newsfeeds with ROME. Now let's move on to newsfeed generation.

7.4 Generating newsfeeds with ROME

Generating RSS and Atom newsfeeds with ROME is easy, thanks to the SyndFeed object model. Generally, all you need to do is create a SyndFeed object and set its properties. Then, add a collection of SyndEntry objects, set their properties, and write the newsfeed out using one of the 10 newsfeed formats supported by ROME. It's easy, but unfortunately, the process does not always result in a valid newsfeed—especially when you generate Atom format, which has some strict requirements about links, ids, and authors.

In this section, you'll learn how to use the SyndFeed model to generate valid RSS and Atom newsfeeds. Then in chapter 8, you'll learn how to check your newsfeeds for validity using FeedValidator.org. Once again, let's dive right into the code. The class GenerateFeed.java, shown in listing 7.5, creates a simple newsfeed with one entry and all the right properties needed to generate a valid RSS or Atom newsfeed. Take a minute to review it and then we'll cover the important points.

Listing 7.5 GenerateFeed.java

```
SyndFeed feed = new SyndFeedImpl();        <--①
feed.setTitle("Example feed");       <--②
feed.setLink("http://example.com/feeds/blog1");
feed.setLanguage("en");
feed.setDescription("Example feed generated by ROME");
feed.setUri("http://example.com/feeds/blog1");        <--③
feed.setPublishedDate(new Date());        <--④

SyndLink selfLink = new SyndLinkImpl();        <--⑤
selfLink.setHref("http://example.com/feeds/blog1.xml");
selfLink.setRel("self");
feed.setLinks(Collections.singletonList(selfLink));
```

```
SyndEntry entry1 = new SyndEntryImpl();
entry1.setUri("http://example.com/blog/entry1.html");      ◄─❻
entry1.setTitle("Entry1");
entry1.setLink("http://example.com/blog/entry1.html");
entry1.setPublishedDate(new Date());
entry1.setUpdatedDate(new Date());      ◄─❼
entry1.setAuthor("Nina");      ◄─❽

SyndContent desc1 = new SyndContentImpl();      ◄─❾
desc1.setValue("Description for test entry #1");
entry1.setDescription(desc1);

SyndContent content1 = new SyndContentImpl();      ◄─❿
content1.setValue("Content for test entry #1");
entry1.setContents(Collections.singletonList(content1));

List entries = new ArrayList();      ◄─⓫
entries.add(entry1);
feed.setEntries(entries);

WireFeedOutput out = new WireFeedOutput();
out.output(feed.createWireFeed(feedType),      ◄─⓬
    new PrintWriter(System.out));
```

Listing 7.5 begins with the creation of a SyndFeed object ❶ feed to represent the newsfeed being generated. Next, we start setting properties. The various versions of RSS together require that we set a title ❷, link, language, and description. Next, we have to satisfy Atom. Atom requires that newsfeeds have an identifier, so we set the feed's uri property ❸, which ROME maps to Atom <id>. Atom also requires that feeds state last update time, so we set the feed's published date property ❹, which ROME maps to Atom <updated>. One last Atom requirement at the feed level is a self link, the URL of the newsfeed itself. We represent that with a Link object ❺, with the right href and rel="self".

Now we move on to the entry. We create a SyndEntry object and start setting properties on it. First, we set the url ❻ to set the Atom entry's <id>. Next, we set the title, link, and published date. Atom requires each entry to have an update time, so we set the updated date property ❼. Since we didn't see a feed level, we must specify an author at the entry level ❽.

The last two entry-level items we need are description and content, each to be represented as a SyndContent object. First, we create the description ❾, which will be mapped to RSS <description> and Atom <summary>. Next, we create the content ❿, which will be mapped to Atom <content> but will be lost if we generate to an RSS format. If you want both content and description in RSS, you'll need to get funky, as we'll explain next.

To wrap up, we create an `ArrayList` to hold our one `SyndEntry`, and we add that to the feed ❶. To generate the XML, we create a `WireFeedOutput` object and call its `output()` method ❷ to write the newsfeed out to the console. The newsfeed format is determined by the `feedType`, which is the ROME feed-type (e.g., "atom_1.0" or "rss_2.0").

Before we wind up this section, let's discuss how to use the Content Module to provide both a description and content for RSS format newsfeeds.

Generating funky RSS

If you want to include both a description and content in an RSS newsfeed, you can use the Content Module. As you learned in section 7.1.2, the Content Module is not included in the core ROME jar. You'll have to download it separately and place it in your application's classpath alongside ROME, but we've done that for you in the online examples that accompany this chapter. If you'd like to see an example, take a look at GenerateFeedFunky.java. It shows how to use the Content Module along with the RSS WireFeed model to generate RSS. At the start of GenerateFeedFunky.java, you'll see the import statement for the Content Module:

```
import com.sun.syndication.feed.module.content.*;
```

After the RSS `Item` object is created, you can see the code that adds the content:

```
ContentModule cm = new ContentModuleImpl();
List encodeds = new ArrayList();
encodeds.add("Content for test entry #1");
cm.setEncodeds(encodeds);
item1.getModules().add(cm);
```

That example shows how to add content via the RSS WireFeed model, but you could use the same code to add content to the SyndFeed model we created in listing 7.5. And with that, we're done with newsfeed generation. Now let's learn how to take advantage of ROME's highly flexible architecture.

7.5 Extending ROME

ROME achieves its design goal of flexibility by providing a comprehensive plug-in architecture. Using ROME plug-ins, you can override and augment ROME's parsing and generation behavior without modifying ROME. You can plug in your own classes to change how ROME parses or generates any of the 10 newsfeed formats it supports, add support for your own newsfeed extensions, and even add support for an entirely new newsfeed format. (With luck, you'll never have to do that.)

In this section, you'll learn by example how to override one of ROME's built-in parsers and how to create and configure a new extension module. But before we start looking at code, you need to understand ROME's plug-in architecture.

7.5.1 The ROME plug-in architecture

In section 7.1.1, you saw how ROME uses parsers, generators, and converters. In section 7.1.2, you learned how ROME uses modules to support newsfeed extensions. The ROME parsers, generators, converters, and modules are all Java classes and they're all *pluggable*, meaning that it's easy for you to replace them with your own Java classes if you want to override the default behavior of ROME. We'll explain how to do that later in this section. First, let's review what those classes do:

- *Parsers*—Each parser is responsible for reading a newsfeed in the form of a JDOM XML document and producing from it a WireFeed object model representing that newsfeed. Each parser is designed to support one specific newsfeed format (e.g., RSS 0.91).

- *Generators*—Each generator is responsible for taking a WireFeed object model and producing from it a newsfeed in the form of a JDOM XML document. Like parsers, each generator is designed to support one specific newsfeed format.

- *Converters*—Each converter is responsible for converting a WireFeed model to a SyndFeed model.

- *Modules*—Each module has a parser that's responsible for parsing the XML elements associated with the module and a generator that's responsible for adding those XML elements to generated XML.

So how does ROME pick which parsers, generators, converters, and modules to use when parsing or generating a newsfeed? It uses a configuration file called rome.properties.

The rome.properties file

The rome.properties file defines the parsers, generators, converters, and modules used by ROME. ROME includes a rome.properties file, and you can add your own to override or augment ROME's default behavior.

When you first use ROME in your application, ROME initializes itself by reading rome.properties. ROME starts by looking in the package `com.sun.syndication` to find its built-in rome.properties configuration file. It loads all of the parsers, generators, converters, and modules defined in that file. Next, ROME searches the root of the classpath for other rome.properties files and loads them in the order defined by the Java classloader.

In rome.properties, three properties define the parsers, generators, and converters available to ROME. These are:

- `WireFeedParsers.classes`: Space-separated list of `WireFeedParser` classes
- `WireFeedGenerators.classes`: Space-separated list of `WireFeedGenerator` classes
- `Converters.classes`: Space-separated list of `Converter` classes

You'll learn how to use those properties to override ROME's built-in parsers later in this section, but what about modules? Modules must be configured for specific newsfeed formats and can work at either the item or feed level. To enable this, ROME uses these four forms of property names to configure modules:

- `<feed-type>.item.ModuleParser.classes`: Space-separated list of `Module-Parser` classes for parsing items of one specific feed-type
- `<feed-type>.item.ModuleGenerator.classes`: Space-separated list of `ModuleGenerator` classes for generating items of one specific feed-type
- `<feed-type>.feed.ModuleParser.classes`: Space-separated list of `Module-Parser` classes for parsing feeds of one specific feed-type
- `<feed-type>.feed.ModuleGenerator.classes`: Space-separated list of `ModuleGenerator` classes for generating feeds of one specific feed-type

We'll see how you can use those properties to add your own new module to ROME in a minute, but first, a word about feed-types.

Feed-type strings

Plug-ins and modules each work with one specific newsfeed format, or feed-type in ROME terminology. ROME uses the following strings to identify feed-types:

- "rss_0.90"
- "rss_0.91U" (the Userland version of RSS 0.91)
- "rss_0.91N" (the Netscape version of RSS 0.91)
- "rss_0.92"
- "rss_0.93"
- "rss_0.94"
- "rss_1.0"

- "rss_2.0"
- "atom_0.3" (the deprecated prerelease Atom format version 0.3)
- "atom_1.0"

Now that you're familiar with the ROME plug-in architecture, let's put it to use by adding a newsfeed extension module to ROME.

7.5.2 Adding new modules to ROME

ROME and its subprojects include module implementations for most of the newsfeed extension modules you'll need to handle now, but extensions are cropping up all the time as companies adapt RSS and Atom for new problem domains. If you want to support new newsfeed extensions with ROME, you'll need to know how to create and configure ROME extension modules. In this section, we'll show you how to do that using a real-world example, the Atom protocol's Publish Control extension.

Atom protocol uses a couple of new XML elements inside each Atom entry to indicate the entry's draft status. For example, if an entry is a draft, its `<entry>` element will include a Publish Control element like so:

```
<app:control>
  <app:draft>yes</app:draft>
</app:control>
```

We'll need to use those Publish Control elements in the newsfeeds we generate and parse in our Atom protocol implementation in chapter 10, so let's develop a ROME module to support that. First, let's discuss how to define a new module for ROME.

Defining a module for ROME

To define a new module for ROME, you might need to define as many as six classes:

- *Module interface*—You must provide an interface that extends ROME's module interface (`com.sun.syndication.feed.module.Module`). This interface should provide properties that represent the values available from the module's XML elements.

- *Module implementation*—You must also provide an implementation of your new module interface.

- *Feed-level module parser*—If your new module adds new XML elements at the feed level or top level of the newsfeed, you should provide a feed-level module parser to read your new XML elements and populate your module implementation.

- *Feed-level module generator*—If you provide a feed-level parser, you probably should provide a feed-level generator to produce an XML representation of your module.
- *Item-level module parser*—If your new module adds new XML elements at the item level of the newsfeed, you should provide an item-level module parser to read your new XML elements and populate your module implementation.
- *Item-level module generator*—If you provide an item-level parser, you'll probably also want to provide an item-level generator.

Since the Publish Control module we're building supports only item-level elements, we won't need to create all of those classes. We'll need only the following classes:

- `PubControlModule`: To define the Publish Control module URI and our one property, draft
- `PubControlModuleImpl`: Implements the `PubControlModule` interface
- `PubContolModuleParser`: So we can parse newsfeeds with Publish Control elements
- `PubControlModuleGenerator`: So we can generate newsfeeds with Publish Control elements

Let's look at the code for those classes, starting with the module interface.

PubControlModule.java

The only things you need to define in a module interface are the URI of the module's XML namespace and properties to represent the data from the module's XML elements. Publish Control defines only one property, draft, so the seven lines of code below are all we need for PubControlModule.java:

```
package com.manning.blogapps.chapter07.modules.pubcontrol;
import com.sun.syndication.feed.module.Module;
public interface PubControlModule extends Module {
    public static final String URI = "http://purl.org/atom/app#";
    public boolean getDraft();
    public void setDraft(boolean draft);
}
```

PubControlModuleImpl.java

Listing 7.6 shows the complete code for class PubControlModuleImpl, which implements our new module's interface. Most of the class is boilerplate—that is, code you have to write to implement any module. The important part is the draft property, which is a boolean **❶**, and its getter **❷** and setter **❸** methods.

Listing 7.6   PubControlModuleImpl.java

```java
package com.manning.blogapps.chapter07.pubcontrol;
import com.sun.syndication.feed.module.ModuleImpl;

public class PubControlModuleImpl
    extends ModuleImpl implements PubControlModule {
    private boolean _draft = false;      ⟵❶
    public PubControlModuleImpl() {
        super(PubControlModule.class, PubControlModule.URI);
    }
    public boolean getDraft() {      ⟵❷
        return _draft;
    }
    public void setDraft(boolean draft) {      ⟵❸
        _draft = draft;
    }
    public Class getInterface() {
        return PubControlModule.class;
    }
    public void copyFrom(Object obj) {
        PubControlModule m = (PubControlModule)obj;
        setDraft(m.getDraft());
    }
}
```

PubControlModuleParser.java

The PubControlModuleParser class, shown in listing 7.7, is responsible for parsing the Publish Control element from within an entry and creating and returning a Module object. Take a minute to examine the code, and then we'll review the important points.

Listing 7.7   PubControlModuleParser.java

```java
package com.manning.blogapps.chapter07.pubcontrol;
import org.jdom.Element;
import org.jdom.Namespace;
import com.sun.syndication.feed.module.Module;
import com.sun.syndication.io.ModuleParser;
```

```java
public class PubControlModuleParser implements ModuleParser {
    public String getNamespaceUri() {
        return PubControlModule.URI;
    }
    public Module parse(Element elem) {          ←①
        Namespace ns = Namespace.getNamespace(PubControlModule.URI);
        PubControlModule module = new PubControlModuleImpl()    ←②
        Element control = elem.getChild("control", ns);    ←③
        if (control != null) {
            Element draft = control.getChild("draft", ns);    ←④
            if (draft != null && "yes".equals(draft.getText()))    ←⑤
                module.setDraft(true);
            else if (draft != null && "no".equals(draft.getText()))
                module.setDraft(true);
            else
                module = null;    ←⑥
        }
        return module;
    }
}
```

The important method here is `parse()`, which takes a JDOM `Element` and returns a `Module` ①. Within `parse()`, we first create a `PubControlModuleImpl` object ②, which will be our return value. Next, we look for a child element named "control" ③ and within that an element named "draft" ④. If we find a draft element with a value of "yes" or "no" ⑤, we return the module object; otherwise, we return null ⑥ to indicate that no Publish Control element was found.

That's it for the parser; now let's move on to the generator.

PubControlModuleGenerator.java

The PubControlModuleGenerator class, shown in listing 7.8, is responsible for generating the XML to represent the Publish Control module element.

Listing 7.8 PubControlModuleGenerator.java

```java
package com.manning.blogapps.chapter07.pubcontrol;
import org.jdom.*;
import com.sun.syndication.feed.module.Module;
import com.sun.syndication.io.ModuleGenerator;
import java.util.*;

public class PubControlModuleGenerator implements ModuleGenerator {
    private static final Namespace NS =
        Namespace.getNamespace("app", PubControlModule.URI);
    private static final Set NAMESPACES;
```

```
static {      ◁━❶
    Set nss = new HashSet();
    nss.add(NS);
    NAMESPACES = Collections.unmodifiableSet(nss);
}
public Set getNamespaces() {    ◁━❷
    return NAMESPACES;
}
public String getNamespaceUri() {
    return PubControlModule.URI;
}

public void generate(Module module, Element element) {    ◁━❸
    PubControlModule m = (PubControlModule)module;
    String draft = m.getDraft().booleanValue() ? "yes" : "no";
    Element controlElem = new Element("control", NS);    ◁━❹
    Element draftElem = new Element("draft", NS);    ◁━❺
    draftElem.addContent(draft);
    controlElem.addContent(draftElem);
    element.addContent(controlElem);    ◁━❻
}
```

PubControlModuleGenerator is slightly more complicated than the parser we just examined, but it's mostly boilerplate. First, we create a static collection of namespace objects ❶ so we can support the getNamespaces() method ❷ efficiently.

The important method in PubControlModuleGenerator is generate() ❸, which takes a Module and a JDOM Element. We add a control element ❹ and a draft element within that ❺, and we add the whole thing to the JDOM element that was passed in ❻.

And that's all for our new module. Let's see how to use it.

Using the Publish Control module

To use the new module in your application, put the module classes and the following rome.properties file in your application's classpath:

```
# Atom Publishing Protocol PubControl extension
atom_1.0.item.ModuleParser.classes= \
    com.manning.blogapps.chapter07.pubcontrol.PubControlModuleParser
atom_1.0.item.ModuleGenerator.classes= \
    com.manning.blogapps.chapter07.pubcontrol.PubControlModuleGenerator
```

Once you've done that, you can parse out a Publish Control draft value from a newsfeed with only a couple of lines of code. For example, you could add the

following code to the ParseFeedAtom.java example in listing 7.3 to parse and
print the Publish Control draft value:

```
PubControlModule pubControl = (PubControlModule)
entry.getModule(PubControlModule.URI);
if (pubControl != null) {
    System.out.print("  Is draft: " + pubControl.getDraft());
}
```

Or if you're working with the Atom WireFeed model, you could use the following
code to add a Publish Control draft value to an Atom element:

```
PubControlModule pubControl = new PubControlModuleImpl();
pubControl.setDraft(true);
entry.getModules().add(pubControl);
```

That takes care of this look at extension modules. Let's turn our attention to how
you can override the ROME parsers, generators, and converters.

7.5.3 Overriding ROME

If you don't like how ROME parses, generates, or converts newsfeeds, you can
override ROME's behavior by providing your own parser, generator, or converter
classes. And that raises a question: "What's not to like?" After all, ROME does a
great job of parsing all forms of RSS and Atom. Why would you ever want to override its default behavior? First, ROME's not perfect. You might find a flaw in
ROME and you might want to fix it without downloading and changing the ROME
source code. (But don't forget to report the flaw to the ROME developers.) And
second, ROME can be too perfect. That's what Nina found to be true.

Nina needs a date

Remember from chapter 5 that Nina is assigned the task of building a simple
newsfeed reader into the FinModler software. Nina wants to include a newsfeed of
recent bug fixes in the aggregator she is building into the FinModler software.
She wants to display title, date, and description for each bug. Unfortunately, the
company's bug-tracking system is old and still uses an RSS 0.91 format newsfeed.
In that newsfeed, each bug is represented as an RSS <item>, and each item has a
<pubDate> field that carries the bug's date. The problem is, the RSS 0.91 specifi-
cation does not allow a <pubDate> field, and ROME, which strictly follows the RSS
specifications, refuses to pick it up. Nina can't get the bug-tracking software to fix
its invalid newsfeed, but she can change ROME.

We'll show you the code needed to solve Nina's date problem, but first let's discuss the different types of parsing and generation plug-ins possible with ROME.

WireFeed parsers

If you want to change the parsing behavior for one newsfeed format, as Nina does, you need to create a parser plug-in. To do that, you implement the Wire-FeedParser interface, which takes an XML Document and returns a WireFeed:

```
public interface WireFeedParser {
    public String getType();
    public boolean isMyType(Document document);
    public WireFeed parse(Document document, boolean validate)
        throws IllegalArgumentException,FeedException;
}
```

Note that the WireFeedParser interface is defined in terms of ROME classes and classes from the JDOM XML parser, the same parser we used in the chapter 5 newsfeed parsing examples. To customize ROME, you'll need to know how to use JDOM. WireFeedParser is a simple interface, but implementing a complete parser is not, so you should avoid that task by extending one of the existing ROME parsers, preferably the one you intend to override.

WireFeed generators

If you want to change the way in which ROME generates a specific format of newsfeed, you need to create a generator plug-in by implementing the WireFeed-Generator interface. This is something Nina doesn't need to do. She needs only to parse <pubDates> from RSS 0.91 newsfeeds, not generate them. But if you find yourself in a situation that does require you to change the way ROME generates a particular newsfeed format, here's the WireFeedGenerator interface.

```
public interface WireFeedGenerator {
    public String getType();
    public Document generate(WireFeed feed)
        throws IllegalArgumentException,FeedException;
}
```

The WireFeedGenerator interface is the opposite of WireFeedParser: it takes a WireFeed and returns an XML Document. Again, you shouldn't write one of these from scratch. Instead, extend one of ROME's built-in generators—the one that you intend to override.

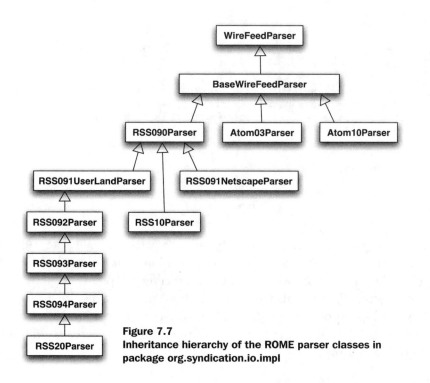

Figure 7.7
Inheritance hierarchy of the ROME parser classes in
package org.syndication.io.impl

Returning to Nina's example, remember that to change the parsing for her RSS 0.91 newsfeeds, she must override ROME's RSS 0.91 parser. To understand how to do this, she needs to download the ROME source code (from http:// rome.dev.java.net). Once she's got the code loaded into her IDE, she looks at the parser and generator classes in ROME's `org.syndication.io.impl` package. She finds that the ROME parsers are organized into the inheritance hierarchy shown in figure 7.7.

Nina realizes that there are two RSS 0.91 parsers, one for the Netscape variant of RSS 0.91 and one for the UserLand variant. She decides that since the bug-tracking system's newsfeed does not declare the Netscape namespace, she needs to override only the UserLand parser. So that's what she does. She studies the code for `RSS091UserLand` and extends it to handle `<pubDate>` elements. Listing 7.9 shows her new parser class.

Listing 7.9   Nina's date-smart RSS 0.91 parser

```
public class RSS091UParser extends RSS091UserlandParser {    ◁—❶
    public RSS091UParser() {    ◁—❷
```

```
        this("rss_0.91U");
    }
    protected RSS091UParser(String type) {      ←─ ❸
        super(type);
    }
    protected Item parseItem(Element rssRoot, Element eItem) {    ←─ ❹
        Item item = super.parseItem(rssRoot, eItem);
        Element e = eItem.getChild("pubDate",getRSSNamespace());
        if (e!=null) {
            item.setPubDate(DateParser.parseRFC822(e.getText()));
        }
        return item;
    }
}
```

Nina's parser is simple. She extends ROME's RSS091UserlandParser ❶. She's studied the source code of that parser enough to know that she needs to define both a default constructor ❷, which sets the correct feed-type of "rss_0.91U", and a type constructor ❸. She also discovered how to override the parseItem() method ❹ to add support for <pubDate>. Hers calls the parent implementation to parse the item, calls JDOM to get the value of the items "pubDate" child, and sets the item's pubDate property.

Converters

If you're overriding one of ROME's built-in parsers and you want to be able to use the results of your new parser in the SyndFeed model, you'll also need to create a converter:

```
public interface Converter {
    public String getType();
    public void copyInto(WireFeed feed,SyndFeed syndFeed);
    public WireFeed createRealFeed(SyndFeed syndFeed);
}
```

The Converter interface goes both ways. The copyInto() method copies a Wire-Feed into a SyndFeed object model. As with parser and generator, you don't want to write a converter from scratch. Instead, extend the one you intend to override.

To accompany her date-smart RSS 0.91 parser, Nina also creates a converter. She first studies the ROME source code in the package org.syndication.feed. synd.impl and finds that the converters are organized into an inheritance hierarchy similar to that of the parsers. She quickly determines that she needs to override the class `ConverterForRSS091Userland`, and that's what she does. The result is shown in listing 7.10.

Listing 7.10   Nina's date-smart RSS 0.91 converter

```
public class ConverterForRSS091U extends ConverterForRSS091Userland { ◁ 1
    public ConverterForRSS091U() {    ◁ 2
        this("rss_0.91U");
    }
    protected ConverterForRSS091U(String type) {    ◁ 3
        super(type);
    }
    protected SyndEntry createSyndEntry(Item item) {    ◁ 4
        SyndEntry entry = super.createSyndEntry(item);
        entry.setPublishedDate(item.getPubDate());
        return entry;
    }
}
```

Nina's converter is tiny, like the parser before. It extends ROME's `Converter-ForRSS091` **1**, it declares a default constructor **2**, and it declares a type constructor **3**. Nina takes a shortcut in her implementation. Since she is interested only in parsing `<pubDates>` from RSS 0.91 and not generating them, she just implements one-way conversion. That is, she overrides only the `createSyndEntry()` method **4**, which takes an RSS `Item` object and returns a `SyndEntry`.

Running the example code

Nina's parser and converter classes are included in the online examples that accompany this book. You can find the complete source code for the two classes, RSS091UParser.java and ConverterForRSS091U.java, in the directory java/ch07/src. In that same directory, you'll also find a rome.properties file that configures ROME to use Nina's classes:

```
# rome.properties file for Nina's date-smart RSS 0.91 parser
WireFeedParser.classes=\
    com.manning.blogapps.chapter07.parsers.RSS091UParser
Converter.classes=\
    com.manning.blogapps.chapter07.parsers.ConverterForRSS091U
```

See the readme file in java/ch07 for instructions on how to build and run the chapter 7 examples. The build process will build Nina's parser, converter, and rome.properties file into the ch07.jar file. Because of this, all of the parsing examples in this chapter support the `<pubDate>` element in RSS 0.91U newsfeeds.

That brings us to the end of another chapter and time to sum up what we've learned.

7.6 *Summary*

- ROME is a free and open source Java class library that supports parsing and generating all of the common RSS and Atom newsfeed formats.

- ROME's primary design goal is to make parsing and generating newsfeeds easy, but it also aims to be complete and highly flexible.

- The primary limitations of ROME are due to its dependence on a DOM-based XML parser. DOM is not the most memory efficient way to parse XML, and DOM-based parsers are not liberal (that is, they can't handle XML that is not well formed).

- With ROME, you can work with an abstract object model known as the SyndFeed model, which masks the differences between newsfeed formats, or you can work with either an Atom- or RSS-friendly WireFeed model.

- The core of ROME is lightweight and depends only on the JDOM parser, but the ROME project also provides a series of subprojects to support most common newsfeed extension modules, efficient newsfeed fetching, and persistence, using other open source Java class libraries (e.g., Hibernate and HTTPClient).

- The ROME Fetcher supports a variety of techniques for efficient fetching and caching of newsfeeds, including HTTP conditional GET, ETags, and compression.

- ROME's plug-architecture makes it possible to add newsfeed extension modules to ROME and to override ROME's default parsing and generating behavior.

How to serve newsfeeds

Learn techniques for efficiently generating and serving Atom and RSS newsfeeds in your web applications.

In the previous chapter, you learned how to read, parse, and make use of newsfeed data. In this chapter, we will cover the other half of the newsfeed story: how to add value to your web applications, web sites, and data sources by generating and serving your own newsfeeds. You'll learn how to produce valid newsfeeds and how to efficiently serve them from your web applications, how to check your newsfeeds for validity, and how to limit the increased load that serving newsfeeds will place on your computer and network resources.

As with the previous chapter, you will get the most out of this chapter if you are knowledgeable in web development, XML, and either Java or C#. The examples in this chapter alternate between Java and C#, but many of the concepts discussed here apply no matter what programming language or environment you are using. Let's get started by checking in with our friends Nina, Rangu, and Otto.

8.1 *The possibilities*

While Nina investigates newsfeed-parsing techniques, Rangu works on devising a plan for serving newsfeeds. It doesn't take long for Rangu to realize that Otto has assigned him the more difficult task. While Nina has only a simple desktop application to worry about, Rangu has to worry about infrastructure because he will need a web server or a web application server to serve the data set distribution newsfeeds. Rangu's mind is filled with questions:

- Should he generate newsfeeds offline and upload them or use a web server to generate them?
- Which newsfeed format should he support—or should he support multiple formats?
- Should he generate newsfeeds using standard XML techniques or something else?
- How can he ensure that the newsfeeds he produces are valid?
- How can he serve newsfeeds efficiently and not bog down his web server?

We'll answer those questions and more in this chapter. First, we'll address the basic questions of static vs. dynamic newsfeed formats and newsfeed validation. Next, we'll show you how to generate both static and dynamic newsfeeds by using a simple file depot example, similar to what Rangu might develop, in both Java and C#. We'll wrap up the chapter by discussing techniques you can use to serve newsfeeds efficiently. In part II, chapter 18, we'll extend the ideas we introduce here to create a simple podcast server.

8.2 *The basics*

Let's start by addressing some of the fundamental questions Rangu faces: which newsfeed formats should he support, how should he indicate that newsfeeds are available, what techniques should he use to generate and serve newsfeeds, and how can he ensure that those newsfeeds are valid? We'll begin with the issue of formats.

8.2.1 *Which newsfeed formats to support?*

Actually, you should support only one newsfeed format. Those who study web site usability have found that offering multiple formats is too confusing for most people. In almost all cases, you should offer newsfeeds in only one format, but which one?

There are a lot of reasons to choose Atom. Atom is the standard, is the technically superior format, and has already been widely adopted. Newsfeed readers from Google, Microsoft, and Yahoo all offer full support of Atom. But despite widespread Atom adoption, RSS 2.0 is still the most widely supported newsfeed format.

To decide which format to support, consider your audience and your requirements. If you're serving newsfeeds to the general public and your newsfeed requirements are simple, RSS 2.0 is good enough. But if you have more sophisticated newsfeed requirements, choose Atom. The logic here is pretty simple. If you want to reach the widest possible audience, use the format that is currently the most widely supported—and that's RSS 2.0. On the other hand, if your requirements are more sophisticated, for instance, if you want to provide both summary and content for each post and you want multi-language enclosures, go with Atom.

Let's return to our friend Rangu, who is most definitely *not* serving newsfeeds to the general public. Rangu is serving newsfeeds of software news, updates, and datasets to a limited audience of FinModler users who are all using the FinModler newsfeed reader. So Rangu should go with Atom.

8.2.2 *How to indicate newsfeeds are available?*

You don't have to be a usability expert to know that newsfeeds are often hard to find and difficult to subscribe to. Let's discuss the common ways in which web developers make newsfeeds available and automate the subscription process, so you can decide which to use for your newsfeeds.

The simplest way to indicate that newsfeeds are available is to display links to each of them. For example, if Rangu is making FinModler company news available in both English and German, he might display the following URLs on his web page:

```
<a href="http://example.com/news-us.xml">
   FinModler news in English</a>
<br/>
<a href="http://example.com/news-de.xml">
   FinModler news in German</a>
```

On newer browsers, such as Internet Explorer 7.0 and Safari 2.0, when you click on one of those links you'll see the newsfeed, nicely formatted, and instructions on how to subscribe. On older browsers, you have to know what to do. To subscribe, you'll have to right-click on one of those links, copy the link, and paste it into your newsfeed reader. If you make the mistake of simply clicking on the link normally, you'll see a page of raw XML, and you'll have no idea what to do next. To work around this problem, Microsoft, Google, and others have decided to use one standard icon to indicate newsfeeds. Figure 8.1 shows what the icon looks like. (You can get it from http://feedicons.com and various other sites.)

**Figure 8.1
The standard feed icon**

So instead of displaying the links above, you'd display them as icons, like so (assuming the feed icon is available at http://examples.com/images/feedicon.png):

```
<a href="http://example.com/news-us.xml">
  <img src="/images/feedicon.png" /></a>: FinModler news in English</a>
<br/>
<a href="http://example.com/news-de.xml">
  <img src="/images/feedicon.png" /></a>: FinModler news in German</a>
```

That's a little bit better, but we're still counting on users to understand that newsfeed links are special and must somehow be copied into a special newsfeed reader. What we need is a way to automate the newsfeed subscription process.

Newsfeed auto-discovery

In addition to displaying newsfeed links using the standard feed icon, you should use newsfeed auto-discovery. Auto-discovery is a technique originally made popular by blogger Mark Pilgrim, which uses the HTML `<link>` element to indicate the newsfeeds available for a web page.

Using auto-discovery is easy. For each of the newsfeeds you are offering, you add a `<link>` element to the head of your web page. The element indicates the content-type of the newsfeed, the title, the language (optional) and the link to the newsfeed itself.

For example, to support his two FinModler newsfeeds, Rangu would add the following two auto-discovery links (shown in bold) to his web page:

```
<!DOCTYPE html PUBLIC "-//W3C//DTD HTML 4.01 Transitional//EN"
    "http://www.w3.org/TR/html4/loose.dtd">
<html>
<head>
    <meta http-equiv="Content-Type" content="text/html; charset=utf-8" >
    <link rel="alternate" type="application/atom+xml"
        title="FinModler news in English" hreflang="en-US"
        href="http://example.com/news-us.xml" />
    <link rel="alternate" type="application/atom+xml"
        title=" FinModler news in German" hreflang="de-DE"
        href="http://example.com/news-de.xml" />
```

Now that we've explained which formats to serve and how to advertise them, let's discuss how to generate them.

8.2.3 Static or dynamic?

Static newsfeeds are served by a web server as static files, just as HTML files are served. Obviously, you don't want your newsfeeds to be truly static. Newsfeeds are meant to change over time, so they must be periodically updated. For example, to produce a newsfeed for a source code management (SCM) system, such as CVS, Subversion, or SourceSafe, you might set up a scheduled task that runs every hour. This task will query the source code system for most recent changes, generate a newsfeed that represents those changes, and then copy the newsfeed file over to the web server so that it can be served as a static file.

Dynamic newsfeeds are produced by application code running within a web server process. This code could be a JSP, an ASP.NET page, or an old-fashioned CGI script. The advantage of these newsfeeds is their dynamic nature. A dynamic newsfeed can be parameterized; that is, it can produce different content based on a web request's parameters or path information. For example, on a personal blog, you might want to allow your newsfeed subscribers to add a category parameter to your newsfeed URL so that they can subscribe to specific categories of your newsfeed. The price to pay is that your application code has to do all of the work that the web server does when it serves a static file, including setting the content-type and writing the newsfeed to the response output stream. We'll show you how to do that with ease later in this chapter.

So how do you decide between static and dynamic newsfeeds? You may have no choice. If you can't run code on the web server, you'll have to generate your newsfeeds offline, upload them, and serve them as static files. Rangu has complete control over his web server, so he chooses dynamic.

8.2.4 *Which generator?*

There are numerous ways to generate newsfeeds; after all, newsfeeds are just XML. Most newsfeed generation techniques are variations of one of the following techniques:

- *Newsfeed library*—A newsfeed library, such as ROME, offers perhaps the easiest way to produce valid newsfeeds, because the libraries are carefully designed for that purpose. You can use this technique for static or dynamic newsfeeds.

- *XML*—Newsfeeds are in XML format, so you can produce them using standard XML techniques, such as DOM serialization, XML data binding, and XML writers. You can use this technique for static or dynamic newsfeeds.

- *Template language*—A template language, such as JSP or Velocity, offers an easy and efficient way to produce newsfeeds and other forms of XML. You get complete control over the XML that is generated because you write the template. You can use Velocity for both static and dynamic newsfeeds, but JSP is suitable only for dynamic newsfeeds because it must execute within a web server.

So how do you choose a technique? If you have a personal preference for XML tools or template languages, choose one of those. Otherwise, pick a newsfeed library. It's the easiest way to produce valid newsfeeds.

8.2.5 *Ensuring well-formed XML*

We don't want the newsfeeds we produce to be among the approximately 10% that fail to pass as XML, so let's review some of the common mistakes found in newsfeeds.

Invalid character escaping

One of the most prevalent mistakes is *invalid character escaping*. Blog entries may contain HTML markup. If special characters are not escaped, as discussed in chapter 4, section 4.1.1 on escaped content, most XML parsers will reject the newsfeed as invalid XML. Newsfeed libraries can help you avoid this problem, but we'll show you how to get this right even if you are not using a newsfeed library.

Incorrect character encoding

Another common mistake is *incorrect character encoding*. XML parsers can handle a wide range of character encodings, including ASCII and UTF-8, but a parser needs to know which character encoding is in use. An XML parser can look for the encoding attribute in the first line of an XML file or, if the file was downloaded from the Web, by looking at the HTTP `Content-Type` header. Unfortunately, many sites that serve newsfeeds make the mistake of either omitting the `Content-Type` header or specifying one that does not match the encoding of the XML file. For example, many sites serve UTF-8 encoded newsfeeds with the content-type `text/xml`, which implies ASCII encoding.

Set the right content-type

We recommend that you use UTF-8 character encoding to write newsfeeds and content-types `application/rss+xml` for RSS newsfeeds and `application/atom+xml` for Atom newsfeeds. UTF-8 is the best choice because it can be used to encode text in all of the world's alphabets. Let's talk about how this can be done for both static and dynamic newsfeeds.

If you are serving static newsfeeds, you must ensure that you generate your newsfeeds with UTF-8 and that your web server is serving newsfeeds with the appropriate content-type. Generating your newsfeeds with UTF-8 encoding is easy, as you will see in the examples that follow in this chapter. The easiest way to ensure that your web server is serving newsfeeds with the right content-type is to name your RSS newsfeed files with the extension *rss* and your Atom newsfeeds with the extension *atom*. You must also configure your web server to recognize these extensions. For example, you can do this for the Apache web server by adding the following two lines to the Mime.types file in the Apache configuration directory:

```
application/atom+xml    atom
application/rss+xml     rss
```

If you are serving dynamic newsfeeds, you must ensure that you generate your newsfeeds with UTF-8 and that your code sets the appropriate `Content-Type` header. We'll show you how to do this in the examples later in the chapter.

8.2.6 Validating newsfeeds

Rangu is a competent programmer, and he is fairly confident that he can produce well-formed XML, but he wants to do better. In all of his previous XML projects, he not only produced well-formed XML but also validated his XML against an XML Document Type Definition (DTD) or XML Schema Definition (XSD). He wants to do the same with the Atom and RSS 2.0 newsfeeds he will be producing, so he starts looking for DTDs and XSDs. Rangu is disappointed when he finds that neither DTDs nor XSDs are part of either newsfeed format's specification.

After some more research, Rangu realizes that even with an XML validation he will not be assured of valid newsfeeds because there are rules in the newsfeed specifications that simply cannot be encoded in a DTD or XSD. The only way to validate a newsfeed format is to use a specially designed newsfeed validator. Fortunately for Rangu, and for us, there is an excellent newsfeed validator—Feed Validator—at feedvalidator.org.

Using Feed Validator is easy. Go to the web site, type in the URL of your newsfeed, click the Validate button, and receive either a congratulatory message of success or a list of the errors and line numbers, as shown in figure 8.2.

Figure 8.2   Feed Validator: The Free Newsfeed Validation Service

Using Feed Validator from the command line

The Feed Validator only works on newsfeeds on the public Internet. If you want to validate newsfeeds on your local network, download Feed Validator and run it on your own computer. Chapter 20 shows how to run Feed Validator from the command line and how to write a script that will automatically validate a set of newsfeeds and send you an email if any fail to validate.

8.3 *File Depot examples*

The examples in this chapter are based on the idea of a *file depot*—a web site that stores files and makes them available for download over HTTP. In our example, called File Depot, we'll provide a newsfeed that users can subscribe to in order to be notified of new files that are available in the depot. When a file is added to the depot, subscribers will see a new entry show up in their newsreaders with a download link to the new file.

We provide several versions of the File Depot example because there are at least several different ways to generate and serve XML, and no one technique is necessarily the best for all situations. Table 8.1 summarizes the various versions. We'll show you how to generate newsfeeds with a newsfeed library in section 8.4, with XML tools in section 8.5, and how to apply caching and compression to those same examples in section 8.6. We don't explain how to generate newsfeeds using a template language, but you can find a couple examples of that in the online examples (depot-rss.jsp and DepotAtomServlet.java).

The last two examples listed in the summary above are not discussed in the book. You can find the Java version of all these examples in the examples directory under java/ch08 and the C# versions in csharp/ch08.

Table 8.1 Summary of the File Depot examples

Section	Technique	Platform	Format
8.4 Generating newsfeeds with Java	Newsfeed library	Java / Servlet	Any
8.5 Generating newsfeeds with C#	XML tools	C# / .NET	RSS 2.0
8.6.5 Caching and compression in Java	Newsfeed library	Java / JSP	RSS 2.0
8.6.6 Caching and compression in C#	XML tools	Java / JSP	RSS 2.0
depot-rss.jsp	Template language	Java / JSP	RSS 2.0
DepotAtomServlet.java	Template language	Java / Servlet	Atom 1.0

Now that we have an overview, let's jump right into the first example, which shows how to generate file depot newsfeeds with Java and the ROME newsfeed library.

8.4 *Generating newsfeeds with Java*

Java can support any of the three newsfeed-generation techniques we discussed in section 8.2.3, but thanks to ROME, the newsfeed library technique is the best choice for most situations. This example shows how you can use the ROME newsfeed library to generate a newsfeed for the File Depot. The advantages to using ROME are many, but the top three are:

- *ROME is easy to use*—You don't need to have a deep understanding of newsfeed specifications to use ROME. You use ROME's easy-to-understand Java API to build a newsfeed object model in memory, and then you use the API to write that object model out to a newsfeed.

- *ROME can generate any format*—Once you have the newsfeed object model in memory, you can write it out to any RSS or Atom newsfeed format. This makes serving multiple newsfeed formats easy.

- *ROME is lightweight*—ROME relies only on Java and the JDOM parser library, so to use ROME you need only two jar files: the ROME jar and the JDOM jar.

The only real disadvantage of using ROME is in dealing with extremely large newsfeeds. Because ROME works by first creating an object model of your newsfeed in memory, large newsfeeds may cause too much object creation, and in a high-volume web application this could become a problem. Generally, newsfeeds are small and this problem does not come into play; but if it does, you should switch to a technique that streams your newsfeeds out item by item. For example, use an approach based on the template language technique, such as JSP or Velocity. The code directory for this chapter includes an example of each.

8.4.1 *Implementing the File Depot in Java*

Before we can generate and serve a newsfeed for the File Depot, we need the File Depot itself, so let's create it. The concept is simple: File Depot is simply a collection of files. For the purposes of this example, we define the depot with a simple Java interface called Depot, shown next:

```
package com.manning.blogapps.chapter08.filedepot;
import java.util.Collection;
import java.util.Date;

public interface Depot {
    public abstract Collection getFiles();
    public abstract Date getLastUpdateDate();
    public abstract void update();
}
```

As you can see, the `Depot` interface allows you to get a collection of files, get the last update time for the files, and update the collection by rescanning the files contained in the depot. The `getFiles()` method returns a collection of `java.io.File` objects.

The `FileDepot` class implements the `Depot` interface, but the actual implementation is not central to our topic, which is generating newsfeeds. We won't discuss the implementation here, but you can find the full source code for it in the examples directory in the file FileDepot.java.

Now that we have our File Depot in place, we are ready to discuss newsfeed generation.

8.4.2 *Generating the File Depot newsfeed in Java*

Now, let's use ROME to create a newsfeed writer that can generate newsfeeds in any RSS or Atom format. We'll design the writer so that it can be used dynamically from within a web application or statically from a command-line invocation. Our new class, `DepotNewsfeedWriter`, is shown in full in listing 8.1.

Listing 8.1   DepotNewsfeedWriter.java

```
package com.manning.blogapps.chapter08.filedepot;
import java.io.*;
import java.util.*;
import com.sun.syndication.feed.WireFeed;
import com.sun.syndication.feed.synd.*;
import com.sun.syndication.io.WireFeedOutput;

public class DepotNewsfeedWriter {                          ❶
    private Depot depot;
    public DepotNewsfeedWriter(Depot depot) {
        this.depot = depot;
    }

    public void write(
            Writer writer, String baseURL, String format)  ❷
            throws Exception {
```

```
SyndFeed feed = new SyndFeedImpl();
feed.setFeedType(format);
feed.setLanguage("en-us");
feed.setTitle("File Depot Newsfeed");
feed.setDescription(
    "Newly uploaded files in the File Depot");
feed.setLink(baseURL);
feed.setUri(baseURL + "/depot-newsfeed");
feed.setPublishedDate(depot.getLastUpdateDate());
```
❸

```
SyndLink selfLink = new SyndLinkImpl();
selfLink.setHref(feed.getUri());
selfLink.setRel("self");
feed.setLinks(Collections.singletonList(selfLink));
```
❹

```
ArrayList entries = new ArrayList();
Iterator files = depot.getFiles().iterator();
while (files.hasNext()) {
    File file = (File) files.next();
```
❺

```
    SyndEntry entry = new SyndEntryImpl();
    String url = baseURL + file.getName();
    entry.setLink(url);
    entry.setUri(url);
    entry.setTitle(file.getName());
    entry.setPublishedDate(new Date(file.lastModified()));
    entry.setUpdatedDate(new Date(file.lastModified()));
```
❻

```
    SyndContent description = new SyndContentImpl();
    description.setValue(
        "Click <a href='"+url+"'>" + file.getName()
        + "</a> to download the file.");
    entry.setDescription(description);
```
❼

```
    entries.add(entry);        ⟵❽
}
feed.setEntries(entries);      ⟵❾
```

```
WireFeedOutput output = new WireFeedOutput();
WireFeed wireFeed = feed.createWireFeed();
output.output(wireFeed, writer);
}
```
❿

```
public void main(String[] args) throws Exception {
    if (args.length < 3)  {
        System.out.println(
            "USAGE: DepotNewsfeedWriter "
          + "[depotDir] [depotUrl] [file] [format]");
        return;
    }
```
⓫

```
        String depotDir = args[0];
        Depot depot = new FileDepot(depotDir);         ⓲
        DepotNewsfeedWriter newsfeedWriter =
            new DepotNewsfeedWriter(depot);

        String depotUrl = args[1];
        String filePath = args[2];                     ⓳
        String format = args[3];
        FileWriter writer = new FileWriter(filePath);
        newsfeedWriter.write(writer, depotUrl, format);
    }
}
```

The code defines a class called DepotNewsfeedWriter that can be used to write newsfeeds for a depot. To construct a DepotNewsfeedWriter, you use the constructor ❶, which accepts a depot object.

Once you have constructed a DepotNewsfeedWriter, you can call its write() method ❷ to write out a newsfeed that references the files most recently added to the depot. To write a newsfeed, you must provide the java.io.Writer to be written to, the base URL to be used in the generated newsfeed, and the type of newsfeed you wish to have generated (for example, rss_0.91, rss_0.92, rss_1.0, rss_2.0, or atom_1.0).

The write() method works by first creating a newsfeed object model in memory and then writing that model out to XML format. We start by creating a ROME SyndFeed object, which represents the feed itself ❸. After we set the feed type to tell ROME which newsfeed format to generate, we start setting the feed-level properties, like title, link, description, and publication date. So that we can support Atom, we add a self link back to the newsfeed itself ❹.

Next, we need to loop through the files in the depot and create a ROME SyndEntry object for each file. We declare an ArrayList to hold the collection of entries we create and we start while looping though the files returned by the depot ❺. Within the loop, we create a SyndEntry for each file, and we set its entry-level properties such as title, link, and published date ❻. The description for each entry is a sentence that contains an HTML hyperlink so that the user can download it. We don't need to escape the HTML because ROME will take care of that for us ❼. We add each new entry to the ArrayList we declared earlier ❽, and when the entry collection is complete, we add it to the SyndFeed object ❾. Finally, we create the ROME WireFeed and WireFeedOutput objects we need and we write out the newsfeed ❿.

The write() method can be called from a Java web application, but we also want to be able to call it from the command line, so we define a standard Java main() method. The user must pass in the four command-line parameters below, and if she does not do so, we print out a usage message to help her along ⓫.

- *depotDir*—The full path to the directory in which the File Depot files exist
- *depotUrl*—The base URL where the File Depot is made available on the Web
- *file*—The filename of the newsfeed file to be generated
- *format*—The name of the newsfeed format to be generated (for example, rss_0.91, rss_0.92, rss_1.0, rss_2.0, or atom_1.0)

Next, we create a File Depot object for the depotDir passed in by the caller and a DepotNewsfeedWriter for that depot ⓬. Finally, we create a java.io.FileWriter to write the filename specified by the user, and we write the newsfeed out to that writer ⓭.

Now we have a Java-based newsfeed writer class that can be used for generating static or dynamic depot newsfeeds. Let's see how to use this class to generate dynamic newsfeeds from a Java web application.

8.4.3 *Serving the File Depot newsfeed in Java*

With DepotNewsfeedWriter, generating the depot newsfeed from within a Java web application is easy. All we have to do is call the writer, pass it a Depot object, and tell it which format we wish to generate. Let's examine how this is done in DepotNewsfeedServlet.java, shown in listing 8.2.

Listing 8.2 DepotNewsfeedServlet.java

```
package com.manning.blogapps.chapter08.web;
import java.io.IOException;
import javax.servlet.*;
import javax.servlet.http.*;
import com.manning.blogapps.chapter08.filedepot.*;

public class DepotNewsfeedServlet extends HttpServlet {

    protected void doGet(HttpServletRequest request,
        HttpServletResponse response) throws ServletException, IOException {

        ServletContext application = this.getServletContext();
        Depot depot = (Depot) application.getAttribute("depot");      ◄─❶
        if (depot == null) {
            depot = new FileDepot(request.getRealPath("/depot"));     ◄─❷
            application.setAttribute("depot", depot);
        }
```

```
    try {
        String format = request.getParameter("format");    ◄─❸
        if (format == null) format = "rss_2.0";
        if (format.startsWith("rss")) {    ◄─❹
            response.setContentType(
                "application/rss+xml;charset=utf-8");
        } else {
            response.setContentType(
                "application/atom+xml;charset=utf-8");
        }
        String url = request.getRequestURL().toString();              ❺
        String depotUrl = url.substring(0, url.lastIndexOf("/"));
        DepotNewsfeedWriter depotWriter =                             ❻
            new DepotNewsfeedWriter(depot);
        depotWriter.write(response.getWriter(), depotUrl, format);
    }
    catch (Exception ex) {
        String msg = "ERROR: generating newsfeed";
        log(msg, ex);
        response.sendError(
            HttpServletResponse.SC_INTERNAL_SERVER_ERROR, msg);
    }
  }
}
```

Let's discuss the code. The DepotNewsfeedServlet class is a run-of-the-mill Java Servlet that can write a newsfeed for a depot. The first thing we do in the doGet() method is either find or create a Depot implementation at the application scope ❶. If we do not find one, we create one in a subdirectory named depot in the application's Servlet Context directory ❷.

We look for a format parameter in the request ❸, which must be one of the standard ROME format types. (Valid options are rss_0.91, rss_0.92, rss_1.0, and atom_1.0.) If we don't find one, we default to rss_2.0.

Next, we use the format to determine which content-type to set. If the format type starts with "rss" ❹, we use the RSS content-type application/rss+xml. Otherwise, we use the Atom content-type application/atom+xml.

Finally, we determine the base URL of the application ❺ and call the depot writer to write out the newsfeed ❻.

And that brings us to the end of our Java example. Now let's discuss how to do the same thing in the .NET world.

8.5 *Generating newsfeeds with C#*

In section 8.2.4 we listed three options for newsfeed generation: newsfeed library, XML, and template language. Unfortunately, only two of those options are really viable for C# developers. Why is that? The Windows RSS platform's Feeds API would be the obvious choice, but supports only newsfeed parsing and offers no support for newsfeed generation. And, there are two open source newsfeed libraries for .NET, but they are incomplete and seem to have been abandoned.

Eventually, Microsoft may introduce a server-side Feeds API for newsfeed generation, but until then, the best option for C# developers is to use the XML classes that are built into the .NET Framework. That's what you'll learn to do in this section.

The .NET framework includes a class called `System.Xml.XmlTextWriter` that makes it easy to write XML to any output stream. As you call the writer's `writeStartElement()` and `writeEndElement()` methods, the XML elements come streaming out, one by one. The advantages of using this technique are:

- Stream style API is well suited for large newsfeeds.

- Simple API makes it easy to write XML elements and attributes.

- The technique takes care of escaping content that is not valid XML.

- The `XmlTextWriter` is built into .NET, so there are no libraries to download and install.

- The technique works for both static and dynamic newsfeed generation.

There are also disadvantages:

- Overall, `XmlTextWriter` is more difficult and error prone than using a newsfeed library.

- Invalid XML is possible because the `XmlTextWriter` does not check for invalid characters in attribute values and element names, improper character encoding, or duplicate attributes.

- Invalid newsfeeds are possible because this approach does not check for conformance to any newsfeed specifications.

Now that we have chosen our technique, let's move on to developing the example.

8.5.1 Implementing the File Depot in C#

As in the Java version of this example, we need a File Depot. In the .NET version, the depot interface is defined in IDepot.cs and the implementation is in File-Depot.cs. Below is the `IDepot` interface:

```
using System;
using System.Collections;
namespace BlogApps_Chapter08 {

    public interface IDepot {
        ICollection getFiles();
        DateTime getLastUpdateTime();
        void update();
    }
}
```

The implementation of the `IDepot` interface is not central to the topic at hand, so we won't discuss it here. Full source code is included in the examples directory that accompanies this chapter.

With our File Depot in place, we can look at how to generate a newsfeed.

8.5.2 Generating the File Depot newsfeed in C#

To support both static and dynamic newsfeed generation, we'll create a news-feed writer class called `DepotRSSWriter`. The writer does not depend on the ASP.NET environment, so it may be used to generate static newsfeeds outside of that environment, or dynamic newsfeeds from within an ASP.NET page. We will illustrate that in a moment, but first let's take a closer look at the source code for `DepotRSSWriter`, which is shown in listing 8.3.

Listing 8.3 DepotRSSWriter.cs

```
using System;
using System.IO;
using System.Xml;
using System.Text;
using System.Collections;

namespace BlogApps_Chapter08 {

    public class DepotRSSWriter {
        private IDepot m_Depot = null;                        ❶
        public DepotRSSWriter(IDepot depot) {
            m_Depot = depot;
        }
        public void write(XmlTextWriter writer, string baseURL) {   ❷
```

```
            writer.Formatting = Formatting.Indented;
            writer.Indentation = 4;                                    ❸

            writer.WriteStartDocument();
            writer.WriteStartElement("rss");
            writer.WriteAttributeString("version", "2.0");             ❹

            writer.WriteStartElement("channel");
            writer.WriteElementString("lastBuildDate",
                m_Depot.getLastUpdateTime().ToString("r"));
            writer.WriteElementString("title",                         ❺
                "File Depot Newsfeed");
            writer.WriteElementString("description",
                "Newly uploaded files in the File Depot");
            writer.WriteElementString("link", baseURL);

            ICollection items = m_Depot.getFiles();                    ❻
            foreach(FileInfo fileInfo in m_Depot.getFiles()) {

                String url = baseURL + fileInfo.Name;
                writer.WriteStartElement("item");
                writer.WriteElementString("title", fileInfo.Name);
                writer.WriteElementString("link", url);                ❼
                writer.WriteElementString("description",
                    "Click <a href='"+url+"'>"
                    + fileInfo.Name + "</a> to download the file");
                                                                       ❽
                writer.WriteElementString("pubDate",
                    fileInfo.LastWriteTime.ToString("r"));

                writer.WriteEndElement();
            }                                                          ❾
            writer.WriteEndElement();
            writer.WriteEndElement();
        }

        static void Main(string[] args) {           ⟵❿
            System.Console.WriteLine("File Depot Newsfeed RSS Writer");
            if (args.Length != 3) {                                    ⓫
                System.Console.WriteLine(
                    "USAGE: DepotRSSWriter [depotDir] [depotUrl] [file]");
                return;
            }
            string depotDir = args[0];
            string outputPath = args[2];
                                                                       ⓬
            IDepot depot = new FileDepot(depotDir);
            DepotRSSWriter depotWriter = new DepotRSSWriter(depot);

            FileStream stream =
                new FileStream(outputPath, FileMode.Create);           ⓭
            XmlTextWriter writer =
                new XmlTextWriter(stream, Encoding.UTF8);
```

```
        string baseURL = args[1];
        depotWriter.write(writer, baseURL);
    }
  }
}
```
⑭

Let's discuss the code in detail. First, we define the `DepotRSSWriter` class and its constructor ❶. To create a `DepotRSSWriter`, you must provide a File Depot object that implements the `IDepot` interface.

Next, we define the `write()` method ❷, which accepts two arguments. These are the `XmlTextWriter` to which the RSS newsfeed is to be written and the base URL to be used in the generated newsfeed. Inside the `write()` method, we set up pretty printing ❸ and start generating the newsfeed by writing out the root `<rss>` element using the writer's `WriteStartElement()` method and the element's version attribute using `WriteAttributeString()` ❹. Inside the `<rss>` element, we write the `<channel>` element and its children ❺. We call the depot to get the value for the `<lastBuildDate>` element, use the base URL for the `<link>` element, and make up some appropriate values for the title and description.

To create the `<item>` elements inside the `<channel>` element, we use a foreach loop to iterate through the `FileInfo` objects from the depot's collection ❻. Inside the loop, we write out the `<item>` element for the current file ❼. We form the link for the file by appending the filename to the base URL, and we also use the filename as the item's title. The item description includes HTML, but we do not need to escape the angle brackets because the `XmlTextWriter` will do that for us ❽. Finally, we use the writer's `WriteEndElement()` method to end the elements we started ❾.

The `write()` method can be called from an ASP.NET web application, but we also want to be able to call it from the command line, so we define a standard C# `Main()` method ❿. The user must pass in the three command-line parameters below, and if she does not do so, we print out a usage message to help her along ⓫.

- *depotDir*—The full path to the directory in which the File Depot files exist
- *depotUrl*—The base URL where the File Depot is made available on the Web
- *file*—The filename of the newsfeed file to be generated

Next, we create a File Depot object for the `depotDir` passed in by the caller and a `DepotRSSWriter` for that depot ⓬. Finally, we create a `FileStream` wrapped with an `XmlTextWriter` ⓫ and hand that over to the depot writer to write out the newsfeed ⓮.

With our `DepotRSSWriter`, we can generate depot newsfeeds with ease. Now let's learn how to use the writer in an ASP.NET web application.

8.5.3 *Serving the File Depot newsfeed with C#*

To use the `DepotRSSWriter` for dynamic newsfeed generation, you just call it from an ASP.NET page. The ASP.NET page does not need to include HTML or any web form controls because the RSS writer will be responsible for all output. All we do is define a standard ASP.NET `Page_Load()` method for the page and call the writer from there. Listing 8.4 shows how this is done.

Listing 8.4   depot-rss.aspx.cs

```
private void Page_Load(object sender, System.EventArgs e) {

    IDepot depot = (IDepot)Application["depoy"];              ❶
    if (depot == null) {
        depot = new FileDepot(MapPath(@"depot"));
        Application["depot"] = depot;
    }
    Response.ContentType = "application/rss+xml";             ❷
    Response.ContentEncoding = Encoding.UTF8;

    XmlTextWriter writer = new XmlTextWriter(                 ❸
        Response.OutputStream, new System.Text.UTF8Encoding());

    DepotRSSWriter rssWriter = new DepotRSSWriter(depot);
    rssWriter.write(writer, "http://"                        ❹
      + Request.ServerVariables["SERVER_NAME"]
      + Request.ApplicationPath + "/");
    writer.Close();
}
```

Let's discuss the code. We need one copy of the `File Depot` object in application scope, so that it is shared across all user sessions and available to all ASP.NET pages in the application. If a depot does not exist in application scope, we create one and put it there ❶. Next, we set the response's character encoding to `application/rss+xml` and its encoding to `UTF-8` ❷, and we create an `XmlTextWriter` to write to the response's output stream using UTF-8 encoding ❸. Finally, we create a `DepotRSSWriter` for our depot and use it to write out the depot newsfeed ❹.

And that brings us to the end of our C# example. Now, we'll switch gears and discuss how to lessen the load that serving newsfeeds places on your web server and other network resources.

8.6 *Serving newsfeeds efficiently*

If you're successful, your newsfeeds become immensely popular, and your subscribers grow from tens, to hundreds, to thousands, you'll know it. Your beeper will notify you of your success when your servers start to stress out. Your accountant will notify you of your success when he gets the big bandwidth bill for it. Newsfeeds will bring more traffic to your web server because newsfeed readers operate by polling your site every hour or so to see if your newsfeeds have been updated.

You might be able to scale your newsfeed-serving web application to meet the increased demand of success by adding servers to your web site, but to keep your hardware bill down, you'll want to use as few servers as possible. What about your bandwidth bill? The best way to control both of these costs is to serve newsfeeds efficiently—to make the most of your computer resources, network resources, and bandwidth allotment.

The secret to efficiently serving newsfeeds, and just about any other web resource, is caching, caching, more caching, and compression. You should cache inside your application, set the right headers to allow proxy servers to cache on your behalf, and handle HTTP conditional GET so that clients can cache intelligently as well. Where possible, you should compress the content you serve to further minimize bandwidth usage.

In this section, we will discuss server-side caching, web proxy caching, client-side caching, and compression in detail. We'll also show you how to add caching and compression to the newsfeed-producing examples we introduced in sections 8.4 and 8.5.

8.6.1 *Server-side caching*

The main purpose of a server-side cache is to reduce load on your system. Each time you generate a newsfeed, you have to use some CPU time, perform disk I/O and network I/O, or all of the above. If you're using static newsfeeds, your web server will take care of caching for you; but if you're dynamically generating your newsfeeds, then you need to use a server-side cache. So each time you generate a newsfeed, you should cache it for later so that you don't have to do the hard work for every request that comes in.

There are plenty of server-side caching choices. If you are using a Java application server, such as BEA Weblogic or IBM Websphere, you can use its built-in caching features. If you are developing a product that must run on multiple Java application servers, you should develop your own caching, use an open source cache, such as OSCache from Open Symphony, or use a commercial caching product, such as Coherence from Tangosol. If you are using ASP.NET, you can use the built-in ASP.NET caching system.

8.6.2 *Web proxy caching*

Many large organizations use a web proxy to cache frequently requested pages for the purposes of reducing network traffic and network latency—and in some cases, to monitor web usage and restrict access to verboten web pages. By setting the right combination of HTTP headers in your newsfeed responses, you can get these web proxies to cache your newsfeeds for you, thus reducing both the load on your servers and the bandwidth consumed by your site. This benefits you, but it also benefits your users because they will experience faster response times if they can pull your content from a local proxy server rather than going all the way to your server.

Web proxies will not cache your content unless they have a way to determine whether your content is fresh once it has been placed into the cache. You can convey freshness information by setting the HTTP `Last-Modified` header or the `ETag` header, which are both described in the client-side caching section below.

You can obtain better control over web proxy caches by using the cache control headers defined in the HTTP 1.1 specification, which can be found at http://www.ietf.org/rfc/rfc2616.txt. You can easily add these headers to your web responses by using either the Java `HttpServletResponse.setHeader()` method or the C# `Response.AppendHeader()` method. Below are a few of the more useful cache control headers:

- *max-age*—Specified in seconds, the `max-age` header allows you to control how long a web proxy will cache content. This is the web proxy cache timeout, so you should set it to be less than or equal to your server-side cache timeout. Once a page has been cached for longer than `max-age`, it is considered to be *expired*.

- *private*—The `private` header indicates that content is private and intended for a single user and should not be cached in a shared public cache.

- *public*—The opposite of `private`, `public` indicates that a page may be cached in a shared public cache and server.

- *must-revalidate*—HTTP allows caches some leniency in obeying the `max-age` rule. By specifying `must-revalidate`, you are telling the proxy servers to strictly follow your rules.

8.6.3 *Client-side caching*

Your browser uses a client-side cache so that web pages, images, and other resources don't have to be downloaded so often. By setting a couple of HTTP headers and adding some supporting server-side logic, you can make these caches work for you as well.

Recall from chapter 5 that client-side caches rely on a technique known as conditional GET. To enable conditional GET caching, set the HTTP Last-Modified header in each newsfeed response to the time when the newsfeed was last modified. This is probably the same as the publication date of the most recent entry in the newsfeed. Whenever you get a request for a newsfeed, check the request for the HTTP If-Modified-Since header. If the newsfeed has not changed since the date specified in the header, don't return the newsfeed. Instead, return only the HTTP 304 Not-Modified response code. If the newsfeed has changed, send the new newsfeed and an updated HTTP Last-Modified header. We'll show you how to do this in the examples that follow.

8.6.4 *Compression*

Another way to reduce bandwidth is to use compression, which has been a part of HTTP since the HTTP 1.1 specification was introduced in 1999. These days, most web browsers and newsreaders support compression. Those that do will indicate support by sending you an HTTP header named Accept-Encodings in each request. Accept-Encodings is a comma-separated list of encodings that are acceptable to the client. If you find the word gzip in a request's Accept-Encodings list, you can respond to that request by sending compressed content.

Returning compressed content is not difficult. In fact, your web or application server may include built-in support for compression and if so, all you have to do is turn it on. If not, it is pretty easy to implement your own compression filter. We'll tell you how to do it later in this section.

Now that we have covered the concepts behind caching and compression, let's take a look at these approaches in practice.

8.6.5 *Caching and compression in a Java web application*

Applying the techniques discussed in the previous section is relatively easy in a Java web application environment. To illustrate this, we will retrofit the example from section 8.4 to support client-side caching via HTTP conditional GET, proxy-caching by use of HTTP cache control headers, and server-side caching by using a simple LRU cache. Then, we'll tell you where to find a filter that lets you add support for compression.

Caching in a Java web application

DepotNewsfeedServletCached is a version of DepotNewsfeedServlet_(listing 8.2) that has been modified to support client-side, proxy, and server-side caching. Let's take close look at the code, shown in listing 8.5.

Listing 8.5   DepotNewsfeedServletCached.java

```java
package com.manning.blogapps.chapter08.web;
import java.io.*;
import java.io.StringWriter;
import java.util.Date;
import javax.servlet.*;
import javax.servlet.http.*;
import com.manning.blogapps.chapter08.*;
import com.manning.blogapps.chapter08.filedepot.*;

public class DepotNewsfeedServletCached extends HttpServlet {
    LRUCache cache = new LRUCache(5, 5400);                           ❶

    protected void doGet(
        HttpServletRequest request,  HttpServletResponse response)
        throws ServletException, IOException {

        ServletContext application = this.getServletContext();
        Depot depot = (Depot) application.getAttribute("depot");     ❷
        if (depot == null) {
            depot = new FileDepot(request.getRealPath("/depot"));
            application.setAttribute("depot", depot);
        }
        depot.update();

        Date sinceDate = new Date(
            request.getDateHeader("If-Modified-Since"));
        if (sinceDate != null) {                                     ❸
            if (depot.getLastUpdateDate().compareTo(sinceDate) <= 0) {
                response.setStatus(HttpServletResponse.SC_NOT_MODIFIED);
                response.flushBuffer();
                return;
            }
        }
        try {
        response.setContentType("application/rss+xml;charset=utf-8");  ⬅❹

            response.setDateHeader("Last-Modified",                  ❺
                depot.getLastUpdateDate().getTime());
            response.setHeader(                                      ❻
                "Cache-Control","max-age=5400, must-revalidate");
```

```
                String url = request.getRequestURL().toString();
                String depotUrl = url.substring(0, url.lastIndexOf("/"));
                if (cache.get(url) == null) {                                  ➐

                    String format = request.getParameter("format");           ➑
                    if (format == null) format = "rss_2.0";

                    StringWriter stringWriter = new StringWriter();            ➒
                    DepotNewsfeedWriter depotWriter =
                        new DepotNewsfeedWriter(depot);
                    depotWriter.write(stringWriter, depotUrl, format);
                                                                               ➓
                    cache.put(request.getRequestURL().toString(),
                        stringWriter.toString());
                }
                response.getWriter().write((String)cache.get(url));     ←⓫
            }
            catch (Exception ex) {
                String msg = "ERROR: generating newsfeed";
                log(msg, ex);
                response.sendError(
                    HttpServletResponse.SC_INTERNAL_SERVER_ERROR, msg);
            }
        }
    }
}
```

In the first block of code ❶, we declare the Servlet and create a cache to be used for server-side caching. Java application servers do not support a standard caching mechanism, so here we use a simple LRU cache. We configure the cache to hold up to five cache entries and expire entries from the cache after 1.5 hours, or 5400 seconds. You can find the source for this cache in the examples directory that accompanies this chapter in the package com.manning.blogapps.chapter08. Next, we override the doGet() method and manage the depot at application scope just as we did in the original example ❷.

To support client-side caches, we have added code to handle HTTP conditional GET ❸. We do this by checking for the HTTP If-Modified-Since header. If the header is included, we convert it to a date and compare it to the last modification date of our newsfeed data. If the newsfeed data has not been modified since the specified date, we return only an HTTP 304 Not-Modified response code, and that's the end of the processing. If not, we continue on, and next we set the content-type, just as we did in the original example ❹.

To help proxy and client caches determine the freshness of our content, we set the HTTP Last-Modified header to the date of the most recently uploaded file in the depot ❺. We tell proxy caches to cache our content for the same period that we cache the content in the server. We do this by setting the HTTP `Cache-Control` header to 5400 seconds ❻.

Finally, we are ready to generate the newsfeed. But wait; we don't need to generate the newsfeed if there is a fresh one available in the cache, so we first check the cache to see if there is an entry for the requested URL ❼. If the cache returns null, we need to generate a newsfeed, so we use the `DepotNewsfeedWriter` to do so. We get the newsfeed format parameter from the request, or use `rss_2.0` if it's not present ❽. Instead of writing the newsfeed directly to the response, we write to a string via a `java.util.StringWriter` ❾, and we put the string in the cache ❿. Once we have ensured that the newsfeed string is in the cache, we write it out to the response ⓫.

That takes care of caching—but what about compression?

Compression in a Java web application

As you may have noticed, the example code above does not do compression. The Java class libraries include support for compression in the package `java.util.zip`, and adding support for compression is fairly easy. But it is even easier to drop in a third-party compression filter—especially when that filter is open source.

You can find an open source compression filter in an article titled "Two Servlet Filters Every Web Application Should Have," by Jayson Falkner. Falkner provides source code for both a compression filter and a cache filter, along with details on how to use them in a Java web application. You'll find the article on the OnJava.com web site at http://www.onjava.com/pub/a/onjava/2003/11/19/filters.html. It's also possible that your web application server supports compression, and all you have to do is find the right configuration setting to turn it on.

Now, let's use the same techniques on our C# example.

8.6.6 Caching and compression in a C# Web application

Applying the efficiency techniques we've discussed in this section is also relatively easy in an ASP.NET environment. To illustrate this, we will retrofit the example from section 8.5 to support client-side caching via HTTP conditional GET, proxy caching by use of HTTP `Cache-Control` headers, and server-side caching by using ASP.NET's built-in cache.

Caching in a C# web application

This is the same `Page_Load` code we saw in section 8.4, but with the additions necessary to support the three forms of caching we have discussed. Let's take a look at the additions in listing 8.6.

Listing 8.6   depot-rss-cached.aspx.cs

```
private void Page_Load(object sender, System.EventArgs e) {

    IDepot depot = (IDepot)Application["depoy"];
    if (depot == null) {                                              ❶
        depot = new FileDepot(MapPath(@"depot"));
        Application["depot"] = depot;
    }

    if (Request.Headers["If-Modified-Since"] != null) {
        depot.update();
        DateTime since =  Convert.ToDateTime(
            Request.Headers["If-Modified-Since"]);
        if (depot.getLastUpdateTime() <= since) {                     ❷
            Response.StatusCode = 304;
            return;
        }
    }
    Response.AppendHeader("Last-Modified",                            ❸
        depot.getLastUpdateTime().ToShortTimeString());
    Response.AppendHeader("Cache-Control",
        "max-age=5400, must-revalidate");                            ❹

    Response.ContentType = "application/rss+xml";
    Response.ContentEncoding = Encoding.UTF8;                        ❺

    if (Cache[Request.Url.AbsolutePath] == null) {        ←❻

        MemoryStream ms = new MemoryStream();
        XmlTextWriter writer =                                       ❼
            new XmlTextWriter(ms, new System.Text.UTF8Encoding());

        DepotRSSWriter rssWriter = new DepotRSSWriter(depot);
        rssWriter.write(writer, "http://"                           ❽
          + Request.ServerVariables["SERVER_NAME"]
          + Request.ApplicationPath + "/");
        writer.Close();

        Cache.Insert(Request.Url.AbsolutePath, ms, null,
            DateTime.Now.AddHours(1.5), TimeSpan.Zero);             ❾
    }

    MemoryStream cachedms =
        (MemoryStream)Cache[Request.Url.AbsolutePath];             ❿
    Response.BinaryWrite(cachedms.ToArray());
}
```

In the first block of code, we get the file depot from application scope or create a new one ❶. Next, we check for the HTTP If-Modified-Since header. If the header is included, we convert it to a date and compare it to the last modification date of our newsfeed data. If the newsfeed data has not been modified since the specified date, we return only an HTTP 304 Not-Modified response code ❷.

Before we write out the newsfeed, we need to set some headers. We set the Last-Modified header to enable proxy and client caches to intelligently cache our content ❸. We set the Cache-Control header to instruct proxy caches to cache our content for an hour and a half (5400 seconds) ❹. We also set the proper content-type and encoding ❺.

Before we generate a new copy of the newsfeed, we check the ASP.NET cache to see if one has already been generated ❻. We use the newsfeed URL as the cache key. If the cache does not contain the newsfeed, we need to generate one.

Instead of writing the newsfeed directly to the response, we write the newsfeed to a MemoryStream object ❼. We write out the newsfeed using the DepotRSSWriter we developed earlier ❽. We store the MemoryStream object in the ASP.NET cache with a timeout of an hour and a half ❾, the same cache timeout we used in the cache control headers. Finally, once we have a copy of our newsfeed in the cache, we write it out to the response and we're done ❿.

Again, we left out compression. Let's discuss why.

Compression in a C# web application

The example code above does not include support for compression, but compression is simple to add. The easiest way to support compression in your ASP.NET-based newsfeeds is to use the compression that is built into IIS. Refer to the Windows Server 2003 documentation Utilizing HTTP Compression for instructions on IIS compression.

If IIS does not give you enough control over the compression process, you might consider implementing compression yourself directly in ASP.NET. In ASP.NET 2.0, you can use the new .NET Framework 2.0 compression classes in the namespace System.Compression to support ZIP and GZIP compression. You can find out how to use ASP.NET 2.0 compression in the article "Compression Support in ASP.Net 2.0" by Bart De Smet. You'll find the article on the Microsoft web site at http://www.microsoft.com/belux/nl/msdn/community/columns/desmet/compression.mspx.

We've covered a lot of ground in this chapter. Let's sum up what we have learned.

8.7 *Summary*

- Dynamic newsfeeds are produced by application code running on a web server, such as an ASP.NET page, a JSP, a Servlet, or an old-fashioned CGI script.

- Static newsfeeds are produced by application code running separately from a web server and then uploaded or copied to a web server to be served as static files.

- We recommend that you generate newsfeeds in Atom format, but in some cases you may also wish to generate RSS 2.0 format, because it is still the most widely supported format.

- Make sure your newsfeeds are valid XML and are valid according to the rules of the newsfeed format you have chosen by using Feed Validator.

- You can generate newsfeeds using a variety of technologies and techniques, including XML tools, JSP, ASP.NET, and newsfeed libraries.

- For most developers, the best approach to generating newsfeeds is to use a newsfeed library, such as ROME for Java.

- Take advantage of client-side caches, proxy caches, server-side caches, and compression to reduce computer, network, and bandwidth usage.

Publishing with XML-RPC based APIs

By using the XML-RPC based Blogger and MetaWeblog APIs, your applications will have the power to post and edit blogs on almost any blog server.

If you need to create a program that publishes to a blog, as Rangu did in chapter 1, you can do the job with XML-RPC based blogging APIs. In this chapter, we'll show you how your programs can connect to a remote blog server, create, retrieve, edit, and delete blog entries, and post multimedia files, such as images and audio clips.

We'll start by giving you the XML-RPC background you need to understand the blogging APIs. Next, we'll introduce the complementary Blogger and Meta-Weblog APIs, which together form the de facto standard among the dozens of XML-RPC based blogging APIs. We'll wrap up the chapter by building a Meta-Weblog and Blogger API-based blog client library you can use to add blogging capabilities to your own programs. In this chapter, we'll be coding in C#, but you can see a Java version of the blog client library in the online examples that accompany chapter 10 (in the directory java/ch10).

In the next chapter, we'll show you how to do the same things covered in this chapter but with Atom, a new web services protocol destined to replace the old XML-RPC based APIs. We'll implement the same blog client library interfaces so that programs that use our library will work with either the XML-RPC based APIs or Atom.

9.1 Why XML-RPC?

XML-RPC is a web services protocol, a way to make remote procedure calls (RPCs) by sending and receiving XML documents over the Web. Nowadays, the standard web services protocol is SOAP, and for most developers SOAP is synonymous with web services. But XML-RPC came first, and the popular MetaWeblog, Blogger, and other blog and wiki APIs were invented during its short reign. To understand them, you have to understand XML-RPC.

Fortunately for us, XML-RPC is relatively simple to understand. The specification, which you can find on the XML-RPC web site at http://xml-rpc.com, is only about two pages long. Let's take a look at how an XML-RPC procedure—or *method*—is called.

9.1.1 Making a method call

With XML-RPC, you call a method on a blog server by posting a specially formatted XML document to the blog server's XML-RPC endpoint URL. The XML document contains the method name and the values of the method's required parameters. For example, to create a new post with the Blogger API, you use the `blogger.newPost` method, which takes the following parameters:

- *appkey*—Your Blogger.com developer application key (no longer required by Blogger.com, so you can pass 0123456789ABCDEF)
- *blogid*—The ID of the blog you are posting to
- *username*—Your username
- *password*—Your password
- *publish*—Publish flag; when true, publishes the post immediately

To call the blogger.newPost method, you would use an HTTP POST to send the XML document shown in listing 9.1 to the destination blog server.

Listing 9.1 XML document sent by a blogger.newPost method call

```
<?xml version="1.0"?>
<methodCall>
    <methodName>blogger.newPost</methodName>
    <params>
        <param>
         <value><string>0123456789ABCDEF</string></value>    ◁┘  Application
        </param>                                                  key
        <param>
            <value><string>784222</string></value>    ◁┘  Blog ID
        </param>
        <param>
            <value><string>rangu</string></value>    ◁┘  Username
        </param>
        <param>
            <value><string>Zoot43star!</string></value>    ◁┘  Password
        </param>
        <param>                                                    Content of
            <value><string>This is the content<string></value>    ◁┘  blog post
        </param>
        <param>                                              Publish
            <value><boolean>false</boolean></value>    ◁┘  flag
        </param>
    </params>
</methodCall>
```

As you can tell just by reading the XML element names, listing 9.1 represents a method call to a method named blogger.newPost, with a list of typed parameters. Parameter names are not included in the list, so parameter ordering is important. The only types in listing 9.1 are string and boolean, but there are more. Let's discuss how XML-RPC encodes type information.

XML-RPC data types

XML-RPC supports primitives `<string>`, `<int>`, `<boolean>`, and `<double>`. It also supports time values in ISO 8601 format as `<dateTime.iso8601>` and Base64 encoded data as `<base64>`. Structures and arrays are also supported. Structures are represented as a list of members, each with a name and a value, which could be any XML-RPC type. Here's an example of a structure with two members, integer parameters `lowerBound` and `upperBound`:

```
<struct>
   <member>
      <name>lowerBound</name>
      <value><int>18</int></value>
   </member>
   <member>
      <name>upperBound</name>
      <value><int>139</int></value>
   </member>
</struct>
```

Arrays are represented as a list of values, which can be of any type. Again from the specification, here's an example of an array with an integer, string, and boolean values:

```
<array>
   <data>
      <value><int>12</int></value>
      <value><string>Egypt</string></value>
      <value><boolean>0</boolean></value>
      <value><int>-31</int></value>
   </data>
</array>
```

As you can see, it's not difficult to make an XML-RPC method call, but working at the XML and HTTP level is tedious. By using an XML-RPC client library, you can work at a higher level.

XML-RPC client libraries

As we learned in chapter 2, using an XML-RPC client library can make calling XML-RPC methods almost as easy as making a normal method call. In listing 2.1, we showed how to call the `metaWeblog.newPost` method from Java using the Apache XML-RPC client library. In listing 2.2, we showed how to do the same thing with the Cook Computing XML-RPC.NET library. In this chapter, we'll use those libraries again, but this time we'll be developing a complete blog client library.

Now that we have the necessary XML-RPC background, let's look at the most widely supported blogging APIs.

9.2 *The Blogger API*

The Blogger API was created in August 2001 by Pyra Labs—the company behind Blogger.com—to allow developers to write programs that blog. Made up of only eight methods, the Blogger API is simple and easy to use, but it has some serious shortcomings. The Blogger API does not support the metadata needed for most blogging applications. For example, when you create a blog entry, you can specify only the text of the entry and the publish flag, which determines whether the entry is to be published on the blog or stored as a private draft. You can't specify a title, publication date, category, or any other metadata. That is simply too limiting for most applications.

Table 9.1   The eight methods of the Blogger API

Method name	Parameters and description
`blogger.newPost`	`string appkey, string blogid, string username, string password, string content, boolean publish` Create a new blog post in the blog specified by `blogid` and content specified by `content`. Some servers interpret `publish=true` to mean publish publicly and `publish=false` to mean save as a private draft. Others interpret it to mean simply publish immediately. Returns a string, which is the `postid` of the new post.
`blogger.editPost`	`string appkey, string postid, string username, string password, string content, boolean publish` Update the blog post specified by `postid` with new content.
`blogger.deletePost`	`string appkey, string postid, string username, string password, boolean publish` Delete the blog post specified by `blogid` and optionally republish the blog.
`blogger.getRecentPosts`	`string appkey, string blogid, string username, string password, int numPosts` Get the most recent blog posts as an array of structures, each having members `dateCreated, userid, postid,` and `content`. Maximum number of posts to return is `numPosts`.
`blogger.getUsersBlogs`	`string appkey, string username, string password` Get the specified user's blogs as an array of structures, each having members `url, blogid,` and `blogName`.
`blogger.getUserInfo`	`string appkey, string username, string password` Get the specified user's information as a structure with members `nickname, userid, url, email, lastname, firstname`.

continued on next page

Table 9.1 The eight methods of the Blogger API *(continued)*

Method name	Parameters and description
`blogger.getTemplate`	`string appkey, string blogid, string username, string password, string type` Get blog's template of the specified type.
`blogger.setTemplate`	`string appkey, string blogid, string username, string password, string template, string type` Change the blog's template of the specified type. The format of blog templates varies depending on the blog server.

Note that each method requires at least three parameters: `appkey`, `username`, and `password`. The `appkey` is an application key. Blogger.com once required you to register for a unique application key for each of your applications that use the Blogger API, but it has eliminated that requirement. Now, you can pass the string "0123456789ABCDEF", and your code will work with just about any server that supports the Blogger API. The `username` and `password` parameters identify the user making the method call. Note another shortcoming here: passwords are sent as plain text with no encryption. Now, let's move on to the more capable MetaWeblog API.

9.3 *The MetaWeblog API*

The MetaWeblog API was created in March 2002 by Userland Software to address the limitations of the Blogger API. The name reflects one of the design goals of the API: to allow metadata for each blog post. These days, most blog services, servers, and clients support both MetaWeblog and Blogger APIs, with the notable exception of Blogger.com, which supports only the Blogger API. Recently, Blogger.com chose instead to support the new Atom protocol, which we will cover in the next chapter.

9.3.1 *The same metadata as RSS*

The MetaWeblog API is far from perfect, but it is preferable to the Blogger API because it supports a more complete set of metadata for each blog post. It is designed to allow the same blog post metadata found in RSS. In the MetaWeblog API, a blog post is represented by an XML-RPC struct with members whose names correspond to those of the XML elements allowed in an RSS <item>. As in RSS, all of these members are optional.

Unfortunately, not all of the `post` struct's members correspond to RSS elements. For example, instead of using the name `pubDate` for the publication date, the MetaWeblog API uses `dateCreated`. Another difference is that RSS uses the RFC-822 date format, while the MetaWeblog API uses ISO-8601. But the date issue will generally not become a problem for you if you use an XML-RPC client library, as we do in this chapter.

9.3.2 *Six new methods that complement the Blogger API*

Table 9.2 lists the six methods of the MetaWeblog API. Note that the MetaWeblog API is not a complete blogging API. It's meant to complement, not replace, the Blogger API. Most blog applications will need to use a mix of both APIs, as we do in the blog client library developed later in this chapter.

Table 9.2 The six methods of the MetaWeblog API

Method name	Parameters and description
`metaWeblog.newPost`	`string blogid, string username, string password, struct post, boolean publish` Creates a new post in the blog specified by `blogid` using the data from the `post` structure. The names in the `post` structure correspond to the names of the XML elements in an RSS `<item>`. Returns the string ID of the newly created post.
`metaWeblog.editPost`	`string postid, string username, string password, struct post, boolean publish` Updates the post specified by `postid` using data from the `post` structure.
`metaWeblog.getPost`	`string postid, string username, string password` Returns the post specified by `postid` as a `post` structure.
`metaWeblog.getRecentPosts`	`string blogid, string username, string password, int numPosts` Returns the most recent blog post as an array of `post` structures. Maximum number of posts to return is `numPosts`.
`metaWeblog.newMediaObject`	`string blogid, string username, string password, struct object` Uploads an image, video, or audio file to the blog specified by `blogid`. The file is specified by the `object` structure with fields `name`, `type`, and `bits`. The `bits` field is the file data encoded as Base64 data. Returns a string, which is the URL of the uploaded file.
`MetaWeblog.getCategories`	`string blogid, string username, string password` Returns the categories available in the blog specified by `blogid` as a structure of structures, each structure representing a category and having members `description`, `htmlUrl`, and `rssUrl`.

Now that we've covered the APIs we need, let's see how they can be used together to implement an XML-RPC based blog client library.

9.4 *Building a blog client with C# and XML-RPC*

The best way to learn a new programming technology is by using it to build something useful, and we're going to build something very useful: a complete XML-RPC based blog client library you can use to add blogging capabilities to any of your programs. We'll define our blog client library as a set of interfaces that allow multiple implementations.

In this chapter, we'll implement the library using a combination of the Blogger and MetaWeblog APIs. In the next chapter, we'll implement it using the new Atom protocol. Comparing the two implementations will help you understand the differences between the XML-RPC APIs and Atom.

In this section, we'll develop our blog client library using C# and XML-RPC.NET. In chapter 10, we'll expand the blog client interfaces to support the Atom protocol and provide Java implementations of those interfaces for both Atom protocol and the MetaWeblog API. On the book's web site, you can find those Java implementations, which use Apache XML-RPC.

We start by defining the interfaces for our library.

9.4.1 *Why a blog client library?*

To understand the usefulness of developing a blog client library, let's put ourselves in Rangu's shoes. After Rangu adds blogging capabilities to his build scripts, other developers in his group want to do the same thing. Otto asks Rangu to do a chalk talk at lunchtime to explain blogging APIs. Rangu prepares a short presentation to explain MetaWeblog API, Blogger API, and Atom to a group of junior programmers who all want to learn how to add blogging capabilities to their programs.

During his presentation, he explains the relationship between the Blogger API and MetaWeblog API, how XML-RPC encodes method calls and data types, and how Atom uses HTTP verbs to post, put, and get XML.

His audience is befuddled and bewildered by the details. They don't understand why things have to be so complicated. One programmer asks, "Why can't I just create a blog object and call its post method?" Another, "Can I make my program blog to both XML-RPC based and Atom-based blog servers?"

Rangu realizes that these programmers are about to run into an ugly learning curve—two ugly learning curves, if you count Atom.

After the presentation, Rangu and Otto decide that the best way to help developers get started with blog application development is to develop an easy-to-use blog client library that abstracts away both the complexities of and the differences between the XML-RPC based APIs and the Atom protocol.

So there are really two reasons we need a blog client library: 1) to make it easy to write a blog application by hiding the complexities of the blogging APIs and 2) to make it possible for our blog applications to work with either the old XML-RPC based APIs or the new Atom protocol.

How easy will we make it? Once we're finished, it will be possible to post a simple blog entry with title and content to a blog server via XML-RPC using just the following code:

```
IBlogConnection blogConn =
    new MetaWeblogConnection(target, username, password, appkey);
IBlog blog = blogConn.GetBlog(blogid);
IBlogEntry entry = blog.CreateEntry();
entry.Title = title;
entry.Content = description;
string result = blog.SaveEntry(entry, true);
```

And once we have an Atom version of the library, all we'll have to do is change the first line to the line shown below, which instantiates an Atom client rather than the MetaWeblog API we were using before:

```
IBlogConnection blogConnection =
    new AtomConnection(url, username, password);
```

Now that we know why we need a blog client library, let's build it. We will start with the most important part: the interfaces.

9.4.2 *Three blog client library interfaces*

Our library will enable programs to perform the basic operations of blogging: creating and editing blog entries. We'll support the following use cases:

- Query a blog server for a list of blogs that the user is allowed to edit
- Create a new blog entry in a blog
- Create a new resource in a blog by uploading a file
- Get a blog entry by ID from a blog
- Get the most recent X number of blog entries from a blog
- Get a list of categories available in a blog
- Update a blog entry from a blog
- Delete a blog entry from a blog

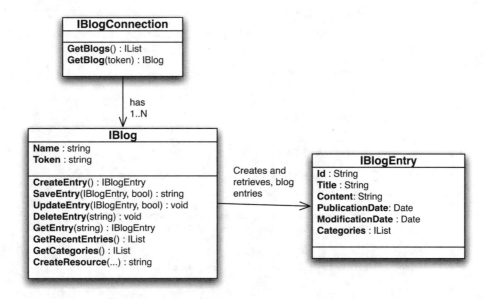

Figure 9.1 **Diagram of blog client interfaces**

To support those use cases, we'll need three interfaces. First, we need an interface to represent a connection to a blog server. We'll call that interface IBlogConnection. To establish a blog connection, you'll need a username, password, and the URL of the blog server's XML-RPC endpoint. Once you've established a blog connection, you can access all of the blogs you have permission to edit. We'll use a second interface called IBlog to represent each of those blogs. Third, we'll need an interface to represent blog entries within each blog, which we'll call IBlogEntry. Figure 9.1 shows our three interfaces and the relationships between them.

We've discussed and diagrammed our blog client interfaces; now let's get down to business and put them down in the form of C# interfaces. Listing 9.2 is the BlogClient.cs file, which defines these three interfaces.

> **Listing 9.2   C# blog client interfaces in IBlogSite.cs**

```
using System;
using System.Collections;
using System.Xml;
using System.IO;

namespace BlogApps_Chapter09 {
```

```csharp
public interface IBlogConnection {

    /** Returns collection of Blogs available from this connection */
    IList GetBlogs();

    /** Get Blog by token */
    IBlog GetBlog(String token);
}

public interface IBlog {

    string Id { get; set; }
    string Name { get; set; }

    /** Create new and empty Entry */
    IBlogEntry CreateEntry();

    /** Create a new Entry, returns ID of saved Entry */
    String SaveEntry(IBlogEntry entry, bool publish);

    /** Update an existing Entry */
    void UpdateEntry(IBlogEntry entry, bool publish);

    /** Delete Entry by id */
    void DeleteEntry(String id);

    /** Get a single Entry by id */
    IBlogEntry GetEntry(String id);

    /** Returns most recent entries as Entry objects */
    IList GetRecentEntries(int max);

    /** Returns list of available categories names as Strings */
    IList GetCategories();

    /** Create a new resource on the server and return its URL */
    String CreateResource(String name, String contentType, FileInfo file);
}

/** A single publishing entry */
public interface IBlogEntry {
    string      Id { get; set; }
    string      Title { get; set; }
    string      Content { get; set; }
    DateTime    PublicationDate { get; set; }
    DateTime    ModificationDate { get; set; }
    IList       Categories { get; set; }
    IDictionary Attributes { get; set; }
}
}
```

Now that we've defined our C# interfaces, we're ready to implement them.

9.4.3 *Implementing the blog client library in C#*

To implement our blog client library, we'll use Cook Computing's XML-RPC.NET, the same XML-RPC client library we used in chapter 2.

XML-RPC.NET makes calling XML-RPC methods on a remote server just as easy as calling normal C# methods. Here's how it works. To call methods in an XML-RPC based API, you must first create a C# interface that defines the methods you need to call. The C# method names and parameters must match the method names in the XML-RPC API. At runtime, XML-RPC.NET reads your interface and creates a dynamic proxy object that implements it. You call this dynamic proxy object as you would any C# object and when you do, the object translates your call into XML-RPC and calls the remote server.

We'll start by defining an interface for the Blogger API.

Blogger API proxy interface

To call the Blogger API via XML-RPC.NET, we must first create a C# interface that defines the Blogger API methods we need. Listing 9.3 shows our Blogger API interface.

Listing 9.3   C# IBlogger interface in BloggerProxy.cs

```
using System;
using System.Collections;
using System.Xml;
using System.IO;
using CookComputing.XmlRpc;

namespace BlogApps_Chapter09 {

    public interface IBlogger {          ←❶

      [XmlRpcMethod("blogger.getUsersBlogs")]     ←❷
      IList blogger_getUsersBlogs(
         string appkey, string username, string password);
          [XmlRpcMethod("blogger.deletePost")]    ←❸
          bool blogger_deletePost(
             string appkey, string postid,
             string username, string password, bool publish);
    }
}
```

Because we are using the Blogger API with the MetaWeblog API, when we define the IBlogger interface ❶, we need to include only the blogger.getUserBlogs ❷ and `blogger.deletePost` ❸ methods. Note that XML-RPC.NET maps XML-RPC arrays to C# lists, and structs to C# dictionaries, so `blogger_getUserBlogs()` returns a list of dictionaries, one for each user blog.

Also note that the mapping between our C# methods and the XML-RPC methods is indicated by a C# attribute named `XmlRpcMethod`, which is provided by XML-RPC.NET.

Let's move on to the MetaWeblog API interface.

MetaWeblog API proxy interface

Just as we did for the Blogger API, we need to define a C# interface for the MetaWeblog API. We'll need to use all six methods in the API, so all six must be included in the C# interface. Listing 9.4 shows the code for the interface.

> **Listing 9.4   C# IMetaWeblog interface in MetaWeblogProxy.cs**

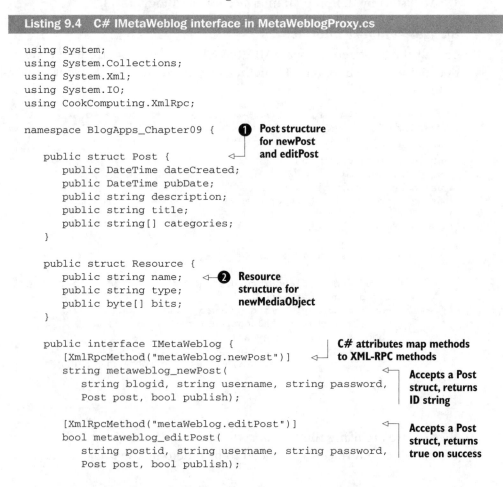

```
using System;
using System.Collections;
using System.Xml;
using System.IO;
using CookComputing.XmlRpc;

namespace BlogApps_Chapter09 {                    ❶ Post structure
                                                     for newPost
    public struct Post {                             and editPost
        public DateTime dateCreated;
        public DateTime pubDate;
        public string description;
        public string title;
        public string[] categories;
    }

    public struct Resource {
        public string name;           ❷ Resource
        public string type;             structure for
        public byte[] bits;             newMediaObject
    }

    public interface IMetaWeblog {                 C# attributes map methods
        [XmlRpcMethod("metaWeblog.newPost")]       to XML-RPC methods
        string metaweblog_newPost(
            string blogid, string username, string password,   Accepts a Post
            Post post, bool publish);                          struct, returns
                                                               ID string

        [XmlRpcMethod("metaWeblog.editPost")]
        bool metaweblog_editPost(                              Accepts a Post
            string postid, string username, string password,  struct, returns
            Post post, bool publish);                         true on success
```

```
[XmlRpcMethod("metaWeblog.getPost")]        ◄┐  Returns post as
IDictionary metaweblog_getPost(                 a dictionary
    string postid, string username, string password);

[XmlRpcMethod("metaWeblog.getRecentPosts")]   ◄┐  Returns list of posts,
IList metaweblog_getRecentPosts(                  each a dictionary
    string blogid, string username, string password, int maxEntries);

[XmlRpcMethod("metaWeblog.getCategories")]   ◄┐  Returns a dictionary
IDictionary metaweblog_getCategories(            of dictionaries
    string blogid, string username, string password);

[XmlRpcMethod("metaWeblog.newMediaObject")]   ◄┐  Returns a dictionary
IDictionary metaweblog_newMediaObject(            with a "url" member
    string blogid, string username, string password, Resource resource);
    }
}
```

The `IMetaWeblog` interface is a little more complicated because it includes some XML-RPC structs. Each one must be passed as a C# struct, so before we define the `IMetaWeblog` interface itself, we define the C# structs we'll need: `Post` ❶ and `Resource` ❷.

Apart from that, the interface works in the same way as the `IBlogger` interface. The best way to see how these interfaces work is to see them in action, so let's move ahead with our blog client implementation.

Blog client implementation in C#

The first part of our blog client library is the entry point, the `IBlogConnection` interface. Let's dive right into the code in listing 9.5.

Listing 9.5   C# MetaWeblogConnection class in MetaWeblogConnection.cs

```
using System;
using System.Collections;
using System.Xml;
using System.IO;
using CookComputing.XmlRpc;

namespace BlogApps_Chapter09 {

    public class MetaWeblogConnection : IBlogConnection {   ◄─❶

        private IDictionary blogMap;   ◄─❷

        public MetaWeblogConnection(   ◄─❸
            string url, string userName, string password, string appkey) {
```

```
                    IBlogger bloggerProxy = (IBlogger)      ◁──❹
                       XmlRpcProxyGen.Create(typeof(IBlogger));
                    XmlRpcClientProtocol bloggerProtocol =
                       (XmlRpcClientProtocol)bloggerProxy;
                    bloggerProtocol.Url = url;

                    blogMap = new Hashtable();
                    IList blogs = bloggerProxy.blogger_getUsersBlogs(   ◁──❺
                                  appkey, userName, password);
                    foreach (IDictionary blog in blogs) {    ◁──❻
                       blogMap.Add(blog["blogid"],
                          new MetaWeblogBlog(
                             (string)blog["blogid"],
                             (string)blog["blogName"],
                             url, userName, password, appkey));
                    }
                 }
                 public IList GetBlogs() {    ◁──❼
                    return new ArrayList(blogMap.Values);
                 }
                 public IBlog GetBlog(String token) {    ◁──❽
                    return (IBlog)blogMap[token];
                 }
              }
           }
```

The class `MetaWeblogConnection` ❶ is our MetaWeblog API-based implementation of the IBlogConnection interface. The only field in the class is `blogMap` ❷, which holds the blogs available from the connection.

To create a `MetaWeblogConnection`, you call the constructor ❸ and pass in the required connection parameters `url`, `userName`, `password`, and `appkey`. In the constructor, we create a proxy interface ❹ so that we can call the Blogger API `getUsersBlogs()` method ❺ to get the list of available blogs. We loop through the list of blogs ❻, create a `MetaWeblogBlog` object for each and add that to the `blogMaps` dictionary using blog IDs as keys.

Once you've created a `MetaWeblogConnection` object, you can access the whole list of blogs by calling `getBlogs()` ❼ or get any one specific blog by passing its blog ID to the `GetBlog()` method ❽.

Blog implementation in C#

While the blog connection represents a single-user connection to a blog server, the blog object represents a single-user session with a specific blog within a blog server. The blog is the primary interface that programmers will use to create, retrieve, update, and delete blog entries.

Our C# and XML-RPC implementation of the `IBlog` interface is the class `MetaWeblogBlog`, shown in listing 9.6. It's a lengthy class made up of eight public methods, but most of them simply call a corresponding method in the MetaWeblog or Blogger API. Let's take a close look at the source and discuss the finer points.

Listing 9.6   MetaWeblogBlog class in MetaWeblogBlog.cs

```csharp
using System;
using System.Collections;
using System.Xml;
using System.IO;
using CookComputing.XmlRpc;

namespace BlogApps_Chapter09 {

   public class MetaWeblogBlog : IBlog {

      private string name;
      private string id;
      private string userName;
      private string password;
      private string blogId;
      private string appkey = null;

      private IMetaWeblog metaWeblogProxy = null;
      private IMetaWeblog getMetaWeblog() {return metaWeblogProxy;}

      private IBlogger bloggerProxy = null;
      private IBlogger getBlogger() {return bloggerProxy;}

      public MetaWeblogBlog(string blogId, string name,      ◄─❶
         string url, string userName, string password, string appkey) {
         this.userName = userName;
         this.password = password;
         this.blogId = blogId;
         this.appkey = appkey;

         metaWeblogProxy = (IMetaWeblog)              ◄─❷
            XmlRpcProxyGen.Create(typeof(IMetaWeblog));
         XmlRpcClientProtocol metaWeblogProtocol =
            (XmlRpcClientProtocol)metaWeblogProxy;
         metaWeblogProtocol.Url = url;

         bloggerProxy = (IBlogger)              ◄─❸
            XmlRpcProxyGen.Create(typeof(IBlogger));
         XmlRpcClientProtocol bloggerProtocol =
            (XmlRpcClientProtocol)bloggerProxy;
         bloggerProtocol.Url = url;
      }
```

```
public string Id {
    get { return id; }
    set { id = value; }
}

public string Name {
    get { return name; }
    set { name = value; }
}

public IBlogEntry CreateEntry() {        ◄─❹
    return new MetaWeblogEntry();
}

public string SaveEntry(IBlogEntry entry, bool publish) {    ◄─❺
    string id = getMetaWeblog().metaweblog_newPost(
      blogId, userName, password, createPostStructure(entry), publish);
    entry.Id = id;
    return id;
}

public void UpdateEntry(IBlogEntry entry, bool publish) {    ◄─❻
    getMetaWeblog().metaweblog_editPost(
        entry.Id, userName, password,
        createPostStructure(entry), publish);
}

public void DeleteEntry(String id) {    ◄─❼
    getBlogger().blogger_deletePost(
        appkey, id, userName, password, true);
}

public IBlogEntry GetEntry(String id) {    ◄─❽
    IDictionary result =
        (IDictionary)getMetaWeblog().metaweblog_getPost(
        id, userName, password);
    return new MetaWeblogEntry(result);
}

public IList GetRecentEntries(int maxEntries) {    ◄─❾
    IList result = (IList)
        getMetaWeblog().metaweblog_getRecentPosts(
        blogId, userName, password, maxEntries);
    ArrayList list = new ArrayList();
    foreach (IDictionary entryHash in result) {
        list.Add(new MetaWeblogEntry(entryHash));
    }
    return list;
}

public IList GetCategories() {    ◄─❿
    IDictionary result = getMetaWeblog().metaweblog_getCategories(
```

```
                blogId, userName, password);
            return new ArrayList(result.Keys);
        }
        public String CreateResource(        ←⓫
            String name, String contentType, FileInfo file) {
            FileStream fs = new FileStream(file.FullName, FileMode.Open);
            int len = Convert.ToInt32(file.Length);
            byte[] bits = new byte[len];
            fs.Read(bits, 0, len);
            fs.Close();

            Resource resource = new Resource();
            resource.name = name;
            resource.type = contentType;
            resource.bits = bits;
            IDictionary result =
                getMetaWeblog().metaweblog_newMediaObject(    ←⓬
                blogId, userName, password, resource);
            return (string)result["url"];
        }

        private Post createPostStructure(IBlogEntry entry) {
            Post post = new Post();        ←⓭
            post.title = entry.Title;
            post.pubDate = entry.PublicationDate;
            post.dateCreated = entry.PublicationDate;
            post.description = entry.Content;
            string[] cats = new string[0];
            if (entry.Categories != null) {
                cats = new string[entry.Categories.Count];
                for (int i=0; i< entry.Categories.Count; i++) {    ←⓮
                    cats[i] = (string)entry.Categories[i];
                }
            }
            post.categories = cats;
            return post;
        }
    }
}
```

Let's start at the beginning of MetaWeblogBlog with the constructor ❶. Note that you won't construct one of these objects directly because the MetaWeblogConnection class will do that for you. In the constructor, after we've stashed away the parameters, we construct the IMetaWeblog ❷ and IBlogger ❸ proxies we'll need to call.

Next, we have simple methods for creating ❹, saving ❺, updating ❻, and deleting ❼ blog entries. The CreateEntry() method constructs and returns a blog entry object. The SaveEntry(), UpdateEntry(), and DeleteEntry() methods all call the corresponding XML-RPC methods. Note that SaveEntry() and UpdateEntry() both use a private helper method, createPostStructure(), to convert the passed-in IBlogEntry object to a post structure suitable for XML-RPC.

The methods for getting blog entries both return MetaWeblogEntry objects, which implement IBlogEntry and can be constructed from a post struct in dictionary form. The GetEntry() ❽ method returns a single one and GetRecentEntries() ❾ returns a list.

The GetCategories() method ❿ calls the corresponding XML-RPC method and then iterates though the resulting dictionary of dictionaries to build and return a list of category name strings.

The CreateResource() method, which uploads a file to the blog, is a little more involved. It reads the file to be uploaded into an array of bytes ⓫, puts that array and the other parameters into a Resource struct, and calls the XML-RPC metaWeblog.newMediaObject method ⓬, which returns the URL of the uploaded resource.

Finally, we have the private CreatePostStructure() method, which we use in both the SaveEntry() and UpdateEntry() methods to convert our IBlogEntry representation to a post struct suitable for the MetaWeblog API. This is mostly a simple matter of copying fields ⓭, but we also have to convert the category list into an array of strings ⓮.

Now that we've got a blog client library, let's put it to use.

9.5 *Using the blog client library*

Using our new blog client library is easy. We've already seen one example in section 9.4.1. If you'd like to see some more extensive examples, take a look at the online ones that accompany the book. First, look at the code for this chapter, which you can find in the directory csharp/ch09. That directory contains a Microsoft Visual Studio solution, which in turn contains three projects. The BlogClient project contains the code for the library itself. The BlogPoster2 project contains a version of the chapter 2 BlogPoster program, rewritten using our new client library. And the BlogClientUI project is a simple GUI client that uses the library.

If you use Visual Studio to open and build the ch09 solution, you'll be able to run the BlogClientUI. But before you do, you should edit the file csharp/ch09/BlogClientUI/App.config to set the connection parameters for your blog server, just as you did with the chapter 2 example. Once you've done that, you

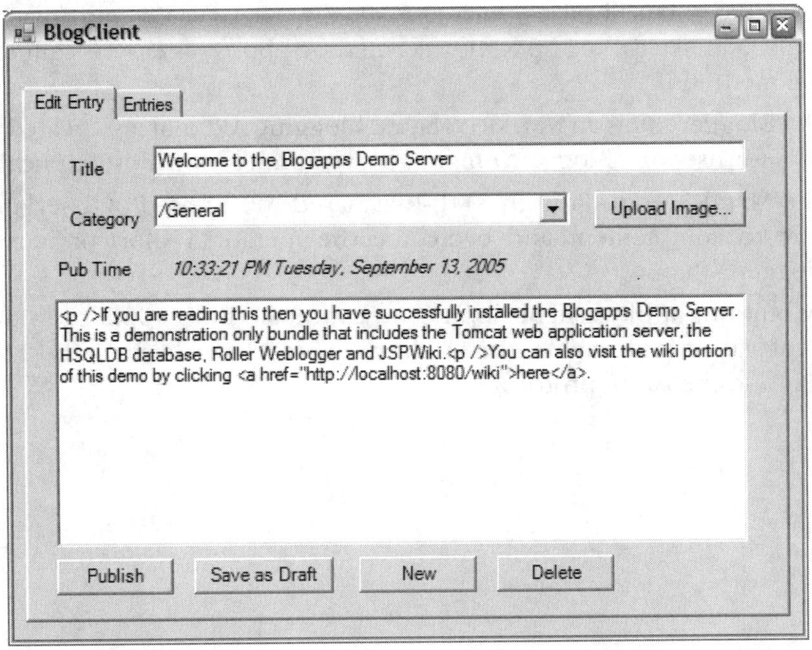

Figure 9.2 The BlogClientUI in action

can run BlogClientUI via the Visual Studio debugger. Figure 9.2 shows the program in action.

There are a number of other blog client examples in the book. We use the blog client library in the example blog apps in part II. Chapters 13 and 14 use the C# version of the library, and chapters 16 and 17 use the Java version (which you can find in chapter 10).

That brings us to the end of our expedition into the world of XML-RPC based blog APIs. Let's summarize what we have learned and then move on to the Atom protocol.

9.6 *Summary*

- If you need to create a program that can blog, you can use either XML-RPC based APIs, such as the Blogger and MetaWeblog API, or you can use the new Atom protocol.

- XML-RPC is a web services protocol that enables you to call remote servers by sending and receiving XML documents over the Web.

- XML-RPC client libraries, such as XML-RPC.NET for C# and Apache XML for Java, make calling an XML-RPC method almost as easy as calling a normal method.

- The Blogger API is an XML-RPC based blogging API that was created by Pyra Labs for use with Blogger.com, but it's too limited for most applications.

- The MetaWeblog API is an XML-RPC based API created by Userland Software to complement and overcome the metadata shortcomings of the Blogger API.

- By building a blog client library, we can make blog application development easier and enable our applications to target both XML-RPC based APIs and the Atom protocol.

Publishing with Atom

Learn how to publish and manage blog entries and file uploads using the new IETF standard Atom publishing protocol.

10

If you've read this far, you already know how to write programs that publish to a blog by using XML-RPC based APIs. Those APIs work for most blog servers today. But moving forward, blog, wiki, and web-publishing systems are adopting the new Atom publishing protocol, which is based on the Atom publishing format. In this chapter, you'll learn why. You'll also learn how to use the Atom protocol, which can do everything the XML-RPC based APIs can and more.

We'll start by describing in detail how Atom works in terms that all web developers should be able to understand, no matter what programming language they use. We'll finish by developing a complete Atom client library for Java that implements the same blog client library interfaces we designed in chapter 9, thus enabling our blog applications to work with both Atom and XML-RPC based servers.

10.1 Why Atom?

Atom was born in 2003 when a group of influential bloggers, blog software developers, and XML experts got together to solve the problems in publishing protocols and newsfeed formats. The Blogger and MetaWeblog API specifications were developed informally, and although they are simple and easy to implement, they are too limited and loosely defined. These problems have led to numerous incompatible server implementations and a handful of server-specific extension APIs, creating, difficulties for blog application developers. The situation is similar to that of the RSS newsfeed formats, where loosely defined standards and political infighting have led to a proliferation of incompatible formats. Atom was created to solve these problems.

The Atom group decided that the best course of action was to start fresh and to design the all-new Atom format and Atom API. In 2004, the group joined with the prestigious Internet Engineering Task Force (IETF) and XML co-inventor Tim Bray to put Atom through the rigorous IETF standards process. Finally, in spring 2005, Atom publishing format became an official IETF standard. The Atom API, now known as the Atom publishing protocol, is expected to follow and become a standard in 2006. All of the major blog software and service vendors have announced support for Atom, including Google, Wordpress, and SixApart. Most are already supporting Atom today, and you should do the same.

10.1.1 Why not XML-RPC or SOAP?

Atom is a web services protocol, but Atom is not based on SOAP. The creators of Atom considered both SOAP and XML-RPC to be too complex and opted instead for a popular new back-to-basics approach to web services known as *Representational State Transfer (REST)*. Instead of defining web services in terms of high-level remote procedure calls, as SOAP does, REST-based web services define their interfaces at a lower level, in terms of HTTP and XML.

Web service providers can specify a REST-based service by defining a set of URLs and a set of XML documents that the service can get, post, put, and delete via those URLs. It's just HTTP and XML. That's why REST-based services are so easy to understand and why, when offered a choice, developers tend to pick REST. For example, Amazon offers both SOAP- and REST-based web services interfaces, and 85 percent of its users choose to use REST. We'll continue our discussion of REST as we examine how Atom protocol works.

10.2 *How Atom protocol works*

Atom protocol works by using the standard HTTP *verbs* GET, POST, PUT, and DELETE to operate on *resources*, which are defined as data objects or services that are available on the Web. Everything you need to do with Atom can be done with those four verbs. From the Atom protocol specification, here's how the verbs are used:

- GET is used to retrieve a representation of a resource or perform a query.
- POST is used to create a new, dynamically named resource.
- PUT is used to update a known resource.
- DELETE is used to remove a resource.

If you know HTTP, there are no surprises in Atom. That's how you'd expect the verbs to work. The same goes for success and error messages, which are returned the standard way: with HTTP status codes. For example, if you try a GET on a resource that does not exist, you'll get status-code 404 "not found." If you don't include the right username and password for a request, you'll receive a 403 "forbidden." If your HTTP POST to create a new blog entry works properly, you'll get a 201 "created" to indicate success. A server-side error will get you a 500, and so on.

10.2.1 *Discovery and collections*

Before you can start HTTP getting, posting, putting, and deleting resources on an Atom server (i.e., a server that supports Atom), you need to know what URLs to use and which types of data to send and receive. In short, you need a way to *discover* the resources and services available. Atom servers manage *collections* of resources, which can contain Atom entries, media files or a mixture of both. So, what you'll be discovering are the URLs you can use to get and post to these collections.

To discover the resources and services of an Atom server, you send an HTTP get request to the server's endpoint URL and receive in return an introspection document, like the one in listing 10.2. An Atom introspection document lists the collections available on the server and for each, its URL and the content-type or types that it accepts.

At the time of this writing, it's not completely clear how discovery and collections will work in the final version of Atom. So we'll show you how it works in what we expect to be the final draft of the specification (draft 9) and we'll provide errata on the web site that accompanies the book once the Atom protocol is finalized. With that caveat in mind, let's learn Atom by exploring a real live Atom server.

10.2.2 *Atom protocol from the command line*

One of the pleasant side effects of using REST for web services is that you can use simple command-line file transfer tools, such as `wget` and `curl`, to interact with your services. Issuing HTTP GETs, PUTs, POSTs, and DELETEs from the command line is a great way to debug a REST-based web service or to obtain a deeper understanding of how it works, so let's give it a try. Since we want to learn how to do Atom using Java and C#, we won't use `curl` and `wget`. Instead, we'll write our own simple command-line tools. We'll write one for each of the four HTTP verbs needed to interact with Atom. Because Atom services are protected by HTTP authentication, our tools will accept username and password arguments. Here are the four tools we'll create:

- `authget.sh <username> <password> <url>`—Sends an authenticated HTTP GET request to a specified URL and prints the response.

- `authpost.sh <username> <password> <filepath> <url>`—Sends an authenticated HTTP POST request and a file to a URL and prints the response.

- `authput.sh <username> <password> <filepath> <url>`—Sends an authenticated HTTP PUT request and a file to a URL and prints the response.

- `authdelete.sh <username> <password> <url>`—Sends an authenticated HTTP DELETE request to a URL and prints the response.

Those are all UNIX shell scripts that call Java, but for Windows users we also provide corresponding BAT files for running the command line-tools. You'll find both the UNIX scripts and BAT files in the directory java/ch10/dist/blogclient.

Let's take a look at the code for each of those tools and use them to explore a
blog server via Atom protocol.

10.2.3 *Discovering Atom resources and services*

We'll start at the beginning, with discovery. The starting point for accessing
an Atom service is the end-point URL. If you do an authenticated HTTP GET
on an Atom service's end-point URL, you'll get an introspection document.
That document will tell you the URLs you need to access and manipulate the
resources available on the server.

A look at AuthGet.java

First, we need a program that can send an authenticated HTTP GET and print out
the result. That program, shown in listing 10.1, is called AuthGet.

Listing 10.1   AuthGet.java

```
package com.manning.blogapps.chapter10.examples;
import java.io.*;
import org.apache.commons.codec.binary.Base64;      ←❶
import org.apache.commons.httpclient.HttpClient;
import org.apache.commons.httpclient.methods.GetMethod;    ❷

public class AuthGet {
    public static void main(String[] args) throws Exception {
        if (args.length < 3) {    ←❸
            System.out.println
                    ("USAGE: authget <username> <password> <url>");
            System.exit(-1);
        }
        String credentials = args[0] + ":" + args[1];
        String url = args[2];

        HttpClient httpClient = new HttpClient();    ←❹
        GetMethod method = new GetMethod(url);    ←❺
        method.setRequestHeader("Authorization", "Basic "      ❻
            + new String(Base64.encodeBase64(credentials.getBytes())));

        httpClient.executeMethod(method);
        System.out.println(method.getResponseBodyAsString());    ❼
    }
}
```

AuthGet is a simple command-line Java program, but it uses a couple of
Apache Commons utilities, so let's break it down. In the imports, we bring in
the Apache Commons Codec Base64 class ❶, which we'll need for HTTP Basic
Authentication. And we bring in Apache HttpClient classes ❷, which we'll use

instead of the standard Java `java.net.URLConnection` classes. We use `HttpClient` because it's more powerful, flexible, and easy to use than the standard `java.net` classes. And we use HTTP Basic authentication because that's what the Blogapps server uses, but other forms of HTTP authentication are possible with Atom, such as Digest and WS-Security (WSSE).

Inside the main method of AuthGet, we first check the number of command-line arguments passed in ❸. We need at least three arguments: a username, a password, and a URL to call. If there are fewer than three, we print a usage message and exit.

Next, we create the `HttpClient` ❹ and `GetMethod` ❺ objects we need to call the URL. We add the username and password authentication by setting a request header with the name "Authorization" and a value that starts with "Basic" and ends with a `Base64` digest of the username and password ❻.

Finally, we execute the HTTP GET request and print out the result that came back in the response body ❼. This works well if we're getting XML or some other text file, but not if we're getting an image or other binary file. We could change AuthGet to save results to a file, but we're trying to keep things simple. We'll use AuthGet for retrieving only XML files.

Getting an introspection document with AuthGet

Let's put AuthGet to work by using it to explore an Atom server. To follow along, you'll have to build the Java examples as explained in the examples readme file. You'll also have to start the Blogapps server as described in chapter 2. When you've done that, you'll be ready to make your first Atom call. Open a command window, change directory to the java/ch10/dist/blogclient directory, and issue this command:

```
$ ./authget.sh admin admin http://localhost:8080/roller/app
```

Or for Windows users:

```
> authget admin admin http://localhost:8080/roller/app
```

This command runs the AuthGet program with username "admin" and password "admin" and the end-point URL of the Blogapps server's Atom implementation. AuthGet will send the request and then print the response, which should look something like the XML in listing 10.2, an Atom introspection document.

Listing 10.2 An Atom protocol draft 9 introspection document

```
<?xml version="1.0" encoding="UTF-8"?>
<service xmlns="http://purl.org/atom/app#">
  <workspace title="Workspace: Collections for adminblog">    ◁—❶
```

```
        <collection title="Collection: Weblog Entries for adminblog"    ⟵❷
                href="http://localhost:8080/roller/app/adminblog/entries">
            <accept>entry</accept>    ⟵❸
        </collection>
        <collection title="Collection: Resources for adminblog"    ⟵❹
                href="http://localhost:8080/roller/app/adminblog/resources">
            <accept>*</accept>    ⟵❺
        </collection>
    </workspace>
</service>
```

The introspection document is likely to change before Atom protocol is finalized, but let's take a closer look anyway so we can better understand the discovery concept. In a nutshell, an Atom introspection document contains a list of workspaces that are available to the authenticated user making the request. Each workspace contains one or more collections of resources.

In listing 10.2, you can see that we have access to one <workspace> ❶, which represents a blog named "adminblog." Within that workspace, we have access to two collections.

The first <collection> ❷ is a collection of entries, indicated by the <accept> element value of "entry" ❸ which is a shorthand way of saying that the collection accepts only Atom entry elements. This collection represents the entries in the blog. The <collection> element's href attribute indicates the URL of the collection, shown below:

```
http://localhost:8080/roller/app/adminblog/entries
```

If you send an HTTP GET request to that URL, the server will send you the entry collection or more likely, just the first portion of the collection, in the form of an Atom feed. To create a new entry in the blog, just post an Atom entry to the entry collection URL.

The second <collection> ❹ is a collection of media files. Note that its <accept> element ❺ contains an asterisk, which indicates that the collection will accept any content-type. The accept element can also be used by the server to restrict collections to specific content-ranges such as image/* for only images or image/gif for only GIF format images. The media collection's URL is shown below:

```
http://localhost:8080/roller/app/adminblog/resources
```

As you might expect, if you send an HTTP GET request to that URL, the server will send you the media collection in the form of an Atom feed. To create a new media file in the blog, post it to the media collection URL.

Now let's use AuthGet again to get one of those collections.

Getting a collection with AuthGet

Based on what we learned from the introspection document in listing 10.2, we know we can fetch the blog entries collection by doing an authenticated HTTP GET on the entries collection URL. We can do this with authget.sh by issuing the following command:

```
$ ./authget.sh admin admin
            http://localhost:8080/roller/app/adminblog/entries
```

The server will respond by sending an Atom feed with the blog entries in reverse chronological order, like the one shown in listing 10.3. Note that the server may not send all of the entries. For bandwidth and performance reasons, most Atom servers will limit the number of entries returned in each request. If you want more, you'll have to ask for them by issuing another GET request.

Listing 10.3   Portion of an Atom protocol entries collection document

```
<?xml version="1.0" encoding="UTF-8"?>
<feed xmlns="http://www.w3.org/2005/Atom"
                 xmlns:app="http://purl.org/atom/app#">            ❶
  <link rel="next" href="http://localhost:
                        8080/roller/app/adminblog/entries/20" />   ❷
  <entry>
    <title>Welcome to the Blogapps Demo Server</title>
    <link rel="alternate"
       href="http://localhost:8080/roller/page/
adminblog?entry=welcome_to_the_blogapps_demo"/>
    <link rel="edit"      ←❸
         href="http://localhost:8080/roller/app/adminblog/entry/
40288127cd75f001f" />
    <category term="/General" />
    <id>
    http://localhost:8080/roller/page/
adminblog?entry=welcome_to_the_blogapps_demo
    </id>
    <updated>2005-09-14T02:38:56Z</updated>
    <published>2005-09-14T02:33:21Z</published>
    <content type="html">&lt;p /&gt;&#xD;
   If you are reading this then you have successfully installed the Blogapps
   Demo Server. This is a demonstration only bundle that includes the Tomcat
     web application server, the HSQLDB database, Roller Weblogger and
     JSPWiki.&lt;p /&gt;
     You can also visit the wiki portion of this demo by clicking
     &lt;a href="http://localhost:8080/wiki"&gt;here&lt;/a&gt; .
    </content>
    <app:control>     ←❹
      <app:draft>no</app:draft>
    </app:control>
```

```
  </entry>
  <entry>
    <!-- another entry ->
  </entry>
  <entry>
    <!-- and another and so on ->
  </entry>
  . . .
</feed>
```

Listing 10.3 is just an Atom feed ❶, but some Atom protocol magic is happening. First, there's a `<link>` element with `rel="next"` ❷. This is only a partial feed and there are more entries available on the server. If you want to retrieve the next batch of entries, send an HTTP GET to the URL in the next link (e.g., http://localhost:8080/roller/app/adminblog/entries/20).

The next bit of magic is a `<link>` with `rel="edit"` ❸, which you can use to retrieve, update, and even delete an entry. To retrieve, you just send an HTTP GET to the link URL. To update, you HTTP PUT a new copy of the entry in Atom format. In the next sections, we'll see those operations in action. And finally, the Publish Control `<app:control>` element ❹ indicates that the first entry is not a draft.

Now that we know how to get collections, let's see how to publish to them.

10.2.4 *Posting and updating blog entries*

To post and update resources on an Atom server, we'll need programs to send authenticated HTTP POST and PUT requests. Those programs are called AuthPost and AuthPut. You can find them in the online examples that accompany the book. The AuthPost and AuthPut programs are identical, except that one uses POST and the other uses PUT, so we'll list only AuthPost here. Let's take a look at AuthPost, shown in listing 10.4.

> **Listing 10.4   AuthPost.java, a program for sending an authenticated HTTP post request**

```
package com.manning.blogapps.chapter10.examples;
import java.io.*;
import org.apache.commons.codec.binary.Base64;        <-❶
import org.apache.commons.httpclient.HttpClient;       <-❷
import org.apache.commons.httpclient.methods.EntityEnclosingMethod;
import org.apache.commons.httpclient.methods.PostMethod;

public class AuthPost {
    public static void main(String[] args) throws Exception {
```

```
            if (args.length < 4) {     ⟵③
                System.out.println(
                    "USAGE: authpost <username> <password> <filepath> <url>");
                System.exit(-1);
            }
            String credentials = args[0] + ":" + args[1];
            String filepath = args[2];
            String url = args[3];

            HttpClient httpClient = new HttpClient();     ⟵④
            EntityEnclosingMethod method = new PostMethod(url);     ⟵⑤
            method.setRequestHeader("Authorization", "Basic "     ⟵⑥
                + new String(Base64.encodeBase64(credentials.getBytes())));

            File upload = new File(filepath);     ⟵⑦
            method.setRequestHeader("name", upload.getName());     ⟵⑧
            method.setRequestBody(new FileInputStream(upload));     ⟵⑨

            String contentType = "application/atom+xml; charset=utf8";
            if (filepath.endsWith(".gif")) contentType = "image/gif";    ⑩
            else if (filepath.endsWith(".jpg")) contentType = "image/jpeg";
            method.setRequestHeader("Content-type", contentType);

            httpClient.executeMethod(method);
            System.out.println(method.getResponseBodyAsString());     ⑪
        }
    }
```

There's a lot more going on with AuthPost than there was with AuthGet, so let's review it in detail. First, we bring in the Apache Commons Base64 ❶ and Apache HttpClient classes ❷, for the same reasons we explained for AuthGet.

Next, we check the argument count ❸. For AuthPost, we need four arguments: the username, password, filepath of the file to be posted, and the URL to post to. We create an HttpClient object ❹. Then, we create a PostMethod object to post to the URL ❺ and add HTTP Digest Authentication ❻, just as we did in AuthGet.

Next, we bring in the file to be posted ❼ and set its name as a request header ❽, and we add the file's contents to the request ❾. Then, we set the content-type ❿. To keep things simple, we assume the Atom content-type (i.e., application/xml+xml), unless the filename indicates that the file is a GIF or JPEG image.

Finally, we execute the HTTP POST request and display the results ⓫. As was the case with AuthGet, displaying the results via System.out.println() works well if the response is XML or some other text file. With Atom protocol POSTs and PUTs, we're safe here—they return only XML.

Now let's post a new blog entry using AuthPost.

Posting a blog entry with AuthPost

To follow along, you'll have to build the Java examples as explained in the readme files included in the online examples, and you'll have to start the Blogapps server as described in chapter 2. To post a new blog entry with AuthPost, you first create the blog entry in a file in Atom format. To make things easy, we've included an example post called testpost.xml in the directory java/ch10/dist/blogclient/etc, which contains the following XML:

```xml
<?xml version="1.0" encoding="UTF-8"?>
<entry xmlns="http://www.w3.org/2005/Atom">
    <id>null</id>
    <title>Atom test post title</title>
    <content>Atom test post content</content>
    <updated>2006-05-16T00:00:00Z</updated>
</entry>
```

Next, you simply post that XML to the collection URL of the target collection. From a command-line prompt in the java/ch10/dist/blogclient directory, issue the following command to post the new entry to the adminblog's entries collection:

```
$ ./authpost.sh admin admin etc/testpost.xml
              http://localhost:8080/ roller/app/adminblog/entries
```

In return, you'll receive a new Atom entry as it is represented on the server, which will look something like this:

```xml
<entry xmlns="http://www.w3.org/2005/Atom">
  <title>Atom test post title</title>
  <link rel="alternate"
    href="http://localhost:8080/roller/page/
  adminblog?entry=atom_test_post_title" />
  <link rel="edit"
    href="http://localhost:8080/roller/app/adminblog/entry/4020590001" />
  <id>http://localhost:8080/roller/page/
  adminblog?entry=atom_test_post_title</id>
  <updated>2005-12-30T17:11:51Z</updated>
  <published>2005-12-30T17:11:51Z</published>
  <content type="html">Atom test post content</content>
  <app:control xmlns:app="http://purl.org/atom/app#">
    <app:draft>no</app:draft>
  </app:control>
</entry>
```

Your new blog entry has been created. Note that the server has filled in the alternate link, edit link, id, updated, and published fields for the entry. Also, the server has added a Publish Control element `<app:control>` to indicate that the entry is not a draft.

Updating a blog post with AuthPut

What if you meant to post testpost.xml as a draft? It's easy to fix that by saving the entry returned by AuthPost, editing it to change the `<app:draft>` element to "yes," and then using an HTTP PUT to update the revised entry to the edit URL provided by the server. Assuming that you've saved the revised blog entry in testpost2.xml, the command to update the entry is shown below. Note: if you're trying this yourself, make sure you use the edit URL that comes back from your server; it will be different from the one printed here.

```
$ ./authput.sh admin admin testpost2.xml
        http://localhost:8080/roller/app/adminblog/entry/4020590001
```

In response, the server will send back the updated entry, and you should see that the value of `<app:draft>` has been changed to yes. Before we move on, let's delete the entry entirely with AuthDelete.

Deleting a blog entry with AuthDelete

Let's say you'd like to delete that test entry you just created. As you might expect, that's easier than updating it. All you have to do is send an HTTP DELETE request to the edit URL provided by the server, like so:

```
$ ./authdelete.sh admin admin
        http://localhost:8080/roller/app/adminblog/entry/4020590001
```

And poof, the entry will be deleted. Now that we know how to deal with blog entries, let's discuss media files.

10.2.5 Posting and updating media files

For media files, Atom protocol outdoes the MetaWeblog API. With Atom, not only can you upload media files to a blog, but you can also list uploaded files and update and delete them from the server. We'll show you how to use those new features, but first we'll cover the most basic operation, uploading a media file.

Posting an image to a blog with AuthPost

We used AuthPost to post a blog entry, and it will work fine for images and other media files too. Assuming that you've compiled the examples and that the Blogapps server is running, here's how you post an image to a blog with Auth-Post. First, open a command-line window and change directory to java/ch10/dist/blogclient. There, you'll find the AuthPost script and a directory called etc, which contains a simple image for you to post. Enter the following command to post that image to the media collection URL we learned about at discovery time (see listing 10.2):

```
$ ./authpost.sh admin admin etc/cover-rssandatom.jpg
                http://localhost:8080/roller/app/adminblog/resources
```

You should see something like this in response:

```
<entry xmlns="http://www.w3.org/2005/Atom">
  <title>cover-rssandatom.jpg</title>
  <link rel="edit"
    href="http://localhost:8080/roller/app/adminblog/
              resource/cover-rssandatom.jpg" />
  <link rel="edit-media"
    href="http://localhost:8080/roller/app/adminblog/
              resource-edit/cover-rssandatom.jpg" />
  <updated>1970-01-01T00:00:00Z</updated>
  <content type="image/jpeg"
    src="http://localhost:8080/roller/resources/adminblog/
                              cover-rssandatom.jpg" />
</entry>
```

The server has accepted the image and sent back an Atom entry to represent it, known as a *media link* entry. The entry includes a `<link>` with `rel="edit"`, which contains a URL you can use to update and delete the media link. The entry also contains a link with `rel="edit-media"`, which you can use to update the image itself. If you want to update the image, simply use AuthPut to PUT a new image to the edit-media URL. The entry also includes a `<content>` element with an src attribute containing the URL where you can find the publicly accessible version of the image.

Listing media files with AuthGet

Now that we've uploaded a file to the adminblog on the Blogapps server, let's use AuthGet to retrieve the list of media files on the server. We've seen what an entry collection looks like, so in fairness, let's do the same for a media collection. Enter the command below to list the members of adminblog's media collection:

```
$ ./authget.sh admin admin http://localhost:8080/roller/
                              app/adminblog/resources
```

You should see something like this in return:

```
<feed xmlns="http://www.w3.org/2005/Atom"
              xmlns:app="http://purl.org/atom/app#">
<entry>
  <title>cover-rssandatom.jpg</title>
  <link rel="edit"
    href="http://localhost:8080/roller/app/adminblog/
              resource/cover-rssandatom.jpg" />
  <link rel="edit-media"
    href="http://localhost:8080/roller/app/adminblog/
              resource-edit/cover-rssandatom.jpg" />
```

```
<updated>2005-12-30T19:46:52Z</updated>
<content type="image/jpeg"
  src="http://localhost:8080/roller/resources/
                                  adminblog/cover-rssandatom.jpg" />
</entry>
</feed>
```

That's the same `<entry>` we saw when we posted the image, but this time it's part of a collection, so it's wrapped in an Atom `<feed>` element. There's no next `<link>` because there's only one item in the collection.

That brings us to the end of our command-line exploration of the Atom protocol. We now understand how Atom works at the lowest level. Let's use that knowledge to build a blog client library for Atom.

10.3 *Building a blog client with Atom protocol*

In chapter 9, we defined the interfaces needed for a simple blog client library and implemented them using the XML-RPC based MetaWeblog API. Our goals were to make it easier to write blog applications and to mask the differences between MetaWeblog API and Atom protocol so that our applications will be able to work with both. But to fully achieve those goals, we need an Atom protocol version of our blog client library, so that's what we'll develop next.

In this section, we'll expand the chapter 9 blog client interfaces to support Atom protocol and explain how to implement them in Java. Since Atom is likely to change before it is finalized, we won't include the source code here, but we will diagram and explain the classes involved. The full source code is available in the online examples that accompany the book, and we'll update it when Atom is finalized.

10.3.1 *Atom does more*

Atom is not complete, but it already does more than the MetaWeblog API. By providing a consistent mechanism for accessing and manipulating large collections, Atom makes it much easier to manage blog entries, uploaded files, and possibly other resources, depending on what the final Atom protocol supports. With Atom, it's possible to iterate or *page* through the items in a collection without fetching the entire collection. As we've seen, it's also possible to list, update, and delete uploaded file resources just as you can list, update, and delete blog entries. And since Atom protocol is based on the well-defined Atom format, it benefits from a richer entry model with common constructs for content, categories, and people.

Let's compare the MetaWeblog API and Atom protocol features that are relevant to our blog client library. Table 10.1 shows them side by side.

Table 10.1 Comparing relevant features of the MetaWeblog API and Atom protocol (Draft 8)

	MetaWeblog API	Atom protocol
Multiple blogs per user	Yes	Yes
Entries: save, update, delete	Yes	Yes
Entries: list (with paging)	Yes, but no paging	Yes
Resources: upload and update files	Yes	Yes
Resources: delete	No	Yes
Resources: list (with paging)	No	Yes
Categories: list	Yes	Yes*

* Categories are part of the Atom protocol charter, but may not be in the final specification.

Let's discuss each of those features:

- *Mutliple blogs per user*—Each user can have one or more blogs. MetaWeblog API supports this via the `blogger.getUsersBlogs()` method. Atom protocol allows multiple workspaces, each representing one blog.

- *Entries: save, update, and delete*—Both MetaWeblog API and Atom protocol fully support saving, updating, and deleting blog entries.

- *Entries: list (with paging)*—MetaWeblog API supports listing recent entries through `metaweblog.getRecentPosts()`, but it is not possible to page through the entries returned or request a specific range. Atom protocol draft 8 supports paging, and the final version of Atom *may* support both paging and indexing.

- *Resources: upload and update files*—Both MetaWeblog API and Atom protocol support uploading and updating uploaded file resources.

- *Resources: delete*—Atom protocol supports deletion of uploaded file resources; MetaWeblog API does not.

- *Resources: list (with paging)*—Atom protocol draft 8 supports listing with paging, and the final version of Atom *may* support both paging and indexing. MetaWeblog API doesn't support either one.

- *Categories: list*—MetaWeblog API can list the categories available in a blog, but it's not clear if Atom protocol will be able to. There seems to be some controversy about the need for category listing in the protocol.

But we don't need it all

You might be wondering how we can complete an Atom blog client library when Atom itself is not complete. In truth, we can't. When Atom is complete, it may also support collections of templates, comments, and even users. If we don't know how those things are defined, we can't include them in our library.

Fortunately for us, the blog applications we'll develop in part II need support only for entries and resources, and those are present in the latest Atom protocol. So for now, we'll implement the Atom protocol "yes" features in table 10.1. Later, when Atom is complete, we'll finish the job by releasing an update to the online examples that accompany this book.

10.3.2 *Expanding the blog client interfaces*

Let's summarize what we learned in the section above: Atom adds the ability to handle entry and resource collections in a consistent way and offers a richer entry model. To benefit from these new features, we'll need to change and expand the blog client interfaces we defined in chapter 9 to match Atom, while still keeping them abstract enough to allow us to continue to support a Meta-Weblog API implementation.

First, let's cover the collections-related changes needed. As you read, you might want to refer to figure 10.1, which shows our expanded blog client library, with new methods and interfaces shown in italics.

Consistent behavior for collections

Remember from chapter 9 that the `Blog` interface allows callers to create, retrieve, update, and delete `BlogEntry` objects. It is essentially a container that holds entries, but with Atom a `Blog` can contain multiple collections, where each collection is represented as an Atom feed and each can hold either blog entries or uploaded file resources. Entry and resource collections are treated in a consistent manner.

To support this new consistent collections model, we'll introduce a new interface called Collection, which you can see in Figure 10.1. Like the `<collection>` element in the Atom introspection document (see listing 10.2), a Collection has a title and an accept string that indicates what content-types of objects are allowed in the collection. A collection has a `saveEntry()` method, so that new entries and resources can be saved and updated, and a `getEntries()` method so that you can access all of the items in the collection.

In Atom protocol, blog entries and resources are treated in a consistent way. In fact, a resource is an entry. To model that, we add a new interface called `Blog-Resource` which extends our existing `BlogEntry` interface.

Expanded entry model

To support Atom's richer entry model, we need a better model for blog entry content, categories, and information about authors and contributors. As you can see in figure 10.1, we'll add three classes associated with the `BlogEntry` interface: `Content`, `Category`, and `Person`.

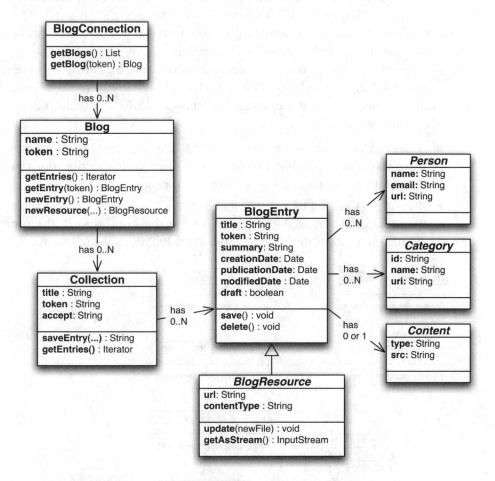

Figure 10.1 Blog client interfaces, expanded to support Atom protocol features

The new interfaces

The new blog client library interfaces shown in figure 10.1 are part of the package com.manning.chapter10.blogclient. You can find the source code for the interfaces under the directory java/ch10/src. You'll also find a complete MetaWeblog API implementation of those interfaces there. Now let's move on to our Atom blog client implementation.

10.3.3 Atom blog client implementation

Since we're working in Java, we have two powerful and flexible libraries to help us write our Atom blog client. We'll use HttpClient to execute our GET, POST, PUT, and DELETE requests. And we'll use ROME to generate the XML we send and to parse the XML that comes back. Thanks to those libraries, our implementation is fairly small: nine classes and about a thousand lines of code, including comments.

Figure 10.2 shows the blog client interfaces and the Atom blog client implementation classes. Let's discuss the key classes in the Atom implementation, which are shaded gray.

- *AtomBlogConnection*—Created by the BlogConnectionFactory, these objects use an AtomService object to parse the Atom introspection document and determine what blogs are available to the caller.

- *AtomBlog*—Created by AtomBlogConnection, an AtomBlog object represents a blog that exists on an Atom server. This is the workhorse of the Atom blog client, where most of the HttpClient and ROME calls are made.

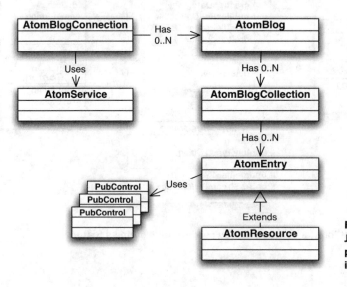

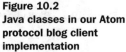

Figure 10.2
Java classes in our Atom protocol blog client implementation

- *AtomBlogCollection*—Created by `AtomBlog`, this class is an inner class of `AtomBlog` that represents a collection of entries, which can be of type `Atom-Entry` or `AtomResource`.

- *AtomEntry*—Created by `AtomBlog`, this class represents an Atom blog entry. The class extends the abstract `BaseBlogEntry` class and implements the `BlogEntry` interface. It calls back to `AtomBlog` to do the work of saving, updating, and deleting. It uses `PubControl`, a custom ROME module, to handle the `<app:draft>` flag.

- *AtomResource*—Created by `AtomBlog`, this class represents an Atom media collection member. It implements `BlogResource` and extends `AtomEntry`, because Atom represents resources as entries.

The new implementation

The new Atom blog client library implementation classes are part of the package com.manning.chapter10.atomclient. You can find the source code for the package under the directory java/ch10/src. You'll also find a complete MetaWeblog API implementation of them there. Now, let's briefly discuss how to use the library.

10.3.4 *Atom blog client in action*

Using the blog client library is easy, and we've included plenty of examples of its use in the rest of the book. You simply put the jars in your classpath, call the `BlogConnnectionFactory` to create a `BlogConnnection` to your blog server, and start blogging with Atom. In the example code for this chapter, we've included a new version of the BlogPoster from chapter 2 that's been rewritten to use our new blog client library. Here's the portion of the new BlogPoster.java that posts to the first blog found on the blog server:

```
BlogConnection con =
    BlogConnectionFactory.getBlogConnection(
        "atom", target, username, password);
Blog blog = (Blog)con.getBlogs().get(0);
BlogEntry entry = blog.newEntry();
entry.setTitle(title);
entry.setContent(new BlogEntry.Content(description));
entry.save();
```

As we did for the C# blog client library we developed in chapter 9, we've developed a simple GUI client that uses the library to support publishing via either the MetaWeblog API or the Atom protocol. Figure 10.3 shows a screenshot of the client. You'll find the code for the GUI client in the example code for the chapter. Refer to the readme file in the examples for instructions on running the client.

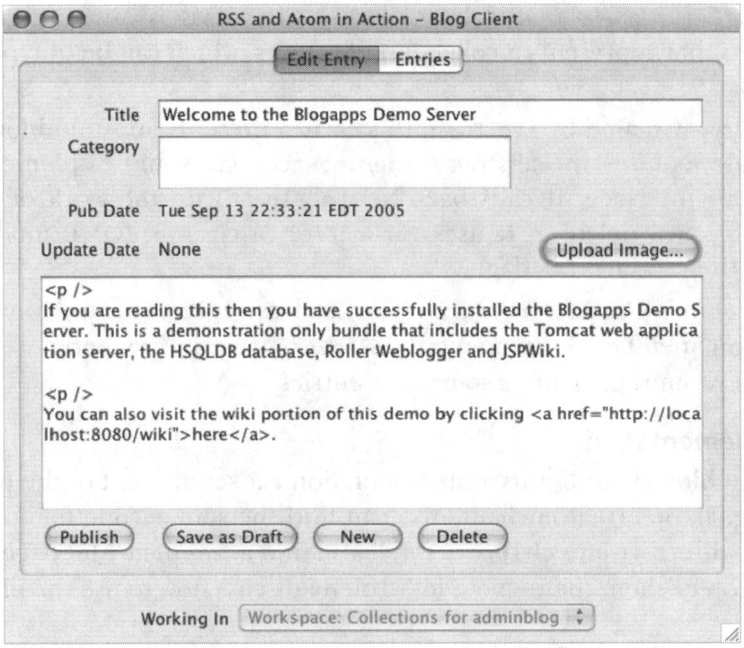

Figure 10.3   Simple blog client GUI based on our blog client library

That brings us to the end of our exploration of the Atom protocol. Let's sum up what we've learned.

10.4 *Summary*

- Atom protocol is a new web services protocol for publishing to blogs, wikis, and other web content management systems.

- Based on the Atom format, Atom protocol is designed to replace the old XML-RPC based protocols, such as the Blogger and MetaWeblog API.

- Atom is not based on SOAP. Instead, it's based on a new back-to-basics approach to web services known as Representational State Transfer (REST).

- Unlike the XML-RPC based blogging protocols, which are defined in terms of remote procedure calls, Atom is defined in terms of URLs, HTTP verbs, and XML.

- It's possible to use Java's built-in HTTP support to blog with Atom, but to implement the Atom version of the blog client library, we used the more powerful and flexible Apache `HttpClient` library.

Part 2

Blog apps

Part II is about putting blog technologies to work. We show you how to use those technologies to build Java and C# blog applications, or blog apps–small applications that use blog technologies to do interesting things. The chapters in part II are short and focused on code. Each blog app is a ready-to-use stand-alone application, and all of them are available from the Blogapps project site on Java.net. To wrap up the book, we present a brainstorming session that includes two dozen additional ideas for useful blog apps.

11

Creating a group blog via aggregation

Create an aggregated group blog to make it easier for readers to follow blogs on one topic or to bring together an online community.

As the number of blogs grows, it becomes more and more difficult for readers to find and follow the ones that cover topics of interest to them. That's what inspired Mike Cannon Brookes, CTO of Atlassian Software, to create Javablogs.com in 2002. Initially, Javablogs.com started as a web page that listed blogs about Java. Mike maintained this list by hand and would add any Java blogger who asked to be included. As Java developers discovered blogs and started searching for kindred spirits, they found Mike's list an invaluable resource.

Eventually, Mike and his co-workers at Atlassian decided to turn their list of blogs into an *aggregator*—a web site that automatically combines multiple separately hosted blogs into one group blog. The new Javablogs.com was an overnight success. Java developers everywhere subscribed to the Javablogs.com newsfeed because it allowed them to read all of the latest Java-related blog posts without having to hunt down and subscribe to individual blogs. Javablogs.com became one of the hubs of the Java developer community.

Javablogs.com was not the first aggregator or the last. These days, you can find aggregators on numerous topics and for many local areas. For example, web developer Roch Smith used an aggregator as the centerpiece of Greensboro101.com, a web site that encourages grassroots journalism, promotes community activism, and provides a community blog for Greensboro, NC. And the popular open source and Python-based Planet-Planet software drives numerous aggregated blogs or *planets* on topics such as Lisp, GNOME, Sun, Python, and the Apache Software Foundation.

In chapter 1, Nina and Rangu included aggregators in their proposed network of blogs and wikis because they knew that their manager would not like the idea of subscribing to—or worse yet, visiting—each of his employees' blogs. Nina and Rangu proposed an aggregated blog for each work group, as well as one at the division level to aggregate the aggregators. They wanted to make it possible for anybody to subscribe to any level of the organization, from individual to division. You can do the same thing in your organization.

In this chapter, we'll explain how to create aggregated group blogs using the example blog app included with this chapter, a Java-based aggregator called Planet Tool. Let's get started.

11.1 *Introducing Planet Tool*

Planet Tool is a command-line Java program that reads a configuration file, downloads newsfeeds, and generates the files needed for an aggregated blog based on those newsfeeds. The source code for Planet Tool is included in the

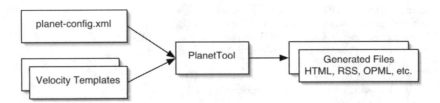

Figure 11.1   Planet Tool inputs and outputs

examples for this chapter, which you'll find in the directory java/ch11. To use it, you first create an XML configuration file that specifies all of the newsfeeds you wish to include and a set of templates that define precisely what output is to be generated.

When you run Planet Tool, it fetches and parses the newsfeeds you specified and then calls the Velocity templates you defined to generate the files you want, as shown in figure 11.1. (More about Velocity templates in a minute.) Planet Tool comes with an example configuration file and templates for generating HTML, RSS, and Outline Processor Markup Language (OPML), which is an XML format commonly used to exchange newsfeed subscription lists. To help you understand how Planet Tool works, let's discuss how to set up and generate an aggregated blog.

11.2 *Configuring Planet Tool*

To configure Planet Tool, you provide an XML configuration file, like the one shown in listing 11.1. This file defines the configuration parameters, subscriptions, and groups to be included in the aggregation. A *subscription* is a newsfeed that is to be included when Planet Tool runs. A *group* is a group of subscriptions that are to be aggregated. By defining multiple groups, you can produce multiple aggregated blogs and feeds. For example, if you're creating a Planet Caribbean blog aggregator, you might want to offer one feed that includes all Caribbean blogs and separate feeds for each of the individual countries. Let's take a closer look at listing 11.1, which defines three subscriptions and one group.

Listing 11.1   A Sample Planet Tool configuration file

```
<?xml version="1.0"?>
<planet-config>
    <admin-name>Dave Johnson</admin-name>          ◄─❶
    <admin-email>dave.johnson@rollerweblogger.org</admin-email>     ◄─❷
    <title>Planet Roller</title>      ◄─❸
    <description>Folks who sometimes blog about Roller</description>   ◄─❹
    <site-url>http://rollerweblogger.org/planet</site-url>    ◄─❺
```

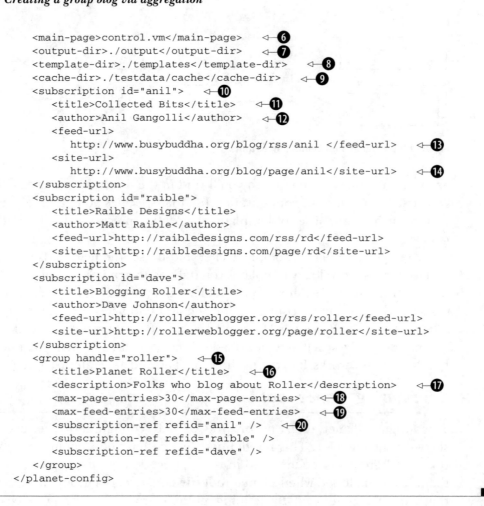

```
<main-page>control.vm</main-page>          ◁─6
<output-dir>./output</output-dir>          ◁─7
<template-dir>./templates</template-dir>       ◁─8
<cache-dir>./testdata/cache</cache-dir>      ◁─9
<subscription id="anil">      ◁─10
    <title>Collected Bits</title>      ◁─11
    <author>Anil Gangolli</author>       ◁─12
    <feed-url>
        http://www.busybuddha.org/blog/rss/anil </feed-url>     ◁─13
    <site-url>
        http://www.busybuddha.org/blog/page/anil</site-url>      ◁─14
</subscription>
<subscription id="raible">
    <title>Raible Designs</title>
    <author>Matt Raible</author>
    <feed-url>http://raibledesigns.com/rss/rd</feed-url>
    <site-url>http://raibledesigns.com/page/rd</site-url>
</subscription>
<subscription id="dave">
    <title>Blogging Roller</title>
    <author>Dave Johnson</author>
    <feed-url>http://rollerweblogger.org/rss/roller</feed-url>
    <site-url>http://rollerweblogger.org/page/roller</site-url>
</subscription>
<group handle="roller">      ◁─15
    <title>Planet Roller</title>      ◁─16
    <description>Folks who blog about Roller</description>      ◁─17
    <max-page-entries>30</max-page-entries>      ◁─18
    <max-feed-entries>30</max-feed-entries>      ◁─19
    <subscription-ref refid="anil" />      ◁─20
    <subscription-ref refid="raible" />
    <subscription-ref refid="dave" />
</group>
</planet-config>
```

Most of the parameters in the configuration are optional, and you need to specify them only if you intend to use them in the templates that define the generated files. The ones that are required are indicated below.

Let's start with the configuration parameters at the start of the file:

❶ The name of the person who administers the aggregated web site

❷ The email address of the person who runs the site

❸ The title for the site

❹ The description of the whole site

❺ The URL where the aggregated web site will be available

❻ The control template to be called to generate the site (**required**)

❼ The directory where generated files are to be placed (**required**)

❽ The directory where the control and all other templates are stored (**required**)

❾ The directory where newsfeed data is to be cached (**required**)

Next, let's examine one of the subscriptions:

❿ Each subscription must be identified by a unique id (**required**)

⓫ The title of the newsfeed source

⓬ The author of the newsfeed source

⓭ The URL of the newsfeed (**required**)

⓮ The URL of the newsfeed source web site

Finally, let's look at the details of the one group defined in the configuration file:

⓯ Each group must be identified by a unique handle. If you're going to use group names in generated filenames, as we do in our example templates, make sure your handles are valid filenames. (**required**)

⓰ The title of the group

⓱ The description of the group

⓲ The number of entries to be displayed in generated HTML pages (**required**)

⓳ The number of entries to be displayed in generated newsfeeds (**required**)

⓴ Include subscriptions in a group by including a `<subscription-ref>` for each, referencing the subscription's id. If you want to include all subscriptions in a group, but you don't want to list them individually you can use `<subscription-ref include-all="true" />` to include them all.

That is all there is to configuring Planet Tool. Now let's define what gets generated.

11.3 Creating templates for Planet Tool

To define the files generated by Planet Tool, you use templates. Planet Tool includes the popular Apache Jakarta Velocity template engine, which makes it easy to generate any sort of text file. For each type of file you want to generate, you must provide a Velocity template. Planet Tool includes sample templates, and it is easy to modify them or create your own from scratch.

Similar to a JSP or ASP page, a Velocity template is a text file that is formatted as you would like the generated output to be formatted. You use Velocity Template Language (VTL) statements and expressions to insert values into the template and to control flow with conditionals and loops. You can call methods and access properties of Java objects. If you want the details, Velocity documentation is available at the Apache Jakarta web site.

The easiest way to learn Velocity is to see it in action, so let's look at a couple of examples. In the configuration file, you specify the control template. The control template governs the generation process and determines which files are generated, but it does not actually generate any files itself. Listing 11.2 shows the sample control template that is included with Planet Tool. It is named control.vm, following Velocity naming conventions.

Listing 11.2   The control template control.vm

```
#set($handles = $planet.groupHandles)
#foreach($handle in $handles)      <-①
   #set($outFile = $strings.concat([$handle, ".html"]))     <-②
   $generator.parse("html.vm", $outFile, "groupHandle", $handle)    <-③
   #set($outputFile = $strings.concat([$handle, ".rss"]))
   $generator.parse("rss.vm",  $outFile, "groupHandle", $handle)
   #set($outputFile = $strings.concat([$handle, ".opml"]))
   $generator.parse("opml.vm", $outFile, "groupHandle", $handle)
#end
```

The control.vm file is short, but it does a lot. Planet Tool puts an object called $planet into the Velocity context. By using the $planet object, we can access all of the data we defined in the configuration file. In control.vm, we get the collection of group handle strings from $planet and loop through that list with a Velocity #foreach statement ①.

For each group, we generate three files: HTML, RSS, and OPML. We use the group handle to form filenames for these three files. For example, we form the name of the HTML file by appending ".html" to the end of the group name ②.

For each file we wish to generate, we call $generator.parse() ③, which is built into Velocity. We pass it the name of the template to be used to generate the file, the name of the file to be generated, the name of an object to be made available to the generating template, and the object. In control.vm, we pass the group handle so that the generating templates know which group they are processing.

Let's examine the HTML template html.vm, shown in listing 11.3.

Listing 11.3   The HTML template html.vm

```
<html>
#set($group = $planet.getGroup($groupHandle))     <-①
#set($entries = $planet.getAggregation($group,$group.maxPageEntries))
<head>
   <meta http-equiv="Content-Type" content="text/html; charset=utf-8" >
   <title>$group.title</title>     <-②
</head>
```

```
<body>
<table>
<tr>
   <td width="80%" valign="top">
      <h1>$group.title</h1>      ←❸
      <p><i>$group.description<i/></p>
      <p>Last updated: $utilities.formatRfc822Date($date)</p>   ←❹
      #foreach($entry in $entries)      ←❺
         <h2>$entry.title</h2>      ←❻
         Blog: $entry.subscription.title <br/>   ←❼
         Date: $entry.published<br/>      ←❽
         <a href="$entry.permalink">Permalink</a><br/>   ←❾
         <p>$utilities.truncate($entry.content, 150, 160, "…")</p>   ←❿
      #end
   </td>
   <td width="20%" valign="top">
      <h3>Other formats</h3>
      <a href="$planet.configuration.siteUrl/${groupHandle}.rss">   ←⓫
         <img src="rss20.png" alt="RSS" border="0"></a>
      <p />
      <a href="$planet.configuration.siteUrl/${groupHandle}.opml">   ←⓬
         <img src="opml.png" alt="OPML" border="0"></a>
      <h3>Subscriptions</h3>
      #foreach ($sub in $group.subscriptions)   ←⓭
         <a href="$sub.siteUrl">$sub.title</a>
         <a href="$sub.feedUrl">(feed)</a><br/>
      #end
   </td>
</tr>
</body></html>
```

The html.vm template does not produce the most beautiful HTML; that is not its aim. It includes only the HTML needed to show you how to write a Planet Tool template. You can see the result of running the html.vm template in figure 11.2. Let's discuss each Velocity statement and expression in the template.

We start by using the $groupHandle that the control template passed to us to fetch the $group object from $planet ❶. On the next line, we use that $group object to get $entries, an aggregation of all entries in that group. In the page header, we use the group's title as the title for the HTML page ❷.

The body of the page contains a table with two columns. The first <td> is the left column, where we will display the aggregated entries. At the start of the first column, we display the title and description of the group ❸. And we use $utilities.formatRfc822Date($date) to display the current date in RFC-822 format ❹. Next, we loop through each of the $entries in the aggregation and #foreach ❺, we display the entry title ❻, subscription title ❼, entry publish date ❽, the entry's permalink ❾, and the content of the entry truncated to between 150 and 160 characters ❿.

In the right column, we display links to the RSS newsfeed ⓫ for the aggregated blog and the OPML file, which lists all of the subscriptions that are included in the aggregated blog ⓬. Below that, we have a #foreach loop that displays the web site and newsfeed link for each blog that is included in the aggregation ⓭.

Now that you understand both Planet Tool configuration and templates, let's run it.

11.4 *Running Planet Tool*

You can run Planet Tool by using one of the scripts provided. Use the planet-tool.sh shell script for UNIX; use the planet-tool.bat script for Windows. To run Planet Tool, open a console window, cd to the Planet Tool directory, and run the appropriate script for your platform, passing the path to your configuration file on the command line. You can find these scripts and instructions for building and running Planet Tool in the online examples directory java/ch11.

If you want your Planet Tool site to be kept up to date, you'll have to run it as either a scheduled task in Windows or a cron task in UNIX so that it runs every hour or whatever frequency you think is appropriate for your readers. Using the configuration data and templates we've examined so far, Planet Tool will generate an HTML, RSS, and OPML file. The HTML file will look something like the one shown in figure 11.2.

Now that you understand the big picture, let's cover some of the details you'll need to know to make the most of Planet Tool.

11.5 *Planet Tool object reference*

If you want to customize the output of Planet Tool, you'll need to know about the Velocity template language, which, as you've seen, is easy to learn. You'll also need to know what objects are available for use in your template code.

Initially, Planet Tool makes three objects available: $planet, $utilities, and $date. From the $planet object, you can gain access to the configuration, subscriptions, and groups defined in the Planet Tool configuration file. You can also call $planet.getAggregation() to create an aggregation for one group.

The $utilities object provides utility methods for escaping HTML, formatting dates, and truncating long text. The $date object contains the current date. It's an object of class java.util.Date, so check the Java API documentation for a description of its properties and methods.

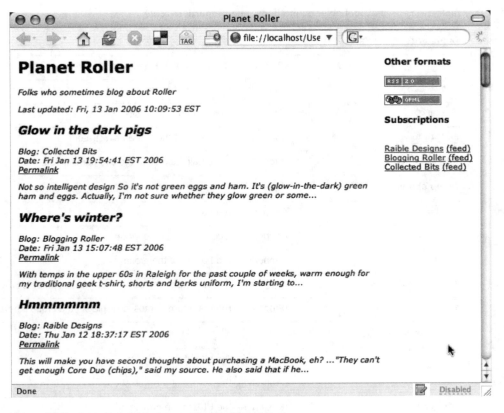

Figure 11.2 Aggregated blog generated by Planet Tool

Table 11.1 lists the properties for each of the six types of objects available to your templates.

Table 11.1 Planet Tool objects, methods, and properties

Planet object (available as $planet)	
`configuration`	(Property)—The Configuration object
`groupHandles`	(Property)—A collection of all available group handles
`getGroup($handle)`	(Method)—Returns the Group object for the specified handle
`getAggregation($group, $count)`	(Method)—Returns an aggregated collection of Entry objects

continued on next page

Table 11.1 Planet Tool objects, methods, and properties *(continued)*

Configuration object	
`url`	(Property)—The URL of the aggregated site
`title`	(Property)—The title of the site
`description`	(Property)—A description of the site
`adminName`	(Property)—The name of the site administrator
`adminMail`	(Property)—The email address of the site administrator
Group object	
`title`	(Property)—The title of the group
`description`	(Property)—A description of the group
`handle`	(Property)—The handle of the group
`maxPageEntries`	(Property)—The maximum entries to display in the group's HTML
`maxFeedEntries`	(Property)—The maximum entries to display in the group's newsfeed
Subscription object	
`title`	(Property)—The title of the web site
`author`	(Property)—The author of the web site
`feedUrl`	(Property)—The URL to the newsfeed
`siteUrl`	(Property)—The URL to the web site
Entry object	
`title`	(Property)—The title of the entry
`permalink`	(Property)—The permanent link to the entry
`author`	(Property)—The author of the entry
`published`	(Property)—The date and time that the entry was published
`updated`	(Property)—The date and time of the last update to the entry
`categories`	(Property)—The category names of the entry, a collection of strings
`subscription`	(Property)—A Subscription object associated with the entry

continued on next page

Table 11.1 Planet Tool objects, methods, and properties *(continued)*

Utilities object (available as `$utilities`)	
`textToHTML($text, $toXml)`	(Method)—An escape string for display in HTML or as an XML page if `$toXml` is true
`formatRfc822Date($date)`	(Method)—Formats a date for display using RFC-822
`formatIso8601Date($date)`	(Method)—Formats a date for display using ISO-8601
`truncate($str, $lower, $upper, $append)`	(Method)—Strips HTML, truncates string `$str` using `$lower` and `$upper` character counts, and appends string `$append` to the end
`truncateNicely($str, $lower, $upper, $append)`	(Method)—Preserves HTML, truncates string `$str` using `$lower` and `$upper` character counts, and appends string `$append` to the end

11.6 *Under the hood*

If Planet Tool doesn't work the way you want, you can change it. The source code and an Ant build script are included in the online examples that accompany this book. Figure 11.3 shows the Planet Tool architecture and what happens when the program runs.

When Planet Tool starts up, it initializes itself by reading the XML configuration file ①. Based on the data in the XML file, Planet Tool creates a configuration

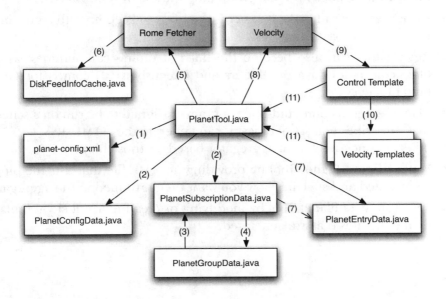

Figure 11.3 Planet Tool architecture

object, as well as subscription and group objects ②. Recall that a subscription can have multiple subscriptions ③, and each subscription can exist in multiple groups ④.

Once initialized, Planet Tool refreshes its subscription data. It does this by calling the ROME Fetcher ⑤ to fetch each newsfeed. ROME Fetcher keeps a cache of newsfeed data ⑥. It uses the conditional GET technique, which we described in chapter 5, to ensure that newsfeeds are fetched only when they have been updated. As each newsfeed is fetched and parsed, Planet Tool adds each entry to the corresponding subscription object ⑦.

Once the newsfeed cache is refreshed and each subscription object has been populated with entries, Planet Tool calls the Velocity template engine, passing in the name of the control template, to generate the files needed for the aggregated web site ⑧. Velocity calls the control template ⑨, and the control template calls other templates ⑩ to generate the files. Both the control template and the other templates have access to the Planet Tool Configuration, Subscription, Group, and Entry objects ⑪, as described in table 11.1.

11.7 *Summary*

- An aggregator is a web site that automatically combines multiple separately hosted blogs into one group blog with its own newsfeeds.

- An aggregator can make it easier for readers to keep up with a growing list of blogs on a topic of interest.

- Aggregators can also become the hubs of online communities, as Javablogs.com is for Java developers and Greensboro101.com is for Greensboro bloggers.

- Planet Tool is a command-line program, designed to be run on a schedule, that subscribes to a set of blogs. It can generate the HTML, RSS, OPML and other files needed for an aggregator based on those blogs.

- You configure Planet Tool by providing an XML file that lists the blogs to be included and specifies how you want them grouped in the aggregation.

- You customize Planet Tool by modifying or creating a Velocity template to define the files that are generated.

12

Searching and monitoring the Web

Use Internet and newsfeed search engines to search the world of blogs and to be alerted whenever a new blog entry matches your search terms.

Searching the Web can be done easily with Google and other Internet search engines, but monitoring is more difficult. If you want timely notification whenever a blogger or news item mentions you, your company, or your products, you may not be able to get that from a search engine that indexes the Web on its own schedule, as traditional search engines do. In addition, visiting your favorite search engine on a daily basis to rerun the same queries is inconvenient and tedious. That's why Google, Yahoo, and a host of other companies are offering new blog and news search services that index newsfeeds instead of web pages. These services can alert you through the magic of Atom and RSS whenever a new search result is found.

In this chapter, we'll tell you how to use one of the first (and still the most popular) blog search engines, Technorati.com. We'll explain how to use Technorati and how to program it via the Technorati API. We'll also give you an overview of competing blog search services from Google, Yahoo, Feedster, PubSub, and IceRocket. Let's get started with Technorati.

12.1 *Technorati.com: Conversation search engine*

Dave Sifry started Technorati in November 2002 to help people "find what's new in the blogging universe, and find out who's linking to whom." Technorati claims to be the authority on the *World Live Web*, a term the company uses to draw a distinction between the old Web of infrequently updated homepages and the new Web of constantly updated blogs and newsfeeds.

By subscribing to millions of newsfeeds (27 million at the time of this writing) and constantly indexing the web pages referenced by those newsfeeds, Technorati is able to give you the timely notification you need to search and monitor blogs.

Technorati tracks blogs. It ranks the *authority* of each blog by counting its *incoming links*—the number of web pages that link to that blog. The more links a blog has, the higher its Technorati ranking will be. Among other things, Technorati uses this ranking to determine the *Technorati 100* list of top bloggers. Technorati also tracks and counts links to each web page. Technorati uses this information to create its News Talk, Book Talk, and Movie Talk lists of the most discussed news stories, books, and movies in the past 12 hours. What can Technorati do for you? Let's start with search.

You can use Technorati to search by keyword or by URL. You simply visit the site and enter your search terms as you would with any other search engine.

For keyword searches, you can enter multiple words and phrases delimited by quotes. You can use boolean expressions with AND, OR, NOT, and grouping with parentheses. Unless you specify AND, Technorati will use OR to combine your search terms. For example, to search for all pages that contain "roller" or "blog" or "server" but do not contain the word "coaster," you'd enter

```
roller blog server NOT coaster
```

Or you could look for the Roller and either "blog server" or "blog software" like so:

```
roller AND ("blog server" OR "blog software")
```

For URL searches, you enter the full URL or a simplified form without an "http://" prefix, and Technorati will search for any page that links to that URL. Figure 12.1 shows the results of a Technorati URL search for my blog, which has the URL http://rollerweblogger.org/page/roller.

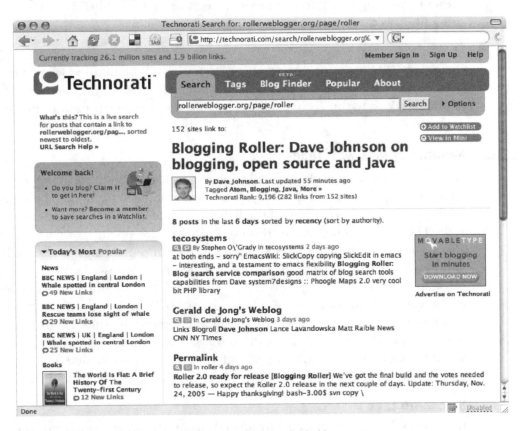

Figure 12.1 Results of a Technorati search on the author's blog

Because I registered as a Technorati user, created a profile, and uploaded my picture, you'll see my smiling face whenever my blog appears in Technorati results. Next to it, you can see that there are 282 links to my site, from 152 separate sources. And below that are links that allow you to sort the results by date or by authority. For each search result, Technorati displays a link and an excerpt. If the result is a blog, it returns a count of the blog's links so that you can gauge its authority.

12.1.1 Subscribing to Technorati watchlists

Whenever Technorati returns search results, it includes an Add to Watchlist option. You can see the link to the right of my mug shot in figure 12.1. If you click that link and you are a registered user, Technorati will create a watchlist and present you with a URL to the RSS newsfeed of that watchlist. It will look something like this (*NNN* will be replaced with an integer):

```
http://www.technorati.com/watchlists/rss.html?wid=NNN
```

Paste that URL into your newsfeed reader, and you'll be notified whenever Technorati finds a new match for your search. Watchlists aren't the only way you can automate access to the Technorati index; you can also write programs that call the Technorati API.

12.1.2 Monitoring tags with Technorati

Since the social bookmarks site Del.icio.us launched in 2003, *tagging* has become an increasingly popular way to organize information on the Web. Tagging means adding category information, in the form of simple keywords, to resources on the Web. There is no standard set of tags and there are no rules for which tags to apply when. You apply the tags you want, others add their tags, and together we build a *folksonomy*—a taxonomy created by the folks who use the Web.

The popularity of tagging makes it even easier to monitor the Web because you're getting help from lots of other citizens. At Del.icio.us, you can listen in to which web sites people are bookmarking and tagging by subscribing to a newsfeed for one or more tags. You can do the same thing at Furl.com, a competing social bookmarks site. You can also follow new photos uploaded and tagged on Flickr.com and Buzznet. If that's too much work for you, Technorati can help.

Technorati tags

In January 2005, Technorati introduced Technorati tags, which not only gives bloggers a way to add tags to blog entries but also brings together tagged content

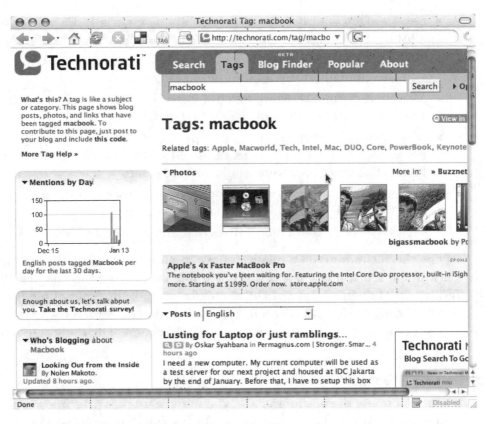

Figure 12.2 The Technorati Tags page for "macbook"

from a wide variety of tagging Web sites. For each tag, Technorati provides a constantly updated page that shows all recent blog posts with that tag; new links on the social bookmarking sites Del.icio.us and Furl.com with that tag; and new photos on the photo sharing sites Flickr and Buzznet.com with that tag. Figure 12.2 shows the Technorati Tags page for "macbook."

To learn more about applying tags to blogs and Web sites, see section 21.3, Tag the Web. Now let's learn how to automate our Technorati searches.

12.2 The Technorati API

The Technorati API is a web services interface to Technorati that allows your programs to retrieve the following types of information from Technorati:

- *Cosmos*—Find out who is linking to a URL. Given a URL, Technorati returns a list of all the pages or blogs that link to that URL.

- *Outbound*—Find out which blogs a specific blogger links to. Given a blog URL, Technorati returns a list of linked blogs.

- *Search*—Perform a keyword search. Given a keyword search string, Technorati returns a list of all of the pages that match.

- *Blog info*—Get information about a specific blog. Given a blog URL, Technorati returns the blog's name, newsfeed URLs, number of inbound links, last update time, Technorati rank, and language.

- *Get info*—Get information about a Technorati user including blog name, blog URL, and geographic information, if available.

- *Tag query*—Get a list of blog entries that link to one specific Technorati tag.

Calling the Technorati API is relatively easy because it's based on the principles of REST (Representational State Transfer), which we discussed in chapter 10. The Technorati API defines a set of URLs, one for each of the types of queries listed above. To call a Technorati method, you send an HTTP GET to its URL. If you need to pass parameters, you can do so via an HTTP request. The results are returned as XML.

12.2.1 *Getting a Technorati API key*

If you want to use the Technorati API, you must register as a Technorati user and request an API key. You can do this at the Technorati developers web site at http://technorati.com/developers. Once you have an API key, you are allowed to make up to 500 method calls per day. You should use the API only for personal and noncommercial purposes. Commercial use is not free. If you need a commercial license, contact the Technorati sales department.

12.2.2 *Calling the Technorati API*

Let's look at an example Technorati API call. We'll call the cosmos method to search for blogs that link to the URL http://atompub.org. To do this, we simply send an HTTP GET request to the following URL (substituting our API key where it says APIKEY):

```
http://api.technorati.com/cosmos?key=APIKEY&url=atompub.org&type=weblog
```

We pass two parameters, url and type. The url is the target URL; in our case, this is atompub.org. The type is weblog, which means that the results will be a list of the blogs that link to the target URL. You can also set the type to link to get a list of the freshest links—typically blog entries rather than blog sites—to the target URL. For the full list of parameters, see the API documentation on the Technorati developers site.

Let's try running that query. It's just an HTTP GET request, so you can use your browser. Enter the URL into your browser's address bar and hit [Enter], and you'll see something like listing 12.1. Let's take a closer look at these results.

Listing 12.1   Results of a Technorati API cosmos query

```
<tapi version="1.0">
    <document>
        <result>        ←①
            <url>atompub.org</url>      ←②
            <inboundblogs>16</inboundblogs>       ←③
            <inboundlinks>36</inboundlinks>     ←④
            <rankingstart>1</rankingstart>      ←⑤
        </result>
        <item>      ←⑥
            <weblog>        ←⑦
                <name>Virtual Projects:</name>       ←⑧
                <url>http://www.vrtprj.com/weblog</url>       ←⑨
                <rssurl></rssurl>       ←⑩
                <atomurl></atomurl>
                <inboundblogs>5</inboundblogs>      ←⑪
                <inboundlinks>5</inboundlinks>
                <lastupdate>2005-02-07 12:11:36 GMT</lastupdate>      ←⑫
            </weblog>
            <nearestpermalink>      ←⑬
                http://www.vrtprj.com/weblog/integrationstd/rss11andatom04.html
            </nearestpermalink>                              ⑭
            <excerpt>well received by selected members
                    of the RSS community</excerpt>
            <linkcreated>2005-02-07 12:10:01 GMT</linkcreated>      ←⑮
            <linkurl>        ←⑯
                http://www.atompub.org/2005/01/10/draft-ietf-atompub-format-
04.html
            </linkurl>
        </item>
    . . .
    </document>
</tapi>
```

Inside the <tapi> and <document> elements that wrap the results, there is a summary in the <result> element ①. This summary includes the target URL ② as well as the total number of blogs ③ and links ④ found.

The <rankingstart> element ❺ requires some explanation. Technorati limits the number of result items returned in each request. You can specify how many to return by using the limit parameter. The default is 20. The maximum is 100. So if you want to retrieve a 1,000-item query result, you do 10 requests. The first will return items 0 through 99. On the second, you set the start parameter to 100 to get the next batch; on the third, start=200; on the fourth, 300, and so on. The <rankingstart> element will contain the value of the start parameter you used in the query.

Following the result summary are the result items. Each represents one blog entry that links to the target URL. For the sake of brevity, only the first <item> ❻ is included in listing 12.1.

Within each <item> is a <weblog> element ❼, which contains information about the blog that links to the target URL. Included is the blog's name ❽, its URL ❾, the URL of the blog's RSS and Atom newsfeeds ❿ (if any were found), and the blog's inbound and outbound links ⓫ so that you can gauge the authority of the blog. Also included is the blog's last-update time ⓬.

Next, after the <weblog> element but still within the <item>, are elements that contain information about how the blog links to the target URL. The <nearest-permalink> element ⓭ contains the closest link to the target URL link (if any), which typically is the permalink of the blog entry that links to the target URL. The <excerpt> element ⓮ contains an excerpt extracted from the area around the link. The <linkcreated> element ⓯ contains the time that the link was created. Finally, the <link> ⓰ element contains the link that the blog entry uses to refer to the target URL.

That's just about all there is to a Technorati API result. We covered only a cosmos query result, but the other queries return the same basic XML format. Let's look next at how you can call the Technorati API from Java and do something useful with the results.

A simple Java Technorati API client

Calling the Technorati API may be easy, but no matter what programming language you are using, sending HTTP GET requests and parsing the XML that comes back is tedious work. If you want to do any serious programming with the Technorati API, you'll want a client library. You can find libraries for C#, Java, Perl, and Python on the Technorati developers web site.

Let's look at Technorati.java, a simple Technorati client library written in fewer than 200 lines of Java code. I wrote Technorati.java shortly after the Technorati API was introduced, and it is now included in the Technorati development

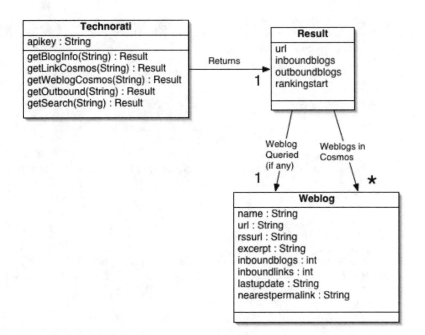

Figure 12.3   Classes defined in the Technorati.java client

kit. I've included an updated version of the code in the examples that accompany this book. You'll find it in the java/ch12 directory.

Technorati.java models the Technorati API using three Java classes: `Techno-rati`, `Result`, and `Weblog`. These classes and the relationships between them are shown in figure 12.3. The `Technorati` class is the entry point of the API. From the Technorati object, you can call any of the four Technorati API methods. Each method returns a Result object. A Result object may contain a Weblog object representing the blog you queried, and it may contain a collection of Weblog objects, one for each search Result item.

Technorati to OPML

Let's say you want to subscribe to all of the blogs recommended by your favorite blogger, the ones listed on his blogroll. You can do this by using the Technorati API to get a list of all the outbound links on his blog, generating an OPML subscription file, and then loading that into your favorite newsfeed reader.

Tapi2opml.java is a simple command-line program that uses Technorati.java to call the Technorati API and creates an OPML file containing the results. Listing 12.2 shows the code.

Listing 12.2   Tapi2opml.java: returns Technorati results in OPML format

```java
package com.manning.blogapps.chapter12;
import java.io.*;
import java.util.Iterator;
import org.jdom.JDOMException;
import org.jdom.input.SAXBuilder;
public class Tapi2opml {
    public static void main(String[] args) throws Exception {
        if (args.length < 3) {          ←❶
            System.out.println(
                    "USAGE: tapi2opml [blogcosmos|linkcosmos|outbound]
                    [search] [filename]");
            System.exit(-1);
        }
        String option = args[0];
        String search = args[1];
        String filename = args[2];
        Technorati tapi = new Technorati();          ←❷
        Technorati.Result result = null;
        if (option.equals("blogcosmos")) {          ←❸
            result = tapi.getWeblogCosmos(search);
            System.out.println("Writing blogcosmos to OPML");
        } else if (option.equals("linkcosmos")) {
            result = tapi.getLinkCosmos(search);
            System.out.println("Writing linkcosmos links to OPML");
        } else if (option.equals("outbound")) {
            result = tapi.getOutbound(search);
            System.out.println("Writing outbound links to OPML");
        }
        FileWriter fw = new FileWriter(filename);
        PrintWriter pw = new PrintWriter(fw);
        pw.println(tapi2opml(result));          ←❹
        pw.close();
        System.out.println("Wrote file ["+filename+"]");
    }
    public static String tapi2opml(Technorati.Result result) {          ←❺
        StringBuffer sb = new StringBuffer();
        sb.append("<?xml version=\"1.0\" encoding='utf-8'?>\n");          ←❻
        sb.append("<opml version=\"1.1\">\n<body>\n");
        Iterator blogs = result.getWeblogs().iterator();          ←❼
        while (blogs.hasNext()) {
            Technorati.Weblog blog = (Technorati.Weblog) blogs.next();
            if (blog.getRssurl()
                != null && blog.getRssurl().length() > 0) {          ❽
                sb.append("<outline text=\"");
                sb.append(blog.getName());
                sb.append("\" xmlUrl=\"");
                sb.append(blog.getRssurl());
                sb.append("\" htmlUrl=\"");
                sb.append(blog.getUrl());
```

```
                    sb.append("\" />\n");
            }
        }
        sb.append("</body></opml>");
        return sb.toString();      ◁─❾
    }
}
```

Inside the main method of Tapi2opml.java, we first check for the presence of three arguments ❶: the type of call to be performed (`blogcosmos`, `linkcosmos`, or `outbound`), the search term (either a URL or a search expression), and the filename to which the resulting OPML is to be written. Next, we create an instance of the Technorati object by calling its default constructor ❷. Note that the Technorati object will look for your Technorati string in a file called technorati.licence, so when you run the program, make sure you have that file in the root of your classpath.

Depending on the type of query that was specified on the command line, we next call either `getWeblogCosmos()`, `getLinkCosmos()`, or `getOutbound()`, passing in the search term ❸. We open up the output file, call `tapi2opml()` to write the query results to a string, and then write that string to the output file ❹. That's all there is to the main method.

In the `tapi2opml()` method ❺, we use a simplistic approach to writing out the OPML: a `java.util.StringBuffer`. First, we write out the `<opml>` and `<body>` elements ❻. Next, we loop through the Weblog objects in the `Result` ❼, and for each one that has an RSS newsfeed URL ❽, we write out an `<outline>` element containing that URL. Finally, we close the OPML and return the string we created ❾.

You can find the source code for the Tapi2opml.java program and instructions for running it in the java/ch12 directory of the examples. That's all it takes to call the Technorati API. Now, let's cover the features of other blog search services.

12.3 *Other blog search services*

Technorati is certainly not alone in the blog search arena. At the time of this writing, at least a dozen blog search engines are competing for your attention. To help you understand what a blog search service can do and to help you find the one that's right for you, let's review the features offered by some of the most popular ones. Table 12.1 shows the features offered by blog search services from Google, Yahoo, Technorati, Feedster, PubSub, and IceRocket.

Table 12.1 Blog search services' features comparison matrix

	Google	Yahoo	Technorati	Feedster	PubSub	IceRocket
Search by keywords	X	X	X	X	X	X
Search by boolean expression	X		X	X	X	
Search by words in title	X				X	X
Search by blog category/tags			X			X
Restrict by author	X					X
Restrict by date range	X	X				X
Restrict to language	X	X	X			X
Adult content filter	X					
Limit search via OPML file				X		
Limit search to one URL			X	X	X	X
Search who links to URL	X		X	X	X	X
Web interface to search	X	X	X	X		X
Sort results by date	X	X	X	X	X	X
Sort results by relevance	X			X		
Sort results by blog authority			X			
Results as newsfeed	X	X	X	X	X	X
Results as email				X		
Blog search API		X	X	X	X	
Open Search support				X		X

Here's a guide to the features listed in the table.

- *Search by keywords*—All blog search services support a simple keyword search that will search for any of these words, for all of these words, or for this exact phrase.

- *Search by boolean expression*—Provide support for powerful boolean search expressions with AND, OR, NOT, and grouping.

- *Search by words in title*—Restrict search to consider only text in entry titles.
- *Search by blog category/tags*—Restrict search to entries with specific words in tags.
- *Restrict by author*—Restrict search by author name.
- *Restrict by date range*—Restrict search by start date, end date, or both.
- *Restrict to language*—Restrict search to entries in one language.
- *Adult content filter*—Filter adult content out of search results.
- *Limit search via OPML file*—Search only web sites or newsfeeds that are listed in an OPML file you provide to the search service.
- *Limit search to one URL*—Limit search to one blog or URL.
- *Search who links to URL*—Search entries that link to a specific URL.
- *Web interface to search*—Provide search results on the Web and not just in newsfeed format.
- *Sort results by date*—Allow sorting by chronological and reverse chronological order.
- *Sort results by relevance*—Sort results by how closely they match search criteria.
- *Sort results by blog authority*—Sort results by how many bloggers link to the blog (e.g., size of Technorati blog cosmos).
- *Results as newsfeed*—Provide results in newsfeed format.
- *Results as email*—Provide email alerts of new search results.
- *Blog search API*—Provide access to search results by web services API.
- *Open Search support*—Support the Open Search API, covered in section 12.4.

Here's a listing of URLs for the blog services compared above:

- *Google Blog Search*—http://blogsearch.google.com
- *Yahoo News Search*—http://search.news.yahoo.com
- *Technorati*—http://technorati.com
- *Feedster*—http://feedster.com
- *PubSub*—http://pubsub.com
- *IceRocket*—http://icerocket.com

So now you know what a good blog search engine can do for you. Before we wrap up the chapter, let's cover a new standard from Amazon.com for newsfeed-friendly search engines.

12.4 *Open Search: The future of search?*

Having lots of choices for search is a good thing, and it would certainly be nice if more Web sites offered search results in newsfeed form. But there's also a problem with having so many search services: The search engines all work differently. They accept different search parameters. Some provide search APIs and some don't. These differences make it difficult to write applications that use search engines. Using RSS or Atom as a standard format for search results is a step in the right direction, but we developers need both a standard way to query and a standard way to receive query results. That's the problem that the A9's Open Search standard is designed to solve.

Open Search is a specification that defines a standard interface for search engines. It was designed by A9, a subsidiary of Amazon, for the A9.com search aggregator. At A9.com, you can search against multiple Web sites, including Amazon.com, Feedster, IceRocket, Flickr, Wikipedia, and any site that supports the Open Search Standard. Let's take a quick look at Open Search and see why you might want to use it in your applications.

12.4.1 *Open Search description format*

A Web site that supports Open Search must provide a description file that defines the search services available at the site. Below is an example description file (taken from the Open Search developers Web site) for a fictional search service at Example.com:

```
<?xml version="1.0" encoding="UTF-8"?>
<OpenSearchDescription xmlns="http://a9.com/-/spec/opensearch/1.1/">
   <ShortName>Web Search</ShortName>
   <Description>Use Example.com to search the Web.</Description>
   <Tags>example web</Tags>
   <Contact>admin@example.com</Contact>
   <Url type="application/rss+xml" template=
      "http://example.com/?q={searchTerms}&amp;
      pw={startPage?}&amp;format=rss"/>
</OpenSearchDescription>
```

The description file contains some simple metadata about the search services, such as name, description, and contact information. The important part of the description is the <url> element, which shows you two things: the type attribute indicates that search results will be returned in RSS format, and the template attribute defines how a search URL must be formed.

To form a search query using this example, you simply replace the words within the curly braces (shown in bold) with your search parameters. In the place of *searchTerms*, you put the keywords to be searched for. In the place of *startPage*, you put the page number, in case you want to iterate through the results page by page.

Now that we know how to form a search query, let's take a look at what comes back.

12.4.2 *Open Search result elements*

If an Open Search result comes back in RSS or Atom format, it may include additional search data in the form of Open Search result elements. Listing 12.3 shows an example of search results in RSS format (also taken from the Open Search developers Web site) with the Open Search result elements shown in bold.

Listing 12.3   Example search results in RSS format with Open Search result elements

```xml
<?xml version="1.0" encoding="UTF-8"?>
<rss version="2.0"
     xmlns:opensearch="http://a9.com/-/spec/opensearch/1.1/">   <-1
  <channel>
    <title>Example.com Search: New York history</title>
    <link>http://example.com/New+York+history</link>
    <description>Search results for "New York history"
                at Example.com</description>
    <opensearch:totalResults>4230000</opensearch:totalResults>   <-2
    <opensearch:startIndex>21</opensearch:startIndex>   <-3
    <opensearch:itemsPerPage>10</opensearch:itemsPerPage>   <-4
    <opensearch:link rel="search"
      href="http://example.com/opensearchdescription.xml"
      type="application/opensearchdescription+xml"/>   5
    <opensearch:Query role="request" searchTerms="New York History" />   6
    <item>   <-7
      <title>New York History</title>
      <link>http://www.columbia.edu/cu/lweb/eguids/
                    amerihist/nyc.html</link>
      <description>
        ... Harlem.NYC - A virtual tour and information on
        businesses ...  with historic photos of Columbia's own New York
        neighborhood ... Internet Resources for the City's History. ...
      </description>
    </item>
    <!-- 9 additional <item> elements appear here -->
  </channel>
</rss>
```

Let's review the Open Search elements in the listing. First, the newsfeed declares the Open Search XML namespace with the prefix opensearch ❶. Next, within the <channel> element of the RSS, we have some top-level search metadata:

❷ <opensearch:totalResults> indicates that there are 4,230,000 search results.

❸ <opensearch:startIndex> tells us that the first item here is actually the 21st search result.

❹ <opensearch:itemsPerPage> indicates that each RSS page will include 10 search items.

❺ <opensearch:link> defines the URL of the Open Search definition file for the search service.

❻ <opensearch:Query> is used here to echo back the search that created the results, but it can also be used to indicate example and alternate queries to the caller.

And finally, after the channel-level metadata, we have the search results each represented as an RSS <item> ❼. Now that you understand the basics of Open Search, let's discuss why you'd want to use it in your applications.

12.4.3 Why Open Search?

For a Web site that provides search services, the benefit of using Open Search is interoperability. Any application that understands Open Search will work with your service. Folks who use Amazon.com's search engine will be able to plug your search service right into the A9.com search portal.

For an application that consumes search services, the benefit of using Open Search is a standard mechanism for querying a variety of search sites. The code you write for working with one search service will work for all of them. And that makes it easier for you to write code that searches and monitors the Web. That brings us to the end of the chapter and time to sum up what we have learned.

12.5 Summary

- Searching the Web is easy with traditional search services, but monitoring the Web is not so simple and convenient.

- New blog search services that index newsfeeds instead of Web pages and return search results in newsfeed form make it much easier to monitor blogs, news, and other frequently updated Web sites.

- Technorati, one of the oldest and most popular blog search services, offers advanced features, including blog authority rankings, tags, and an extensive web services API.

- The Technorati API example in this chapter, Tapi2opml.java, can be used to find the blog and newsfeed URLs on a blog and write them out in OPML format for use in your newsfeed reader.
- The blog search service market is heating up, as Google, Yahoo, and a host of smaller companies compete to provide the best blog search service.
- A9.com's Open Search specification provides a standard interface for issuing queries against and retrieving results from search engines and is supported by Feedster, IceRocket, Flickr, Wikipedia, and others.

13

Keeping your blog in sync

Use a simple command-line program
to keep your main blog updated with
posts from your secondary blogs.

Rangu, whom we met in chapter 1, developed quite an interest in blogging and started a number of blogs. He started one on Blogger.com to write about software development issues. He started one on Typepad.com to write about photography and to host his photographs with Typepad's integrated photo gallery feature. He also participates in a group blog, where he and six co-authors write about local politics and community activism. To top it all off, he has his own personal blog running on a PC at his house, which he considers his primary blog.

When Rangu posts to one of his secondary blogs, he often posts a note on his primary blog to let his readers know about it. But what he'd really like to do is to capture all of the posts on his secondary blogs and copy them to his primary blog, keeping his primary blog in sync with the others. That way, readers of his main blog would get everything he posts to his secondary blogs, and his primary blog could serve as an archive of all his posts, regardless of where they were posted.

What Rangu needs is what blogger and author Ben Hammersley calls a *cross poster*. Hammersley's Perl-based CrossPoster works by parsing each of his secondary blog's newsfeeds, looking for posts authored by him during the last 24 hours, and posting them to his primary blog via the XML-RPC based Movable Type API. Unfortunately, Hammersley's CrossPoster can parse only RSS newsfeeds and can post only to Movable Type blog servers. It won't work for Rangu because he uses Roller for his primary blog.

Since Hammersley's cross poster won't do for Rangu, we'll write a new one. In this chapter, we'll show you how to write a cross poster in C# that can handle either RSS or Atom newsfeeds and can post to any blog server that supports the MetaWeblog API.

13.1 Designing Cross Poster for C#

The design for Cross Poster for C# is simple. It runs once a day and processes a list of blogs in a configuration file, each specified by a newsfeed URL and an optional author name. For each blog in the list, Cross Poster checks the blog's newsfeed. If the newsfeed has been modified in the last 24 hours, Cross Poster will parse it. For each item in the newsfeed, Cross Poster will check the publication date and the author. If the item was published in the last 24 hours and the author matches the one specified for the blog, Cross Poster will post that item to a destination blog.

13.1.1 *Design limitations*

Cross Poster uses HTTP conditional GET to determine which newsfeeds have been updated. Newsfeeds that do not support HTTP conditional GET will be fetched and reparsed every time Cross Poster is run. That is a waste of bandwidth and processing time, but it does not prevent Cross Poster from working.

Cross Poster uses item-level publication dates, <pubDate> in RSS and <published> in Atom newsfeeds, to determine which items should be included in the daily blog digest. Newsfeeds that do not provide this information will not work in Cross Poster. That includes all RSS newsfeeds in formats older than RSS 0.93 and some post-0.93 newsfeeds that omit the optional <pubDate> element. Before you use an RSS newsfeed in Cross Poster, check to make sure it includes item-level publication dates.

Now that we know how Cross Poster will work, let's discuss how it will be configured.

13.2 *Configuring Cross Poster for C#*

To configure Cross Poster, we'll use a simple XML file consisting of a list of subscription elements, one for each secondary blog, and a destination element for the primary blog. Listing 13.1 shows an example of a Cross Poster configuration file.

Listing 13.1 Cross Poster configuration file CrossPoster.config.xml

```
<?xml version="1.0" encoding="utf-8" ?>
<cross-poster>        ←❶
   <subscription>    ←❷
      <feed-url>http://blogger.com/rangu/atom.xml</feed-url>    ←❸
      <author>Rangu</author>      ←❹
   </subscription>
   <subscription>
      <feed-url>http://localscene.typepad.com/rss.xml</feed-url>
      <author>rangu</author>
   </subscription>
   <destination>    ←❺
      <metaweblog-url>
         http://rangu.example.com/blog/xmlrpc      ←❻
      </metaweblog-url>
      <username>rangu</username>      ←❼
      <password>tiger</password>      ←❽
      <blogid>rangublog</blogid>      ←❾
      <category>General</category>      ←❿
   </destination>
</cross-poster>
```

Inside the root element `<cross-poster>` ❶, you can define any number of `<subscription>` elements ❷. In this configuration file, we have two. The first one is for Rangu's Blogger.com blog. Each subscription element must include a `<feed-url>` element ❸ containing a newsfeed URL and may include an optional `<author>` element ❹, but only if you wish to limit the items to those by a specific author. The newsfeed URL may point to either an RSS or an Atom newsfeed; Cross Poster can handle either format.

At the end of the file is the `<destination>` element ❺, which specifies the MetaWeblog API connection parameters for the destination blog. The connection parameters are the MetaWeblog API URL ❻, username ❼, password ❽, blog ID ❾, and category ❿. That's all we need to configure Cross Poster. Now let's take a look at the code.

13.3 *The code for Cross Poster for C#*

Cross Poster is a small program, designed to be invoked daily as a Windows Scheduled Task. It's small, in part, because it does not have any user interface. Another reason for its small size is reuse. We are reusing two components we developed in earlier chapters: the AnyFeedParser.cs newsfeed parser from chapter 5 and the MetaWeblog API blog client library from chapter 9. Let's look at the code, shown in listing 13.2.

Listing 13.2 Source code for Cross Poster for C#

```
using System;
using System.Xml;
using System.Net;
using System.Collections;
using BlogApps_Chapter05;      ←❶
using BlogApps_Chapter09;      ←❷

namespace BlogApps_Chapter13 {

   public struct Subscription {      ←❸
      public string feed_url;
      public string author;
   }

   public class CrossPoster {
      static string metaweblog_url = null;   ←❹
      static string username = null;
      static string password = null;
      static string blogid = null;
      static IList categories = new ArrayList();
      static IList subs = new ArrayList();   ←❺
```

```
public static void Main(string[] args) {        ◄─❻

    System.Console.WriteLine("CrossPoster for C#");
    try {
        InitFromXml();        ◄─❼
    } catch (Exception e) {
        System.Console.WriteLine(
            "ERROR: reading config file: " + e.Message);
        return;
    }
    IFeedParser feedParser = new AnyFeedParser();        ◄─❽

    IBlog blog = null;
    try {
        IBlogConnection con = new MetaWeblogConnection(        ◄─❾
            metaweblog_url, username, password, blogid);
        blog = con.GetBlog(blogid);        ◄─❿
    }
    catch (WebException e) {
        System.Console.WriteLine(
            "ERROR: connecting to destination server: " + e.Message);
        return;
    }
    if (blog == null) {
        System.Console.WriteLine(
            "Blog not found with blogid: " + blogid);
        return;
    }

    DateTime since = DateTime.Now.AddDays(-1.0);        ◄─⓫

    foreach (Subscription sub in subs) {        ◄─⓬

        HttpWebRequest request =
            (HttpWebRequest)WebRequest.Create(sub.feed_url);        ◄─⓭
        request.IfModifiedSince = since;

        try {        ◄─⓮
            HttpWebResponse response =
                (HttpWebResponse)request.GetResponse();        ◄─⓯
            IDictionary feedMap =
                feedParser.ParseFeed(response.GetResponseStream());        ◄─⓰

            IList itemsList = (IList)feedMap["items"];        ◄─⓱
            foreach (IDictionary itemMap in itemsList) {        ◄─⓲
                string author = (string)itemMap["author"];        ◄─⓳
                if (author == null) {
                    author = (string)itemMap["dc:creator"];
                }
                DateTime pubDate = (DateTime)itemMap["pubDate"];        ◄─⓴
                if (itemMap["pubDate"] == null) {
                    pubDate = (DateTime)itemMap["dc:date"];
                }
```

```
            if (pubDate > since                                    ㉑
                && sub.author != null
                              && sub.author.Equals(author)) {
                string title = (string)itemMap["title"];
                string content = (string)itemMap["description"];  ← ㉒
                if (content == null) {
                    content = (string)itemMap["content:encoded"];
                }
                IBlogEntry entry = blog.CreateEntry();    ← ㉓
                entry.Title = title;
                entry.PublicationDate = pubDate;
                entry.Content = content;
                entry.Categories = categories;
                blog.SaveEntry(entry, true);
            }
        }
    }
    catch (WebException e) {
        HttpWebResponse res = (HttpWebResponse)e.Response;
        if (res != null) {
            if (res.StatusCode == HttpStatusCode.NotModified) { ← ㉔
              System.Console.WriteLine("Not modified: "+sub.feed_url);
            }
        }
        else {
            System.Console.WriteLine(    ← ㉕
                "ERROR: connecting to destination server?");
            System.Console.WriteLine(e.Message);
            System.Console.WriteLine(e.StackTrace);
        }
    }
  }
}
private static void InitFromXml() {
    // . . .
}
  }
}
```

The code starts with the usual preamble of using statements. We include the chapter 5 namespace ❶ so that we can use the IFeedParser interface and the AnyFeedParser.cs implementation of that interface. We also include the chapter 9 namespace ❷ so that we can use the MetaWeblog API implementation of the blog client library.

Inside the chapter 13 namespace, we define a subscription struct ❸, which we will use to represent the subscriptions specified in the configuration file.

Next, we define the CrossPoster class and its member variables. We define member variables for each of the destination connection parameters ❹ from the configuration file. We also define a list ❺ to hold a Subscription structure for each of the subscriptions to be processed.

Next, we define the main method of the class ❻. Before we do anything else, we initialize the class by calling the initFromXml() method ❼ to read the XML configuration file and initialize the member variables. We don't include the code for initFromXml() here because it is just routine XML parsing code, but the complete source code is available in the online examples. After that, we create the IFeedParser ❽ necessary to parse the newsfeeds, establish a blog connection ❾ and get the blog object ❿ we need to post the destination blog.

Before processing the subscriptions, we define a DateTime variable called since and set it for one day in the past ⓫. We'll use this variable to ensure that we only download newsfeeds and post blog entries that have changed in the last day.

Now we come to the heart of the program: the foreach loop that processes subscriptions ⓬. The first step in processing a subscription is to fetch it with a web request. So we set up a web request for the subscription's newsfeed URL ⓭ and set the request's IfModifiedSince field so that an HTTP conditional GET is used to fetch the newsfeed, as described in chapter 5, section 5.5.1.

Within the subscription processing foreach loop, we do our work inside a try block ⓮ so that an error processing one subscription will not prevent us from continuing with the rest. Inside the try block, we first get the web response ⓯. If the newsfeed has not changed since the IfModifiedSince time, request.getResponse() will throw an exception. That's no problem. The newsfeed hasn't been updated in the last 24 hours, so we just continue with the next subscription.

Once we get a response, we hand the response stream over to the IFeedParser to parse the newsfeed into dictionary representation ⓰ in feedMap. We don't care about the rest of the feed, just the items; so we get the items collection from feedMap ⓱ and loop through the items in the feed, each represented by an IDictionary ⓲.

For each item, we need to check the author and the publication date. We have to play some games here because the publication date and author may be specified using the ordinary RSS elements <pubDate> and <author> or they may be specified by the Dublin Core elements <dc:date> and <dc:creator>. We don't have to worry about Atom element names here because, as you may remember from chapter 5, an IFeedParser maps the Atom elements to RSS element names.

So here we check for the author element **⓳** and determine whether it is a match. Then, we check for the publish date **⓴**.

If the item was published in the last 24 hours and the author matches **㉑**, we post the item to the destination blog. First, we have to get the title and the content, searching for the content in either a `<description>` field or a `<content:encoded>` field because RSS allows both **㉒**. Once we get those, we are ready to post using the blog client library **㉓**. After that, we loop again to process the next subscription.

The `catch` block at the end caches both `HTTP_NOT_MODIFIED` responses and errors. For the former, we just write out a simple "Not Modified" message **㉔**. For the latter, we print out an error message and a stack-trace to help the user debug the problem **㉕**.

That's all there is to the Cross Poster. Now let's discuss how to run it.

13.4 *Running Cross Poster for C# and Java*

You can find instructions for building and running Cross Poster for C# in the readme.html file in the examples directory csharp/ch13. We have also included a Java version of Cross Poster, which you can find in the directory java/ch13.

13.5 *Summary*

- Bloggers who post to multiple blogs will find Cross Poster useful in keeping their primary blog up to date with postings from their secondary blogs.
- Ben Hammersley's CrossPoster for Movable Type is written in Perl. It can read RSS newsfeeds and post to Movable Type based blogs.
- Cross Poster for C# can read RSS and Atom newsfeeds and can post to a blog server that supports the MetaWeblog API.
- Cross Poster for C# can be run from the command line, but it's designed to be run every 24 hours as a Windows Scheduled Task.

Blog by sending email

14

Post to your blog from a cell phone or any device that can send e-mail.

Nina, whom we met in chapter 1, realized her addiction to blogging one summer morning when she had the sudden urge to post a message to her blog—while sitting in a canoe in the middle of Lake Crabtree. She had her mobile phone with her, but its limited web browser made it impossible to log in to her blog server. Her phone couldn't handle complex web sites very well, but it could send email. It took Nina only a couple of seconds to realize that with her knowledge of blogging APIs, it would be easy to write a simple blog app that would allow her to blog by sending email.

In this chapter, we'll look at an example program, which we'll call Mail Blogger for C#, that you can use for *moblogging*, blogging from your mobile phone.

14.1 Designing Mail Blogger for C#

Mail Blogger runs every hour or half-hour, checks a POP3 email mailbox, and posts any blog messages it finds. How does Mail Blogger know which messages are blog messages? And how does it prevent others from posting to your blog? Mail Blogger searches for email messages whose first line begins with "MailBlogger:" followed by a codeword. If it finds that and the codeword is correct, it will strip off the first line and post the rest of the message to a blog.

14.2 Configuring Mail Blogger for C#

To configure Mail Blogger, we'll use a simple XML configuration file like the one in listing 14.1.

Listing 14.1 Mail Blogger configuration file MailBlogger.config.xml

```xml
<?xml version="1.0" encoding="utf-8" ?>
<mail-blogger>
   <codeword>panther</codeword>      <-1
   <mailbox>      <-2
      <username>nina</username>      <-3
      <password>leopard</password>      <-4
      <pop-server>pop-server.example.com</pop-server>      <-5
   </mailbox>
   <destination>
      <metaweblog-url>http://blogs.example.com/xmlrpc</metaweblog-url>  6
      <username>nina</username>      <-7
      <password>tiger</password>      <-8
      <blogid>47562</blogid>      <-9
      <category>General</category>      <-10
```

```
        <category>General</category>
    </destination>
</mail-blogger>
```

A Mail Blogger configuration specifies a mailbox to be monitored and a blog to which messages are to be posted. Let's cover the important elements of the configuration file XML, so you will be able to write your own.

First, within the root `<mail-blogger>` element, we find the `<codeword>` element ❶, which contains the codeword for posting. Pick any codeword you want, but for security's sake, make it different from your email or blog password.

Next, we have the `<mailbox>` element ❷, which contains the information needed to connect to and monitor your mailbox for incoming blogs. You must specify your mail server username ❸, password ❹, and the hostname of your POP3 mail server ❺.

Finally, we have the `<destination>` element, which specifies the blog to which posts are to be made. First, we specify the MetaWeblog API target URL ❻ for the blog server. After that, we specify the username ❼, password ❽, and blog ID ❾ of the blog. At the end of the `<destination>` element, you can specify a list of blog categories ❿ to be applied to posts made by email. (This is optional.).

That's all there is to Mail Blogger configuration, so let's move on to its implementation.

14.3 *The code for Mail Blogger for C#*

With the blog client library we developed in chapter 9, implementing Mail Blogger for C# is relatively easy. The tricky part is monitoring the mailbox for new posts, and it's tricky only because .NET does not have built-in support for retrieving mail. After looking at a number of alternatives, we finally decided on Pawel Lesnikowski's Mail Namespace for C# because it is the one used in Das Blog, a popular open source and ASP.NET-based blog server. Listing 14.2 shows the code.

> **Listing 14.2   Source code for Mail Blogger for C#: MailBlogger.cs**

```
using System;
using System.IO;
using System.Xml;
using System.Collections;
using BlogApps_Chapter09;           <--❶
using Lesnikowski.Pawel.Mail.Pop3;   <--❷
```

```
namespace BlogApps_Chapter14 {

    public class MailBlogger {        ◄─❸
        string codeword;
        string mail_username;
        string mail_password;
        string mail_pop_server;
        string dest_metaweblog_url;
        string dest_username;
        string dest_password;
        string dest_blogid;
        IList dest_categories = new ArrayList();        ◄─❹

        static void Main(string[] args) {        ◄─❺
            MailBlogger mailBlogger = new MailBlogger();
            mailBlogger.InitFromXml();
            mailBlogger.run();
        }
        private void run() {
            IBlog blog = null;
            try {
                IBlogConnection con = new MetaWeblogConnection(        ◄─❻
                    dest_metaweblog_url, dest_username, dest_password,
                    "0123456789ABCDEF");
                blog = con.GetBlog(dest_blogid);
            } catch (Exception e) {
                System.Console.WriteLine(
                  "ERROR: problem connecting to destination blog: " + e.Message);
                return;
            }
            Pop3 pop = null;
            try {
                pop = new Pop3();        ◄─❼
                pop.userName = mail_username;
                pop.password = mail_password;
                pop.host = mail_pop_server;
                pop.Connect();
                pop.Login();
                pop.GetAccountStat();
            } catch (Exception e) {
                System.Console.WriteLine(
                    "ERROR: problem connecting to POP3 mailbox:" + e.Message);
                return;
            }

            int count = pop.messageCount;        ◄─❽
            for (int i=count; i > 0; i--) {        ◄─❾
                Pop3Message message = pop.GetMessage(i);        ◄─❿
                string body = message.body;        ◄─⓫
                StringReader reader = new StringReader(body);        ◄─⓬
```

```
        String first = reader.ReadLine();
        if (first != null && first.StartsWith("MailBlogger:")) {   ⬅❶③
            string cw = first.Substring(12);   ⬅❶④
            if (cw.Equals(codeword)) {   ⬅❶⑤
                string line = reader.ReadLine();
                string content = "";
                while (line != null) {   ⬅❶⑥
                    content += line;
                    line = reader.ReadLine();
                }
                string title = message.subject;
                Console.WriteLine("title: "+title);
                Console.WriteLine("content: "+content);

                IBlogEntry entry = blog.CreateEntry();   ⬅❶⑦
                entry.Categories = dest_categories;
                entry.Title = title;
                entry.PublicationDate = DateTime.Now;
                entry.Content = content;
                blog.SaveEntry(entry, true);   ⬅❶⑧

                pop.DeleteMessage(i);   ⬅❶⑨
            }
        }
    }
    pop.Close();   ⬅②⓪
}
private void InitFromXml() {
    // . . .
}
    }
}
```

MailBlogger.cs starts with the typical preamble of using declarations. After the standard system namespaces, we declare that we are using the BlogApps_Chapter09 namespace ❶ so that we can use the blog client library. We also use Lesnikowski's Mail namespace ❷.

Next, we declare the MailBlogger class ❸ and within that, the fields needed to hold the information read from the configuration file. Note that the categories are stored as an IList of strings ❹.

In the main method for Mail Blogger ❺, we create an instance of the Mail-Blogger class, call the InitFromXml() method to read the configuration file, and then call the run() method to start processing the mailbox contents. We didn't include the code for InitFromXml() method here because it is just simple XML parsing code and not important to the topic at hand.

In the run() method, we first initialize the XML-RPC version of the blog client library ❻. Next, we initialize and connect to the POP server mailbox using the configuration parameters mail_username, mail_password, and mail_pop_server ❼.

Now that all of the initialization is done, we get to the heart of the matter. We get a count of the incoming messages available in the mailbox ❽ and we loop through them ❾, going in reverse order because we will be deleting any messages we post.

Inside the message-processing loop, we first get the message ❿. Then, we get the body of the message as a string ⓫ and wrap it with a string reader ⓬ so that we can read it line by line. We read the first line and check to see whether it begins with "MailBlogger:" ⓭. If so, we get the remainder of the first line ⓮ and compare it to the codeword specified in the configuration file ⓯. If it matches, we read in the remaining lines of the message and put them in the string content ⓰. We then use the blog client library to create a blog entry ⓱, set its fields, and post the message to the blog server ⓲. We want to make sure that we don't post the message again, so we delete it from the mailbox ⓳.

Once we finish processing messages, we close the mail server connection ⓴, because it is the nice thing to do, and we are done.

14.4 *Running Mail Blogger for C# and Java*

You can find instructions for building and running Mail Blogger for C# in the readme.html file in the examples directory csharp/ch14. We have also included a Java version of Mail Blogger, which you can find in the directory java/ch14.

14.5 *Summary*

- You can use Mail Blogger to blog from mobile devices that have limited web access.

- Mail Blogger monitors a mailbox and posts any messages that are tagged as blog messages and that contain the correct codeword.

- .NET does not support retrieving email, but Lesnikowski's open source Mail Namespace for C# can retrieve mail from any POP mail server.

15

Sending a daily blog digest by email

Produce a daily summary of one or more blogs for readers who want to follow your blog but don't want to use a newsfeed reader.

As Nina and Rangu worked to bring to life the grand plan they began in chapter 1, they encountered some resistance. Some FinModler employees were too attached to using email and didn't want to learn to use a newsfeed reader to keep up with blogs and newsfeeds. They wanted to be notified by email of new blog posts instead. Nina and Rangu tried to convince them that using a newsfeed reader would be a much better option. Rangu even showed the resisters how the Thunderbird e-mail client could be configured to read newsfeeds, but they were not convinced.

Nina did some research and found that some blog servers support email notification, but she knew that this would not be a complete solution because many newsfeeds at FinModler were produced by aggregators and other software. Eventually, Nina and Rangu realized that the only way to hook the resisters on blogs and newsfeeds was to give them what they wanted. So the pair developed a program that monitors a set of blogs and sends out a daily digest of new blog entries, a *blog digest*, at the end of each day. In this chapter, we'll show you how to do the same in C#.

15.1 Designing Blog Digest for C#

Much like Cross Poster for C# in chapter 13, Blog Digest for C# is a simple command-line program that's designed to run once a day as a scheduled task. It processes a list of blogs in a configuration file, each specified by a newsfeed URL. For each blog in the list, Blog Digest will check the blog's newsfeed. If the newsfeed has been modified in the last 24 hours, Blog Digest will parse it. For each item in the newsfeed, Blog Digest will check the publication date. If the item was published in the last 24 hours, Blog Digest will add that post to an email message. After processing all of the blogs in the list and building an email containing them, Blog Digest will send that email to a specified address.

15.1.1 Design limitations

Blog Digest uses publication dates to determine which blog entries are new, so it has the same design limitations as Cross Poster for C#. These limitations are covered in chapter 13, section 13.1.1.

15.2 Configuring Blog Digest for C#

To configure Blog Digest, we'll use a simple XML configuration file. The file defines the newsfeeds to be monitored, which we'll call subscriptions, and the email destination for the daily blog digest. Listing 15.1 shows an example configuration file.

Listing 15.1   Blog Digest configuration file BlogDigest.config.xml

```
<?xml version="1.0" encoding="utf-8" ?>
<blog-digest>      ◄━❶
   <subscription>    ◄━❷
      <feed-url>http://blogs.example.com/blog/otto/rss</feed-url>    ◄━❸
   </subscription>
   <subscription>
      <feed-url>http://blogs.example.com/blog/rangu/rss</feed-url>
   </subscription>
   <destination>    ◄━❹
      <smtp-server>smtp.example.com</smtp-server>    ◄━❺
      <username>rangu</username>    ◄━❻
      <password>tiger</password>    ◄━❼
      <to-address>bloglist@example.com</to-address>    ◄━❽
      <from-address>rangu@example.com</from-address>    ◄━❾
   </destination>
</blog-digest>
```

Inside the root element `<blog-digest>` ❶, you can define any number of `<subscription>` elements ❷. In this configuration file, we have two. The first one is for a blog written by Rangu's manager, Otto. The second `<subscription>` element is for Rangu's Blogger.com blog. Each `<subscription>` element must include a `<feed-url>` element ❸ containing a newsfeed URL. The newsfeed URL may point to either an RSS or an Atom newsfeed; Blog Digest can handle either format.

At the end of the file is the `<destination>` element ❹, which specifies the email destination of the daily blog digest. The parameters are the SMTP server hostname ❺, mail server username ❻, mail server password ❼, the address to send to ❽, and the address to send from ❾. That's all we need in order to configure Blog Digest. Note that we allow the specification of only one email address. If you need to send to more, you can send to an email alias.

Now that we have defined the configuration for Blog Digest, let's take a look at the code.

15.3 *The code for Blog Digest for C#*

The code for Blog Digest for C# , shown in Listing 15.2, is similar to the Cross Poster for C# code covered in chapter 13.

Listing 15.2 Source Code for Blog Digest for C#: BlogDigest.cs

```csharp
using System;
using System.Xml;
using System.Text;
using System.Net;
using System.Collections;
using BlogApps_Chapter05;        ← ❶
using System.Web.Mail;           ← ❷

namespace BlogApps_Chapter15 {

    public class BlogDigest {     ← ❸
        string username;
        string password;
        string to_address;
        string from_address;
        string smtp_server;
        IList subs = new  ArrayList();    ← ❹
        string auth_key =
            "http://schemas.microsoft.com
                        /cdo/configuration/smtpauthenticate";    ❺
        string username_key =
            "http://schemas.microsoft.com/cdo/configuration/sendusername"; ❻
        string password_key =
            "http://schemas.microsoft.com/cdo/configuration/sendpassword"; ❼

        static void Main(string[] args) {    ← ❽
            BlogDigest blogDigest = new BlogDigest();
            blogDigest.InitFromXml();
            blogDigest.run();
        }

        public void run() {
            System.Console.WriteLine("BlogDigest for C#");
            IFeedParser feedParser = new AnyFeedParser();    ← ❾
            DateTime since = DateTime.Now.AddDays(-5.0);    ← ❿

            StringBuilder sb = new StringBuilder();    ← ⓫
            foreach (string sub in subs) {    ← ⓬

                HttpWebRequest request =
                    (HttpWebRequest)WebRequest.Create(sub);    ← ⓭
                request.IfModifiedSince = since;

                try {
                    HttpWebResponse response =
                        (HttpWebResponse)request.GetResponse();    ← ⓮
                    IDictionary feedMap =
                        feedParser.ParseFeed(response.GetResponseStream());    ← ⓯

                    sb.Append("-----------------------------\n");    ← ⓰
```

```
            sb.Append("Blog: ");
            sb.Append(feedMap["title"]);
            sb.Append("\n\n");

            IList itemsList = (IList)feedMap["items"];          ◁─⑰
            foreach (IDictionary itemMap in itemsList) {
                DateTime pubDate = (DateTime)itemMap["pubDate"];      ◁─⑱
                if (itemMap["pubDate"] == null) {    ◁─⑲
                    pubDate = (DateTime)itemMap["dc:date"];
                }
                if (pubDate > since) {       ◁─⑳
                    string title = (string)itemMap["title"];
                    string content = (string)itemMap["description"];
                    if (content == null) {
                        content = (string)itemMap["content:encoded"];
                    }
                    sb.Append("Title: ");
                    sb.Append((String)itemMap["title"]);       ◁─㉑
                    sb.Append("\n");
                    sb.Append(itemMap["link"]);         ◁─㉒
                    sb.Append("\n\n");
                }
            }
        }
        catch (WebException e) {
            HttpWebResponse res = (HttpWebResponse)e.Response;
            if (res != null) {
                if (res.StatusCode == HttpStatusCode.NotModified) {  ◁─㉓
                    System.Console.WriteLine("Not modified: "+sub);
                }
            }
            else {
                System.Console.WriteLine(         ◁─㉔
                    "ERROR: connecting to destination server?");
                System.Console.WriteLine(e.Message);
                System.Console.WriteLine(e.StackTrace);
            }
        }
    }
    string text = sb.ToString();        ◁─㉕
    if (text.Length > 0) {
        try {
            MailMessage Message = new MailMessage();       ◁─㉖
            Message.To = to_address;        ◁─㉗
            Message.From = from_address;         ◁─㉘
            Message.Subject = "Daily Blog Digest";
            Message.Body = text;          ◁─㉙
            Message.Fields.Add(auth_key, "1");
            if (username != null && password != null) {       ◁─㉚
                Message.Fields.Add(username_key, username);
                Message.Fields.Add(password_key, password);
            }
```

```
            SmtpMail.SmtpServer = smtp_server;
            SmtpMail.Send(Message);      ←❸❶
        }
        catch(Exception ex) {
            Console.WriteLine("ERROR: " + ex.ToString() );
            while( ex.InnerException != null ) {     ←❸❷
                Console.WriteLine(
                    "ERROR" + ex.InnerException.ToString() );
                ex = ex.InnerException;
            }
        }
    }
}
    private void InitFromXml() {
        // . . .
    }
    }
}
```

BlogDigest.cs starts with the familiar preamble of using statements. We include the BlogApps_Chapter05 namespace ❶ so that we can use the AnyFeedParser class, and we include the System.Web.Mail namespace ❷ so that we can use .NET's built-in support for sending mail via SMTP protocol.

Just inside the BlogDigest class ❸, we define fields for each of the parameters we will read from the configuration file. We use a list to hold the newsfeed URL strings ❹. We also include keys that we'll use later for setting email connection authentication ❺, username ❻, and password ❼.

In the main method of the class, we create an instance of the class called the InitFromXml() method to read the configuration file ❽ and then we use the run() method to start processing.

In the run() method, we first create an instance of the AnyFeedParser class ❾ and create a DateTime object set to one day in the past ❿. Next, we create a StringBuilder, which we'll use to build the digest email message. ⓫

Using a foreach loop ⓬, we iterate through each of the subscriptions specified in the configuration file. In the loop, we create an HttpWebRequest to fetch the subscription's newsfeed ⓭ and then set the IfModifiedSince property to perform an HTTP conditional GET. Next, inside a try block, we attempt to get the response from the web server ⓮. If the newsfeed has not been modified since the since date, the call to request.getResponse() will throw an exception. If that happens, we'll move on to process the next subscription. If we get a response, we hand the response stream to the feed parser ⓯.

Once we have parsed a newsfeed, we add a header to the email message with the newsfeed's title ⑯ and loop through the items in the newsfeed ⑰.

For each item in the newsfeed, we get the publication date ⑱. If we don't find it under the key pubDate ⑲, we look for a Dublin Core date using the key dc:date. If the item's date is more recent than the since date ⑳, we add the item's title ㉑ and link ㉒ to the email message.

Still inside the foreach loop, we have a catch block to catch any web exceptions that occur during the processing of one subscription. If the response status code is HTTP_NOT_MODIFIED ㉓, we print out a "Not Modified" message and proceed to the next feed. Otherwise, we print out the exception ㉔ and continue with the next subscription.

Once we finish processing subscriptions and we're out of the foreach loop, we convert the StringBuilder to a string ㉕. If that string is not empty, we create a mail message ㉖ and set its to ㉗ and from ㉘ fields based on configuration parameters. We set the text of the message ㉙ using the email message we built. If the configuration specified a mail server username and password ㉚, we set those fields in the message too. Finally, we send the message on its way ㉛.

Note that we set up and send the message in a try-catch block, and we take special care to print out any exceptions that are thrown ㉜. The .NET System. Web.Mail classes do not have the best exception handling, and sometimes the only way to debug problems with them is to examine the inner exceptions.

15.4 Running Blog Digest for C# and Java

You can find instructions for building and running Blog Digest for C# in the readme.html file in the examples directory csharp/ch15. We have also included a Java version of Blog Digest, which you can find in the directory java/ch15.

15.5 Summary

- For users who refuse to use a newsfeed reader, use a blog server that supports email notification of new blog entries.
- If your blog server doesn't support email notification of new blog entries or if you want to provide email notification of new entries in newsfeeds not produced by blog servers, use Blog Digest.
- Blog Digest can read multiple RSS and Atom newsfeeds and notify you of new posts by sending email via any SMTP-based mail server.
- Blog Digest is designed to be run every 24 hours as a scheduled task.

16

Blog your software
build process

Automatically announce new soft-
ware builds and publish test results to
your blog using a custom blogging
task for the popular Ant build system.

In chapter 1, Otto asked Rangu to announce new software builds on the development group's blog for the benefit of the quality and sales teams. Rangu responded by modifying the group's build script so that it could automatically post build announcements. But because Rangu also wanted to use the group's blog to provide feedback to the development team, he modified the build script again so that it could report nightly build results and upload unit-test reports to the blog server. Developers were pleasantly surprised to find that they could subscribe to Rangu's development blog and receive a fresh set of build and test results in their newsfeed reader every morning.

Rangu found these things easy to do because he uses the Ant build system to execute his build scripts. Ant builds use a set of predefined *tasks* for doing things like compiling Java code, copying files, and running JUnit tests. You can provide your own custom Ant tasks by extending the Ant `org.apache.tools.ant.Task` class. Just define a property setter for each attribute you want your task to support and an execute method that Ant will call when your task is invoked. For more information on Ant and developing custom tasks, refer to *Java Development With Ant* by Erik Hatcher and Steve Loughran.

16.1 Blogging from Ant

In this chapter, we'll develop two new Ant tasks: `<post-blog-entry>` for posting a blog entry and `<post-blog-resource>` for uploading a file to a blog. Let's look at how these two tasks are used in an Ant script that uploads a new build and announces it by posting a blog entry. listing 16.1 shows how you would invoke these new tasks in an Ant build script.

Listing 16.1   Using the Ant blogging tasks

```
<post-blog-resource      ◄─❶
    username="admin"      ◄─❷
    password="admin"
    blogid="adminblog"
    apitype="metaweblog"
    targeturl="http://localhost:8080/roller/xmlrpc"
    filename="./dist/ch16.jar"      ◄─❸
    contenttype="application/x-jar"      ◄─❹
    resourcename="ch16.jar"      ◄─❺
    urlproperty="url" />      ◄─❻

<post-blog-entry      ◄─❼
    username="admin"
    password="admin"
```

```
blogid="adminblog"
category="Build"
apitype="metaweblog"
targeturl="http://localhost:8080/roller/xmlrpc"
title="New build of BlogTasks available"    ←8
content="&lt;a href='${url}'&gt;Click to Download&lt;a&gt;" />    ←9
```

In this Ant script fragment, we first use the `<post-blog-resource>` task to upload a file ❶. The task attributes specify the blog server connection parameters ❷: username, password, blogid, apitype, and targeturl. We also specify the name of the file to be uploaded, which in this case is a relative path to a jar file called ch16.jar ❸. We specify the content-type of the file, which is `application/x-jar` ❹, and the name we want to assign to the file once it is uploaded ❺.

After `<post-blog-resource>` uploads the file, it receives the URL of the uploaded file from the blog server. If we're going to create a blog entry that refers to that file, we need to know that URL. By default, the task stores the URL in an Ant property named `uploadurl`, but in our example, we ask that the URL be stored in a property named `url` ❻.

Once we upload the jar file, we blog about it using the `<post-blog-entry>` task ❼. We specify the same set of blog connection parameters. Next, we pass in the blog title ❽ and content ❾. Special XML characters in the content attribute are escaped, so it's difficult to tell that the content is simply a link to the jar we just uploaded, with the words "Click to download." Without escaping, the content would look like this:

```
<a href="${url}">Click to Download</a>
```

The variable reference `${url}` refers to the URL of the jar we uploaded with the `<post-blog-resource>` task.

Now that we know how we want the new Ant tasks to work, let's discuss how to implement them.

16.1.1 *Base blog task*

Because the two Ant blogging tasks we're developing in this chapter each need the same set of blog server connection attributes and the same connection logic, it makes sense for them to share a common base class that handles those concerns. Once we have a common base class, it will be easy to develop other Ant tasks for blogging.

First, we'll create an abstract base class `BaseBlogTask.java`. We'll make it easy for subclasses to blog by providing a `getBlog()` method, which returns a `Blog`

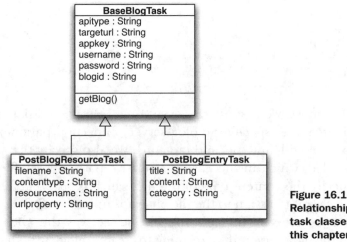

**Figure 16.1
Relationship between the
task classes developed in
this chapter**

object that supports all of the methods needed for interacting with a blog. Our abstract class will require the following attributes:

- *apitype*—This is the type of API, either "metaweblog" or "atom."
- *targeturl*—This is the URL of the blog server's web services interface.
- *appkey*—This is the application key (may be required for some older blog servers).
- *username*—This is the username for logging into the blog server.
- *password*—This is the password for logging into the blog server.
- *blogid*—This is the ID of the target blog.

Figure 16.1 illustrates the relationship between the BaseBlogTask class and the other task classes we'll develop in this chapter.

BaseBlogTask.java is short and sweet, just a method and some properties, so let's take a look at the whole class, shown in listing 16.2.

Listing 16.2 Source code for the custom Ant BaseBlogTask.java

```
package com.manning.blogapps.chapter16;
import org.apache.tools.ant.*;
import com.manning.blogapps.chapter10.blogclient.*;
import java.util.*;

public abstract class BaseBlogTask extends Task {          ◀━❶
    protected String apitype = "metaweblog";    ◀━❷
```

```
    protected String targeturl = null;
    protected String appkey = null;
    protected String username = null;
    protected String password = null;
    protected String blogid = null;

    protected Blog getBlog() throws Exception {    ◁─❸
        BlogConnection con =    ◁─❹
            BlogConnectionFactory.getBlogConnection(
                apitype, targeturl, username, password);
        if (appkey != null) {
            con.setAppkey(appkey);    ◁─❺
        }
        return con.getBlog(blogid);    ◁─❻
    }
    public void setApitype(String apitype) {    ◁─❼
        this.apitype = apitype;
    }
    public void setTargeturl(String targeturl) {
        this.targeturl = targeturl;
    }
    public void setAppkey(String appkey) {
        this.appkey = appkey;
    }
    public void setUsername(String username) {
        this.username = username;
    }
    public void setPassword(String password) {
        this.password = password;
    }
    public void setBlogid(String blogid) {
        this.blogid = blogid;
    }
}
```

The file starts with the usual package imports. The class itself, BaseBlogTask, extends the Ant org.apache.tools.ant.Task class ❶. Inside the class, we define a member field for each of the task attributes and we set the default apitype to "metaweblog" ❷.

In the task's getBlog() method ❸, we call the BlogConnectionFactory to get a BlogConnection suitable for the apitype we have ❹. Once we have a Blog-Connection, we set its apikey, if we have one ❺. Only Blogger.com requires an apikey, but it no longer requires a unique one—anybody can use the apikey "0123456789ABCDEF".

Finally, we use the blogid to fetch and return a Blog object ❻, ready for use by the calling subclass. The rest of the class is the setters, one for each of the attributes supported by the task, starting with the apitype ❼. Now, let's put `Base-BlogTask` to use.

16.1.2 *Post blog entry task*

We'll implement `<post-blog-entry>` as a Java class `PostBlogEntryTask.java` by extending `BaseBlogTask`. We'll inherit the blog server connection attributes, so we need to add only the three new attributes listed below. All of these attributes are optional arguments, but you should set at least one title and one content attribute—otherwise, there will be nothing to your blog entry.

- *title*—This is the title of the blog post. It should be plain text without HTML markup.
- *category*—This is the category for the blog post.
- *content*—This is the content for the blog post. It may include HTML markup, but any characters with special meaning in XML must be escaped.

Because we're simply extending the `BaseBlogTask`, the code for `PostBlogEntry-Task.java` is pretty brief, only about 50 lines. listing 16.3 shows it in its entirety.

Listing 16.3   PostBlogEntryTask.java

```java
package com.manning.blogapps.chapter16;
import org.apache.tools.ant.*;
import com.manning.blogapps.chapter10.blogclient.*;
import
    com.manning.blogapps.chapter10.metaweblogclient.MetaWeblogConnection;
import com.manning.blogapps.chapter10.atomclient.AtomBlogConnection;
import java.util.*;

public class PostBlogEntryTask extends BaseBlogTask {          ◁─❶
    protected String title = null;       ◁─❷
    protected String category = null;
    protected String content = null;

    public void execute() throws BuildException {         ◁─❸
        try {
            System.out.println("Posting to blog");
            System.out.println("    username=" + username);
            System.out.println("    targeturl=" + targeturl);
            System.out.println("    apitype=" + apitype);
            System.out.println("    title=" + title);
            System.out.println("    content=" + content);
            System.out.println("    category=" + category);
```

```
        Blog blogSite = getBlog();
        BlogEntry entry = blogSite.newEntry();     ◄─④

        if (title != null) {
            entry.setTitle(title);     ◄─⑤
        }
        if (category != null) {
            List categories = new ArrayList();
            categories.add(
                new BlogEntry.Category(category));
            entry.setCategories(categories);    ◄─⑥
        }
        if (content != null) {
            entry.setContent(
                new BlogEntry.Content(content));    ◄─⑦
        }
        entry.setPublicationDate(new Date());    ◄─⑧
        entry.save();    ◄─⑨
        String id = entry.getId();
        System.out.println("New post id is " + id);    ◄─⑩

    } catch (Exception e) {
        throw new BuildException(e);    ◄─⑪
    }
}
public void setTitle(String title) {    ◄─⑫
    this.title = title;
}
public void setCategory(String category) {
    this.category = category;
}
public void setContent(String content) {
    this.content = content;
}
}
```

We start by declaring the class `PostBlogEntryTask` ❶ to extend `BaseBlogTask`. Inside the class, we declare a member field for each of the attributes we discussed above: title, category, and content ❷.

In the `execute()` method ❸ and within a try-catch block, we first print out the key attributes so that they will appear in the Ant log file. Next, we call `BaseBlogTask`'s `getBlog()` to get a `Blog` object and then use that to create a `BlogEntry` ❹.

Once we've created a `BlogEntry`, we need to set the title, content, and category specified by the task attributes. Again, we must be forgiving here because all three arguments are optional. If we have a title, we set it on the entry ❺. If we have a category, we create a `BlogEntry.Category` object, add it to a `java.util.List`, and set the entry's categories property ❻. If we have content, we create a `BlogEntry.Content` object and use it to set the entry's content property ❼. We set the entry's publication date to the current time ❽ and, at last, we are ready to post by calling its `save()` method ❾. To verify that a new blog entry was posted, we print the ID returned by the blog server ❿. And finally, we close the `try-catch` block. If anything went wrong, we throw an Ant `BuildException` ⓫ so that Ant's error handler can take over.

That's really all there is to posting to a blog from Ant. The rest of the class consists of property setters, one for each attribute of the Ant task, starting with the title attribute ⓬.

Now let's move on to the post blog resource task.

16.1.3 *Post blog resource task*

The `<post-blog-resource>` task also extends `BaseBlogTask`. To enable the uploading of a file to a blog, the task adds four attributes:

- *filename*—This is the name of the file to be uploaded. It may be an absolute or relative path.
- *contenttype*—This is the content-type of the file. Its value must be a MIME media type; for example, `text/plain` for plain text, `text/html` for HTML, or `application/x jar` for a Java jar file.
- *resourcename*—name to be assigned to uploaded file on server.
- *urlproperty*—This is the name of the Ant property in which the URL of the uploaded file should be stored. It defaults to `url` if not specified.

Let's turn our attention now to the source, shown in listing 16.4.

Listing 16.4   Source code for custom Ant task PostBlogResourceTask.java

```
package com.manning.blogapps.chapter16;
import java.io.*;
import org.apache.tools.ant.*;
import com.manning.blogapps.chapter10.blogclient.*;

public class PostBlogResourceTask extends BaseBlogTask {     ◄─❶
    private String filename = null;     ◄─❷
    private String contenttype = null;
    private String resourcename = null;
    private String urlproperty = "uploadurl";
```

```
    public void execute() throws BuildException {      ←❸
        try {
            System.out.println("Posting file resource to blog");   ←❹
            System.out.println("   username=" + username);
            System.out.println("   targeturl=" + targeturl);
            System.out.println("   apitype=" + apitype);
            System.out.println("   filename=" + filename);
            System.out.println("   contenttype=" + contenttype);
            System.out.println("   resourcename=" + resourcename);

            Blog blog = getBlog();   ←❺
            BlogResource resource = blog.newResource(
                resourcename, contenttype, new File(filename));   ←❻
            resource.save();
            getProject().setProperty(urlproperty,
                resource.getContent().getSrc());              ❼

        } catch (Exception e) {
            throw new BuildException(e);
        }
    }
    public void setFilename(String filename) {    ←❽
        this.filename = filename;
    }
    public void setContenttype(String contenttype) {
        this.contenttype = contenttype;
    }
    public void setResourcename(String resourcename) {
        this.resourcename = resourcename;
    }
    public void setUrlproperty(String urlproperty) {
        this.urlproperty = urlproperty;
    }
}
```

After the familiar set of package `import` statements, we start by declaring the `PostBlogResourceTask` class ❶, which extends `BaseBlogTask`. Next, we declare a member field for each of the attributes mentioned above ❷.

In the `execute()` method ❸, we first print out the key attributes so that they'll appear in the Ant log ❹. Next, we call `getBlog()` to get a `Blog` object ❺. Once we have a `Blog` object, all it takes is one call to `Blog.newResource()` ❻ to upload the file specified by the task attributes. The `newResource()` method returns a `BlogResource` object representing the newly uploaded file. We store the URL of the uploaded file as an Ant property by using the task's `getProject()` method to get the Ant project object and the project's `setProperty()` method to set the property ❼.

That's all there is to the implementation of the `<post-blog-resource>` task. The rest of the class consists of property setters, one for each attribute of the Ant task, starting with the filename attribute ❽.

16.2 *Summary*

- A blog can be used to automate the announcement of new software builds, to log build results, and to post unit-testing reports.

- It's easy to add custom tasks to the Ant-based build system by extending the Ant `org.apache.tools.ant.Task` class.

- Our custom Ant `<post-blog-entry>` task can be used to post a blog entry to any blog server that supports the MetaWeblog API or Atom Protocol.

- Our custom Ant `<post-blog-resource>` task can be used to upload files to those same types of servers.

- If you want to implement your own custom Ant tasks for blogging, do so by extending `BaseBlogTask` and using `getBlog()` to establish a connection with a blog server.

Blog from a chat room

A chatbot that enables participants in an online chat to post messages to a blog using wiki syntax.

In Internet Relay Chat (IRC) channels where geeks and hackers gather to discuss the issues of the day, share links, and provide informal technical support, you'll find that many have implemented their own *chatbots*. A chatbot is a program that responds to commands entered in a *chat channel*, or room. Some chatbots act as knowledge bases, storing the definitions of common terms. Some just meet and greet new visitors to the channel. Recently, developers have been creating chatbots that know how to blog.

In the #mobitopia channel on Freenode (irc.freenode.net), where mobile developers gather to chat about programming techniques for phones and other mobile devices, a chatbot named mobibot provides a number of helpful services. It performs Google searches, provides weather reports, and retrieves stock quotes. It also collects all URLs mentioned in the channel and formats them as an RSS newsfeed, so that anybody can subscribe to the interesting links discussed in the channel. In the #rtpbloggers channel on Freenode, a chatbot named hughbot does something similar: it looks for URLs and whenever it sees one, it uses the MetaWeblog API to post it to a blog. We can do the same thing.

17.1 A wiki-blogging chatbot

There is probably no business case for blogging from a chat room, but chatbots are fun, and a blogging chatbot is a good example of how any program can be made to blog. Besides, sometimes the most crazy and seemingly useless ideas can lead to great things. In that spirit, let's use the blog client library we developed in chapter 10 to develop Chat Blogger, our very own blogging chatbot. To make things even more interesting, we'll enable Chat Blogger to understand wiki syntax, so that we can easily add formatting and links to the posts we create.

Figure 17.1 illustrates how Chat Blogger will work once we have completed it. The screenshot shows the Mac-based Fire chat program, which is logged in to an IRC channel named #testchannel. Chat Blogger joins the channel at 8:44 PM using the nickname *blogbot* and is greeted by *snoopdavey*. Next, snoopdavey greets blogbot, posts a short blog message using wiki syntax, issues the undo command to unpost the blog message, and then terminates blogbot by asking it to exit.

17.1.1 Chat Blogger design

Here's how Chat Blogger works. A configuration file specifies which IRC chat server and channel is to be monitored for commands and which blog server is to be used for blog posts. When Chat Blogger starts, it logs into the specified chat server, enters the specified chat channel, and waits for commands. A Chat

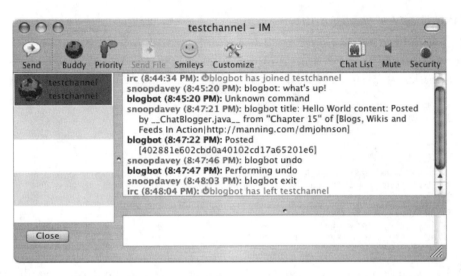

Figure 17.1 A chatbot in action

Blogger command must begin with the Chat Blogger's nickname (which is configurable). Chat Blogger responds to the following commands:

- *<nickname>* *title:* *<title text>* *content:* *<content text>*—This posts a blog entry with the specified title and content. The title text should be plain text (no HTML) and the content may contain JSPWiki syntax.

- *<nickname>* *undo*—This deletes the most recently posted blog entry, but only if that entry was posted in the past 30 seconds.

- *<nickname>* *exit*—This causes the Chat Blogger to exit and shut itself down.

17.1.2 *Chat Blogger guidelines*

Since anybody in the chat channel can issue commands to the chatbot, you should be careful. Let's discuss some guidelines for using Chat Blogger.

First, you should establish a blog especially for your Chat Blogger. You probably don't want random chat participants posting to your personal or corporate blog. The Chat Blogger's blog should be clearly labeled so that readers know it is not the work of one individual author. Second, unless you have a private, password-protected chat channel, you'll probably want to accompany the Chat Blogger by logging in to the same chat channels the Chat Blogger does. If somebody commands Chat Blogger to exit, you'll want to be there to restart it.

17.1.3 *Chat Blogger configuration*

To configure Chat Blogger, we'll use a simple properties file that specifies blog server and chat server connection parameters. Here is an example Chat Blogger properties file:

```
chat_port=6667
chat_hostname=irc.freenode.net
chat_channel=#testchannel
chat_nick=blogbot
chat_altnick=_blogbot
blog_apitype=metaweblog
blog_username=admin
blog_password=admin
blog_id=adminblog
blog_category=Chat
blog_url=http://localhost:8080/roller/xmlrpc
wiki_url=http://localhost:8080/wiki
```

Below is an explanation of each of the properties in the file. Note that all properties are required.

- *chat_hostname* is the hostname of the chat server to be used.
- *chat_port* is the port number of the chat server to be used.
- *chat_channel* is the chat channel to join when the chatbot connects to the server.
- *chat_nick* is the nickname to be used by Chat Blogger.
- *chat_altnick* is the alternate nickname to be used if your first choice is already in use.
- *blog_apitype* is either "atom" or "metaweblog."
- *blog_username* is the username for login to your blog server.
- *blog_password* is the password for login to your blog server.
- *blog_id* is the ID of the blog where messages should be posted.
- *blog_category* is the category for new blog entries.
- *blog_url* is the target URL of your blog server's Atom or MetaWeblog API interface.
- *wiki_url* lets you specify the base URL of your wiki site. Use this if you have a JSPWiki and you want wiki-words you use in your posts to post to that wiki.

Now that we know how Chat Blogger works and how it will be configured, let's discuss the components necessary to implement it.

17.1.4 *Chat Blogger construction*

Fortunately, all of the components needed to create Chat Blogger are available as open source Java class libraries. We'll use our blog client library from chapter 10 to do the blogging; we'll use the Relay-IRC Chat engine to do the chatting; and we'll use the JSPWiki *wiki rendering engine* to turn wiki syntax into HTML. By putting these pieces together, we'll be able to implement Chat Blogger with a very small amount of Java code.

Figure 17.2 shows the object classes involved in the Chat Blogger. The main class is ChatBlogger, which extends the Relay-IRC ServerAdapter class so that it can hook into messages coming from the Relay-IRC Server. As soon as Chat Blogger is notified of an IRC server connection, it creates a ChannelBlogger object, which extends the Relay-IRC ChannelAdapter to listen to messages in the chat.

When ChannelBlogger gets commands, it calls back to ChatBlogger to perform the requested actions. ChatBlogger calls its JSPWiki WikiContext to format the entry and its Blog to post the entry to the blog server. Now that we've defined the design, let's examine the implementation.

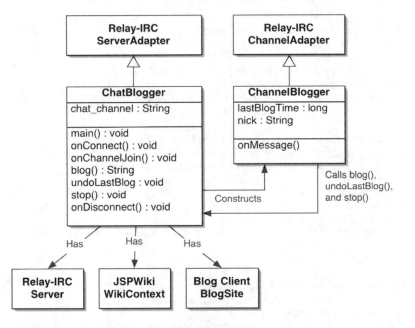

Figure 17.2   Chat Blogger classes and relationships

17.1.5 *Chat Blogger implementation*

Chat Blogger is implemented in two Java class files, ChatBlogger.java and ChannelBlogger.java. We'll start by examining the main class, ChatBlogger. java, shown in listing 17.1.

Listing 17.1   Source code for main class ChatBlogger.java

```java
package com.manning.blogapps.chapter17;
import java.io.*;
import java.util.*;
import com.ecyrd.jspwiki.*;
import org.relayirc.chatengine.*;
import com.ecyrd.jspwiki.providers.FileSystemProvider;
import com.manning.blogapps.chapter10.blogclient.*;


public class ChatBlogger extends ServerAdapter {        ◄—❶
    private Blog blog;        ◄—❷
    private Server server;
    private WikiContext context;
    private String chat_channel;        ◄—❸
    private List categories = new ArrayList();


    public static void main(String args[]) throws Exception {        ◄—❹
        new ChatBlogger();
    }
    public ChatBlogger() throws Exception {        ◄—❺
        Properties config = new Properties();
        config.load(new FileInputStream("config.properties"));        ◄—❻
        chat_channel = config.getProperty("chat_channel");

        String blog_apitype =  config.getProperty("blog_apitype");
        String blog_username = config.getProperty("blog_username");
        String blog_password = config.getProperty("blog_password");
        String blog_id =       config.getProperty("blog_id");
        String blog_url =      config.getProperty("blog_url");
        String category =      config.getProperty("blog_category");
        if (category != null) {
            BlogEntry.Category cat = new BlogEntry.Category(category);
            cat.setName(category);
            categories.add(cat);
        }
        BlogConnection con = BlogConnectionFactory.getBlogConnection(        ◄—❼
            blog_apitype, blog_url, blog_username, blog_password);
        blog = con.getBlog(blog_id);
        String wiki_url = config.getProperty("wiki_url");
        Properties wikiprops = new Properties();
        wikiprops.setProperty(
          "jspwiki.fileSystemProvider.pageDir",".");
```

```java
      wikiprops.setProperty(
        "jspwiki.basicAttachmentProvider.storageDir",".");
      wikiprops.setProperty(
        "jspwiki.baseURL", wiki_url);
      wikiprops.setProperty("jspwiki.pageProvider",
        "com.manning.blogapps.chapter17.PageProvider");
      WikiEngine engine = new WikiEngine(wikiprops);
      context = new WikiContext(engine, new WikiPage("dummy"));     <-8

      String chat_hostname = config.getProperty("chat_hostname");
      String chat_port =    config.getProperty("chat_port");
      String chat_nick =    config.getProperty("chat_nick");
      String chat_altnick = config.getProperty("chat_altnick");
      int port = Integer.parseInt(chat_port);
      server = new Server(chat_hostname, port, "n/a", "n/a");     <-9

      server.addServerListener(this);     <-10
      server.connect(chat_nick, chat_altnick, chat_nick, chat_nick);     <-11
   }
   public void onConnect(ServerEvent event) {     <-12
      System.out.println("Connected!");
      server.sendJoin(chat_channel);     <-13
   }
   public void onChannelJoin(ServerEvent event) {     <-14
      Channel chan = (Channel)event.getChannel();
      System.out.println("Joined "+chan);
      chan.addChannelListener(
         new ChannelBlogger(this, server.getNick()));     <-15
   }
   public String blog(String title, String content) throws Exception {  16
      StringReader reader = new StringReader(content);
      TranslatorReader tr = new TranslatorReader(context, reader);
      BlogEntry entry = blog.newEntry();     <-17
      entry.setTitle(title);
      entry.setCategories(categories);
      entry.setContent(
         new BlogEntry.Content(FileUtil.readContents(tr)));     <-18
      entry.save(true);     <-19
      return entry.getId();     <-20
   }
   public void undoLastBlog() throws Exception {     <-21
      List entries = blog.getRecentEntries(1);
      BlogEntry entry = (BlogEntry)entries.get(0);
      entry.delete();     <-22
   }
   public void stop() {     <-23
      System.out.println("Stopping...");
      server.disconnect();
   }
   public void onDisconnect(ServerEvent event) {
      System.out.println("Disconnected: good-bye!");
```

```
        System.exit(0);
    }
    public class PageProvider extends FileSystemProvider {    ◁─㉔
        public boolean pageExists(String pageName) {
            return true;
        }
    }
}
```

To create a chatbot with the Relay-IRC chat client library, you extend the `ServerAdapter` class and write the code to respond to server events, such as connection, channel joins, channel parts, and disconnections. So `ChatBlogger` extends `ServerAdapter` class ❶. We add fields for the `Blog`, Relay-IRC `Server`, `WikiEngine`, and `WikiContext` objects we'll need later ❷. We also add a field for the `chat_channel` configuration parameter ❸ because we'll need it when we get the `onConnect()` callback from the chat server.

The main method ❹ creates an instance of the class using its one constructor ❺.

The constructor reads the properties file config.properties ❻ and instantiates the blog, wiki, and chat components. Here we use the `BlogConnectionFactory` to create a `BlogConnection` suitable for the apitype we have ❼. Creating a JSPWiki `WikiContext` is a little tricky ❽. Because of the way that the JSPWiki engine works, we must configure a storage directory, a page directory, and even a page provider class.

After we create the chat server object ❾, we add the `ChatBlogger` object itself as a server listener ❿ and establish a connection ⓫ with the IRC server.

Once the connection is in place, the Relay-IRC Chat engine will notify us by calling the `onConnect()` method ⓬. When that happens, we use the chat server object to join the target chat channel ⓭.

Once we've joined the channel, Relay-IRC will call our `onChannelJoin()` method ⓮, and that's where we create the `ChannelBlogger` object ⓯ to monitor the channel for chatbot commands.

Next we have a method for each of the three chatbot commands. First is the `blog()` method ⓰, which creates a `BlogEntry` object ⓱, formats its content ⓲, posts it to the blog server ⓳, and returns the post's ID ⓴. Second is the `undoLastBlog()` method ㉑, which deletes the most recent blog entry ㉒. And third, we have the `stop()` method ㉓, which requests disconnection from the chat server.

That's it for the main class. The `PageProvider` class ❷⓪ is needed only for the creation of the `WikiContext` in the constructor. Now, let's move on to the `ChannelBlogger` class, shown in listing 17.2.

Listing 17.2 Source code for ChannelBlogger.java

```java
package com.manning.blogapps.chapter17;
import org.relayirc.chatengine.*;

public class ChannelBlogger extends ChannelAdapter {      ◄—❶
    private ChatBlogger chatBlogger;
    private String nick;
    private long lastBlogTime = 0L;
    public static final String TITLE = "title:";
    public static final String CONTENT = "content:";

    public ChannelBlogger(
            ChatBlogger chatBlogger, String nick) {      ◄—❷
        this.nick = nick;
        this.chatBlogger = chatBlogger;
    }
    public void onMessage(ChannelEvent event) {      ◄—❸
        Channel channel = (Channel)event.getSource();
        try {
            String line = (String)event.getValue();
            if (line.startsWith(nick+" exit")) {      ◄—❹
                chatBlogger.stop();
            }
            else if (line.startsWith(nick+" undo")) {      ◄—❺
                long currentTime = System.currentTimeMillis();
                if (currentTime - lastBlogTime < 30*1000) {
                    channel.sendPrivMsg("Performing undo");
                    chatBlogger.undoLastBlog();
                    lastBlogTime = 0L;
                }
                else {
                    channel.sendPrivMsg("Too late to undo");
                }
            }
            else if (line.startsWith(nick+" ")) {
                String input = line.substring(nick.length()+1);
                int titleloc = input.indexOf(TITLE);
                int contentloc = input.indexOf(CONTENT);
                if (titleloc != -1 && contentloc != -1) {      ◄—❻
                    String title = input.substring(
                        titleloc +TITLE.length(),contentloc-1);
                    String content = input.substring(
                        contentloc + CONTENT.length());
```

```
                String id = chatBlogger.blog(title, content);   ⟵❼
                lastBlogTime = System.currentTimeMillis();
                channel.sendPrivMsg("Posted [" + id + "]");   ⟵❽
            } else {
                channel.sendPrivMsg(
                    "Ignoring, need title: and content:");
            }
        }
        else if (line.startsWith(nick)) {
            channel.sendPrivMsg("Unknown command");
        }
    } catch (Exception e) {
        if (e.getCause() != null) {
            System.out.println(e.getCause().getMessage());
        }
        channel.sendPrivMsg("ERROR processing command");
    }
  }
}
```

To listen to a specific channel with a Relay-IRC based chatbot, you extend the
ChannelAdapter class. So that's what we do with ChannelBlogger ❶. In the class,
we have fields for the chatbot's nickname and the associated ChatBlogger class,
both passed into the constructor ❷, and the lastBlogTime, which we'll use to
enforce the 30-second undo limit.

The only method in ChannelBlogger is onMessage() ❸, which is called whenever a chat message appears in the chat channel. The method uses a series of
else-if statements to handle the three Chat Blogger commands. For the exit
command ❹, we call the ChatBlogger.stop() method. For the undo command
❺, we check lastBlogTime. If it was less than 30 seconds in the past, we call the
ChatBlogger.undoLastBlog() method; otherwise, the command is ignored. For
the blog command, we extract the title and content ❻, post it to the blog ❼, and
send a message to the chat channel to confirm success ❽.

17.1.6 *Running Chat Blogger*

You can find instructions for building and running Chat Blogger in the
readme.html file in the examples directory java/ch17.

17.2 *Summary*

- Chatbots can provide helpful services to people in a chat room, such as performing Google searches, querying knowledge bases, and even posting messages to a blog.

- Our Chat Blogger chatbot uses the blog client library from chapter 10 to do the blogging, the Relay-IRC Chat engine to do the chatting, and the JSPWiki wiki rendering engine to turn wiki syntax into HTML.

- You can use our new Chat Blogger chatbot to blog from an IRC chat channel, but be aware that anybody can issue commands to Chat Blogger.

- It's easy to create a chatbot by extending the Relay-IRC `ServerAdapter` and `ChannelAdapter` classes.

18

Distribute files
podcast style

Use podcasting to distribute files of
any sort to newsfeed readers, podcast
clients, and other applications with
a simple JSP-based web application.

In chapter 5, our friends at the fictional FinModler technology firm decided to use podcasting to distribute dataset files to customers of the FinModler financial modeling software. While Nina worked on adding podcast download capabilities to FinModler, Rangu worked on creating a podcast server. He started by meeting with the technical support staff to define high-level requirements for the server. He came up with the following list of required features:

- A web interface so that FinModler support staff can easily add new files to be distributed

- A file-upload capability so that new files can be uploaded to the server

- The ability to distribute files on remote web servers whose location is specified by a URL

- An RSS 2.0 format newsfeed containing podcast `<enclosure>` elements

In this chapter, we'll develop FileCaster, a simple JSP web application, which meets Rangu's requirements. In the next chapter, we'll develop a Podcast client that can be used to subscribe to and download files from the newsfeed produced by FileCaster.

18.1 Designing FileCaster

Distributing files podcast style is easy. All you have to do is place the files somewhere on the Internet where they can be accessed via URL. You also provide a newsfeed, which notifies folks when you have made a new file available. Each new file appears as an `<item>` in the newsfeed with an `<enclosure>` element that specifies the URL, content-type, and content-length of the file. For example, here is an RSS item containing a podcast enclosure (with the enclosure shown in bold):

```
<item>
    <title>InfoWord Article on blogs and wikis</title>
    <description>
       Local copy, downloaded from the InfoWorld site [&lt;a href=
       "http://localhost:8080/filecaster/uploads/13SRblogwiki.pdf"
        &gt;Download&lt;/a&gt;]
    </description>
    <enclosure url="http://localhost:8080/filecaster/uploads/
    13SRblogwiki.pdf"
       type="application/pdf" length="675329" />
     <pubDate>Sun, 15 Jan 2006 11:33:35 EDT</pubDate>
</item>
```

If a user subscribes to your podcast newsfeed with a newsfeed reader that supports podcasting, each new enclosure will be automatically downloaded. Depending on how the newsfeed reader is configured, downloaded files might be copied to different directories according to their type. For example, the popular iPodderX software can be configured to copy all downloaded music files to your Apple iTunes music player directory and all downloaded image files to your photo archive directory. Now that we understand the basics of podcast-style file distribution, let's talk server design.

18.1.1 *The podcast server*

To support the needs of a web interface and an RSS newsfeed, we'll implement FileCaster as a simple JSP-based web application. The web interface will consist of one JSP that allows users to add new file-casts and one that produces an RSS newsfeed. The web interface will interact with some Java classes to store and retrieve metadata about each file-base and any files that are uploaded to the server. Figure 18.1 shows how FileCaster will work.

On the left side, you can see the types of clients that work with FileCaster. In the center is the web server, where FileCaster runs. Below that, a rectangle represents other web servers that may host your file-casts.

Let's follow the numbers, which illustrate the basic FileCaster use case. First, you use your browser to create a file-cast by either uploading a file or pointing at a remote file that already exists on the Web ①. The web interface works with the FileCaster backend ② to store metadata information about your file-cast ③. If you uploaded a file, FileCaster stores that as well ④. At this point, you have successfully created a file-cast.

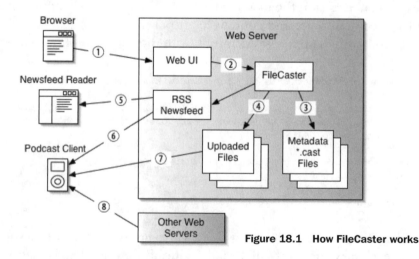

Figure 18.1 How FileCaster works

Now that the file-cast is available, your subscribers who use newsfeed readers ⑤ and podcast clients ⑥ will see the new file-cast. If you created the file-cast by uploading a file to your server, the clients will download it from your server ⑦. If you pointed to a remote file on the Web, they'll download it from there ⑧. Now that we have basic requirements and design in mind, let's implement FileCaster.

18.2 *Implementing FileCaster*

The first step in implementing FileCaster is to develop the Java classes needed to store and retrieve file-cast metadata and uploaded files. We'll define an interface `FileCaster`, which our JSP pages will use to add, remove, and retrieve file-casts from the system. Our implementation of this interface is `FileCasterImpl`. We'll develop a class `FileCast`, which will store the metadata we need to track for each file-cast. Figure 18.2 shows these classes.

First, let's discuss the `FileCast` class, starting with the properties:

- *title* is the title of the file-cast, to be included in the RSS item's `<title>` element.

- *description* is the description of the file-cast, to be included in the RSS item's `<description>` element.

- *filename* is the filename to be used to store the uploaded file (if it's not a remote file).

- *remoteUrl* is the URL of the file-cast (if it's not an uploaded file).

- *contentType* is the MIME Media Type of the file-cast file.

- *contentLength* is the length (in bytes) of the file-cast file.

- *uploadTime* is the time that the file-cast was added to the system.

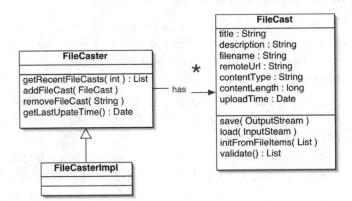

Figure 18.2
FileCaster object model

We'll use a simple XML format to store each `FileCast` object. An example is shown below.

```
<?xml version="1.0" encoding="UTF-8"?>
<file-cast>
    <title>InfoWord Article on blogs and wikis</title>
    <description>Local copy, downloaded from the InfoWorld site</
description>
    <filename>13SRblogwiki.pdf</filename>
    <content-type>application/pdf</content-type>
    <content-length>675329</content-length>
    <upload-time>Jan 16, 2006 11:33:35 AM</upload-time>
</file-cast>
```

Now let's look at the public methods of the `FileCast` class:

- `save(OutputStream)` saves the object's properties to XML format.

- `load(InputStream)` reads the object's properties from XML format.

- `initFromFileItems(List)` initializes file-cast metadata from multipart form data posted from the `FileCaster` web interface. Data is represented as a collection of Jakarta Commons File Upload `FileItem` objects. We use the File Upload library because, as you'll soon see, it makes implementing File Upload amazingly easy.

- `validate()` determines whether the object's file-cast metadata is correct. If `removeUrl` is specified, the method will send an HTTP `Head` request to the URL to get its content-type and content-length. It returns a collection of error strings, one for each problem found. If the object is valid, the collection will be empty.

Let's look at the `FileCaster` interface. This interface will be used by the code in our JSP pages to add, remove, and retrieve file-casts from the system. Here's how the `FileCasterImpl` interface implements the methods:

- `getRecentFileCasts(int max)` returns a collection of the most recently uploaded `FileCast` objects, up to the limit specified by the integer argument max. The method does this by reading file-cast metadata files from disk, so it is a relatively expensive operation.

- `addFileCast(FileCast)` adds a file-cast to the system. If the file-cast contains an uploaded file, that file is saved to disk. The `FileCast` object is also saved to disk in XML format.

- `removeFileCast(String filename)` removes a file-cast specified by filename from the system by removing its metadata file and the upload, if any, associated with it.

- `getLastUpdateTime()` returns the upload-time of the most recently added file-cast.

`FileCaster` and `FileCast` are all we need to implement the Web interface, so let's move on to the JSP code.

18.3 FileCaster upload page

Figure 18.3 shows the FileCaster user interface, a single web page that allows you to manage the file-casts in the system. The top half of the page is a form in which

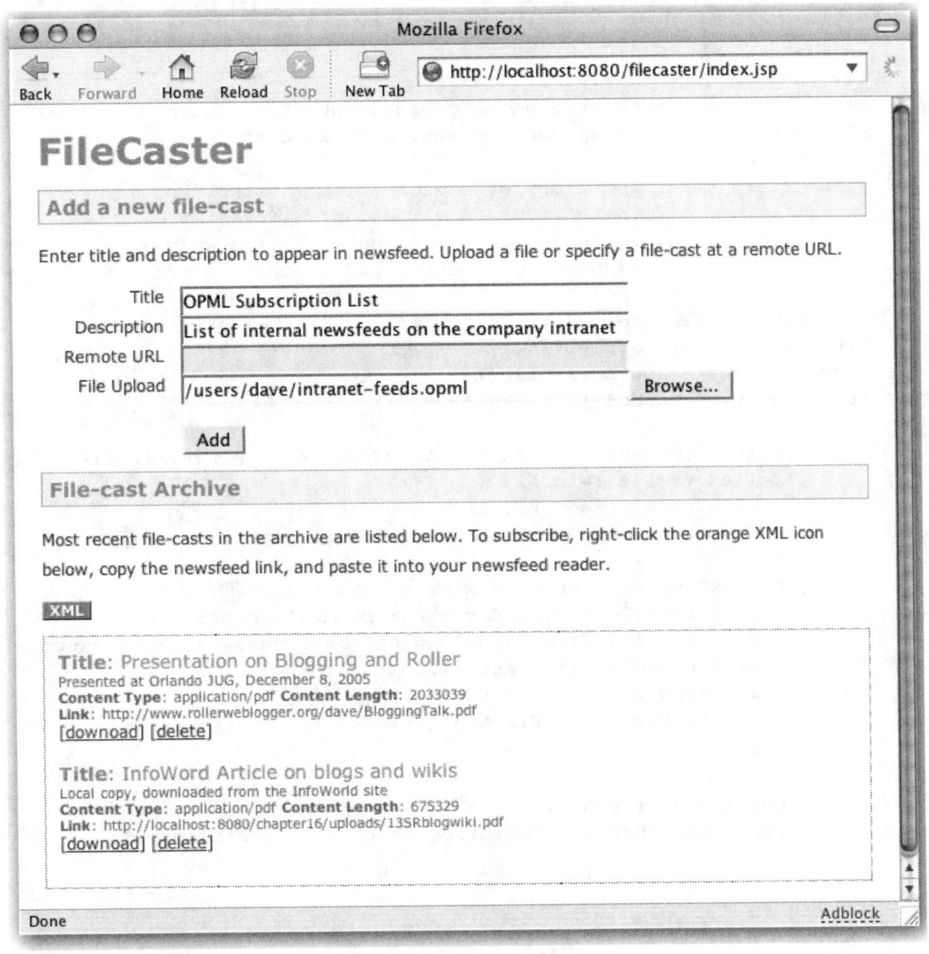

Figure 18.3 FileCaster web user interface (index.jsp)

you can enter the title and description of a new file-cast. To add a file-cast, you
must upload a file or enter the URL of a remote file.

The bottom half of the page is the File-cast Archive, a listing of the 30 most
recent file-casts that exist in the system. You can download file-casts or delete
ones you no longer want in the newsfeed. The orange XML icon links to the RSS
newsfeed of the most recent file-casts.

Now that we know what the final product will look like, let's dive into the JSP
code for the FileCaster main page, shown in listing 18.1. JSP code is shown in bold
to set it apart from the HTML that makes up the rest of the page.

Listing 18.1   index.jsp

```
<html>    ←❶
<%@ page import="java.util.*" %>
<%@ page import="com.manning.blogapps.chapter18.filecaster.*" %>
<%@ page import="org.apache.commons.fileupload.*" %>
<head>
<link href='<%= fileCaster.getAbsoluteUrl() + "/rss.jsp" %>'
         rel="alternate" type="application/xml+rss" />
<link href="blogapps.css" rel="stylesheet" type="text/css" />    ←❷
<script type="text/javascript" src="filecaster.js"></script>    ←❸
<%
FileCaster fileCaster = FileCasterImpl.getFileCaster(request);    ←❹
List errors = new ArrayList();    ←❺
List messages = new ArrayList();
if (request.getMethod().equals("POST")) {    ←❻
   try {
      String removeFile = request.getParameter("removeFile");    ←❼
      if (removeFile != null) {
         fileCaster.removeFileCast(removeFile);    ←❽
         messages.add("SUCCESS: removed file-cast");    ←❾
      } else {
         FileCast fileCast = new FileCast();    ←❿
         DiskFileUpload uploader = new DiskFileUpload();
         fileCast.initFromFileUpload(uploader.parseRequest(request));    ←⓫
         errors.addAll(fileCast.validate());
         if (errors.size() == 0) {    ←⓬
            fileCaster.addFileCast(fileCast);    ←⓭
         }
      }
   } catch (Exception e) {
      errors.add("ERROR: processing post" + e.getMessage());    ←⓮
   }
} %>
</head>
<body>    ←⓯
<h1>FileCaster</h1>
<h2>Add a new file-cast</h2>
```

```
<% if (messages.size() > 0) { %>        ←⑯
<span class="messages">
<% for (int i=0; i<messages.size(); i++) {
   out.write(messages.get(0).toString() + "<br />"); } %>
</span>
<% } %>


<% if (errors.size() > 0) { %>          ←⑰
<span class="errors">
<% for (int i=0; i<errors.size(); i++) {
   out.write(errors.get(0).toString() + "<br />"); } %>
</span>
<% } %>


<p>Enter title and description to appear in newsfeed.
Upload a file or specify a file-cast at a remote URL.</p>

<form name="addFileCast" action="index.jsp" method="post"      ←⑱
   enctype="multipart/form-data">
   <div class="row">
      <label class="leftcol" name="title">Title</label>
      <input type="text" name="title" size="40" />
   </div>
   <div class="row">
      <label class="leftcol" name="description">Description</label>
      <input type="text" name="description" size="40"URL />
   </div>
   <div class="row">
      <label class="leftcol" name="remoteUrl">Remote URL</label>
      <input type="text" name="remoteUrl" size="40"
         onkeyup="validate()" />        ←⑲
   </div>
   <div class="row">
      <label class="leftcol" name="fileUpload">File Upload</label>
      <input type="file" name="fileUpload" size="40"
         onchange="validate()" onkeydown="validate()" />      ←⑳
   </div>
   <br />
   <div class="row">
      <span class="leftcol"> </span>
      <input name="add_button" type="submit" value="Add" disabled="true" />
   </div>
</form>


<h2>File-cast Archive</h2>    ←㉑


<p>Most recent file-casts in the archive are listed below.
To subscribe, right-click the orange XML icon below, copy
the newsfeed link, and paste it into your newsfeed reader.</p>
<p><a href="rss.jsp">
```

```
      <img src="images/rssbadge.gif"" border=0 />      ←㉒
</a></p>

<div style="padding: 10px; border: grey 1px dotted">
<% Iterator list = fileCaster.getRecentFileCasts(30).iterator();      ←㉓
while (list.hasNext()) {
   FileCast loopcast = (FileCast)list.next();
   String url = loopcast.getUrl(
      fileCaster.getAbsoluteUrl() + "/uploads/");
%>
<span class="title">
   <b>Title</b>: <%= loopcast.getTitle() %>
</span><br />
<span class="details">
   <% if (loopcast.getDescription().length() > 0) {
      out.write(loopcast.getDescription() + "<br />"); } %>
   <b>Content Type</b>: <%= loopcast.getContentType() %>
   <b>Content Length</b>: <%= loopcast.getContentLength() %><br />
   <b>Link</b>: <%= url %>
</span><br />
[<a href="<%= url %>">downoad</a>]
[<a href="#" onclick=
   "removeFileCast('<%= loopcast.getSaveFilename() %>')">remove</a>]  ㉔
   <br /><br />
<% } %>
</div>

<form name="removeForm" action="index.jsp" method="post">      ←㉕
   <input type="hidden" name="removeFile" value="" />
</form>
</body>
</html>
```

Let's discuss the JSP in detail. The page starts with the usual opening <html> tag, followed by the Java imports needed by the Java code contained in the page ❶. Next, we have a link to the blogapps.css stylesheet, which sets our attractive fonts and gives the page its nice orange and yellow color scheme ❷. That's followed by a <script> tag that brings in the filecaster.js, which includes a couple of helpful JavaScript functions that we'll discuss later ❸.

We start the main body of JSP scriptlet code by creating the objects we'll need on the rest of the page. We get the FileCaster object by calling a static method getFileCaster(), which either returns the existing object from application scope or creates a new one ❹. Next, we create errors and messages collections to hold messages we create during processing ❺.

If the request is a POST ❻, that means the user hit the Add button to add a new file-cast or clicked a delete link on an existing file-cast.

If the request parameter `removeFile` is set ❼, the user clicked a remove link. We respond by calling the `fileCaster` object to remove the specified file-cast ❽ and adding a success message to the messages collection ❾.

If the request is not a remove request, the user clicked the Add button to add a new file-cast. We respond by creating a `FileCast` ❿ and initializing it using the Jakarta Commons File Upload `DiskFileUpoad` class to parse the request parameters and any uploaded file data ⓫. If calling the `fileCast.validate()` method returns no error messages ⓬, we have a valid file-cast and we call the `fileCaster.addFileCast()` method to save it ⓭. If there are error messages, we'll display them later in the body of the page.

At this point, we're through with the posted form data and ready to display the body of the HTML page. We did everything in a `try-catch` block, so if an exception occurs, we simply add a message to our error collection ⓮, which will be displayed later in the page.

In the `<body>` ⓯, we welcome the user by displaying the `FileCaster` header and the "Add a new file-cast" options. Since we're at the top of the page and we have the user's attention, we display any success and error messages we have collected so far. We display them ⓰ in a span with a CSS class "messages" so we can style them with a light green box and a green outline. We do the same thing for any error messages ⓱, except we display them in a light red box.

Next we present the file-cast form ⓲ with encoding type `multipart/form-data`, which is required for posting file-uploads. It's just a standard HTML form with fields for title, description, remote URL, and a file-upload. There's no magic or JSP code involved, but the form does have one special feature. The form will not allow you to click the Add button until you have entered either a remote URL or a file-upload—and it will allow you to enter only one or the other, not both. We do this by using `onkeyup`, `onkeydown`, and `onchange` event handlers in the `remoteUrl` ⓳ and `fileUpload` ⓴ fields, which call a `validate()` method (defined in filecaster.js) to enable and disable form elements.

After the file-cast form, we display an informative listing of the most recent file-casts. First, we display a File-cast Archive heading ㉑ and explain how to subscribe to the file-cast newsfeed. We provide a link to the file-cast newsfeed with the standard orange XML icon ㉒.

We're also going to display a list of the 30 most recent file-casts. For each one, we'll display title, description, a download link, and a remove link. We start by calling the `FileCaster` object's `getRecentFileCasts()` method ㉓ to get an iterator. We iterate through the collection of `FileCast` objects and emit the HTML needed to display each. The remove link ㉔ uses a JavaScript method removeFileCast() (defined in filecaster.js) to remove the file-base by setting the removeFile parameter on the removeForm form ❷❺ and submitting that form.

That brings us to the end of the JSP that defines the FileCaster web UI. Now, let's move on to the JSP for the RSS newsfeed.

18.4 *FileCaster newsfeed*

The FileCaster newsfeed is a standard RSS 2.0 newsfeed, which includes an <enclosure> element in each item. Let's examine listing 18.2 and see how the JSP code produces the newsfeed. Here again, JSP code is shown in bold to differentiate it from the HTML that makes up the rest of the page.

Listing 18.2   rss.jsp

```
<?xml version="1.0" encoding="utf-8"?>      ◁─❶
<%@ page import="java.util.*" %>      ◁─❷
<%@ page import="com.manning.blogapps.chapter18.*" %>
<%@ page import="com.manning.blogapps.chapter18.filecaster.*" %>
<%
FileCaster fileCaster = FileCasterImpl.getFileCaster(request);      ◁─❸
Utilities utilities = new Utilities();
Date sinceDate = new Date(request.getDateHeader("If-Modified-Since"));
if (sinceDate != null
   && fileCaster.getLastUpdateDate().compareTo(sinceDate) <= 0) {
   response.setStatus(HttpServletResponse.SC_NOT_MODIFIED);      ◁─❹
   response.flushBuffer();
   return;
} else {
   response.setDateHeader("Last-Modified",      ◁─❺
      fileCaster.getLastUpdateDate().getTime());
   response.setContentType("application/rss+xml;charset=utf-8");      ◁─❻
} %>
<rss version="2.0">      ◁─❼
<channel>
   <language>en-us</language>
   <title>FileCaster</title>
   <description>Most recent file-casts</description>
   <link><%= fileCaster.getAbsoluteUrl() %></link>      ◁─❽
   <lastBuildDate>
      <%= utilities.formatRfc822Date(fileCaster.getLastUpdateDate()) %>❾
   </lastBuildDate>
   <% Iterator fileCasts =
      fileCaster.getRecentFileCasts(30).iterator();
   while (fileCasts.hasNext()) {      ◁─❿
      FileCast fileCast = (FileCast)fileCasts.next();
      String url = fileCast.getUrl(
```

```
                    fileCaster.getAbsoluteUrl() + "/uploads/");
            %>
            <item>
                <title><%= fileCast.getTitle() %></title>          ←⓫
                <description>
                    <%= fileCast.getDescription() %>
                    [&lt;a href="<%= url %>"&gt;Download&lt;/a&gt;]      ←⓬
                </description>
                <link><%= url %></link>      ←⓭
                <guid isPermaLink="true"><%= url %></guid>
                <pubDate>
                    <%= utilities.formatRfc822Date
                                 (fileCast.getUploadTime()) %>          ⓮
                </pubDate>
                <enclosure url="<%= url %>"      ←⓯
                           type="<%= fileCast.getContentType() %>"
                           length="<%= fileCast.getContentLength() %>" />
            </item>
        <% } %>
    </channel>
    </rss>      ←⓰
```

The first line of rss.jsp is the standard XML declaration ❶. It's followed by the necessary package imports ❷.

Next, we create the FileCaster and Utilities objects ❸ we'll need later in the page, and we handle HTTP conditional GET. If the file-cast newsfeed has not changed since the time specified in the request's If-Modified-Since header, we return the HTTP Not-Modified response code ❹ and exit the page with a call to return. If the page has changed, we set the HTTP Last-Modified header ❺ and set the correct content-type for UTF-8 encoded RSS newsfeed application/rss+xml;charset=utf-8 ❻.

We start RSS generation with the <rss> element ❼. Within that element, we have the <channel> element, with newsfeed metadata including the newsfeed title, description, and the link to the FileCaster site. We use the FileCaster object's getAbsoluteUrl() method for the <link> element ❽. We use the getLastUpdateDate() method to get the <lastBuildDate> value, but we first use the utilities object to put the date in RFC-822 format ❾.

We use a while loop to iterate through the most recent FileCast objects ❿, and for each we emit title ⓫, description ⓬, link ⓭, and publication date, which we convert to RFC-822 format ⓮. The item's file-cast is represented as an RSS <enclosure> element ⓯. We wrap up by closing the channel and RSS elements ⓰. That's all it takes to generate a file-cast newsfeed.

18.5 *Running FileCaster*

You can find instructions for building and running FileCaster in the readme.html file in the examples directory java/ch18.

18.6 *Room for improvement*

FileCaster is a simple example application, and it's missing some important features you might want to add, depending on how you want to use file-casting. Here are some suggestions for improvement:

- *Security*—FileCaster allows anybody to upload and delete file-casts. You'll probably want to make the management page private, with access by username and password only.
- *Categorization*—Make it possible to specify the category of each file-cast and to subscribe to a newsfeed for each category.
- *View all file-casts*—Make it possible to page through the file-casts in the system (instead of listing the most recent 30, as we do now).
- *Proxy support*—Make it possible to configure a proxy host and port used by `FileCast.validate()` when sending an HTTP `Head` request.
- *Better storage for uploaded files*—Instead of storing uploaded files in the server file-system, store them in a distributed data-store.

18.7 *Summary*

- Although podcasting is commonly used to automatically download audio files to personal music players, the technique can be used to automate the download of any type of file.
- Distributing files podcast-style is easy; just make the files available on the Web and reference them as enclosures in your newsfeed—or use FileCaster to do the job.
- A podcast may be included in an RSS newsfeed `<item>` element by using the RSS `<enclosure>` tag to specify the podcast URL, content-type, and content-length.
- FileCaster is a simple JSP-based web application, which you can use to manage a podcast newsfeed. You can add a new podcast by uploading a file or by referencing a file somewhere on the Web.
- FileCaster uses the Jakarta Commons File Upload library, which makes the difficult task of implementing file upload easy.

19

Automatically download podcasts

Build a simple console program that will download podcast files for you and route them to the applications that use them.

In the previous chapter, we developed FileCaster, a simple web application that enables you to distribute files podcast-style, as RSS enclosures. In this chapter, we'll develop a client for FileCaster called FileCatcher: a simple console program that can be used to subscribe to a podcast newsfeed from FileCaster or any other podcast server.

In chapter 5, our fictional friend Nina was assigned the task of adding podcast client capabilities to the FinModler software so that new datasets could be automatically downloaded. Nina was intimately familiar with the FinModler dataset download process, so she had no problem coming up with requirements for a podcast-style download program. Here are the requirements she put together:

- Must be able to subscribe to multiple newsfeeds
- Must use HTTP conditional GET to avoid parsing newsfeeds that have not changed
- Must not download files that have already been downloaded
- Should download only files of a specific set of content-types
- Must be able to copy files of different types to different destination directories

FileCatcher meets all of Nina's requirements. Let's discuss how it works.

19.1 Designing FileCatcher

FileCatcher is designed to run as a Scheduled Task, working off an XML file that lists newsfeed subscriptions and destination directories for different types of files. To configure FileCatcher, all you have to do is provide that XML file. Listing 19.1 shows an example.

Listing 19.1 Example XML file

```
<file-catcher>
<subscription>      ⊲—❶
    <feed-url>http://FinModler.com/FinModler-updates.rss</feed-url>
    <last-modified>Fri, 08 Apr 2005 13:20:40 GMT</last-modified>
</subscription>
<subscription>      ⊲—❷
    <feed-url>http://example.com/radioshow.rss</feed-url>
    <last-modified>Fri, 08 Apr 2005 08:52:03 GMT</last-modified>
</subscription>
<destination>      ⊲—❸
    <content-type>application/FinModler</content-type>
```

```
        <directory>c:\\FinModler\datasets</directory>
    </destination>
    <destination>     ←④
        <content-type>audio/x-mpeg</content-type>
        <directory>c:\\personal\podcasts</directory>
    </destination>
</file-catcher>
```

Our FileCatcher XML file contains two subscriptions, one to the FinModler software update newsfeed ① and one to a newsfeed at example.com ②. You can add as many subscriptions as you like. Subscriptions must be listed before destinations.

You should add a destination for each type of file you want to download. In listing 19.1, we have two destinations, one for FinModler files ③, specified with FinModler's custom content-type `application/FinModler`, and one for MP3 files ④, which have content-type `audio/x-mpeg`. Files of other types will not be downloaded.

19.2 *Implementing FileCatcher*

With the `AnyFeedParser` class we developed in chapter 5, implementing File-Catcher is pretty easy. Listing 19.2 shows the C# code for FileCatcher.

Listing 19.2   Source code for FileCatcher

```
using System;     ←①
using System.Xml;
using System.IO;
using System.Text;
using System.Net;
using System.Collections;
using BlogApps_Chapter05;     ←②

namespace BlogApps_Chapter19 {     ←③

    public class Subscription {     ←④
        public string feed_url;
        public DateTime last_modified;
    }

    public class FileCatcher {     ←⑤
        IList subscriptions = new ArrayList();     ←⑥
        IDictionary destinations = new Hashtable();     ←⑦

        static void Main(string[] args) {     ←⑧
            FileCatcher fileCatcher = new FileCatcher();
            fileCatcher.InitFromXml();
```

```
        fileCatcher.run();
        fileCatcher.UpdateXml();      <--9
    }
public void run() {    <--10
    System.Console.WriteLine("FileCatcher for C#");
    IFeedParser feedParser = new AnyFeedParser();      <--11

    foreach (Subscription sub in subscriptions) {    <--12
        HttpWebRequest request =
            (HttpWebRequest)WebRequest.Create(sub.feed_url);    <--13
        request.IfModifiedSince = sub.last_modified;    <--14
        try {
            HttpWebResponse response =
                (HttpWebResponse)request.GetResponse();    <--15
            IDictionary feedMap =
                feedParser.ParseFeed(response.GetResponseStream());    <--16
            sub.last_modified = response.LastModified;    <--17

            IList itemsList = (IList)feedMap["items"];
            foreach (IDictionary itemMap in itemsList) {    <--18

                IDictionary enclosure =
                            (IDictionary)itemMap["enclosure"];    |
                if (enclosure == null) continue;    <--20           19

                try {
                    string dir =
                            (string)destinations[enclosure["type"]];    |
                    if (dir == null) continue;    <--22                  21

                    HttpWebRequest dl_request = (HttpWebRequest)
                        WebRequest.Create((string)enclosure["url"]);
                    string name = dl_request.RequestUri.LocalPath;
                    string path = dir + @"\" + name.Replace("/","_");    23

                    if (!File.Exists(path)) {    <--24
                        Console.WriteLine("Downloading "+enclosure["url"]);
                        HttpWebResponse dl_response =
                            (HttpWebResponse)dl_request.GetResponse();
                        writeInputToOutput(    <--25
                            dl_response.GetResponseStream(),
                            File.OpenWrite(path));
                    } else {
                        Console.WriteLine("Skipping: "+enclosure["url"]);
                    }
                }
                catch (Exception e) {
                    Console.WriteLine("Bad URL: "+enclosure["url"]);
                }
            }
        }
    }
```

```
        catch (WebException e) {
            HttpWebResponse res = (HttpWebResponse)e.Response;
            if (res != null) {
                if (res.StatusCode == HttpStatusCode.NotModified) {   26
                  System.Console.WriteLine("Not modified: "+sub.feed_url);
                }
            }
            else {    <-27
                System.Console.WriteLine(
                    "ERROR: connecting to destination server");
                System.Console.WriteLine(e.Message);
                System.Console.WriteLine(e.StackTrace);
            }
        }
    }
  }
  private void writeInputToOutput(    <-28
      Stream inputStream, Stream outputStream) {
      // omitted
  }
  private void InitFromXml() {    <-29
      // omitted
  }
  private void UpdateXml() {    <-30
      // omitted
  }
  }
}
```

Let's walk through the code. We start with the usual preamble of using statements to declare the namespaces we need for the program ❶. Except for
BlogApps_Chapter05 ❷, which contains the AnyFeedParser class we'll use for newsfeed parsing, we need only built-in .NET namespaces.

Inside the BlogApps_Chapter19 namespace ❸, we declare a small class
Subscription ❹, which we'll use to hold the URL and last-modified date of
each newsfeed in the subscriptions list.

Next, we declare the FileCatcher class ❺ and inside that, the subscriptions
collection ❻, which will hold a Subscription object for each subscription we need
to process. We'll store destinations as a dictionary ❼ containing directory path
strings keyed by content-types.

In the Main() method ❽ of the class, we create the FileCatcher object, initialize it from XML, and call its run() method. When it has finished running, we
update the last-modified dates in the XML file ❾.

The run() method ❿ is where everything happens. First, we construct an AnyFeedParser to use for parsing ⓫. Next, we loop through the subscriptions ⓬. For each subscription, we create a WebRequest for the subscription's newsfeed URL ⓭ and set its IfModifiedSince property ⓮. If a newsfeed has not been modified since the IfModifiedSince date, the request will throw an exception when we try to get the response ⓯. If that happens, no problem; we'll move to the next subscription.

If the subscription's newsfeed has been modified, we parse it into dictionary form using feedParser ⓰ and stash the last-modified date for the next time we run ⓱.

Now we're ready to look for files to download, so we loop through the newsfeed items ⓲, each being a dictionary. For each item, we check for an enclosure ⓳. If none is found, we skip to the next item ⓴.

If we do have an enclosure, we attempt to look up a directory for it in our dictionary of destination directories ㉑, using the enclosure type as the key. If no directory is found, we're not interested in this type of enclosure, so we skip to the next item ㉒.

If we do have a destination directory, we still have one more check to perform before we download the file. We create a local filename for the file by replacing the forward slashes in the file's path with underbars ㉓, and we check to see whether that file already exists on disk ㉔. If it doesn't, we download it and save it to disk by calling writeInputToOutput() ㉕. Still within the loop is a catch block to handle any WebException that is thrown during processing. Whether it's an HTTP Not-Modified exception ㉖ or something else ㉗, we want to log it and keep on going through the list of subscriptions.

There are three more methods in the file, and we've already used them. We used writeInputToOutput() ㉘ to handle file-download, we used InitFromXml() ㉙ to read the FileCatcher XML file, and we used UpdateXml() ㉚ to save the XML file. We won't discuss the implementations because they're not central to the topic at hand.

19.3 *Running FileCatcher for C#*

You can find instructions for building and running FileCatcher for C# in the readme.html file in the examples directory csharp/ch19.

19.4 Summary

- This chapter's example FileCatcher is a simple console-based podcast client that can automatically download files from FileCaster or any other podcast server.

- With a simple newsfeed parser and the .NET class libraries, developing a podcast download client is a simple exercise.

- By using HTTP conditional GET as described in chapter 5, section 5.5.1, it's possible to avoid parsing newsfeeds more often than necessary.

20

Automatically validate newsfeeds

Use a simple script to monitor your newsfeeds and receive notification via email when any are found to be invalid.

If your blog's newsfeed is invalid for a short period of time because you forgot to escape an ampersand, it's probably no big deal. But if you're using newsfeed syndication to notify customers of critical software patches and new datasets, as our friends Nina and Rangu are doing at the fictional FinModler technology firm, invalid newsfeeds can be a much more serious issue.

You should do whatever you can up-front to ensure that your newsfeeds are valid, but it also makes sense to monitor your newsfeeds so that you are notified quickly when they become invalid.

In this chapter, we'll show you how to write a newsfeed auto-validator, a simple command-line script you can run on a schedule to check each of your newsfeeds for validity and to send you an email if any are found to be invalid.

20.1 Getting started

To implement our auto-validator, we'll use Mark Pilgrim's and Sam Ruby's Feed Validator, which provides a comprehensive set of validity checks for every type of RSS and for Atom. When we introduced Feed Validator in chapter 8, we discussed how to use its web interface at feedvalidator.org, but there are a couple of other ways to use it. You can call Feed Validator via a SOAP-based web services interface, but that won't work for newsfeeds on a private intranet because feedvalidator.org can reach only newsfeeds on the public Internet. You can also download the source code for Feed Validator and run it on your own computer, where it can easily access newsfeeds on your private network. That's what we'll do. Let's start by setting up Feed Validator to run locally.

20.1.1 Setting up Python

First, make sure you have Python 2.2 or later. If you have a Linux or Mac OS X based computer, Python 2.2 or later is probably already installed. If not, you can get Python and its documentation at http://python.org/. Download the version of Python that is appropriate for your operating system and run through the Python installation process. Once you have Python on your path, you'll be able to run any Python script by simply typing *python* and the name of the Python script on the command line.

20.1.2 Setting up Feed Validator

When you have Python, the next step is to install Feed Validator. To get the latest version, you'll need to use a CVS client to get the source code from the project's

CVS server. You can find instructions for doing this on the project's SourceForge web site at http://sourceforge.net/cvs/?group_id=99943.

To make life a little easier for you, we have included a copy of the Feed Validator in the online examples that accompany this book. You'll find it in the directory python/ch20/feedvalidator. To use Feed Validator, open up a command window, change directory to the Feed Validator directory, and run the Python script demo.py. For example, here's what you'd do on Windows to validate a newsfeed (assuming that your examples are in c:\blogapps):

```
c> cd \blogapps\python\ch20\feedvalidator\src
c> python demo.py http://example.com/index.rss
Validating http://example.com/index.rss
No errors or warnings
```

If there had been any errors, you'd see a list of the specific errors and warnings. Now that we have Python and Feed Validator, we are ready to write the code for our auto-validator.

20.2 *Implementing auto-validator*

All our auto-validator has to do is read a list of newsfeeds to be validated, run Feed Validator against each one, and if there are any problems, send us an email with the details.

Our script needs two inputs: a list of newsfeed URLs and the email configuration. To keep things simple, we'll store the newsfeed URLs as a simple text file with one newsfeed per line and we'll define the email configuration in the auto-validate script itself. Here is an example auto-validator input file containing a list of newsfeed URLs:

```
http://blogs.example.com/index.atom
http://blogs.example.com/index.rss
http://example.com/news.rdf
```

We'll specify the email parameters at the start of the Python script, which is shown in listing 20.1.

Listing 20.1 auto-validate.py, a Python script that monitors newsfeeds for validity

```
smtpserver = 'smtp.FinModler.com'      ←—❶
smtpuser =   'rangu'
smtppass =   'tiger'
subject =    "Feed Validation Errors and Warnings"    ←—❷
sender =     'rangu@FinModler.com'     ←—❸
recipients = ['nina@FinModler.com','rangu@FinModler.com']    ←—❹
```

```
import sys      ◄─⑤
import string
import smtplib    ◄─⑥
import feedvalidator     ◄─⑦
from feedvalidator import compatibility
from feedvalidator.formatter.text_plain import Formatter
report = 0
if len(sys.argv) < 2:     ◄─⑧
    print "No input file specified"
    sys.exit(-1)     ◄─⑨
else:     ◄─⑩
    input = open(sys.argv[1])     ◄─⑪
    while True:
        link = input.readline().strip()     ◄─⑫
        if link and not link.startswith("#"):     ◄─⑬
            try:
                results = feedvalidator.validateURL(\     ◄─⑭
                            link, firstOccurrenceOnly=1)
                events = results['loggedEvents']     ◄─⑮
            except feedvalidator.logging.ValidationFailure, vf:
                events = [vf.event]
            filter = "AA"
            filterFunc = getattr(compatibility, filter)
            events = filterFunc(events)     ◄─⑯
            output = Formatter(events)     ◄─⑰
            if output:     ◄─⑱
                if not report:
                    report = ""
                report = report + ("<%s>\n" % link)     ◄─⑲
                for event in output:     ◄─⑳
                    report = report + event + "\n"
        else:
            break

if report:     ◄─㉑
    msg = "Subject: %s\r\nFrom: %s\r\nTo: %s\r\n\r\n%s" \     ◄─㉒
            % (subject,sender, string.join(recipients,","),report)
    session = smtplib.SMTP(smtpserver)     ◄─㉓
    session.login(smtpuser, smtppass)
    smtpresult = session.sendmail(sender, recipients, msg=msg)     ◄─㉔
    if smtpresult:
        errstr = ""
        for recip in smtpresult.keys():     ◄─㉕
            errstr = "Error sending to: %s\r\nMessage: %s\r\n%s\r\n%s" \
            % (recip, smtpresult[recip][0], smtpresult[recip][1], errstr)
        raise smtplib.SMTPException, errstr
```

The first email parameter is the SMTP server hostname ❶, followed by the user-name and password for connecting to the server. Next is the subject of the email message ❷, the address of the sender ❸, and a list of the recipient addresses to which notification emails are to be sent ❹.

We then import the Python packages and classes we will need in the program, starting with the sys and string packages ❺. To send mail, we'll use Python's built-in smtplib package ❻. Finally, we import feedvalidator ❼.

With the imports out of the way, we're ready for the application logic. We start by checking len(sys.argv) ❽, which gives us the number of arguments passed in. We expect there to be two arguments, the name of the script and the name of the input file. If there are fewer than two, we print an error message and exit ❾.

Otherwise ❿, if an input file is specified on the command line, we open it ⓫ and loop to read it, line by line, stripping off any leading or trailing white-space ⓬. If the line starts with a hash, it's a comment and we ignore it ⓭. Otherwise, the line is a newsfeed URL and we call Feed Validator to validate it ⓮. We pass first-OccurenceOnly=1 so that we are notified only once for each type of error that is found. We collect the error and warning messages in the events collection ⓯.

Next, we filter the error and warning messages using the filter string AA ⓰, which has special meaning. These possible filter values can be used:

- *A* is the most basic level of validation.
- *AA* mimics the online validator (i.e., the one at feedvalidator.org).
- *AAA* is experimental. (Rules may change in a future release of Feed Validator.)

We call Feed Validator's built-in formatter to format the filtered messages for output ⓱. If there is any output ⓲, we add the offending newsfeed URL to our error report ⓳ and then add the list of errors and warnings ⓴ reported by the validator.

Once we finish looping through the input file and validating each newsfeed, we check the report. If the report is not empty ㉑, we need to send out an email to notify everybody of the problem. We format the email ㉒, connect to the SMTP mail server ㉓, and send the email ㉔. If there are any problems sending the email ㉕, we print an error message and raise an exception.

That's all there is to our auto-validator. Now let's discuss how to put it into use.

20.3 *Running auto-validator*

To prepare to run auto-validator, edit the source code file and enter the email parameters for your SMTP server, your email sender address, and the email addresses of the people who should be notified when an error or warning is encountered. Create a text file that lists the URLs of the newsfeeds you'd like to auto-validate, one per line.

You're almost ready. But before you can run auto-validator.py, you must define the environment variable PYTHONPATH to include the directory where the Feed Validator source code can be found. For example, on a Windows-based computer with the example code installed in the directory c:\blogapps and an input file named *files* you would do the following:

```
c> cd \blogapps\python\ch20
c> set PYTHONPATH=c:\blogapps\python\ch20\feedvalidator\src
c> python auto-validator.py files
```

And on a UNIX-based computer in the bash shell, with the examples installed in /usr/local/blogapps, you'd do the following:

```
$ cd /usr/local/blogapps/python/ch20
$ set PYTHONPATH=/usr/local/blogapps/python/ch20/feedvalidator/src
$ python auto-validator.py files
```

That's all it takes to configure and run auto-validator.py, but we don't want to have to launch it manually like that. Let's discuss how to run it on a schedule, first with Windows.

20.3.1 *Using Windows Scheduled Tasks*

On Windows, you can use the Windows Scheduled Tasks facility to run the auto-validator as often as you like. First, you need to set the PYTHONPATH environment variable so Python can find Feed Validator. Open the Windows Control Panel and double-click the System icon to edit System Properties. Choose the Advanced Tab, click the Environment Variables button at the bottom of the dialog box, and add a PYTHONPATH variable. Assuming you have installed the examples in c:\blogapps, you would set the variable to this value:

c:\blogapps\python\ch20\feedvalidator\src

Next, add a scheduled task to run the auto-validator. Go back to the Control Panel, double-click the Scheduled Tasks icon, and double-click Add Scheduled Task. Use the wizard to set up a new task and then, before you click the Finish button, select Open Advanced Properties so that you can set the Run command and the Startup directory. Assuming c:\blogapps again, you would set the Run command to:

python c:\blogapps\python\ch20\auto-validate.py files

And the Startup directory would be:

c:\blogapps\python\ch20

Now, use the Schedule Tab to set the auto-validator to run as often as you'd like.

20.3.2 *Using UNIX cron*

On UNIX, the standard way to automatically schedule tasks is to use cron. Since we need to set the PYTHONPATH environment variable first, and some versions of cron do not run shell startup files, we'll need to write a small shell script to launch our auto-validator. You can find a copy of the script auto-validate.sh in the online examples for this chapter in the directory python/ch20. Here is the script:

```
export AUTOVALIDATOR_HOME=/usr/local/blogsapps/python/ch20
export PYTHONPATH=${AUTOVALIDATOR_HOME}/feedvalidator/src
python ${AUTOVALIDATOR_HOME}/auto-validator.py ${AUTOVALIDATOR_HOME}/files
```

You'll need to modify the script if your examples are installed somewhere other than /usr/local/blogapps. Also, you may need to make the script executable using the UNIX chmod command. For example:

```
$ cd /usr/local/blogapps/python/ch20
$ chmod +x auto-validator.sh
```

Once you've set up the shell script, you can run it from cron. Start the cron editor (usually invoked by the command crontab -e) and add the following line to run validation every hour on the half-hour:

```
30 * * * * /usr/local/blogapps/python/ch20/auto-validate.sh
```

20.4 *Summary*

- Invalid newsfeeds can cause data loss, unhappy customers, and other ill effects, so monitor your newsfeeds to ensure that they are valid.

- Feed Validator provides a comprehensive set of validity tests for all of the commonly used newsfeed formats.

- Feed Validator is open source and available under the terms of the GNU Public License (GPL).

- The Python source code for Feed Validator can be downloaded from the project's CVS archive, and we include a copy in the book's online examples.

- It's easy to set up auto-validator.py to automatically check your newsfeeds at regularly scheduled intervals and to send you an email when any of the newsfeeds become invalid.

The best of the rest

21

Once you start brainstorming, you can come up with all sorts of ideas for blogs, wikis, newsfeed syndication, and publishing protocols.

So far in part II, we've presented you with 10 blog apps, each wrapped in a tidy little chapter with diagrams, source code, and usage instructions. There are, of course, many more ways to apply blog technologies, but we're limited by time, space, and even imagination. So, in this last chapter of *RSS and Atom in Action*, we're going to present some great ideas that wouldn't fit into the book, and we're going to brainstorm—with some help from the blogosphere—for as many new ideas about applying blog technologies as we can. You can pick up where we leave off by using the knowledge you've gained from this book to put these ideas into action or to extrapolate and imagine even better ones.

We'll keep the discussion of each idea brief, so that we can cover as many as possible. And we'll illustrate those that require some integration or software development with the same type of building block diagrams we used in chapter 0 to illustrate the part II blog apps. Let's start, as we did in chapter 1, with monitoring.

21.1 *Monitor anything*

In chapter 1, we introduced Carl, a marketing strategist at the fictional Finmodler technology firm. Carl used a newsfeed reader and newsfeed search engines to keep up with his three vertical market segments, but you can use newsfeeds to monitor just about anything you can imagine. Let's start with the most mundane of topics, the weather.

21.1.1 *Monitor the weather*

Weather feeds allow you to read the latest weather reports in your newsfeed reader or display them on your web site. WeatherUnderground.com offers RSS 2.0 newsfeeds of current conditions and daily forecasts for each city it serves.

RssWeather.com also offers RSS 2.0 weather newsfeeds, but it goes further and allows you to create a customized feed by specifying Celsius or Fahrenheit, frequency of update, and type of report. The service includes a special feature designed just for webmasters: it also allows you to specify the content of the newsfeed. You can choose plain text, encoded HTML, or XHTML. If you specify XHTML, it will use the XHTML namespace as an RSS extension module. Each RSS <item> element will include an XHTML <body> element with the content.

For the United States only, the National Weather Service offers RSS 2.0 newsfeeds of weather alerts and current observations at weather.gov, although, at this time, the feeds are marked as experimental.

If you're not interested in weather, you can go shopping.

21.1.2 *Shop with your newsfeed reader*

By using newsfeeds from vendors such as Amazon, Buy.com, Yahoo Shopping, Dealnews.com, and many other web sites, you can monitor new product listings and daily promotions and sales. If your newsfeed reader allows keyword searches, you can look for deals on specific items of interest.

For example, if you use the newsfeed reader that is built into the popular Thunderbird email program, you can setup *message filters* to route news items that contain specific combinations of keywords to different folders. Let's say you're interested in buying a new disk drive for your computer and a new Treo phone. You'd create two filter folders, one for disk drives and one for Treo. Then, you'd use the Thunderbird Filter Rules dialog-box, shown in Figure 21.1, to set up the rules for moving items into those folders based on specific keywords.

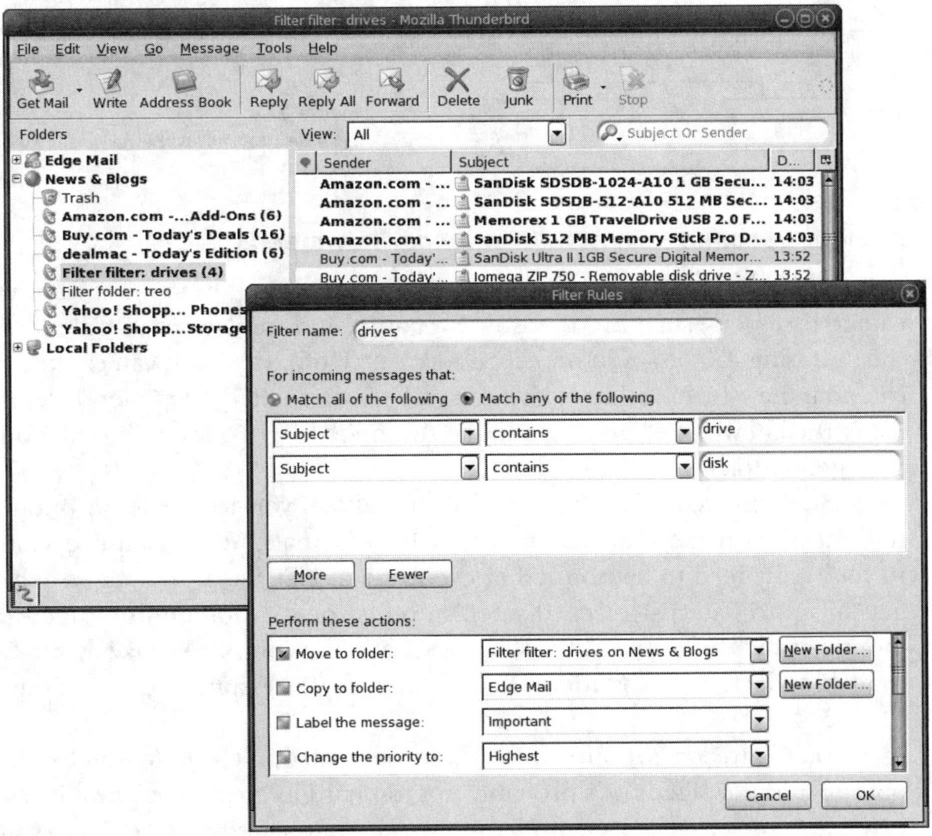

Figure 21.1   Searching for deals on disk drives via Thunderbird

21.1.3 *Use newsfeeds to monitor eBay auctions*

Monitoring eBay is a little different from monitoring a normal shopping site because eBay is an auction site. You might want to monitor new items, just as we did disk drives and Treos above, but you'll also want to monitor bids.

Unfortunately, eBay does not currently offer newsfeeds, so you'll have to turn to third-party services, such as RssAuctions.com, or use eBay's web services API to develop your eBay syndication service. RssAuctions.com allows you to create your own custom eBay newsfeeds for different categories of items or for bids in a specific auction.

RssAuction.com uses the eBay API to get the data required to generate newsfeeds, and there's no reason you can't do the same thing using what you've learned in this book. You would need an eBay client component that reads data from eBay, some application logic to decide which items to include, and a newsfeed generator, as shown in Figure 21.2.

**Figure 21.2
Newsfeed generator
for eBay**

21.1.4 *Monitor upcoming events via calendar newsfeeds*

Newsfeeds can also be used to monitor calendars. It's only a matter of time before calendar servers, such as Microsoft Exchange and the Netscape Calendar server, start offering calendars in newsfeed formats. Until then, you can create your own calendar newsfeeds using a commercial service called RSSCalendar.com or by using the knowledge you've gained in this book to write your own calendar newsfeed generator.

RSSCalendar.com is a free service that allows you to create an online calendar and then make it available in newsfeed formats. Your friends can subscribe to your daily feed to be notified of events on a daily basis; to your weekly feed to get an up-to-date list of each week's events; or to your monthly feed to get a month's worth of entries at a time. RSSCalendar.com also makes your calendar available in Microsoft Outlook VCal format or IETF standard iCalendar format (RFC-2445).

If you've already got calendar software and you don't want to wait for the developer to add newsfeeds, it's probably not too hard to create your own calendar-to-newsfeed converter. For example, many calendar systems make data available in iCalendar format, which is a simple text format consisting of name-value pairs

**Figure 21.3
iCalendar-to-newsfeed
converter**

separated by line feeds. So to create a converter, you'd need an iCalendar reader, some application logic to decide which data items to include, and a newsfeed generator, as shown in Figure 21.3.

21.1.5 *Turn mailing lists into newsfeeds*

You can't use newsfeeds to monitor something if no newsfeeds are available. And unfortunately, some online services still don't offer newsfeeds. Many of these services, however, do offer email notifications. One way to create newsfeeds for a service that lacks them is to use an email-to-newsfeed gateway to convert a mailing list into a newsfeed.

For example, you can use the free email-to-newsfeed gateway service at www.mailbucket.org. Any mail you send to *name*@mailbucket.org will be made available in a mailing list at www.mailbucket.org/*name*.xml.

Or you can create your own email-to-newsfeed gateway. That's what we did in chapter 12, where we developed Mail Blogger, a program that monitors a mailbox for new email messages and posts them to a blog where they can be accessed in newsfeed form.

If you want to monitor anything, you'll want your applications and services to syndicate everything, so let's discuss that next.

21.2 *Syndicate everything*

Newsfeed syndication makes possible unanticipated applications, applications you haven't yet imagined. By making your data available in newsfeed form, you make it easy for others to add value and create new applications with that data. And now that browsers and mail programs can read and filter newsfeeds, people might not even have to write any code to build a useful application.

Look at your existing applications. If you're sending out email notifications, provide newsfeeds with the same information. If your application logs status, warnings, or errors, provide newsfeeds that deliver the same information. In fact, anything that changes is a candidate for a newsfeed. Here are some examples.

21.2.1 *Syndicate operating system and network events*

Operating system errors, warnings, and information messages should be made available via syndication to enable easier monitoring. Newsfeeds won't replace the robust Simple Network Management Protocol (SNMP) or Java Management Extension (JMX) for system and network monitoring, but they can provide an easier way for people and programs to monitor what is going on in a network of computers.

21.2.2 *Syndicate vehicle status*

Many vehicle fleets are now equipped with wireless Internet connectivity and global positioning system (GPS) receivers. Vehicles in such fleets periodically beam status and location information back to a central server for allocation, management, and tracking purposes. By making newsfeeds available for each vehicle and making aggregated newsfeeds available for each geographical zone, you can make it easy for other people and programs to monitor fleet status and to create those unanticipated applications.

21.2.3 *Syndicate your logs*

Many applications use logging to record status, warnings, and errors. So one way to enable existing applications to produce newsfeeds is to hook in at the log level.

For example, by creating an *appender* plug-in for the popular Apache Log4X logging system, you can have each log message posted to a blog, where it will be made available in newsfeed form. To create an appender that blogs, you'll need to implement the appender interface so you can plug into the Log4X configuration, and you'll need a publishing client so you can post log messages to a blog. Figure 21.4 illustrates a Log4X appender.

Log4X is highly configurable, so you may be able to hook in this type of blogging capability without making any code changes in your existing application. For more information on Log4X, which is available for both Java and .NET, see the Apache Logging Services web site at logging.apache.org.

Now that we've covered syndication from both the consumer's and producer's perspectives, let's move on to a new topic: tagging.

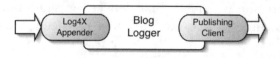

**Figure 21.4
Log4X appender that
logs to a blog**

21.3 Tag the Web

Tagging and folksonomies are not perfect, and some see them as too messy and imprecise, but they work amazingly well. Like blogs and wikis, they make it easier for ordinary people to collaborate in new ways—in this case, to add some meaning to the Web. In this section, we'll discuss the intersection of tagging and blog technologies and we'll explore some ways you can use tagging in your blog and your blog apps.

21.3.1 Create a tagged link blog with del.icio.us

The word *weblog* can be taken literally to mean a *log of the Web,* and many of the earliest blogs were just that—daily listings of links to cool new sites and articles found on the Web. Today, most blogs focus on commentary, and blogs that include only links are known as *link blogs.* Some bloggers maintain both a blog and a link blog, which is often displayed in the sidebar of a blog site and has its own separate newsfeed.

Perhaps the best way to create a link blog is to use a social bookmarking service, such as del.icio.us. Once you've registered at del.icio.us, it's easy to save bookmarks to the site by using a simple *bookmarklet* (a small JavaScript program encoded in the text of a URL) provided with the service. As you explore the Web, you bookmark the sites you find to be interesting. You add a title and (optional) description for each. Most important, you add tags to organize your bookmarks. You're creating a link blog and helping to build the del.icio.us folksonomy. Anybody can subscribe to your link blog's primary newsfeed or to one (or more) of your tags, if they are interested only in specific categories of links.

If you'd like to include your del.icio.us bookmarks on your primary blog, you can use an experimental feature called Daily Blog Posting to post a list of each day's bookmarks.

Del.icio.us is programmable, too. It provides a REST-like web services interface so that your programs can create, retrieve, update, and delete bookmarks. Now let's move from link blogs to photo blogs and do for photos what we did for links.

21.3.2 Create a tagged photo blog with Flickr.com

The popular photo-sharing site Flickr.com, which was recently acquired by Yahoo, allows you to use tagging to organize the photos you upload to the service. A Flickr account is essentially a photo blog: new photos are displayed in reverse chronological order; photos are categorized; visitors can leave comments; and newsfeeds are provided.

Flickr can be configured to accept new photos via email, making it possible to post new photos directly from a camera-phone. It can also be configured to post each new photo to one or more other blogs using a variety of publishing protocols (including MetaWeblog and Atom). For developers, there's an extensive REST-like web services interface.

One problem with the folksonomies that are being developed in the social bookmarking and photo-sharing services is that they exist as separate islands of information. For example, if you searched for the tag *Jamaica* in del.icio.us, it would be really nice to receive in return links from both del.icio.us and other tagging sites—plus photos from Flickr. That brings us to the topic of Technorati Tags, which were, in part, designed to solve that problem.

21.3.3 *Tag your blog entries with Technorati Tags*

Technorati's new Tags service, available at http://www.technorati.com/tag, enables you to search for tagged items across multiple social bookmarking sites, Flickr photos, and blogs—as long as those blogs are tagged with category information.

Technorati will look for the `<category>` or `<dc:subject>` elements in your news-feed and use those as your tags. If you'd like to specify other tags, you can include some additional HTML in your blog entries. For example, if you'd like to tag an entry with *Jamaica*, include the following link somewhere in the blog entry HTML:

```
<a href="http://technorati.com/tag/Jamaica" rel="tag">Jamaica</a>
```

Technorati Tags is a useful service but not nearly as useful as it would be if it offered newsfeeds. At this time, you can't subscribe to Technorati Tags. Now let's talk about something else that's in need of improvement: geotagging.

21.3.4 *Geotag the Web*

Currently, it's not very easy to search for blogs or blog entries about a specific geographic area. Eventually, *geotagging* will change this. You can see a proof-of-concept of this idea at geourl.com, a service that indexes web sites by longitude and latitude. If you want to add your web site to the index, you must first add your Intercontinental Ballistic Missile (ICBM) coordinates to the HTML `<head>` element of your web page. For example:

```
<html>
<head>
   <meta http-equiv="Content-Type" content="text/html; charset=utf-8" >
   <meta name="ICBM" content="35.87832,-78.61950">
   <meta name="DC.title" content="Blogging Roller">
   . . .
```

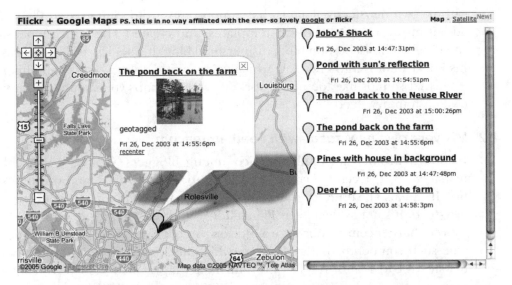

Figure 21.5   Geotagging of Flickr.com photos via geobloggers.com

Once you've added the ICBM tag to your blog and registered at geourl.org, your blog will be included when people search geourl.org for blogs by location.

You can find another proof-of-concept of geotagging at geobloggers.com, a site that combines Google Maps with Flickr.com to enable the geotagging of photos. Instructions are available at the geobloggers.com web site, but basically all you have to do is add latitude and longitude tags to each of your photos when you upload them to Flickr.com. Figure 21.5 shows the geobloggers.com interface, which borrows heavily from Google Maps, and a list of pictures that all share the same location.

21.4 Aggregate yourself

If your personal online presence is spread across multiple blogs, social bookmarking sites, and Flickr, how do people subscribe to *you*? You don't want your friends, family, and your other fans to have to subscribe to multiple newsfeeds to receive your latest posts. In this section, we'll discuss a couple of ways to aggregate your own multiple newsfeeds.

21.4.1 Create an aggregated blog with Planet Tool

You can use the Planet Tool program we presented in chapter 11 to generate an aggregated blog that combines the newsfeeds from all of your sites into one blog with its own newsfeeds. That's what Simon Phipps did. Simon used Planet Tool, added his own HTML and CSS templates, and created The Mink Dimension, a site that combines his Sun blog, his personal blog, his del.icio.us bookmarks, and his Flickr photos into one blog, which you can find at http://www.webmink.net.

If that sounds like too much work for you, perhaps you should just mix your own custom newsfeed.

21.4.2 *Mix your own newsfeeds with Feedburner.com*

Feedburner.com is a popular service among bloggers because it can enhance newsfeeds by correcting errors, converting to other formats, and tracking statistics. It can also be used to *splice* your del.icio.us links and Flickr photos into your newsfeed. It's not as flexible as Planet Tool, but it is much easier to use.

Feedburner.com has been around long enough to spawn some competitors. One such competitor is RssMix.com, which allows you to enter any number of newsfeed URLs and receive in return an aggregated newsfeed containing them all.

Now, let's move away from the topic of personal blogging and discuss how blogs and syndication can be used in public relations.

21.5 Get the word out

Blogs are great for public relations. By allowing the members or employees of your organization to speak freely about their work (with reasonable limitations, of course), you can get the word out about the interesting things you are doing, make sure your side of the story is heard, and humanize your organization. Whether you're a corporation or a nonprofit, there are a number of ways you can use syndication technologies to blog more effectively and to build a spirit of community around your organization.

21.5.1 *Bring your bloggers together with aggregation*

If your bloggers are spread out across the Internet, it's harder to get the feeling of a community. A group aggregator like the one we developed in chapter 11 will help bring your bloggers together as one big aggregated blog.

21.5.2 *Bring bloggers together with tagging*

If your organization's bloggers want to focus on some key issues, you can use tagging as a way to promote your content and your blogs. Agree on a set of tags to use for your issues and encourage your bloggers to use these tags on whatever folksonomy sites they use. Tags will help ensure that people will find your blogs when they're looking for information on those key issues. In addition, links to your blogs from the tagging sites will help boost your blogs' search engine rankings.

21.5.3 Track news and blogs to find the conversations

Use blog search engines as we described in chapter 12 to be alerted whenever a news article or blogger mentions your organization or your key issues. That will allow you to respond quickly to bad press or to join the conversation when people have questions about your organization or products. Respond on your blog and, if possible, use trackback to tie your blog post into the conversation.

21.6 Open up your web site

This is an extension of the "syndicate everything" philosophy introduced in section 21.2. Even if you're not using blogs, you can and should use blog technologies, such as newsfeed syndication, to open up your web site and make it more accessible to your fans, customers, and constituents.

21.6.1 Open up your site with newsfeeds, protocols, and tagging

By adding newsfeeds, web services protocols, and support for tagging, you allow your users to add value by creating new and unanticipated uses for your site. This is the model that Flickr.com uses for photo sharing and eBay uses for auctions. It makes sense for other sites and services as well. For example, the British Broadcasting Corporation (BBC) is applying the same principle by introducing backstage.bbc.co.uk, a site for developers that features newsfeeds, podcasts, and soon, a web services API to make it easy for anybody to remix and repurpose BBC content.

21.6.2 Syndicate your search results with A9 Open Search

If your site includes a search feature, make your search results available in newsfeed form so that your users can easily subscribe. Better yet, when you add newsfeed support to your search engine, implement the Open Search specification, which we covered in chapter 12, to give developers a uniform interface to your search engine and to enable your users to plug your site right into the A9 search portal.

Now that we've discussed some ways to use syndication, aggregation, and tagging on the public Internet, let's see how the same techniques can be applied on your private intranet.

21.7 *Build your own intranet blogosphere*

Just as blogs, wikis, and newsfeeds are taking root on the public Internet, they're sprouting up like weeds on the private intranets of the world. Organizations are using blogs for internal department web sites, project web sites, operations logs, and status reports. Because of this, the same techniques that work on the public Internet can be applied on private intranets as well. Here are some examples.

21.7.1 *Unite internal communities with aggregation*

By using group aggregators to bring together the blogs of each organizational unit, you can create a hierarchy of aggregated blogs. You can then subscribe to blogs at any level: individual, group, department, or division.

You can also use group aggregation to bring together communities of practice (e.g., accountants, engineers, or project managers) whose individual members work in different organizations.

21.7.2 *Build a folksonomy of your intranet*

We learned about how social bookmarking and tagging allows Internet users to share interesting links and build a folksonomy of the Internet. You can do the some thing on your intranet. If your organization has a large and complex intranet, you'll benefit from having at least one del.icio.us-like social bookmarking site.

It's probably not that hard to write your own social bookmarking application, but if you're not up to the task, try Rubric, a del.icio.us clone that's written in Perl. You can get it for free at the Perl CPAN.org archive.

21.8 *Blog your software project*

By setting up blogs, aggregators, and wikis for your software project, you can create a sort of development dashboard for your team—a place where team members can get the latest information about new builds, test results, new bugs, new enhancement requests, new articles on the project wiki, and changes to the code base.

The beauty of the project blog concept is automation—all of the content is created, posted, or aggregated automatically. As we learned in chapter 16, your build script can post messages, unit test results, and other build artifacts automatically via blog publishing protocols. An aggregator can bring together newsfeeds from your issue-tracking system, wiki, and other systems.

Here are a couple more ideas you can use to enhance your project blog.

21.8.1 *Use newsfeeds to syndicate source code changes*

At the time of this writing, most source code control systems do not provide newsfeeds. With the knowledge you've gained in this book, creating such a newsfeed should be a fairly easy project.

If you use the ubiquitous CVS source code control system, one approach to creating a newsfeed is to periodically create a CVS history report, parse the report, and generate a newsfeed based on the report data. Figure 21.6 shows this approach.

Figure 21.6
Create a CVS newsfeed by parsing history

Since CVS and other source code control systems can be configured to send email on each change, you can use an email-to-blog program to post changes to a blog server, where they are made available in newsfeed form. Figure 21.7 illustrates this technique.

Figure 21.7
Create a CVS newsfeed using an email-to-blog program

21.8.2 *Pull software documentation from a wiki*

If you're using a wiki for your product documentation and you'd like to include those documents in your software distribution, you can use the XML-RPC based WikiRPCInterface to automate the process. For example, you could create an Ant task that can be invoked like this:

```
<copy-wiki-page url="http://example.com/wiki/rpc"
    pagename="UserGuide" version="34" destdir="${build}/docs" />
```

Here, the `copy-wiki-page` task copies a specific version of a wiki page, in this case, version 34 of the page named UserGuide, to a directory. In this example, the directory is specified by `${build}/docs`. The `url` attribute is the WikiRPCInterface URL.

21.9 *Summary*

It's difficult to summarize a chapter like this because we've presented so many ideas and concepts. If there is a theme that runs through this chapter—and the book as a whole—it's this: just as you can use newsfeeds and publishing protocols provided by others to build interesting new applications, you can also use them to enable others to remix, repurpose, and add value to the things you create. Or more simply: share and share alike.

index

MANNING BESTSELLERS

Ajax in Action
   by David Crane and Eric Pascarello
      with Darren James
   ISBN: 1-932394-61-3
   680 pages
   $44.95
   October 2005

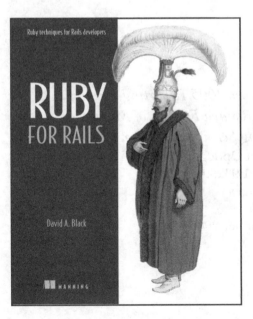

Ruby for Rails: Ruby Techniques
for Rails Developers
   by David A. Black
   foreword by David Heinemeier Hansson
   ISBN: 1-932394-69-9
   532 pages
   $44.95
   May 2006

For ordering information please go to www.manning.com

MORE TITLES FROM MANNING PUBLICATIONS

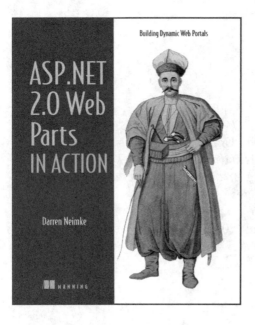

ASP.NET 2.0 Web Parts in Action: Building Dynamic Web Portals
  by Darren Neimke
  ISBN: 1-932394-77-X
  450 pages
  $44.95
  September 2006

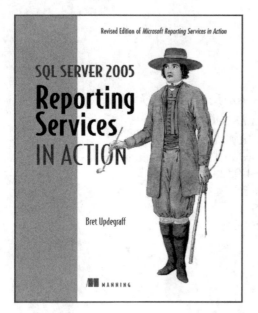

SQL Server 2005 Reporting Services in Action: Revised Edition of Microsoft Reporting Services in Action
  by Bret Updegraff
  ISBN: 1-932394-76-1
  650 pages
  $49.95
  September 2006

For ordering information please go to www.manning.com

MORE TITLES FROM MANNING PUBLICATIONS

C++/CLI in Action
 by Nishant Sivakumar
 ISBN: 1-932394-81-8
 400 pages
 $44.99
 December 2006

Groovy in Action
 by Dierk Koenig, Guillaume Laforge,
   and Andrew Glover
 foreword by James Gosling
 ISBN: 1-932394-84-2
 420 pages
 $44.99
 January 2007

For ordering information please go to www.manning.com